T0314313

VERNACULAR INDUSTRIALISM IN CHINA

Studies of the Weatherhead East Asian Institute, Columbia University

STUDIES OF THE WEATHERHEAD EAST ASIAN INSTITUTE,
COLUMBIA UNIVERSITY

The Studies of the Weatherhead East Asian Institute of Columbia University were inaugurated in 1962 to bring to a wider public the results of significant new research on modern and contemporary East Asia.

For a complete list of titles, see page 397.

Vernacular Industrialism in China

Local Innovation and Translated Technologies in the Making of a Cosmetics Empire, 1900–1940

Eugenia Lean

Columbia University Press   New York

COLUMBIA
UNIVERSITY
PRESS

Columbia University Press gratefully acknowledges the generous support for this book provided by a member of our Publisher's Circle on behalf of Ms. Monica Shu-ping Chen Yü in memory of the late Professor James Pusey.

Columbia University Press wishes to express its appreciation for assistance given by the Wm. Theodore de Bary Fund in the publication of this book

Columbia University Press wishes to express its appreciation for assistance given by the Chiang Ching-kuo Foundation for International Scholarly Exchange and the Council for Cultural Affairs in the publication of this series.

Columbia University Press
Publishers Since 1893
New York   Chichester, West Sussex
cup.columbia.edu
Copyright © 2020 Columbia University Press
All rights reserved

Cataloging-in-Publication Data available from the Library of Congress.
ISBN 978-0-231-19348-1 (cloth)
ISBN 978-0-231-55033-8 (ebook)
LCCN 2019032862

Printed in the United States of America

Cover image: Courtesy of the author
Cover design: Chang Jae Lee

To Paize and Inez

Contents

Acknowledgments

Appreciating Chen Diexian, a witty individual in all his complexity, has been a collaborative journey from the start. Over the years, friends, colleagues, students, and seminar audience members have helped shape this project. Some did so with an in-depth reading of a chapter (or, in some cases, chapters), a source, a probing question, or even an offhand remark that nonetheless profoundly informed my thinking. Others generously shared their work in progress or invited me to workshops where I could develop my project further. Yet others have brainstormed on the book title or debated key concepts. I thank Dan Asen, Weihong Bao, He Bian, Kim Brandt, Danni Cai, Mia Carter, Janet Chen, Chu Ping-yi, Debbie Coen, Rob Culp, Will Deringer, Alex Des Forges, Ben Elman, Marwa Elshakry, Jacob Eyferth, Fa-ti Fan, Li Feng, Karl Gerth, Peter Hamilton, Marta Hansen, Michael Hill, T. J. Hinrichs, Xiaoqian Ji, Joan Judge, Paize Keulemans, Dorothy Ko, Liza Lawrence, Hsiang-lin (Sean) Lei, Elaine Leong, Sylvia Lindtner, Weijing Lu, Miaw-fen Lü, Yue Meng, Projit Mukherji, Rebecca Nedostup, Ying Qian, Christopher Rea, Christopher Reed, Lukas Rieppel, Tristan Revells, Bruce Rusk, Ori Sela, Victor Seow, Kavita Sivaramakrishnan, Grace Shen, John Tresch, Jing Tsu, Joseph Ulichny, Sebastian Veg, Nicolai Volland, Richard von Glahn, I-Hsien Wu, Grant Wythoff, Matti Zelin, Ying Zhang, and Zhang Zhongming.

I no doubt should have included many others in this list, discussants and participants of workshops, conferences, and talks where I have presented portions of my project. In the United States, these conversations took place at Princeton University; Harvard University; Bowdoin College; University of Chicago; Massachusetts Institute of Technology; University of Pennsylvania; Bard College; New York University; Stanford University; Chemical Heritage Foundation; Yale University; Ohio State University; University of San Francisco; Cornell University; Institute for Advanced Studies; University of Texas, Austin; University of California, Los Angeles; and Columbia University, as well as abroad at the Institute for Modern History at the Academia Sinica, Fudan University, Freie University, National Taiwan University, Tel Aviv University, the Max Plank Institute, the National University of Singapore, and the University of Toronto. They have also occurred on panels at conferences held by the Association for Asian Studies, the Association for Asian Studies in Asia, the History of Science Society, the American Historical Association, and the International Society for the History of East Asian Science, Technology, and Medicine. Participants in these conversations have pushed me to refine the analysis and to think in bolder ways as well as to be ever more responsible in mobilizing my evidence and crafting my argument.

I also thank several cohorts of graduate students at Columbia who read and commented on drafts of the project in class. Their views and opinions, always given in polite and gentle terms, have influenced this product in more ways than they can probably imagine. I have been lucky to have hardworking and talented research assistants as well. Gaoziyan Cui, Yingtian He, and Yize Hu deserve special thanks on this front. Yanjie Huang recently stepped in to wrap up some loose ends, for which I am grateful.

I have benefited from multiple sources of support. I was able to conduct research with an American Council of Learned Societies/Charles A. Ryskamp Research Fellowship, two Taiwan Fellowships of the Ministry of Foreign Affairs, and internal Columbia University research funding and sabbatical support. A Chiang Ching-kuo Research Fellowship, a National Endowment for the Humanities Fellowship, and a fellowship from the Institute for Advanced Studies, School of Historical Studies Membership (funded by the Starr Foundation East Asian Studies

Endowment Fund) provided me with the precious gift of time. With that generous support, I was able to take leave from my teaching and administrative responsibilities to complete the writing of the book.

Christine Dunbar, Christian Winting, and the rest of the team at Columbia University Press were more than patient with me as they expertly shepherded the book through publication. Fa-ti Fan, Sigrid Schmalzer, and one other reviewer for the press provided trenchant criticism where needed and raised excellent suggestions about how to tighten the manuscript, add comparisons, and push on the conceptual front. As always, all mistakes and deficiencies remain mine alone.

Material in chapter 2 was first explored in "Recipes for Men: Manufacturing Make-up and the Politics of Production in 1910s China," in the special issue "Masculinities in Science/Sciences of Masculinity," *Osiris* 30, no. 1 (Fall 2015): 134–157 (© 2015 by the History of Science Society). Portions of chapter 1 and 5 are drawn from "The Butterfly Mark: Chen Diexian, His Brand, and Cultural Entrepreneurism in Republican China," in *The Business of Culture: Cultural Entrepreneurs in China and Southeast Asia, 1900–65*, edited by Christopher Rea and Nicolai Volland (Vancouver: University of British Columbia Press, 2015). An earlier version of part of a section in chapter 4 was previously explored in "The Making of a Chinese Copycat: Trademarks and Recipes in Early Twentieth-Century Global Science and Capitalism," *Osiris* 33, no. 1 (2018): 271–93 (© 2018 by the History of Science Society). Finally, two sections of chapter 6 appeared in "Proofreading Science: Editing and Experimentation in Manuals by a 1930s' Industrialist" in *Science and Technology in Republican China*, edited by Benjamin Elman and Jing Tsu (Leiden: Brill 2014).

My daughter, Inez, has enriched my and my husband's lives in immeasurable ways. Her birth in 2007 coincided with the publication of my first book. Her arrival completed our family and brought joy and fulfillment in ways that cannot be described. Although it has not been easy balancing the needs of work and family, I would not have it any other way and am that much richer because I have done so with my family's support and inspiration. It is to Inez, my beautiful daughter, and Paize, my partner in life, that I dedicate this book.

VERNACULAR INDUSTRIALISM IN CHINA

Introduction

> The founder of the Association for Household Industries, Mr. Chen
> [Diexian] is . . . not only accomplished in music, chess, calligraphy,
> and painting, performing stringed as well as wind instruments, but
> also versed in the three religions and the nine schools of thought.
> There is nothing he cannot do; he is even well educated in all fields
> of modern science. His writings are thus broad in scope: he can
> write fiction, compose poetry, discuss politics and economics, as
> well as expound upon modern physics and chemistry. He not only
> knows (*zhi*) [these subjects] but can also put them into practice
> (*xing*). The various products of [his pharmaceutical company],
> the Association for Household Industries, are the result of his
> experimentation. . . . Perhaps we cannot call a man like him China's
> Edison, but to call him a remarkable man rare in modern society
> would probably not be exaggerated praise.
>
> —"JIATING GONGYESHE" (ASSOCIATION FOR
> HOUSEHOLD INDUSTRIES) 1935

This hagiographical description is of Chen Diexian (1879–1940), a cosmopolitan man of letters, industrialist, and practitioner of science. He is
presented as someone notable not only for his talent and knowledge but
also for his ability to do an array of things, from literary work to hands-
on science and industry building. He is lauded for being both deeply
knowledgeable and able to apply his knowledge in practice. He writes
prolifically and experiments with science. He also founds companies. Although remarking that Chen might not be China's Edison, the
commentator nonetheless extolls him as a "remarkable man" (*qiren*) of
modern times.

At first blush, Chen's biography seems to support such characterizations. As a young man in Hangzhou in the final decades of the Qing

dynasty (1644–1911), Chen turned his literati studio into a chemistry lab, where he polished his literary skills, composed poetry about new forms of technology, and dabbled in chemical experiments. As a professional writer and editor in Shanghai after 1913, he amassed considerable money and literary fame by publishing serialized romance novels. At the same time, he compiled and edited influential newspaper and journal columns on "common knowledge" (*changshi*) that notably included an abundant amount of industrial and manufacturing information. As a budding entrepreneur, Chen ground cuttlefish bones to harvest local ingredients for powder-based cosmetics. In 1918, he established what was to become one of Republican China's most successful domestic pharmaceutical empires, the Association for Household Industries Co., Ltd. (Jiating gongyeshe gufen lianhe gongsi; hereafter, Household Industries). Its most notable product, Butterfly Toothpowder, was as versatile as its inventor, unique among toothpowders in its ability to double as face powder. The item proved able to outmaneuver Japanese and Western brands in Chinese and Southeast Asian markets throughout the 1920s and 1930s. And in an era when words and things were not just mass-produced but also widely counterfeited, Chen vigorously protected his brand domestically by promoting emerging global laws on trademark infringement even while championing Chinese native products by advocating the "emulation" (*fangzhi* or *fangzao*) of technologies from abroad.

If there is some overlap between hagiographical accounts and Chen's biographical profile, this study is not interested in providing a celebratory account of a unique individual who somehow transcended his time. Nor is it invested in drawing analogies between Chen and individual, heroic inventors, as the epigraph seems to do when noting somewhat apologetically that Chen was not quite China's Edison. Rather, this book uses Chen's industrial, commercial, *and* literary pursuits to explore the broader conditions under which a range of lettered if commercially oriented elites in early-twentieth-century China engaged in building industry and pursued science and commerce. Figures such as Chen navigated a transitional period around the fall of the Qing, leveraging their classical education to find success in the newly commercial world of letters and the emerging sphere of industrial manufacturing.[1] At a moment when China's involvement with global commerce was shaped by economic imperialism within its own borders, Chen Diexian's industrious activities constituted a form of what I call "vernacular industrialism." This industrialism was local and "homegrown" (as opposed to imperialist or foreign), informal and part of China's consumer cultures (rather than state sponsored or located in academia), as well as artisanal in spirit and family run even if eventually situated in factories. It included equal parts material work—to produce ingredients and manufacture gadgets—and knowledge work, including the compilation of how-to columns on manufacturing knowhow in magazines, newspapers, and other publications. Certain endeavors of Chen's vernacular industrialism served nonindustrial and even seemingly "frivolous" purposes (including showcasing literary wit in the poetry circles of Hangzhou and shaping an emerging taste and lifestyle market in Shanghai). Others fall more squarely in what we consider the parameters of industrial modernity and resulted in the building of China's pharmaceutical industry. This vernacular industrialism, furthermore, came to transcend any individual effort and overlapped with the ethos of the National Products Movement (NPM, Guohuo yundong, 1935–1937), a "buy and manufacture Chinese goods" campaign of the period. Yet even though promoted as local and native, vernacular industrialism also often depended on access to global circuits of law, science, and commerce.

Vernacular industrialists such as Chen stand as a powerful rebuke to the characterization of China's traditional lettered men as narrowly interested in textual knowledge and the Confucian classics and concerned only with frivolous and fanciful pursuits. The educated men of this period have often been characterized as scornful of commerce and the pursuit of profit, effete and unprepared to face the challenges of modernity and capitalism, and unwilling or unable to engage in hands-on activities and to take up technology and science.[2] Early-twentieth-century intellectuals associated with the New Culture Movement (1915–1919) criticized these "old-style literati" (*jiu wenren*) as hopeless connoisseurs who, if interested in gadgets or technology, appreciated them merely as precious curios or fanciful marvels.[3] As such, they were unable to adapt to new forms of knowledge, including science, and meet the demands of the modern world. By focusing on Chen, this book fundamentally challenges such a depiction and sheds light on the role he and others like him assumed in China's emerging spheres of not only modern print culture but also industry, science, and capitalism.[4]

If Chen was remarkable in the degree of success he achieved, his endeavors are nonetheless typical of the transitional period in Chinese history in which he found himself. His life spanned a period during which China witnessed remarkable change. The ravages of the Taiping Uprising (1850–1864) deeply unsettled the Qing Empire. In 1905, the civil-service examination system, the institutional mechanism that had long tethered China's educated elites to the bureaucracy, was dismantled. With its abolition, state privileging of the Confucian canon and its moral text-based knowledge came to an abrupt end. The year 1911 saw the fall of the empire, and the first decade of the new republic (1912–1949) started off with great promise but quickly disintegrated into political disarray. The goals of the revolution of 1911—including the establishment of a legitimate constitution and a parliamentary government—proved elusive, and internecine warfare engulfed China and crippled the central government by the late 1910s. The political chaos emboldened imperialist powers, and the Japanese in particular deepened their penetration into China, extracting humiliating demands from the fledgling and vulnerable nation. Paralyzing court politics and widespread factionalism and corruption drove many away from national politics.

Yet even as such a scenario shows a period characterized by decline, chaos, and instability, the early twentieth century was also a period when unprecedented opportunities appeared. Although the epigraph's mention of Edison is a rhetorical flourish more indicative of the commentator's hagiographical agenda than of anything else, it does point to how both Thomas Edison and Chen Diexian were part of a global trend where entrepreneurial types could take advantage of new opportunities in societies experiencing increasing industrial development. In China, disenfranchised and dislocated literati leaving the moribund political center in the North and traditional centers of learning in Jiangnan in the South found unprecedented prospects in vibrant treaty ports (see Reed 2004; Meng 2006). As they migrated to these new centers, they leveraged their cultural skills to pursue new avenues in burgeoning commercial print industries, emerging entertainment cultures, and even mercantile and light manufacturing. With institutions of knowledge production, social occupations, and political power structures in flux, a generation of urban actors adapted a host of entrepreneurial strategies to deal with the changes. Regional elites, urban connoisseurs (male and female), maverick entrepreneurs and industrialists, amateur scientists, Chinese "medicine men," professional editors, and taste "experts"—all took advantage of new possibilities.[5] This transformation was not limited to China. Self-made inventors in colonial Korea of the 1920s, for example, were able to apply successfully for patents from the Imperial Patent Office in Tokyo despite having no scientific or technical education or institutional support.[6]

Chen Diexian provides a compelling example of the new-style industrial entrepreneurs who emerged around the world at the turn of the twentieth century and navigated the transition to industrial modernity. Chen did so with considerable aplomb. He engaged in what were often unconventional and homegrown ways to build industry, dabbled in scientific activity, and developed commercial enterprises, both lettered and material. He translated texts on and explored regimes of chemical and legal knowledge, adapted foreign technologies, and openly pursued profit—activities once deemed unthinkable for respectable men in late-imperial China. Productive in the making and selling of words and things, Chen was able to reinvent and update the man-of-letters persona. Finally, it is worth emphasizing that Chen Diexian's endeavors were at once cultural and commercial, imaginative and industrial, lettered and material.

Previous examinations of Chen have tended to regard his literary and industrial activities as separate and unrelated. Scholars of literature have explored his prolific production in the literary arena (see, e.g., Hanan 1999; H. Lee 2007b) and his editorial efforts as a high-profile professional editor in Shanghai (see, e.g., Meng 1994; H. Lee 2007a). Popular hagiographic biographies have dwelled on Chen's commercial and industrial activities, often to celebrate him uncritically as a heroic captain of industry (e.g., Chen Dingshan [1955] 1967). This segregated approach to Chen stems from contemporary categories of analysis that rest on our own historical ways of understanding occupation and knowledge fields. In contrast, this book examines how Chen's activities confound these epistemological and occupational divisions. To be sure, it does not cover Chen's life comprehensively. Nor does it explore his novels, plays, essays, and poetry in depth, mentioning only a few. Nor does it consider all aspects of his industrial work. The study instead examines select literary, editorial, industrial, and manufacturing practices to demonstrate how in a period when things and words were increasingly mass-produced, multiple aspects of Chen's life were intertwined. It takes an in-depth look at some of the poetry composed by Chen that features new technologies, how-to columns he compiled in women's journals, translated recipes that he tinkered with, and collectanea he used to impose order on the newfound materiality of the age.[7] In terms of the material practices, the book explores a scientific appliance shop Chen opened as a young man, the gadgets he tinkered with throughout his career, and the legal and marketing tactics he deployed to protect his brand as a mature industrialist.

Indeed, Chen found success both as a professional writer and editor in urban China's burgeoning cultural markets *and* as a modern industrialist and nativist manufacturer. He straddled the worlds of literary production, editorial work, industrial capitalism, technological connoisseurship, and amateur science. His success in navigating different circles stemmed from his ability to reinvent himself in new settings and to adapt resources and skills from one circle to another, bringing tactics from his literary and editorial endeavors to his industrial and manufacturing enterprises. Thus, his story sheds light on the interaction of the world of letters and the world of commerce during a period when both were increasingly being reshaped by technologies of mass production and mechanical reproduction. It showcases how both knowledge work and material undertakings constituted Chen's vernacular industrialism and more broadly reflected the variegated terrain of industrial activities in China at the time.

VERNACULAR INDUSTRIALISM

A central concept in this study is "vernacular industrialism." This concept is analytical but inspired by a specific term, *xiao gongyi*, which commentators of the day often used to describe Chen's publications on manufacturing items such as dyes and cosmetics.[8] *Xiao gongyi* is difficult to translate because its meaning has shifted over time. In modern Chinese, the main compound, *gongyi*, can mean "craftsmanship" and "technical arts," such as printing or textile manufacturing. It is often combined with *shou*, "hand," to make the compound *shou gongyi*, "handicraft." In the 1930s, *gongyi*, especially in combination with *shou*, could evoke nostalgia for Chinese tradition and often referred to handmade handicraft goods that were set in contradistinction to foreign-made factory goods (Fernsebner 2003, 269–271, 285–291). But before the 1930s, *gongyi* referred to the industrial arts, especially industrial manufacturing that involved chemistry and physics. With the additional character *xiao*, "small," the longer term *xiao gongyi* meant "minor industrial arts" or "light industrial arts" and was used to describe practices relevant to light industry or manufacturing, especially of chemical-based goods.

Renderings of the compound *xiao gongyi* as "minor industrial arts," however, might risk the connotation that such activities were frivolous and somehow less important.[9] It is precisely this connotation that this study seeks to avoid. The book instead takes Chen's interest in *xiao gongyi* seriously, even as it demonstrates how this interest initially emerged as part of a turn-of-the-twentieth-century culture of play (*youxi*) that took delight in new literary forms and technologies.[10] Chen's writings on *xiao gongyi* did not initially appear in specialist or industry journals but were published in new-style columns in women's leisure magazines and later in the literary supplements of daily newspapers. In these new forms of media, Chen promoted the experimentation needed for manufacturing cosmetics and other daily-use items and stipulated that such production was suitable first for genteel women to conduct in inner chambers (*guige*) of the household as entertainment and later for the lettered urbanite to do in modern homes (*jiating*). In practice, too, Chen engaged in *xiao gongyi* outside of formal laboratories. He casually tinkered with gadgets such as the chemical fire extinguisher and while writing poetry on the shores of Ningbo discovered cuttlefish bones as a source of calcium carbonate, a key ingredient of powder-based cosmetics.

Rather than interpret Chen's unorthodox pursuits in manufacturing and chemistry as frivolous, it is better to understand how their informal, ad hoc nature was reflective of the early twentieth century, when the ownership of scientific knowledge, technology, and industry was not yet fixed. Questions of who was responsible for adapting and producing new knowledge related to chemistry and industrial manufacturing, where such knowledge was to be applied, and for what purposes remained open-ended. Chemistry and manufacturing were not yet firmly ensconced in factories, laboratories, or the research halls of academia.[11] Academics, professional industrialists, and the state did not yet monopolize science and industry as they would in later periods.[12] Meanwhile, with industrial-property regimes still nascent worldwide, corporations and individuals had difficulty claiming exclusive legal ownership over any recipe or manufacturing formula. The exploration of light industry thus took place in seemingly apolitical, unprofessional, and inconsequential spaces, including literati studios, reading rooms, domestic and private spaces, and scientific-appliance shops as well as in how-to columns in women's magazines. Plenty of emulation, adaptation, and domestic sourcing took place, as did local ingenuity and homespun innovation.

This informal, playful approach to science and industry belied its serious undertones. With political orthodoxy crumbling during the late Qing and political chaos threatening to engulf China in the early Republic of China, this broader culture of lettered and amused engagement with technology opened up new avenues for educated men and women alienated from conventional politics. Chen's delight with things both literary and technological did not simply pass quickly as a whimsical fad but would serve as the basis of multiple endeavors in industry and commerce throughout his life. His interest in *xiao gongyi* thus provides us with a starting point to examine the broader analytical category "vernacular industrialism" in order to capture the variegated range of light-industrial and manufacturing-related activities in turn-of-the-twentieth-century China. Such activities might not conform to our understanding of industrial development based on what we have learned from American or European history. They instead exemplify the heterogeneous engagement with manufacturing, science, and commerce that existed in modern China (and probably in many other parts of the world as well). It casts light on sets of unlikely actors who built light industry in unexpected ways, especially when faced with considerable obstacles as well as a lack of resources and state support.

From a contemporary vantage point, Chen's decidedly unconventional industrialism might seem to be riddled with contradictions. It was commercial in nature yet drew from a classical literary tradition. It relied on the production of "common knowledge," which included sharing brand recipes, and aspired at least in principle to be more democratic as it exhorted a larger consuming audience to engage in chemical experimentation and apply medicinal and chemical recipes in their daily lives. At times, Chen's endeavors had little to do with the establishment of industry and far more to do with his desire to establish his status as a tastemaker and lifestyle expert. For readers of his publications and fellow practitioners of *xiao gongyi*, engagement with forms of vernacular industrialism functioned to demarcate social standing, showcase their gentlemanly (and gentlewomanly) curiosity and wit, and facilitate exploration of the chemistry behind manufacturing elixirs of longevity. Yet at the same time aspects of Chen's vernacular industrialism could and did prove directly relevant to the establishment of formal industry. His "playful" experimentation with brine on China's eastern seaboard was crucial for him to find ways to produce magnesium carbonate on an industrial scale. He tinkered with materials and vetted recipes with the aims to remake and improve translated technologies and manufacturing practices. As his ad hoc enterprising turned into an established business, his industrial work became situated in factories and thus was more proprietary in nature. But it is precisely these seemingly contradictory elements of vernacular industrialism that are of interest. They force us to question exactly what constitutes legitimate industrial activity and provide us with the opportunity to consider alternative paths of industrial modernity.

The concept of vernacular industrialism draws inspiration in part from historians of science who use the terms *vernacular* and *everyday* to provincialize universalizing epistemological claims often associated with the rise of industry and science. These scholars often focus on practices that fall outside of modern industry or industrial settings. Some use the term *vernacular science* to describe informal, artisanal, embodied, and nonacademic ways of knowing in early-modern European workshops. By demonstrating how artisanal methods of pursuing knowledge through the sense and the body were crucial to habits and practices of modern science, they challenge the tendency to privilege theoretical and abstract dimensions of modern science and disembodied, "rational" ways of engaging with the natural world (see, e.g., P. Smith 2004). Others use *vernacular science* to describe the codification of "native" or "indigenous" knowledge as constructed by colonial anthropologists and ethnologists in places such as late-nineteenth- and early-twentieth -century Africa. Thus, they expose gaps of uncertainty and doubt in the universalizing epistemologies of colonial science (see, e.g., Tilley 2011). Yet others advance the concept of "everyday technology" to showcase how imported small machines and consumer goods were appropriated for daily use in unanticipated ways in places such as late-nineteenth- and early-twentieth-century India. By doing so they reshape the thinking about class, race, and politics in the colonial and postcolonial context.[13] These revisionist studies of "vernacular science" and "everyday technology" are powerful for a host of reasons. They question the modernist prioritization of abstract knowledge over bodily ways of knowing. Some rightly work to rescue nonindustrial production from modernization narratives that privilege industrialization over craft or indigenous knowledge. Others cast aside the usual accounts of invention and origins to explore the unanticipated and ingenious *uses* of technology (Edgerton 2007). They underscore the process by which the localization of technologies generates often unexpected adaptation of imported technologies. These studies are compelling in their potential to decenter narratives of dissemination that persist in understanding modern technology as being transmitted unchanged from the West to the rest of the world.

This book is inspired by these recent studies of the vernacular and the everyday but adds to them with an unapologetic focus on a modern, lettered Chinese industrialist. It hopes to offset some of this scholarship's emphasis (and arguably even romanticization) of handwork, handicraft, artisanal, indigenous, or peasant production that might inadvertently perpetuate the handicraft–mechanization, rational–embodied, and indigenous–metropole dichotomies generated by the very modernization narratives the scholarship seeks to challenge.[14] The notion of "vernacular industrialism" may employ the term *vernacular*, but it does not conceptualize this type of industry as somehow subaltern or noncosmopolitan. Nor does it assume a fixed understanding of the "everyday" as something located only in the daily, familial realm that is distinct from formal industry, manufacturing, and commerce. Instead, vernacular industrialism combines two terms that at first glance might fit together somewhat uncomfortably. But this uncomfortable combination is valuable and generates a productive conceptual tension. It is useful insofar as it functions to caution us against reifying analytical categories and binaries. It allows us to see how "vernacular" should not always be understood as being dichotomously opposed to or somehow derivative of "cosmopolitan" or "modern" forms of industrialization and that "everyday" need not be juxtaposed in contrast to formal industrial development.

Indeed, Chen's vernacular industrialism spanned both formal and informal industrial endeavors, casual tinkering and factory-based work, local homegrown experimentation and active adaptation of global trends, as well as the material building of industry and lettered knowledge work. It can shed light on the question of formal industrialization even while insisting on the exploration of more prosaic, ad hoc practices of production and making that might fall outside of any conventional path toward industry building.

RETHINKING SCIENCE AND INDUSTRY IN CHINA AND BEYOND

Examining vernacular industrialism in the history of modern China means focusing on unusual and makeshift practices of manufacturing and industry and ways of knowing. Such an approach adds an important if understudied vector to our understanding of Chinese industrialization and modern science. The history of modern Chinese industry and science often begins with the Self-Strengthening Movement (c. 1861–1895), a state-endorsed, formal attempt to develop technology and industry to strengthen China. Weakened by half a century of internal rebellion and Western imperialist aggression, the Qing state engaged in eleventh-hour reforms in the latter part of the nineteenth century to save the moribund dynasty. In response to a perceived political and technological crisis, Chinese provincial statesmen worked closely with Western missionaries and experts as well as with Chinese artisans to launch a range of projects that involved the building of arsenals, shipyards, technical schools, and translation bureaus in Guangzhou, Ningbo, Beijing, and Shanghai. Earlier scholarship on the Self-Strengthening Movement, although importantly casting light on the key role it played in the history of China's industrialization, tends to take the modern West's experience with capitalism and industrialization as an implicit standard to evaluate success. James Reardon-Anderson (1991), a historian who writes about the emergence of modern chemistry in China, characterizes China's foray into Western technology with the Self-Strengthening Movement as incomplete and delayed. These industrial developments in China, Reardon-Anderson posits, originated in the West and were transplanted to China, often imperfectly and with considerable resistance.[15] It was not until the Nanjing decade and with the Nationalist state's support that a truly modern chemical industry—one that most resembled industrial enterprises in the West—emerged.

More recent revisionist histories, however, demonstrate how the Chinese engagement with technology and industry in the latter part of the nineteenth century was, in fact, more complex. Introducing technology and science to help bolster a flagging Qing Empire, the manufacturing of armaments in arsenals and related mining projects, they argue, were hybrid in nature, shaped by developments both within China and from abroad (Meng 1999; Elman 2005; Shellen Wu 2015). Arsenals employed Chinese translators, working closely with foreign missionaries, to translate the most up-to-date scientific and technological knowledge.[16] At the same time, innovation at these sites also drew from the local knowledge of mathematicians and technicians located in the Jiangnan area. Literati became conversant with science and technology as they joined these Chinese technicians, engineers, and skilled artisans in the arsenals' endeavors. The textual activity that was a central component of the work at the arsenals helped legitimate the idea that technical and scientific prowess was just as important as moral aptitude in ensuring the strength of the nation. Finally, the Self-Strengthening Movement was not merely a transitional period before the inevitable stage of "mature" industrialization that was to come. Rather, it was only with the defeat of the Qing in the Sino-Japanese War in 1895 that the Self-Strengthening agenda was suddenly deemed insufficient (Elman 2005, 355, 392–395).

Even with the discrediting of the Self-Strengthening project, the efforts to build industry and pursue science did not come to a halt in the late nineteenth and early twentieth centuries. Despite a weak central state during this period, a host of nonstate actors emerged to build industry outside of the state's purview.[17] Salt merchants and rural paper manufacturers continued to dominate indigenous industries (see Zelin 2005; Eyferth 2009). New cultural enterprises, including vibrant, fiercely competitive, modern presses and print industries, emerged in cities such as Shanghai (Reed 2004; Culp 2016). This was also a time when regional entrepreneurs founded modern business empires, such as the Dasheng textile mills (Köll 2003). A natural outgrowth of studying industrialization through industry-sector analysis or company-based histories, however, has been that much of this work has focused only on formal industry and its relevant technologies. Company-based studies, for example, tend to examine company-specific activities or, if they do examine extra-company practices, tend to focus on aspects that eventually "led" to the founding of the company or industrial success. In some studies, moreover, a distinction is drawn between "modern" corporate structures based on Western standards as constituting formal industrial practice and "traditional" practices of the Chinese family business (e.g., Köll 2003).

The study of modern science in China has similarly focused on the making of formal fields and professions that came to constitute "science," *kexue.* Supplementing earlier forms of scholarship that adopted primarily the history-of-ideas approach, these studies that examine the formal institutions and practices of *kexue* importantly identify a variety of initial steps toward professionalizing and providing an institutional identity to modern science in China.[18] As mentioned earlier, the translation of scientific work had already started to take place at the Self-Strengthening arsenals (Elman 2005). With the relative absence of state action during the twilight years of the Qing Empire and the dawn of the Republican period, scholarly societies of the late Qing and new scientific organizations of the 1910s, such as the Science Society of China, emerged as sites where science was explored.[19] The publication of scientific journals, such as *Science* (*Kexue*), served to elevate science as a transcendent truth divorced from the everyday (H. Wang 2006). The 1920s would then see the further institutionalization of modern science with the rise of academic disciplines in Chinese universities and the development of professional "fields" more broadly. A recent spate of studies on the emergence of formal fields of geography, forensics, and traditional Chinese medicine has contributed tremendously by fleshing out how this institutionalization started occurring in the 1920s and 1930s and by showing how ways of knowing that had long been in existence became folded, at times uncomfortably, into these new disciplines.[20] Invested in understanding the formation of formal knowledge, however, these studies have been less concerned with how more unorthodox, hybrid, or ill-fitting aspects or ways of knowing might assume different or varied historical functions.

This primary focus on professional, organized, or formal fields of modern science resonates with narratives inherited from actors of the time. The May Fourth Movement began with students and citizens of

Beijing marching on May 4, 1919, to protest the humiliating treatment of China in the Versailles Treaty and to call for the strengthening of the Chinese nation domestically against warlords and internationally against imperialists. As part of a global trend promoting the authority of science for modern societies, the movement's participants drew from the related New Culture Movement to argue that the old ways should be rejected and a "new culture" introduced, including Western science and democracy. In a *New Youth* (*Xin qingnian*) essay published in January 1919, Chen Duxiu, the dean of Peking University, and a key leader of the New Culture Movement, promoted "Mr. Science" (Sai Xiansheng) and "Mr. Democracy" (De Xiansheng) as antidotes to the superstitions of the past and the oppressive shackles of Confucianism and traditionalism (Chen Duxiu 1919). The two imported ideals, "Mr. Science" and "Mr. Democracy," became a central slogan for May Fourth protesters and were consecrated as iconic of and essential to China's modernity.[21] These intellectuals did not see "Mr. Science" as something only professionals or specialists could be in practice but rather an ideal to be pursued by cosmopolitan intellectual citizens like themselves. Yet at the same time their pursuits need to be understood as an attempt to claim ownership over a well-organized and distinct field of "science," to define its parameters in lofty (often academic or philosophical) terms, and to articulate its primary purpose as helping build the Chinese nation-state.

Scholarship that emphasizes the history of formal industry and science in China has been vital insofar as it helps push back against narratives that evaluate Chinese industrialization and science as incomplete or even failed industrialization. The rich empirical studies on the formalization of science and industry have done much to demonstrate how, despite the inhospitable conditions of imperialism and political decline, modern China has been tremendously flexible and adaptable and quick to industrialize and establish fields of modern science. What appears to receive less attention, however, are the manufacturing and production practices that fell outside of formal industrialization or formal "science." The vernacular-industrialism approach adopted here thus builds on the foundation laid by studies that have documented state-sponsored technological growth, formal institution building, company-centered development, and the rise of modern science, but it adds to the picture by attending to seemingly extraneous practices. It thus provides a particularly effective vantage point from which to appreciate how the varied industrial activities in China diverged from an inexorable path toward formal industrialization and modern science.

Chen Diexian's story illustrates several of these alternative paths. Take, for example, how the story of Chen's formal *and* informal manufacturing and chemical activities departs from the usual straightforward narrative of a company evolving from small enterprise to big industry. Small-scale companies ranging from handicraft workshops to modestly mechanized mills and foundries dominated the light-manufacturing sector in early-twentieth-century China (Dikötter 2007). There were also large-scale industrial complexes. Giant foreign multinationals such as British American Tobacco were present. So, too, were domestic companies such as Dasheng textiles, founded by regional industrialists who were stepping in where the late-imperial state had once led industrial development (Köll 2003; Benedict 2011). At first glance, Chen's company, Household Industries, seems to provide a typical example of a small-scale, family-based enterprise that evolved to become a successful vertically integrated factory. Yet upon closer examination Chen's industrialism maps onto the history of industry in early-twentieth-century China in unanticipated ways, never entirely fitting into our previous understandings of what constituted small-scale or large industrial enterprises.

The unorthodox elements of Chen's vernacular industrialism were multiple. When state support was not particularly substantial yet economic imperialism was increasingly perceived as a grave threat, Chen used the thriving print market to promote patriotic manufacturing and channeled proceeds from his writing to start his daily-goods company (chapters 2 and 3). In an era when materials and resources needed for building industry, including key raw ingredients, were scarce and often hard to come by, Chen experimented with local source materials such as cuttlefish bones and sea brine as substitutes for expensive imported ingredients (chapter 3). He pursued a broad range of practices in chemistry and manufacturing, including unconventional activities, whether exploring new technologies and industry in bamboo-branch poetry (chapter 1) or reverse-engineering brand cosmetics to identify chemical ingredients (chapter 4). These unorthodox industrial efforts were not simply residual "premodern" artisanal practices associated with family-based workshops that relied on unskilled or semiliterate labor.[22] They were neither useless literati dabbling that obstructed professionalization nor armchair lettered activities that never translated into hands-on productive or scientific engagement. Rather, Chen built on seemingly inconsequential tinkering with gadgets such as the foam fire extinguisher from his days as a "connoisseur" in Hangzhou to later manufacture industrially the Butterfly brand extinguisher (chapter 3). The compilation of his business letters as forms of "model correspondence," a distinct pedagogical genre with a long history in China, ensured that his reach would go beyond simply the founding of Household Industries to encourage and enable small start-ups and young industrialists. Such efforts—some of which were seemingly capricious—functioned to generate curiosity about and actual material engagement with industry, manufacturing, and chemistry.

At the same time, Chen's informal, contingent, nonsystematic, and variegated practices need to be understood not *solely* from the perspective of their role in modernizing Chinese industry or in making modern chemistry. His endeavors occurred during a period when methods for building industry and pursuing science were variable and still being formed. Thus, one might characterize his amateur dabbling, his playful how-to writings, and his "copycat" practices as simply the necessary stage or "initial steps" of an inexorable development toward "real" and formal chemical industry in China. Such an interpretation, however, does injustice to the multifaceted nature of these practices and obfuscates how even as some of these activities did play a role in Chen's (and others') industry building, they also assumed alternative purposes and functions. By situating Chen's practices of leisurely dabbling or his prolific promotion of amateur chemistry in his commercial writings, we can see how some aspects of his vernacular industrialism facilitated the self-cultivation of urban readers or helped define status and taste. Other aspects helped foster new forms of sociability around chemical experimentation.

The express cultivation of Chen's industrial activities as vernacular, local, and artisanal in spirit was moreover a very modern and relevant strategy in the age of nativist manufacturing. The exact parameters of "vernacular industrialism" shifted over the course of Chen's career: it emerged first as a creative necessity in a period of scarce resources and inhospitable conditions and then evolved into a deliberate branding strategy. A central aspect of Chen's industrialism, especially in the early part of his career, was making a virtue out of necessity and turning the scrappy and meager resources he had at his disposal into strengths. His initial efforts in industry building were decidedly modest and family based and turned on informal tinkering and resourceful experimentation. Chen's approach in the early years might even be characterized as tactics of the "weak" and included strategic "piracy," adaptation of foreign technologies, local sourcing, and the improvement of existing technologies rather than engagement in wholesale invention. Chen's vernacular industrialism thus involved efforts to engage in copying (*fangzhi* or *fangzao*), experimenting (*shiyan*), and improving (*gailiang*) small technologies.

As Chen became an established and seasoned industrialist in the late 1920s and 1930s, he no longer embodied the traits of vernacular industrialism the way he had as a learned amateur and aspiring manufacturer. His industrialism gained new meaning over time. Its key practices of "tinkering," emulating, and improving, which had been born out of necessity, became the basis of Chen's strategies to brand his company as nativist and to dominate markets at home and abroad. In an era when the ideal of patriotic manufacturing and an ethos of nativist industrialism defined the NPM (of which Chen was a leading participant), Chen and eventually the Nationalist (Guomindang, GMD) state hailed copying, experimenting, and improving as skills that were exemplary in virtue (chapter 4). The vernacular industrialism of Household Industries was furthermore portrayed as a patriotic and virtuous alternative to global capitalism and economic imperialism. The company's reputation for autarky and localism (even though in reality it had from the beginning been integrated with global circuits) allowed it to position itself competitively against global competitors in China and Chinese diasporic markets throughout Southeast Asia.

In short, a study of vernacular industrialism can remind us that factory-based manufacturing and formal industry did not constitute the only form of industrial practice at the time and allows us to convey more fully the heterogeneity of the historical reality that was China's industrialization. Myriad reasons and interests (political, cultural, and social) lay behind the array of industrial, chemical, and manufacturing practices in early-twentieth-century China, some of which led to considerable success in industry and some of which assumed wholly different historical functions. An expansion of our definition of industrial work and a broader focus on the variegated strategies of industrialization, both formal and informal, serve, furthermore, as a powerful antidote to characterizations that continue to see the period as one of stalled industrialization when inferior, less-substantial engagement with science and manufacturing took place. Nor was this period merely a "transitional" stage in which China was simply a latecomer on an inevitable and desirable course toward modernity. This is an important corrective of the portrait of China as an imperfect or incomplete industrial developer that continues to inform comparativists' and world historians' identification of the Western origins of modern capitalism in the making of the modern world.[23]

WAYS OF KNOWING AND BRANDING IN AN ERA OF MASS TECHNOLOGIES

During a period when knowledge work and material work were increasingly defined by technologies of mass production, Chen engaged in industrial work by assuming both lettered and manufacturing activities. His efforts in both realms were linked. For Chen, building industry was predicated just as much on the production of textual and conceptual knowledge as it was on the production of raw materials and finished goods and the building of factories. As industrialization engendered the mass proliferation of things and words, new strategies became necessary to guarantee both objects and knowledge about objects. When a sea of goods threatened consumers' ability to discern a genuine article from a fake one or a nativist product from a foreign, "enemy" product, Chen sought to authenticate the nativist value and guarantee the trustworthiness of products he made and his commercial endeavors more generally. In an era when texts and words were mechanically reproduced, he took pains to assure readers of the reliability of the publications he sold and of his acts of knowledge production.

As a maverick entrepreneur who blended for-profit activities across the worlds of letters and industry, Chen Diexian complicates the recent "material turn" in historical writing. This "turn" has provided a needed corrective to the poststructuralist-inspired linguistic analysis of the 1990s, prompting historians to reexamine material and institutional aspects of the past. Yet this endeavor to unearth the materiality of things and uncover bodily practices has at times come at the expense of the examination of cultural concerns, politics, and textual endeavors. For instance, revisionist work that posits how the West's fortuitous windfall of coal and access to resources in the American colonies explain the eighteenth-century "great divergence" between industrial and economic development in the West and China rests on the assumption that if Chinese (or any other actors) had had access to coal, they would have industrialized (Pomeranz 2000). Such an approach, however, underappreciates the "human factor," the conditions of imperialism, and politics, all of which helped shift the Chinese worldview from appreciating coal as a resource upholding livelihood (*minsheng*) to defining coal as a fuel necessary for an industrial nation-state's survival in a new world order (Shellen Wu 2015).

Recent work in the history of science has also taken a material turn. Revisionist historians of science have increasingly been attentive to the practices of physical and intellectual labor that produce the knowledge identified as scientific forms of knowledge. Real contributions have been made in emphasizing how these "ways of knowing" not only are constituted by abstract knowledge and theoretical forms of engagement but also include forms of embodied knowing and material practice (see, e.g., Pinkstone 2000). A recent trend in the study of material culture deliberately employs terms such as *craft* and *handwork* to examine embodied skill and knowledge production.[24] This turn toward matter has been exceptionally powerful in how it eschews the analytical framework that privileges theory over bodywork and that has long informed studies on the scientific revolution. Yet appealing as this corrective is, it can at times risk going too far by looking exclusively at the material and the embodied without considering, for example, how cultural, conceptual, and textual aspects of knowing are also related to the material world and are manifested materially. As a critique of the epistemic regimes of the post–Industrial Revolution and modern world, this trend can also lead to the privileging of the nonmodern, nonmechanized ways of knowing over both cultural and material ways of knowing in the modern era of mechanized production.

As a lettered entrepreneur and modern industrialist, Chen serves as an effective case study to cast light on what may be underemphasized in this recent materialist turn. Specifically, Chen's vernacular industrialism allows us to examine more closely the exact interrelationship between thought and toil, epistemology and matter, and culture and commerce in a modern and increasingly mechanized era. It showcases the mutually constitutive relationship between material and mental labor. As this introduction's epigraph notes, Chen sought both to know (*zhi) and* to practice (*xing*) industry. Although hagiographic, the epigraph does point to how Chen was productive in the industrial world while also prolifically documenting his industrial activities and advocating the need to know (often through texts) new forms of knowledge. In other words, his "knowledge work" played a crucial role in his material endeavors. This study thus uses the term *knowledge work* self-consciously to emphasize that Chen's engagement of ideas was not just abstract.[25] His production of knowledge and ways of knowing were material in nature. His cognitive labor included epistemic practices that can be historicized, including experimenting, emulating, and improving. Concrete material conditions and institutional settings and distinct forms of labor shaped the textual practice, whether compilation, translation, or editing, through which he produced knowledge.

Throughout his career, Chen blended his knowledge work with his industrial work. As a young man, Chen was already conducting chemical experiments in his Hangzhou literati studio, undertaking hands-on pursuits and experimentation, and fiddling with gadgets such as the foam fire extinguisher (chapters 1 and 3). After he moved to Shanghai in 1913, he continued to explore methods for manufacturing cosmetics, raw ingredients, and a host of other light-industry items (chapters 2 and 3). Moreover, this ongoing hands-on experimentation was never far removed from textual modes of knowledge. To secure knowledge about manufacturing and industry, he translated information, recipes, and formulas from abroad and published these translations widely. In applying the translated recipes locally, he found that he often had to innovate to conform to local conditions and to rely on ingredients available at hand. So he often drew from the long-standing practices of mixing and assembling ingredients associated with herbal medicine that he was familiar with, just as his father had done in practicing medicine (chapter 4). In turn, he would publish his findings as exemplary "model correspondence" to share them with young workers and emerging manufacturers.

Chen's textual work was often practiced with an eye toward convincing fellow lettered men and women of the merit of industrial and commercial endeavors and hands-on engagement with production and technical work. With the spread of print globally, transmission of knowledge to larger and far-flung readerships was increasingly common. In nineteenth-century England, Victorian writers, pastors, and journalists served as popularizers of science (Lightman 2007).[26] Chen's textual work similarly functioned to transmit knowledge about chemistry and manufacturing. But it also did more. In a postimperial era, industry and the pursuit of profit remained unsettling for many lettered elites. Chen was aware that his exploration of technology, industry, and profit had the potential to generate social anxiety and discomfort and could be perceived as a challenge to accepted social order and convention. Much of his textual work thus aimed to alleviate these concerns, not merely by straightforwardly transmitting knowledge, but rather by reworking and presenting the knowledge in new ways and genres to make it more appealing to his readership. In Hangzhou, he wrote bamboo-branch poetry to domesticate newfangled technology among lettered circles (chapter 1). By the time he moved to Shanghai, he continued to exhibit skill in introducing manufacturing know-how in a palatable manner. A column on manufacturing cosmetics in a woman's journal in 1915 deployed powerful gendered assumptions of virtuous domestic production to help legitimate industrial pursuits as proper and patriotic. This tactic also helped assuage concerns about women and consumption and the dangers of commodification (chapter 2). During his editorship of the newspaper column "Common Knowledge for the Household" ("Jiating changshi," 1918–1927), Chen presented manufacturing and technical knowledge as "common knowledge," thus appealing to an audience imagined as "generalist" in nature and carving out a market niche for this knowledge in an era when lines of expertise and specialization in industry and manufacturing were starting to be drawn by emerging academics and professionals (chapter 3).

Chen proved particularly attentive to how the presentation of knowledge and the media technology of the day could elicit the consumer's sensorial engagement with either the story at hand, the knowledge being featured, or the product being sold. For instance, he paid attention to the linguistic register in which he presented information. Chen wrote and published mostly in a new-style classical Chinese, a commercially viable style of writing in early-twentieth-century China's burgeoning print market. This hybrid mode of the classical language incorporated some of the spoken language in writing and was arguably more "vernacular" than the new and national vernacular (*baihuawen*) being promoted at the time. Already in the late Qing (1890s–1910s), high-minded editors and political activists promoted *baihuawen*, or written Mandarin based on colloquial speech, as a means to expand China's community of educated citizens. Such an effort to replace the classical language was key in the lofty goal of making knowledge accessible to new readers, including women, children, and petty urbanites through primers, textbooks, and vernacular newspapers. By the late 1910s, in conjunction with the iconoclastic New Culture and May Fourth Movements, intellectuals such as Hu Shi (1891–1962), a Beijing University philosophy professor, pronounced modern *baihuawen* as *the* new national vernacular. This promotion accompanied an intensification of the ongoing assault against the classical language, which was increasingly deemed effete, obsolete, and at fault for holding back the Chinese nation. Yet, as scholars have shown, despite the urgency of New Culture claims that the new national vernacular would shape a new citizenry, the *baihuawen* movement remained accessible only to a relatively rarefied sector of the intellectual elite in the late 1910s and 1920s. Against this backdrop, the hybrid classical Chinese that Chen preferred was a commercial vernacular (as opposed to the more elite national vernacular), dominating China's vibrant print markets and reaching a far greater audience.[27]

Chen widely published, branded, and marketed his products in this commercial vernacular.[28] Tremendously popular and produced at a quick clip, his for-profit serialized novels written in this linguistic register in particular earned the wrath of New Culture and May Fourth intellectuals. Highbrow intellectuals derogatorily referred to his fiction publications (and others like them) as "Mandarin duck and butterfly fiction" (*yuanyang hudie pai xiaoshuo*; hereafter, butterfly fiction), referring to the novels' unabashed use of the romantic duck and butterfly literary tropes. They targeted the novels as worthless commercial entertainment rather than serious national literature. Chen's columns and writings on minor industrialism were also written in this commercialized form of classical Chinese and, like his novels, probably drew the ire of May Fourth intellectuals.[29] May Fourth figures were promoting *kexue*, "modern science," as serious noncommercial knowledge written in the new national vernacular and necessary for saving the nation. In contrast, Chen's publications asserted the epistemological authority of modern scientific knowledge such as chemistry but interpreted the social, cultural, and political value of such a regime in a way that diverged from what professionals or highbrow academics might have wanted. His portrayal of chemistry and manufacturing knowledge was at times playful, at times patriotic; occurred outside of academia or credentialed fields of professional knowledge making; and was often for sale. At a time when professional knowledge, expertise, and authority over the definition of "science" were only starting to be established, his writings allowed him to participate in the larger debate over who had the authority to determine what constituted valuable manufacturing and chemical knowledge and how to consume and apply such knowledge. In contradistinction to emerging forms of professionalized, specialist knowledge and academic, highbrow "Mr. Science" discourses, Chen presented himself as a fashionable adviser in media columns, providing practical if tasteful tips, "common knowledge," and vernacular know-how to his readers—for a price.

As author and editor *and* man of industry, Chen was furthermore fully aware of the surfeit of words and things in China's markets. In the late nineteenth and early twentieth centuries, an increasingly competitive market of both words and things meant that producers of both had to invest in strategies to guarantee and legitimate their range of products for sale. Mechanized reproduction of texts meant that false information, overabundance of knowledge, and the seduction of words threatened epistemological certainty. With the rise of mass-produced foreign and domestic brands, counterfeits, fakes, and recycled products became rampant (Benedict 2011). The NPM was symptomatic of the growing apprehension that fraudulent enemy products from abroad were threatening China's sovereignty.[30] In response to some of this anxiety, the movement sought to promote native goods as authentic, genuine, and central to China's national survival.

It was in this context that Chen realized the value of generating the illusion of the real.[31] He achieved this illusion in multiple ways. Featuring the trope of the butterfly, Chen's fiction and the marketing for his

Butterfly brand cosmetics exploited the nostalgia for a sentimental dreamscape world, which, though fictional or illusory, nonetheless evoked a sense of being untainted by prosaic, commercial, or sundry concerns (chapters 1 and 5). His knowledge products—from his how-to columns (chapters 2 and 3) to his collected series on nativist goods (chapter 6)— were pitched to be authoritative in their ability to provide readers with the expertise to discern which commodities on the market were quality objects and uncounterfeited native goods and thus trustworthy and genuine. The "authentic" nature of products was thus not only about their not being counterfeits but also about their being "native" goods. Several of the items that Chen's company manufactured, including toothpowder, soap, and modern cosmetics, had in the latter part of the nineteenth century been identified as *yanghuo*—literally "ocean goods" but often translated as "foreign goods"—in the Self-Strengthening Movement. By the twentieth century, Chen and other NPM leaders helped turn such *yanghuo* objects into "native products" (*guohuo*). Chen's technical manuals in the 1930s, discussed in chapter 6, articulated how the domestic production process—executed by Chinese merchants, even if often involving the copying of foreign technologies—was at the crux of defining a genuinely nativist object, distinct from foreign, enemy commodities. Cognizant of cutting edge marketing and advertising strategies emerging worldwide, Chen did not hesitate to launch ambitious advertising campaigns and deploy new laws on trademark infringement to claim exclusive ownership over its highly compelling Butterfly mark.

In an era when an individual could become a brand, all of these endeavors helped Chen craft his persona as a new-style industrialist. This persona rested on being genuine and sincere as well as authoritative and authentic, and it evolved over the course of his career. He started as a new-style lettered man dabbling in profit, a tastemaker in the Shanghai lifestyle markets, and then became a brand-name author. He was also an advocate of chemistry and an aspiring manufacturer who ended up a patriotic captain of industry. In each of these roles, he pushed conventional boundaries of what was acceptable and was always cognizant of the need to legitimate his efforts. This cognizance was evident even in his serialized fiction, where he sought to present himself as an author of genuine feeling who could make his readers weep even as he had them navigate new ideas about profit and technology and as he sold his lettered work for a price, as discussed in chapter 1. Chen expanded such early efforts to bolster not only his creative labor but also his industrial endeavors and to portray himself as a sincere man of feeling even as he engaged in cold-hearted capitalism.

Yet lest we take his self-branding too literally, it should be noted that behind the self-promotion and crafting of personae Chen was often ruthless, cunning, and willing to make shifty deals and engage in duplicity to navigate the darker sides of the business and political worlds. There are hints of this more cutthroat side in the source materials. This behavior includes the bullying of local denizens in Ningbo to secure ingredients needed to manufacture magnesium (chapter 4), the duplicitous strategies his company assumed to avoid taxation (chapter 4), and the hardball legal maneuvering it engaged in to monopolize the brand name "Butterfly" (chapter 5).[32] Chen also had his fair share of failures, including a less than successful foray into paper production (Chen Dingshan [1955] 1967, 180, 186). The more opportunistic and shady side of Chen's career needs to be pointed out precisely because of his superior skills in branding and marketing.

Finally, the importance of the linguistic terrain and the media environment upon which Chen operated brings us back to the relevance of "vernacular" in "vernacular industrialism." In its most mundane sense, the term *vernacular* refers to local languages that are often deemed less scholarly or learned than a classical or cosmopolitan language. However, scholars in various disciplines have used this term to conceptualize the complexities of localized, regional, or noncosmopolitan cultural forms to avoid the negative connotations associated with analytical categories such as "popular" or "mass culture," which are somehow seen as inferior to and analytically distinct from "elite" or "learned" culture (e.g., Pollack 2000). Film scholars have built on this scholarship to use the term *vernacular modernism* to characterize the mass-mediated and mass-consumed modernity of early-twentieth-century Shanghai, especially in terms of understanding the interaction between China's domestic film industry and global Hollywood in the context of industrial modernity and colonialism.[33] Thoughtful critiques, to be sure, have emerged cautioning how these conceptualizations of "vernacular modernism" still risk indexing the West and Hollywood as the cosmopolitan/global and render China's vernacular modernity as somehow provincial, if not simply derivative.[34] Yet, although these critiques are important, I none-theless contend that a revised notion of the "vernacular" accommo-dates these concerns and remains compelling. The linguistic and media-related connotation is directly relevant for understanding Chen's knowledge production and marketing practices. Chen wrote in com-mercialized classical Chinese in his *xiao gongyi* publications, and his marketing tactics drew directly from the translocal Shanghai and Southeast Asian cinema cultures, as discussed in chapter 5. Although in the mode of the vernacular modern, Chen's industrial activities were moreover never merely local. Nor were they derivative even as they took place within the context of the uneven power relations of colonial moder-nity. His actions were a constituent part of worldwide developments of capitalism and linked inextricably to far-flung circuits of knowledge and goods. His industrial pursuits targeted regional and global markets and resulted in his outmaneuvering of transnational brands in China and beyond. And, if we keep in mind how the "vernacular" is never fixed but constantly constructed vis-à-vis shifting notions of the "cosmopoli-tan," the term captures what was on Chen's part a conscious attempt to build a nativist reputation vis-à-vis imperialist "enemy" goods that reso-nated with the NPM and allowed him to compete with global brands.

TINKERING AND GLOBAL REGIMES OF INNOVATION AND OWNERSHIP

Nowhere is the entanglement between knowledge work and material work more evident than with Chen's deployment of what I call "tinker-ing." As a writer and editor, Chen crafted, combined, and played with words in an era of mechanical reproduction of print. As a dabbler in chemistry, he mixed and matched ingredients, and as a start-up manu-facturer he tinkered with gadgets such as the offset printing press and the foam fire extinguisher. The interrelationship between his crafting of words as a wordsmith and his experimentation as both an amateur chem-ist and an emerging manufacturer informed his practices of innovation at a time when regimes of industry and industrial property rights were not yet fixed. The practice of tinkering with words and things was at the basis of his improving (rather than inventing) light-manufacturing technologies, which resulted in industrial innovation and considerable commercial success. Chen's approach thus sheds light on the modern significance of practices of improvisation and emulation of circulating technologies.

By employing the term *tinker* and flagging "tinkering" as a central component of Chen's vernacular industrialism, I seek to evoke the colloquial associations of the term as well as to tap into historiographical debates about technology, innovation, and industrial development. The term *tinkerer* originally referred to an itinerant mender of pots and pans who would seek to improve or repair things.[35] Its meaning has since expanded to include those who experiment with and repair mechanical parts. In colloquial terms, *tinkering* frequently refers to experimenting or playing around with something, often if not always to repair or improve the item, though the results are not always a product that is as good as new. The term can thus elicit negative connotations. In British studies, for example, the practice has often been uncritically associated with Gypsies or the Irish as itinerant tinkerers who engage in lowbrow technology and eke out a meager living by repairing tin pots. The repair furthermore is often portrayed as desultory and temporary.[36]

For my purposes here, however, I would like to reclaim the concept of "tinkering" as useful to rethink practices of innovation and production. With respect to the historiographical implications of "tinkering," the choice of this term is hardly neutral. It evokes, for example, debates in history about the nature of innovation in technological and industrial development. Historians such as Joel Mokyr have noted that the knowledge economy (open and public and characterized by "useful knowledge"), a culture of creativity, and the "mental and political diversity" of the West created the perfect confluence of forces to generate quantum leaps in technological innovation that singularly constituted the Industrial Revolution and the West's ensuing sustained technological superiority (1990, 302).[37] Seeking to link Newtonian physics to the Industrial Revolution, others argue for a unique "scientific culture" that turned on practical acts involving mechanical knowledge and that informed early-modern British engineers and merchants (Jacob and Stewart 2004). Revisionist approaches, however, not only have cautioned against the triumphalist nature of such rise-of-the-West narratives but have also suggested alternative ways of thinking about technological development and innovation. Some have rejected the idea of revolutionary macroinvention and instead have promoted the idea of gradual, nonlinear, and nonte-leological change in technology that was then diffused beyond the West.[38] Others have added that such innovation based on practices of incremental improvement were hardly specific to the Western case.[39] And, more recently, postcolonial scholars and global historians have demonstrated even more concretely how the making of science and industry has always involved transnational exchanges and encounters and how knowledge transfers where the knowledge was necessarily adjusted, altered, and modified, often incrementally, in forms of trans-mission occurred not in any smooth, diffuse fashion but across uneven terrains of power and through processes of local adaptation, translation, and contestation.[40] The term *tinkering*, as used here, builds on this cri-tique of wholesale innovation and ex nihilo invention by highlighting the contingent, haphazard, and experimental fashion in which innovation happens and as technology exchange occurs around the world.

In addition to its significance in historiographical terms, tinkering in this twenty-first-century moment is becoming positively associated with do-it-yourself (DIY) and start-up cultures that underlie high-technology industries (or, certainly, their founding myths). It is associ-ated, for example, with practices in manufacturing-design hubs in places such as Shenzhen, China, where attempts at cloning and "ripping off" are now understood as helping to beget innovation and experimentation (Stevens 2018).[41] As seen with the opening of the Tinkering Studio at San Francisco's science museum explOratorium in 2014, the twenty-first-century digital era is witnessing and, indeed, helping generate a revival of DIY culture.[42] This culture is in large part made possible by access to information on the internet and is informing makers' communities, who now celebrate their hands-on acts of tinkering as working at the inter-section of art, science, and technology. In these contemporary discourses, "tinkering" and the DIY ethos have emerged as conceptual tools with which to rescue practices that might be demonized by modern intellec-tual property rights or corporate manufacturing regimes. Acts of adap-tation, collaborative sharing of knowledge (or open sourcing), and improving (not inventing) are increasingly seen as legitimate elements of creativity.[43]

To be sure, critics have recently cautioned that some contemporary endorsements of makers' cultures and start-ups are uncritical and overly rosy and fail to expose the potential neoliberal biases that lie behind the discourses surrounding these makers' communities, something I discuss in more detail in the conclusion. These caveats are indeed important to keep in mind, but the turn to DIY practices is not entirely without value and has been generative, prompting scholars to explore alternative cultures of production. In this vein, tinkering has drawn attention as both a historical topic and a conceptual category. The introduction to a recent compilation of the writings of Hugo Gernsback, for example, treats tinkering not simply as an engaging hobby but also as a special form of intuition or creativity and as a means of advancement for a self-educated working class (Wythoff 2016). Gernsback was a science-fiction writer in early-twentieth-century America, an avid tinkerer with radios and gadgets, and a proponent of a hands-on, bottom-up approach to technology, writing for a series of periodicals, including the *Electro Importing Catalog, Modern Electric* (1908), *The Electrical Experimenter* (1913), and *Radio News* (1919). Central to his approach was the emphasis on incremental modification and a belief that tinkering involved innovation and creative expression, expertise, and skill. This vision was notably distinct from the assumptions of ownership and invention at the heart of the emerging regimes of industrial property being promoted by capitalist corporations and corporate-based industrial-research laboratories at that time. This culture of making, moreover, turned on a system that advocated the free sharing of knowledge and skills rather than exclusive and corporate ownership of intellectual property.

The cultural, industrial, and innovative practices of Chen Diexian and his readers (who, as we explore in chapter 2, included both men and women) resonated with much of what defined Gernsback's community of (mostly male) radio aficionados. In fact, the convergences, it should be noted, were hardly accidental. Both communities were symptomatic of a global moment made possible precisely by the far-reaching nature of both the mass production of things and its correlate, the mechanical reproduction of words. Just as the rise of turn-of-the-twenty-first-century virtual technologies are informing contemporary DIY practices and makers' communities, the mass technologies that characterized material and textual production in the early twentieth century were key contexts for both Chen and Gernsback. Both were lettered workers, compiling, editing, and, in Chen's case, translating and adapting texts. Both also incrementally mended and improved things—often by hand—in a period of increasing mechanical and industrial production. Gernsback worked on radios and other electronics. Chen tinkered with the foam fire extinguisher, toothpowder, and other gadgets and daily-use items. Both used the power of print to mobilize followers and fellow makers. The lettered work they produced enabled them to provide the necessary knowledge and resources to promote techniques of making that could emerge as alternatives to the growing monopolization over industrial and scientific work by big corporations, academics, and the state. By compiling manufacturing know-how, including brand recipes and domestic and foreign formulas, as "common knowledge" and freely repurposing such information for different publications, Chen defied any claim of exclusive possession over the information. His goal of rendering such knowledge transparent and "common" was a response to the hoarding behavior among traditional merchants but also defied assumptions of ownership associated with emerging practices of modern intellectual property.

If both Chen and Gernsback were indicative of a singular global moment, it is important to keep in mind what was historically specific and local in their efforts. In Chen's case, tinkering as a conceptual approach is particularly effective in illuminating how the amateur ideal of literati dabbling in leisurely pursuits was hardly at odds with the "tinkering" that characterized his manufacturing work. The conventional "amateur ideal" of the traditional man of letters was one who dabbles in an array of textual activities, such as composing poetry and writing plays in the imperial era as well as editing and compiling newspapers and writing serialized fiction in the modern era. The amateur connoisseur also had a hand in an array of "manual activities"—farming, practicing calligraphy, gardening, and exploring technologies/crafts—as long as they were for purposes of self-cultivation rather than for subsistence. The term *tinkering* is furthermore useful in that it points to the materiality of acts of bricolage in both Chen's adaptation of the manufacturing of raw ingredients *and* his textual work. Drawing from global circuits of industrial knowledge and chemical materials, Chen was epistemologically promiscuous in his *xiao gongyi* publications, where, as explored in chapter 3, he eclectically compiled entries on folk knowledge, indigenous pharmacology, global chemistry, physics, and other subjects—all in one column. He mixed and matched materially as well, innovating by drawing from Chinese pharmacology and by adapting translated recipes.

Gernsback and Chen, however, differ notably in the geopolitical significance of their tinkering. The practices advocated by Gernsback and his community of radio amateurs gained pointed meaning domestically with the rise of large corporate manufacturers of consumer technologies, such as RCA and AT&T. For Chen Diexian, the domination of domestic corporate entities was less significant. (Chen's own company was to become a powerful nativist corporation by the mid-1920s, and its products were, in turn, "pirated" by smaller companies.) Rather, Chen's community secured industrial and technical know-how not as working-class tinkerers but as new urban elites and emerging manufacturers invested in building nativist industry vis-à-vis imperialist multinational corporations. In an age of global capitalism, when the concept of intellectual-property rights was only unevenly starting to develop globally, macro-invention often did not represent the most strategic path. Many instead sought to improvise by sourcing locally, emulating foreign technologies, reverse-engineering brand products from abroad, and improving upon existing small technologies. Chen did these things precisely to challenge both Western and Japanese competitors within Chinese markets and beyond.

For a period when new global regimes of industrial property were only starting to emerge, the term *tinkering* is effective in teasing out how Chen understood and pursued strategies of copying and staking ownership over both knowledge and objects. His lettered work turned more on transmission, compilation, and adaptation than on original authorship. So, too, did his industrial innovation. Yet a characterization of him as merely blindly and literally copying others fails to capture the complexity of his entrepreneurial, editorial, and chemical practices. Like many of his generation, he adapted texts liberally, whether they were formulaic romance narratives or translated pharmaceutical recipes. Just as he recycled and repurposed content from publication to publication, he tapped into myriad sources and manufacturing traditions to develop industrial goods.[44] He resisted evolving norms of ownership that were increasingly associated with modern industrial-property regimes by promoting emulation of foreign technologies as a form of import substitution needed for building nativist manufacturing. In his marketing endeavors, he adapted global advertising campaigns launched by competing Western pharmaceutical multinationals to pitch his Butterfly brand cosmetics in Southeast Asia and to outmaneuver the very brands he was copying.

In short, these practices were not examples of ignorance or deviousness but instead demonstrate how copying and innovation were not always at odds. As a result of such approaches, Chen won recognition in China's manufacturing world for his ability not to "invent" but to "improve" (*gailiang* or *gaizao*) existing (foreign and domestic) technologies (chapter 4). His liberal adaptation and improvement of foreign technologies might appear to contradict his adoption of aggressive, brass-knuckle tactics—including the promotion of trademark-infringement laws of modern intellectual property—to stamp out domestic infringers and counterfeiters to guarantee Household Industries' dominance. However, for Chen, there was no contradiction between his pursuit of counterfeiters of his own products and infringers on his Butterfly trademark, on the one hand, and his adaptation of foreign technologies, on the other. His views on ownership were those of an industrialist competing on a global commercial stage, aware of and contributing to shifting norms of ownership, and appropriating those technologies that served his immediate goals.

A GLOBAL MICROHISTORY

At a moment when "deep" and "big" history has gained considerable attention in academia, a study of an individual entrepreneur—one who, despite the many translations he published, did not speak a single foreign language and resided in one region of China for most of his life—seems an odd choice.[45] It is, moreover, not an obvious case study from which to address broad phenomena such as China's industrialization and negotiation with modern science and global capitalism. Previous approaches to the study of science, industry, and commerce in China—if they did engage with world history—tended to favor the *longue durée* method and a comparative historical perspective. The founding father of the study of Chinese science, Joseph Needham, for example, famously promoted the idea that Chinese civilization had generated unique

Chinese forms of science that streamed into the universal river of modern science alongside European sciences.[46] Recent influential histories of Chinese industrialization have similarly been conducted from a world-history perspective and through a comparative approach (e.g., Pomeranz 2000).

To be sure, both the civilizational and the comparative approaches have been challenged.[47] Postcolonial and global-history approaches have been particularly effective at moving away from any residual civilizational analysis in comparative approaches by advocating for a focus on transnational connections.[48] In the history of science, this move has led to the consideration of the myriad networks and connected pathways along which material items and knowledge have historically flowed. Alternatively, some scholars zero in on nodes of exchange on such networks. Go-betweens and mediators are seen as coauthors of global science rather than merely as agents who have localized the global or transplanted "science" from the West.[49] Such mediators are now identified as key participants in transnational circuits of knowledge and materials that helped constitute global capitalism and science. By examining linkages, practices of translation, points of convergence, and globally circulating networks of expertise and material, these studies fundamentally question how we demarcate "Chinese" and "Western" science and industrialization (e.g., Tilley 2011; Shellen Wu 2015). This is not to say that the knowledge and practices traveled and flowed freely. Some scholars rightfully warn against using "hydraulic" metaphors of circulation too uncritically. They argue for the need to keep in mind how uneven power relations and local conditions can generate friction that might fragment encounters and stymie the free travel of ideas and things.[50]

This book draws from these ongoing discussions about the history of science and industry that are conducted from more globally oriented perspectives, but it does so somewhat counterintuitively by conducting a microhistory. Specifically, it seeks to exploit the opportunities accorded by focusing on an individual. Company-centric studies and sector-based or discipline-focused histories tend to examine exclusively the formal aspects of industry or science and as their end goal desire to explain how the company, sector, or field developed. Focusing on an individual, however, sheds light on relevant activities that might be located outside of a particular field or company or beyond formal industrial or scientific work. Through Chen's activities, we are able to locate unexpected practices and myriad sites of industrial activity. We see how knowledge making and textual work bear upon the material and bodily practices of industry. Following the myriad pathways that Chen took allows us to think of the transits of knowledge and materials he engaged in, which were local, regional, and even global in scope. Through practices of collaborative translation where fidelity came second to the adaptation of texts to local concerns, Chen selectively facilitated "technology transfer" from abroad and drew from global circuits of legal knowledge. But these endeavors were not simply acts of smooth transmission and localization. They included hands-on vetting and were points where circulation of information was at times facilitated and at times obstructed. They served as sites of alteration, improvement, and innovation that enabled resourceful local sourcing to produce finished products that could engage competitively in global markets. The study of a multifaceted, ambiguous individual such as Chen thus helps us challenge easy oppositions and binaries that have in the past closed down intellectual options regarding lettered versus industrial work, commerce versus culture, and local versus global. What follows is a locally embedded yet nonetheless globally linked account of vernacular industrialism.

PART ONE

Gentlemanly Experimentation in Turn-of-the-Century Hangzhou

CHAPTER ONE

Utility of the Useless

Zhuangzi was walking on a mountain when he saw a great tree with huge branches and luxuriant foliage. A wood cutter was resting by its side, but he would not touch it and when asked the reason said that it was of no use for anything. Zhuangzi then said to his disciples, "This tree, because its wood is good for nothing, will succeed in living out its natural term of years."

—ZHUANGZI, "THE MOUNTAIN TREE"

As a young man in turn-of-the-century Hangzhou, Chen Diexian started to turn to new kinds of endeavors—exploring imported technologies and new forms of media, promoting chemical and technical knowledge, openly pursuing money, and reckoning with the emergence of industrialization and mechanical reproduction at the level of daily life. The emergence of modernity in China (whether cultural, technological, industrial, or commercial) is often identified as taking place in treaty ports such as Shanghai. Although Chen eventually moved to Shanghai in the 1910s to pursue a range of cultural, industrial, and commercial activities, he did not begin those pursuits upon his arrival there. His formative experiences in exploring new practices and ideas took place in Hangzhou during his youth, where he adopted an array of strategies to domesticate the newfangled and to pursue profit. Even as he introduced and explored activities and new technologies in daily life in Hangzhou, he drew on familiar cultural practices to authenticate his endeavors. In an era when mass production was increasingly informing the everyday, his ability to evoke a sense of sincerity and genuineness by choosing appropriate pen names and sobriquets, writing poetry, and holding elegant gatherings was important for his lettered, industrial, and commercial work in Hangzhou and beyond. His exploration of new things and gadgets, alongside his experimentation in literary forms and endeavors, was part and parcel of a contemporary culture of play and whimsy in urban centers in Jiangnan that gained significance in a period when "serious" politics was mired in dysfunction, the Qing dynasty was waning, and the chaotic period of the early republic was beginning.[1]

Chen's biographical background and the local context in which he explored new technological delights are important in understanding his pursuits. Chen was born in 1879 in Qiantang, near Hangzhou.[2] He came from a well-to-do family. His father, Chen Fuyuan, practiced medicine, and his uncle served as an official.[3] Chen's father died in 1885 when Chen was only six, and his uncle died in 1897, setting off an inheritance dispute that split the family (Hanan 1999, 2). His mother, Ms. Dai, a concubine who had borne four children, was left to fend for the immediate family and saw that Chen Diexian was married to Zhu Shu, who had been selected for him years earlier. Chen and Zhu had three children (Wan 2001, 10). The eldest son, Chen Qu (1897–1989), whose sobriquets include "Xiaodie" and later "Dingshan," became a writer and industrialist in his own right in Shanghai and then in Taiwan. Chen's second son, Chen Cidie (1905–1948), became an artist.[4] His daughter, Chen Xiaocui (1902–1968), became a famous artist and professor in Shanghai.

Chen's upbringing had provided him with a classical literary education and the knowledge and skill set typical of a gentry doctor's household.[5] This background was helpful in enabling him to move with ease among different circles of society, including the official, literary, publishing, commercial, and industrial circles—many of which were new and evolving in the early twentieth century. Like many of his generation, he initially sought positions in officialdom, if rather reluctantly. He took the licentiate examination in Hangzhou and in 1893 became a *xiucai*-level candidate, successfully passing the county-level imperial examination.[6] From 1909 to 1913, he served in lower-level offices or as an assistant to a ranking official in Zhejiang and Jiangsu Provinces, including at one point secretary to the commissioner of customs (Chen Xiaocui, Fan, and Zhou 1982, 210). However, he was always dabbling in alternative endeavors. Some of these endeavors—such as writing and publishing poetry—were typical of educated men at the time. Some were more unconventional. Many were entrepreneurial. He opened up a publishing house for poetry and founded an early newspaper in Hangzhou. Chen's entrepreneurial efforts in the world of letters were furthermore paralleled by his efforts outside the literary arena. He bought a share in a tea and bamboo dealership in 1899 and then opened up Hangzhou's first scientific-appliance shop. After these brief forays into commerce in Hangzhou, he proceeded to take advantage of new opportunities arising in Shanghai to become a professional writer and editor and eventually a captain of industry.

Chen's life story provides an interesting case study with which to understand how an educated man started to experiment with new pursuits and to expand boundaries of convention in post-Taiping Uprising Hangzhou. In the twilight years of the Qing empire, the decline of orthodoxy resulted in shifting mores and opened up space so that novel opportunities could emerge. Ambitious young men started to blur the boundaries between the worlds of literati officialdom (*wen, guan*) and the realm of merchants (*shang*). To be sure, such blurring was hardly new. In the late Ming, the hybrid identity of the gentry merchant (*shishang*) had already brought together arenas of activity commonly associated with literati, merchants, and businessmen, thus shaping and animating trends in book publishing (Chow 2004). In nineteenth-century Shanghai, local gentry, such as the Gu family, acted as local entrepreneurs— purveyors of peaches, embroidery, inkstones, and preserved vegetables (Swislocki 2008).

Certain conditions shaping this blurring of identities were new. Fresh epistemological regimes and institutional spaces came to frame and radically reconfigure the intermingling of commerce and culture by the turn of the twentieth century. Educated elites increasingly disenchanted or alienated from officialdom and from traditional literati activities started to engage openly in the once taboo realm of commerce, many of them specifically turning to treaty-port publishing, commercial entertainment, and leisure.[7] As noted in the introduction, the dismantling of the civil-service examination system had a profound impact on elite strategies of cultural, social, and political reproduction and levied a serious challenge to the values of examination-oriented literati culture. New paradigms included novel forms of knowledge and culture (e.g., science rather than statecraft), newfound institutions through which to legitimate such knowledge (e.g., mass media, modern schools), and an array of practices that urban elites developed to navigate these new forms of knowledge and the new media associated with them (e.g., entrepreneurism and the pursuit of profit, nation building, and social reform). The last decades of the Qing dynasty constituted a critical juncture in Chinese history when elites' identity, paths of social mobility, and ways of knowing and navigating the world were up in the air. The institutions of empire that had once determined social mobility and direction were defunct, and new, unprecedented opportunities were emerging, often with little guarantee or certitude of success or promise.

In this context, Chen, along with fellow colleagues and family members, sought to push acceptable boundaries in multiple ways, including the appreciation of what had once been considered unorthodox, unconventional, or valueless. This push included expressing curiosity about imported objects, such as the gramophone, and establishing Hangzhou's first newspaper with friends. Later, this same trait of searching for value in what might appear useless drove Chen to realize that the vast amount of discarded cuttlefish shells that washed onto China's seashore could serve as an ingredient for toothpowder, the key commodity that would bring him industrial success. More broadly, we will see how Chen came to see the value in pursuing light industry and manufacturing, something that was still often deemed déclassé at the turn of the twentieth century.

Chen moreover sought to justify his tendency to play with and stretch convention and to find utility if not profit in what appeared frivolous. To this end, he employed an array of strategies that used the familiar to authenticate the new and the unconventional. He took advantage of Hangzhou's literati networks and elegant gatherings and adopted the disinterested stance of the lettered connoisseur to promote new ideas, information, and pursuits. Through thoughtfully chosen sobriquets and pen names, he created the persona of an eccentric figure who could dabble in the somewhat unorthodox. He opened up a familiar cultural institution, the reading room, but at the same time founded a more controversial institution—a scientific-appliance shop. He employed familiar literary genres such as bamboo-branch poetry to domesticate and explore new technologies and institutions in the landscape of his hometown, Hangzhou. At the same time, he pushed literary boundaries by exploiting new genres, such as the serialized romance novel, to explore anxiety-provoking themes, including money. He established himself as a serial author who, although writing for profit, was nonetheless a sincere man of sentiment. All of these choices and actions were indicative of an entrepreneurial and enterprising personality. For Chen, this ability to recognize the utility of that which appears to have little value was to become the basis of innovation and eventually profit.

CHOICE NAMES

Like other men of his generation, Chen had multiple names over the course of his life. His original personal name was "Chen Shousong," though he changed it to "Chen Xu" early on. He also had several *zi*, courtesy names, and *hao*, sobriquets.[8] One of his best-known sobriquets was "Diexian," or "Butterfly Immortal," which he had already started using in Hangzhou by 1900. A related *hao* was "Taichangxiandie," "Immortal Butterfly of Taichang" (Xu Shoudie 1948, 43).[9] His courtesy names included "Xuyuan," which can be translated literally as "Garden of Vitality" but evokes the meaning "dreamscape."[10] Multiple pen names included "Xihongsheng," the "Master of Studio Xihong," which he used when publishing poetry,[11] and "Chaoran," the "One Who Transcends," a pen name he used when writing a social exposé of officialdom (Chen Xiaocui, Fan, and Zhou 1982, 212).[12] He was best known in the literary world, however, as "Tianxuwosheng," "Heaven Bore Me in Vain."[13] He had already adopted this name around 1900 when he was a young man in Hangzhou and used it when publishing his romance fiction and serving as an editor in Shanghai.

With several of these names, Chen sought to cultivate a particular and strategic reputation, which is conveyed in the chapter epigraph. The epigraph is from chapter 20, "The Mountain Tree," in the basic writings of Zhuangzi, the early Chinese thinker (b. c. 369 BCE). Related to Daoism, Zhuangzi's thought expressed skepticism for man-made norms and yet was highly idealistic in its promotion of an understanding of the spontaneity of the universe and thus freeing oneself from worldly expectations and demands. Daoism and Zhuangzi's thought stood in contrast to schools of thought that centered on this-worldly social and political reform and prescription, such as Confucianism, Legalism, and Moism. This particular passage is representative. In it, Zhuangzi characteristically questions what we mean by utility with a parable involving a mountain tree. In the parable, Zhuangzi passes a huge tree with thick, lush branches and leaves and a wood cutter lying by the tree. When the wood cutter makes no move to cut down the big old tree, explaining that the tree is useless, Zhuangzi disagrees and argues for its value: "This tree, because its wood is good for nothing, will succeed in living out its natural term of years." Herein lies its utility.

Chen Diexian was drawn to the twin impulses of idealism and skepticism in Zhuangzi's thought. With his pen names, he sought to evoke Zhuangzi's tradition as he emerged as a new-style entrepreneur and dabbler in new things in late-Qing Hangzhou. His pen name "Tianxuwosheng," "Heaven Bore Me in Vain," was a self-effacing pun and allusion to the seventh line of the poem "Bring on the Wine" ("Jiang jin jiu") by one of China's most famous Tang dynasty (618–907) poets, Li Bai (701–762):[14] "Since heaven has given me life, it must be put to use (*tian sheng wo cai bi you yong*)." In a biographical account of her father, Chen's daughter confirmed the genealogy of the pen name, noting that her father had stated that his name "is that which is said by Li Bai, namely, if heaven has given birth to my talent, it must have use; if this is true, then I was born in vain; therefore, I call myself Tianxuwosheng, as I have no use" (quoted in Chen Xiaocui, Fan, and Zhou 1982, 210). The self-effacing modesty evoked by the pen name was not simply typical of the virtues valued by the literati at the time but also useful in allowing Chen to present himself in as humble a manner as possible and to conjure Zhuangzi through Li Bai. Li Bai had held office during his lifetime but nonetheless cultivated a reputation of being an eccentric immortal. Chen sought to present himself in a similar manner. He was "the one whom Heaven produced in vain" (a different rendering of the pen name), who dabbled in endeavors not seen as immediately useful or perceived as unconventional and yet still with potential value.

Chen also fostered a reputation of eccentric curiosity with the sobriquet "Diexian." "Diexian" can be translated as "Butterfly Immortal." As with the name "Tianxuwosheng," Zhuangzi was the direct source of inspiration for the name "Diexian." According to Chen's daughter, Chen stated that this name referred to a classical Zhuangzi parable titled "Zhuangzi Dreamed He Was a Butterfly" ("Zhuang Zhou meng die") (Chen Xiaocui, Fan, and Zhou 1982, 210). In this parable, Zhuangzi first dreams that he is a butterfly and then, when he awakes, starts to wonder whether he, the man, was dreaming or the butterfly is now dreaming he is Zhuangzi. This passage quintessentially captures the romanticism and the skepticism regarding knowledge and reality in Zhuangzi's thought. Chen's choice of the name "Diexian," "Butterfly Immortal," was hardly accidental. For Chen, the name suggested that he was unencumbered and could engage in a romantic dalliance with all forms of knowledge and activity—whether they were orthodox or not. Whereas Zhuangzi was still dreaming within a dream, Chen, by adopting the persona of an immortal, sought to achieve transcendence from the corruptions of the real world (Chen Xiaocui, Fan, and Zhou 1982, 210). The romantic impermanence evoked by Chen's butterfly-themed names could be juxtaposed to what had once been certain but by the late Qing had become hollow—mainly Qing officialdom and its Confucian orthodoxy.

In a period when attributes, titles, and careers that once had seem so useful became increasingly useless, Chen employed Daoist-inspired names to render the opposite effect: to mark opportunity in areas that had previously seemed uselessly peripheral. From an early age, Chen sought to mark himself as someone able to recognize the value in what others failed to appreciate during a period when values were in flux. Through the savvy choice of a string of public and pen names, he relished in challenging convention and orthodoxy and consistently displayed an appreciation for the seemingly worthless, often turning it into something with value. He established a persona of virtuous eccentricity that would allow him to cloak, or rather to present as permissible, some of his more controversial and cutting-edge ambitions.

POST–TAIPING UPRISING HANGZHOU: WESTERN LEARNING IN ELEGANT GATHERINGS

By the late Qing, after the Self-Strengthening Movement, curious literati and newly rising merchant-industrialists in cities in the Jiangnan area continued to explore scientific and industrial knowledge. Local elites such as Chen adapted the ideals of literati versatility and "broad learning" (*boxue*) in vogue to legitimate experimentation and innovation with new ideas and endeavors associated with industry and commerce, pursuits once deemed undesirable for respectable elites to participate in. Lettered men had long engaged with the material world but had often done so only textually by incorporating insights from artisans into their learned treatises. Or if they did engage in hands-on work, they presented any actual engagement with the material world as an endeavor of connoisseurship to deflect long-standing ambivalence toward production and manufacturing as well as class suspicion of certain skills and forms of knowledge associated with toiling workers. They engaged in hands-on work mostly out of philosophical interest or for purposes of self-cultivation, but not for subsistence. Such an approach continued in post–Taiping Uprising Hangzhou as lettered men such as Chen employed a stance of disinterested curiosity to engage in chemistry and explore modern scientific equipment in respectable homes, literati studios, and gardens where elites gathered. Late-Qing dabbling and connoisseurship in such spaces served as the grounds for both experimentation and entrepreneurism.

This growing interest in approaching the material world in this manner emerged alongside a concerted effort on the part of the government to continue industrial development in China's light-industry sector after the Self-Strengthening Movement's state sponsorship of heavy armaments. The late-Qing New Policies worked to reinforce developments that were already occurring in treaty ports and urban centers. From 1903 to 1907, Yuan Shikai (1859–1916), for example, established the Bureau of Industry in Zhili to develop industry in the region.[15] By 1908, a policy of developing industry served as the key policy framework during the Qing's closing years. The industrial intendant, who reported to the governor-general or governor of the province and received instructions from the Ministry of Agriculture Industry and Commerce, sought to reorganize Chinese industry.[16] During this period, state units worked with private actors to establish higher-education facilities in industry, to organize displays, and to run workshops, lectures, and night classes to teach trade and industry. They printed educational materials and visited factories to encourage and develop what they deemed to be desirable industrial practices. Already in the late Qing, spectacular and pedagogically driven displays were featured in expositions targeted to merchants, industrialists, academics, journalists, and officials. Men of letters in more traditional urban centers such as Hangzhou were hardly immune to these developments and started to engage with science and industry through existing cultural and social frameworks, including the tradition of "broad learning" and practices of elegant gatherings.

Scholars have characterized the explorations of new knowledge among educated communities in Jiangnan at this time as evidence of proto-science or the start of modern science in China. Some, for example, have identified individuals such as Xu Shou (1818–1884), who emerged from natural-studies (*bowu*) networks fostered in Jiangnan academies, as being fundamental to the eventual making of modern chemistry.[17] Such accounts, however, risk interpreting the turn-of-the-century scholarly activity and its practices and institutions anachronistically and in terms of the teleological unfolding of "modern science."[18] A more accurate portrayal of these activities includes understanding their significance as part of the gentlemanly tradition of broad learning, or *bowu*. In this tradition, lettered men and women explored a broad range of topics, some of which happened to include new knowledge and practices that would later become identified as "scientific knowledge," whereas others did not (Elman 2005).

The founding of China's first modern museum by early industrialist Zhang Jian (1853–1926) in Nantong in 1905 demonstrates how *bowu* proved to be an effective frame through which to domesticate new ideas and things. The Nantong museum came to be called a *bowuyuan* or *bowuguan*, compounds that include the term *bowu*, "broad learning." With this designation, Zhang Jian signaled how the institution was generating a new vision characterized by an awareness of the full if chaotic scope of the collection. The museum featured new objects and fields of knowledge. Natural history was a major emphasis. Modern industrial tools and machines were also displayed (Shao 2003, 157–158). This was an institution where radically new *and* old ways of seeing were fostered (Claypool 2005, 590–599). The museum encouraged the unfolding of a new vision known as *bolan*. This compound, fusing the terms *bo*, "to study," and *lan*, "looking" as in surveying a landscape, can be translated as "studious and adventuring eye" and captured how new-style exhibits were to be studied. To make the new-style museum and the new way of viewing more accessible to local elites, Zhang made sure to include familiar literati aesthetics and display styles as well as to hold intimate and elegant soirees.

In late-Qing Hangzhou, networks of literati schooled in the tradition of *boxue* often congregated in "elegant gatherings" (*yaji*). In these gatherings, lettered men shared tasteful artifacts in intimate settings, explored new knowledge and things, built community, and renewed the vitality of the area after the destruction of the Taiping Uprising. These gatherings held great cultural prestige and further proved to be a potent means by which to fend off the discomforting new reality of the commercialization of literati cultural activity, a trend clearly evident in nearby Shanghai but also encroaching into Hangzhou. The famous Xiling Seal Society in post–Taiping Hangzhou, for example, renewed its corporate identity and local literati culture by facilitating the "congregation of like-minded, cultured men for purpose of socializing, drinking, composing poetry, playing games and engaging in connoisseurship" (Lawrence 2014, 15–45). These congregations took place on the physical site of the Xiling Seal Society, which happened to be located next to Chen's publishing house on the West Lake. The society sought to preserve not just seals and metal-and-stone artifacts but also specific modes of social interaction, such as the exclusivity and amateurism that ideally characterized literati scholarship, which was rapidly disintegrating at the turn of the twentieth century.[19]

Gentlemanly congregations focused specifically on Western learning emerged in Hangzhou at this time. New-style literati reform activity flourished under the aegis of Lin Qi (1839–1900), the prefect of Hangzhou starting in 1895. Lin supported the establishment of reform-oriented groups that centered on the Fujian native-place network (Lin Qi was from Fujian), including the well-known Cansang Academy (or Silkworm Breeding and Mulberry Growing Academy).[20] This group avidly promoted a reformist agenda in the new-style *Hangzhou Vernacular Daily* (*Hangzhou baihuabao*). Late-Qing reformists and radicals often founded vernacular dailies (*baihuabao*) to promote new ideas, forward their political agendas, and radicalize young readers. Zhuang Yumei, a young intellectual from the Ningbo group that included anti-Manchu radicals, writes about the *Ningbo Vernacular Daily* (*Ningbo baihua ribao*) in his autobiography (Zhuang 1963). This new-style newspaper, Zhuang notes, was inspired by the *Women's Vernacular Daily* (*Funü baihuabao*), published in Shanghai in 1904, and like its predecessor actively promoted new knowledge (*xinxue*) as well as new social and political ideas, including progressive gender norms. Radicals—including Zhong Xianchang (1868–1940), the anti-Manchu founder of the China Educational Supply Association Ltd. (Kexue yiqi guan, a name whose more literal translation would be "Science Apparatus Shop"), a Shanghai-based scientific-appliance shop, and close compatriot of revolutionary leader Cai Yuan-pei (1868–1940)—were involved with the Ningbo paper and served as both contributors and consumers. The *Hangzhou Vernacular Daily* and the affiliated Cansang Group were similarly oriented toward new learning and may have served as an incubator for radicalism.

There is no direct evidence that Chen Diexian was a member of the Cansang Academy or participated directly in these Western-learning scholarly networks. However, he was no doubt familiar with the late-Qing Hangzhou vogue of "elegant gatherings," both real and imagined, as well as with the groups and newspapers associated with Western learning and the reformist, even radical agenda. Chen advertised some of his commercial endeavors, including his scientific-appliance shop, in the *Hangzhou Vernacular Daily*.[21] We also know that later on he collaborated in Shanghai with famous translator and editor Lin Shu (1852–1924), who was in Hangzhou in the late Qing and part of the Western-learning group (Hill 2013, 176). This larger culture of lettered exploration of new things was the backdrop against which Chen Diexian combined his literary skills with an entrepreneurial spirit.

ELEGANT EXPERIMENTATION AND THE GATHERING OF BENEFIT

Embedded in local networks of connoisseurship, Chen opened a scientific-appliance shop and reading room on the West Lake right next to the Xiling Seal Society. There he hosted intimate "elegant gatherings" similar to those given by his esteemed neighbors around the West Lake, including the members of the Xiling Seal Society. Whereas society members shared seals and scrolls at their gatherings, Chen introduced new gadgetry and scientific objects and even put some on sale, which proved unsettling to some. This experimentation with the new and flirtation with profit was what prompted Chen to find ways to present his endeavors in the guise of a gentlemanly pursuit.

Chen had already taken such an approach when he built a chemistry lab in his home with the guidance of a Japanese consul who was posted in Hangzhou. After the Sino-Japanese War of 1895, Japan gained considerable international power. It was able to expel privileges of extraterritoriality for Chinese in Japan, whereas the Qing state had to continue to grant Japanese communities extraterritoriality and cede more extraterritorial privileges over time. Japan could also participate in the International Mixed Court in Shanghai with equal footing as other treaty powers, sending assessors to "intervene" and defend Japanese interests against the Chinese (Cassel 2011, 149–178). In smaller cities such as Hangzhou, the presence of the Japanese was similarly strengthened during this period. The reformist *Hangzhou Vernacular Daily* devoted a full and regular section to news for the overseas Japanese student community, which suggests a substantial Japanese community overall.[22]

In this context, the Japanese came to be seen as bearers of new, cutting-edge knowledge. An ad for the Hangzhou Photography Company (Hangzhou zhaoxiang gongsi), a new kind of business at the time, was posted in the *Hangzhou Vernacular Daily* and boasted about having a famous Japanese teacher onboard as an adviser.[23] Chen, too, seemed to appreciate the prestige that would come with associating with the Japanese in Hangzhou. He started exploring chemistry through his personal connections with the local Japanese diplomatic community. In 1896, at the age of twenty-seven, he invited a Japanese consul stationed in the city to tutor him in chemistry and help him turn his traditional literatus studio into a domestic laboratory (Chen Dingshan [1955] 1967, 180–181).[24] In a memoir, Chen's son Dingshan recounts one of his most vivid childhood memories not only of running in his family compound while playing hide-and-seek with cousins but also of being introduced to the Japanese man whom his father had invited to his home as his chemistry tutor.[25] It was this Japanese gentleman who left Chen Diexian a cache of Japanese publications on manufacturing and industry that later became the source of many of Chen's publications and columns on light manufacturing (Chen Xiaocui, Fan, and Zhou 1982, 212).

Chen pursued chemistry and science in multiple registers, including amateur fascination. He tinkered with gadgets such as the chemical foam fire extinguisher (discussed in chapter 3) and at one point enthusiastically dragged peers up a hill in Hangzhou to witness his attempts to extinguish bales of hay that he had set on fire (Chen Dingshan [1955] 1967, 192). (The extinguisher apparently failed to function in this instance, and Chen presumably had to rely on more traditional techniques to quell the conflagration.) However, the register of his endeavors moved rather quickly beyond leisurely curiosity. By 1901, Chen founded the Gather Benefit Company (Cuili gongsi), the first store in Hangzhou to sell scientific appliances. As someone who understood the power of a sobriquet, Chen seemed to have chosen the store's name carefully. The first character, *cui*, "gather," functioned to evoke the culture of "elegant gatherings" discussed earlier. Other scholars have translated the second character, *li*, as "profit,"[26] but I prefer rendering it as "benefit." *Profit* evokes crass material and monetary pursuits, whereas *benefit* better conveys what Chen no doubt sought to convey—namely, that the store's goal was not simply self-interest but also benefit to society.

The establishment was located in the Qinghefang, a famous neighborhood in Hangzhou. The area was filled with medicine shops, handicraft shops, and other small commercial stores selling products from ham to tea leaves and was frequented by literati and commoners alike for leisurely entertainment. The store sold a range of items for profit, though it was to close in only a few years. An ad for the company was posted in the *Hangzhou Vernacular Daily* and described the "'Gather Benefit Company' as specializing in instruments for the academy."[27] It listed goods on sale, such as stationary items (paper, leather and cloth book covers, double-sided wax paper, map-making paper, and carbon paper), musical instruments (both a stand-up and a grand piano—given the newness of the instrument in China, the word *piano* was written phonetically in the ad—a variety of stringed instruments, two kinds of flutes, a bugle, and drums), as well as pen and ink, books, and utensils for the literatus studio. That the store was advertised in the *Hangzhou Vernacular Daily* suggests that the targeted audience included reformminded individuals in the area. Whereas books and stationary were certainly familiar, the musical instruments listed in the ad, along with other even more foreign goods in the store, such as imported scientific instruments, chemical apparatuses, and related appliances, were new. Its pioneering inventory included Hangzhou's first imported gramophone. In his retrospective biography, Chen's son Dingshan recalls hearing a foreigner's laugh and early Western music on the imported gadget for the first time when he was nine (Chen Dingshan [1955] 1967, 181).

Given the reformist tinge of the imported knowledge and goods that the Gather Benefit Company sought to sell, it caused consternation among more conservative types. Chen's son bitterly notes that the store brought his father considerable ridicule from his peers, who were less comfortable with things foreign and the open pursuit of money (Chen Dingshan [1955] 1967, 182). Cognizant of the potentially threatening nature of the shop, Chen set up a lithographic publishing company in conjunction with the shop in 1902 and then followed that in 1906 with a public library cum reading room known as the Read-to-Your-Heart's-Content Society (Baomushe). Chen's primary and explicit goal in opening up the publishing company and reading room was to make knowledge readily available—including newly published books and new forms of learning (Chen Xiaocui, Fan, and Zhou 1982, 211). Whether intentionally or not, the reading room and the publishing arm of the company also assumed a strategic function. As familiar institutions, both were more acceptable to local elites and helped Chen strike a less overtly foreign or commercial pose. As if in anticipation of some of the hesitation or opposition that the Gather Benefit Company would face among fellow literati, Chen echoed the strategy that Zhang Jian had pursued in Nantong by presenting potentially threatening new objects and knowledge in familiar settings. Reading rooms that introduced translations on science and technology could be found in Shanghai arsenals and polytechnic institutes as new spaces to learn about science.[28] These Shanghai-based reading rooms would feature translations on science and technology, maps, models, and devices alongside Chinese classics (Biggerstaff 1956, 129–30). They would also hold lectures. Similarly, Chen's Read-to-Your-Heart's-Content Society drew Hangzhou intellectuals together to pore over not only books but also the newfangled apparatuses and gadgets for sale at the Gather Benefit Company. They were there to discuss if not to experiment with the chemical formulas and recipes, just as they would share a painting or the experience of carving a seal at the Xiling Seal Society or observe a specimen in a gathering at the new Nantong museum.

Ultimately, both the store and reading room folded. Chen's daughter's explanation for the closing was that they were not able to sustain themselves financially (Chen Xiaocui, Fan, and Zhou 1982, 211). However, according to his son Dingshan, although Chen Diexian entertained many Hangzhou intellectuals, in return all he received was derision. The son claimed that local intellectuals stated, "Diexian has truly become a foreign devil and dared to bring this kind of spiritually polluting stuff to Hangzhou" (Chen Dingshan [1955] 1967, 182). Writing retrospectively in the 1950s in Taiwan, Dingshan was clearly invested in portraying his father as a heroic maverick, prescient for his times, especially in comparison with the local literati, who were more conservative and cautious. Yet even if his account is biased, we can nonetheless discern from it how there was room for exploring new things in the post–Taiping Uprising Hangzhou, even as that exploration might have generated anxiety.

Chen was not alone. Others were contemporaneously establishing scientific-appliance shops and bookshops in China.[29] In 1903, Wang Mengzou (1877–1953) opened the Wuhu Science Book Company (Wuhu kexue tushushe) in Anhui. Like Chen, Wang was a member of the last generation of scholars who had risen through the civil-service exam system and had grown disillusioned with pursuing traditional routes of officialdom. Also like Chen, Wang entered the publishing business by founding the Wuhu Science Book Company with the support of his fellow Anhui natives. The enterprise was a new-style bookshop that aimed to promote fresh knowledge by selling new-style textbooks, atlases, and scientific specimens and instruments.[30]

Some of these stores were quite expansive. Founded in the late Qing in Shanghai, the China Educational Supply Association Ltd. was a particularly interesting operation. It grew out of the Four Brights Practical Studies Association (Siming shixue hui), a Ningbo academy that focused on new learning, such as practical studies. After the Reforms of 1898, a group of patriotic Ningbo intellectuals near Zhenhai gathered together to organize the Ningbo Native-Place Association (Ningbo tongxianghui), where they were united in their opposition to the civil-service examination and in their belief in the need to engage in the study of science and to invest in industry in order to save the nation. Among this group was Ningbo native Zhong Xianchang, who went on to found the China Educational Supply Association in Shanghai not only to provide materials of science to build Chinese industry but also to promote a radically new culture and to instruct others in chemistry and physics.[31]

The China Educational Supply Association offers fascinating evidence of the intimate link between radical politics and the legitimacy of modern science in late-Qing China. From the start, its owner, Zhong Xianchang, saw science—especially the science behind bomb and explosives making as well as the chemistry involved in making poisons to be used for political assassination—as a key means to incite revolution and bring down Manchu rule.[32] Behind its neutral name and ostensible claim that it was opened to provide science materials for Chinese schools and educational facilities, the store thus quickly came to serve as a hub for anti-Manchu activity, functioning to supply revolutionaries with key materials and hardware, much of it imported from Japan.

One account colorfully illustrates the link between this institution and political revolution. In a retrospective account of the revolutionary Retrocession Association (Guangfu hui), Yu Ziyi (1990) describes in detail the kind of chemical tinkering and experimentation he engaged in for purposes of revolution and how he frequented the China Educational Supply Association. He tells how the revolutionary Cai Yuanpei (who was also a close associate of store founder Zhong Xianchang and eventually worked with Yu to found the Retrocession Association) knew he was interested in chemistry and urged him to study the manufacturing of poisons. To do so, Yu obtained the necessary materials from the China Educational Supply Association, which he described as "Shanghai's only organization run by Chinese that supplied chemistry and physics appliances and materials." Most goods were imported from Japan. Zhang Zhimin (1872–1945), a Ningbo industrialist living in Japan, served as the buyer for the store and secured the imported goods.[33] However, Chinese factories almost immediately started to manufacture local substitutes for expensive imports as well as to repair and supply replacements for imported appliances.[34] The China Educational Supply Association also printed translations of chemistry books and was considered a great boon for those researching physics and chemistry.

The store sourced ingredients that were to be used for revolutionary purposes. Among the ingredients Yu Ziyi purchased there was cyanic acid (Yu Ziyi 1990, 332), which he used to make a liquid poison with which to assassinate Manchu officials. Although Yu tested this particular poison successfully on a cat, Cai Yuanpei apparently felt that the liquid poison was inadequate and requested solid poisons in powder form. Yu manufactured these poisons once he mail-ordered from Japan books on materia medica, pharmaceuticals, and forensics. Yu also dabbled in explosives. Late-Qing revolutionary activists were using explosives in their efforts to destabilize Qing rule. As part of this movement, Yu and his colleagues would meet in alleyways, swear oaths of alliance by smearing their mouths with a blood sacrifice, and then experiment with guncotton, or nitrocellulose, a flammable compound, to make nitroglycerin for low-order explosives. Yu describes their laboratory as being quite humble; aside from tables and chairs, it featured little more than medicine bottles and glass utensils. He recalls how they would study the science behind their experiments at a set time every day and then launch into the actual experiments. Failures often resulted in billowing smoke, but they nonetheless persevered and continued to hone their methods. When the acids available at the China Educational Supply Association proved too weak, Yu and his colleagues disguised themselves as Japanese and wore Western suits to secure more potent acids from the foreign pharmacy, the Anglo-Chinese Dispensary (Hua-Ying yaofang), and extra-pure glycerin at the KOFA Dispensary or Koelkel & Schroeder Ltd. (Kefa da yaofang), both in Shanghai. The sources from which they learned how to manufacture explosives included a single copy of a Jiangnan Arsenal translation of a Western chemistry book and whatever Japanese books on explosives they could get. Reportedly, those books were not as easy to get as texts on poisons.

This small group of explosive and poison experimenters was part of a larger network of revolutionaries affiliated with Cai Yuanpei and the China Educational Supply Association. As part of the revolutionary movement, it was imperative that each group labor in secrecy, and Yu notes that he knew only the three individuals with whom he worked, but no others.[35] The China Educational Supply Association would thus serve as a broker in instances where knowledge had to be shared beyond any immediate cell. The institution would transfer the findings or drawings from one group to others in the network. Yu Ziyi found this out when he worked on manufacturing shell cases for explosives. He was asked to share his designs and drawings in a letter composed in English, which the China Educational Supply Association would post on his behalf to others involved in the revolution.

Ultimately, it was the revolutionaries' failure to grasp or apply the chemistry being imported through organizations such as the China Educational Supply Association that led to the fateful string of events that were to topple the empire and shape the political future of modern

China. Essentially tinkerers in their pursuit of destabilizing poisons and explosives, anti-Qing revolutionaries quite literally sparked the Revolution of 1911. On October 9, 1911, a bomb that two local revolutionary groups were building accidentally went off in the Russian concession in Hankou. It was this explosion that then alerted the Qing authorities to the secret cell. On October 10, 1911, the revolutionaries, to preempt the Qing (who had grabbed revolutionary registers in the raid) from killing fellow radicals, felt they had no choice but to launch the revolution.

After the revolution, the China Educational Supply Association was no longer a hub for revolution. However, it continued to be an important source for Chinese industrialists and educators to purchase scientific equipment and materials. Its commitment to science education persisted into the Republican period. An advertisement for the store during the Hangzhou West Lake Expo in 1929 boasted about its past accomplishments: "Opened for 29 years on Shanghai's Qipan Road, the store was one of the earliest to introduce inventions dealing with chemistry and physics. It opened a factory on Hefeng Street in the Zhabei section of Shanghai to manufacture chemical and physics apparatus, museum specimens and replicas, musical instruments, stationary, and pharmaceutics. In previous competitions, it has repeatedly received awards. Domestic educators and industrialists unanimously sing its praises."[36] Chen Diexian was to become a regular customer after he moved to Shanghai. He purchased the store's ingredients, glass appliances, and gadgets for his own experiments. He also became an avid supporter and advocate of the store, urging readers of his how-to columns to shop there.[37] He would eventually become its competitor, though. Deciding that the imported ingredients at the store were too expensive, he would establish China's Number One Magnesium Factory (Zhongguo diyi zhimei chang) in 1921 to manufacture magnesium domestically.

But while still in Hangzhou prior to moving to Shanghai, Chen and the Gather Benefit Company did not appear to be involved with revolutionary activity. Nor were they linked to the Shanghai-based China Educational Supply Association. Chen's local operation was comparatively more modest than the Shanghai store and catered predominantly to members and students of the (local) academy. There is scant evidence of a revolutionary pedigree. However, Hangzhou and Shanghai were only about one hundred miles apart, so Chen likely knew about his store's counterpart and its reputation, along with other similar operations in Jiangnan. His local Hangzhou institution was indeed part of a larger network of stores that circulated scientific books, ingredients, and appliances and that supported the tinkering by revolutionaries, amateur chemists, and budding industrialists. Information and goods were imported from Japan, translations of Japanese publications helped transmit knowledge, and direct mail ordering from Japan ensured the transmission of ingredients, materials, and textbooks. Chinese radicals in Japan or Japanese figures in China (such as Chen's tutor in Hangzhou) also helped with the transnational circulation of knowledge and things. Chen's store, despite being locally situated in Hangzhou, was part of larger national and transnational circulations, some of which proved to be quite radical.

BAMBOO-BRANCH POETRY AND A NEW TECHNOLOGICAL LANDSCAPE

In addition to organizing new kinds of elegant gatherings and scientific appliance shops, Chen Diexian also used his perch in the Hangzhou literary scene to forge imagined gatherings via texts to explore and disseminate knowledge about new technologies and institutions that were remaking daily life in late-Qing Hangzhou. Chen was a prolific a writer throughout his life. *The Collected Works of Xuyuan* (*Xuyuan conggao*) (Chen Diexian n.d.), a collection of Chen's writings, consists of ten full volumes. The range of his work was also considerable. One account notes that over the course of his life Chen composed several thousand poems, authored more than one hundred novels, and on the side wrote countless essays on music (Chen Xiaocui, Fan, and Zhou 1982, 210). Noted not just for his wide range, Chen also proved willing early on to link cultural work with profit. In 1899, he entered the new profession of journalism in Hangzhou. With two friends, He Gongdan and Hua Chishi, he founded the daily newspaper *Grand View* (*Daguanbao*), and in 1900 they established the Grand View Publishing House (Daguanbao guan).[38] They came to be known as the Three Western Rarities (Xiling sanjia) and authored together works such as *Odes of Three Rarities* (*Sanjia qu*), published in

1900. The press also published Chen's bamboo-branch poetry (*zhuzhici*) and rhyme ballads (*tanci*).[39] The newspaper ran serial novels, a newly emerging commodified genre, including Chen's own 120-chapter-long series *Teardrop Destiny* (*Leizhuyuan*) in 1900 (Hanan 2000, 264). In 1906–1907, Chen organized the Twentieth-Century Writing Forest Association (Ershi shijie zhuzuolin she) and founded the monthly journal the *Writing Forest* (*Zhuzuolin*), which featured poetry and published contributions from both local Chinese writers and writers as far away as Manchuria, Korea, and Japan. One to two thousand copies of each issue were produced and sold widely, reaching even Hong Kong.[40]

During the late nineteenth century, both long-standing literary genres and new forms of media were being used to produce and legitimate new forms of knowledge and imported technologies. China's turn-of-the-century press, for example, expanded the potential audience that could read about and consume technology. Lithographically and photolithographically produced, the famous new-style urban pictorial the *Dianshizhai Pictorial* (*Dianshizhai huabao*) visually transmitted to a Jiangnan-based readership the excitement of new technologies and other spectacles of urban life, including curious customs and religious practices, fighting courtesans, and accounts of the strange and fantastic.[41] Published for fourteen years from 1884 to 1898, the pictorial was the product of new printing technologies and produced new ways of viewing. In it, coverage of modern science and technology sat side by side with depictions of strange and fantastic events, the latter of which can be traced back to the literary tradition of reports of the strange (*zhiguai*). The journal was read for both enjoyment and edification, the same reasons why literati had in the past consumed literary accounts of the strange (Huntington 2003). The marvelous tales of the strange from the Chinese tradition arguably helped domesticate the new marvels of technology being imported in the present. The pictorial's preface literally likens the new genre of the illustrated journal to the more familiar scrolls long consumed by cultivated men and women. It states that, like looking at scrolls, reading the journal "for amusement after wine and tea could also suffice to increase one's pleasure" (quoted in Huntington 2003, 344). The lithographically printed pictorial allowed the more anonymous audience to mimic the more intimate "elegant gatherings" where more conventional cultural objects—from seals to scrolls—were enjoyed.

Yet even as the *Dianshizhai Pictorial* resonated with familiar and long-standing viewing practices, it also engendered a distinctly modern visuality. Editors of the pictorial might have sought to invoke the hand scroll to legitimate the new illustrated newspaper. However, the modes of viewing that the two kinds of texts elicited were quite different. The technology of the production of the journal, including photolithography, and its mode of publication, which was serial in format yet not relating the content of each illustration, created a new protocinematic perceptual mode that Weihong Bao calls "panoramic perception" (2005). This perception could evoke an experience of modern travel among the readers, allowing them to view a continuous flow of discontinuous images from China and the world. What further distinguished the mass-produced pictorial from earlier art scrolls and other objects of literati consumption was how it enabled a far larger, more anonymous urban audience to consume the illustrations. This new form of consumption and visual mode was nicely captured and represented in the visuals, with large groups of spectators gawking at amazing sights ranging from large blazing fires to hot-air balloons. New-style pictorials invested in generating knowledge about the everyday served as a "new documentary practice" to introduce new forms of technology.

Chen similarly realized that both familiar and new literary genres and forms of media were useful in allowing him to explore new things. Later in this chapter, I examine how he utilized the serialized novel to explore the issue of profit. Here, I turn to how he perceived the genre of bamboo-branch poetry, a long-standing ethnographic genre, as something that could be updated to document new developments. Dating back to the Tang dynasty in China, bamboo-branch poetry was not a completely new genre like the illustrated journal. As a genre, bamboo-branch poetry was relatively brief, accessible, often witty, and even whimsical, exploring themes of everyday life that might have been seen as too informal for other poetic forms. The poetry focused on a specific place and the customs of ordinary people and provided a verbal snapshot or postcard of the locale and its daily life. It was furthermore characterized by a curiosity for a locality while exhibiting a sense of authorial distance that could allow for slight satire of what was being featured and for the author to show off his cleverness and wit (D. Wang 2003). Amusing and short at four lines long, with each line consisting of seven characters, bamboo-branch poems were easy to memorize. They allowed Chen to reach a fairly broad audience of readers and beyond that other consumers, especially if the poems were read aloud.

In his collected poems, *Bamboo-Branch Poetry from the Gongchen Bridge* (*Gongchen qiao zhuzhici*), published in 1900, Chen Diexian provided snapshots of the people, customs, and institutions and technologies of Hangzhou.[42] The poems covered local places, public bureaus, ancestral shrines, stores, theater, types of people, attire, and brothels. They also dealt with technology, industry, as well as new-style institutions and practices of officialdom dotting and shaping the Hangzhou landscape. Among those poems featuring new-style technologies, there were ones on photography, a "Japanese-style" carriage, the bicycle, rubber-wheeled carriages, a small steamship, a ferry, and street lamps. Poem number 48 of the collection is titled "The Bicycle" ("Jiaotache"):

On the winch, [a pair of] swift feet pedal quickly;
With two dots of aqua and crimson light.[43]
In the middle of the night, it rushes across the Gongchen Bridge.
Some surmise that it is the will-o'-the-wisp.

By the 1890s, this imported mode of transportation, cycling, was somewhat limited because the rickshaw still proved more widespread and preferred. But cycling was becoming increasingly common, and the craze for the two-wheeler began in Shanghai, though it quickly spread to other cities, including Hangzhou. Bicycles could be found on the streets of urban centers as well as in urban media depicting the modernity of China's cities. They were a fad and a sign of the new. As a result, even though more Chinese were using the bicycle, bicyclers belonged primarily to more exclusive or fashionable groups, including missionaries, returnees from abroad, and elite courtesans (Rhoads 2012, 95–99). The breeziness of Chen's poem speaks to the bicycle's relative newness and its continued status as a curiosity. At the same time, the reference to the will-o'-the-wisp, *qinglin*, belies that very breeziness and even conveys a bit of a warning. The reference to the *qinglin*, a traditional spirit that lights up, allows Chen to liken the bike, with its flashing red and aqua lights, to a classical, fantastical spirit in a light-hearted manner.

A sense of the newness of technology is also conveyed in the poem titled "Rubber-Wheeled Carriage" ("Xiangpiche"),

Rubber-tired wheels, black-oiled hood,
Rolling soundlessly, leaving no trace.
When [another] carriage comes from the opposite side, there is no need
    to cup one hand in the other and greet [the oncoming carriage]
Ding Dong, the carriage's bell rings a warning.

The first automobile would not be introduced to Hangzhou until 1917, so here the term *xiangpiche*, literally the "rubber-wheeled vehicle," refers to carriages with rubber wheels, which were found in Hangzhou at the time, including near the Gongchen Bridge.[44] The lines of the poem introduce this new form of transportation, describing the sensorial presence of the carriage or, more precisely, the lack thereof. The carriage's rubber wheels make no sound and leave no trace. Like the bicycle as a will-o'-the-wisp, the noiseless carriage comes and goes breezily and is thus rendered into something intriguing. As the fourth line suggests, the carriage, precisely because of its stealthy silence, features a bell, a new technology that can enable communication among drivers. Rather than the driver's cupped hands, the carriage's bell, rung by the driver's foot, becomes the means to greet and warn oncoming vehicles.[45] New technologies, the poem says, shape social custom such as ways of greeting. The poem presents the object of focus as fun and intriguing, amuses the reader, and provides him or her with a quick ditty about how new technologies were changing daily life in Hangzhou. New institutions also caught Chen's attention. His curiosity about the city's new factories and industries inspired him to compose a bamboo poem about a local cotton mill, titled "Gongyi Cotton Mill" ("Gongyi shachang"):

Up high, down low, electric lights glow brightly.
Sounds of the machine whir an unfathomable din.
At dusk, the weaving girls are released [from work]
As the steam whistle over the eaves brays like a donkey.

Although the title of the poem refers to the Gongyi Cotton Mill, it seems likely that Chen's subject was the Tongyi Cotton Mill, a famous mill located at the head of the Gongchen Bridge. Ding Bing (1832–1899) and Pang Yuanji (1864–1949) founded this mill with four hundred thousand tales of silver in 1889 (Zhong 2013, 58–60).

The poem features weaving girls. The female factory worker was a new kind of figure that was born with the rise of modern factories around the world. She was not only a familiar sight in Shanghai and other industrializing cities by the turn of the twentieth century but also an emerging cultural icon.[46] She was representative of a new regime of labor developing in the newly industrial parts of the world, where gender norms, the ordering of time, and the idea of work were being radically reconfigured. As such, she had become the source of reformist concern as well as an omnipresent trope in urban media and film in industrializing societies. In what has often been identified as the first projected film, Louis Lumière featured female factory workers exiting the main gate of his own factory. The brief, forty-five-second, black-and-white silent film made in 1895 was aptly titled *Workers Leaving the Lumière Factory in Lyon* (*La Sortie de l'Usine Lumière à Lyon*), only five years prior to the publication of Chen's poems. Lumière's short film sought to emphasize the significance of such a moment by having the new technology of film gaze upon the outpouring of factory women as they were released from work.

Just as Lumière found the image of the women leaving the factory gates to be pregnant with meeting, Chen apparently sought to capture the meaning of a similar scene through poetry. To create a sense of the uncanny, he did not have the lens of a camera to dictate the "gaze," so he played with sound in the poem and juxtaposed images to create a sense of the jarring nature of the moment. The mention of the whistle, a synecdoche of the new industrial technology that was the factory, is central to Chen's description of how the mill left an imprint not simply on Hangzhou's physical landscape but also on its aural economy. The likening of steam pipes (modern technology) to the braying of donkeys—a mundane, mournful, slightly annoying, yet amusing sound— functions to evoke a somewhat comical, if ambivalent tone. In this way, the poem de-naturalizes the image of flowing women emerging from a factory by making the reader take note of the unprecedented nature of the phenomenon, just as Lumière's film does. There is no evidence that Chen saw Lumière's film, but, given the global circulation of cultural products, including film, into China at the time, it is entirely possible that he at least knew of it. The uncanny overlap in what was being portrayed in both film and poem seems to suggest that this was the case. Regardless of whether he saw Lumière's film, the spectacle and anxiety surrounding the new phenomenon of women working in factories was worldwide, and the trope of factory girls exiting a factory served as a powerful means for Chen to capture the developments of industrialization that he and his peers were witnessing daily in Hangzhou.

Chen's poetry also specifically featured technologies of mass reproduction. Take, for example, "Bright Moon Mirror Photography" ("Mingyuejing zhaoxiang"):

Ah, who is calling for Zhen Zhen in the portrait?
Pointing wildly, the woman in the portrait seems like the (real) person
I blame the hazy moon mirror,
It merely delivers the appearance and not the spirit.

The first line refers to a woman, Zhen Zhen, who appears in the portrait. The calling for Zhen Zhen is a literary allusion to a Tang dynasty tale by Du Xunhe that was part of his collection *Pine Window Jottings* (*Song chuang zaji*).[47] In the story, a degree holder named Zhao Yan is in an artist's studio and sees a painting featuring a beautiful woman named Zhen Zhen. The artist describes the painting as a *shenhua*, a portrait that is capable of truly capturing a person's authentic spirit. The tale then describes how Zhen Zhen comes alive after Zhao calls her name for a hundred days, exits the picture, and bears him a son. When Zhao starts to suspect she is a demon, Zhen Zhen takes the son and returns into the painting, which then includes the child. By asking who is calling for Zhen Zhen in the portraiture, the first line of Chen's poem alludes directly to the Tang dynasty tale. The second line affirms that the portrait does indeed capture the person's real spirit. As in the tale, the name "Zhen Zhen" functions as a pun: it is the beautiful woman's/spirit's name but also means "to be vivid and lifelike."

The pun on "truth" or the "genuine" is important because that is what is at stake in this poem. The poem is essentially contrasting new media technology such as the camera with the genre of *shenhua*, portraiture in Chinese art, which had long been celebrated not for its realism but for its ability to grasp and convey the truest essence of a person's spirit, *shen*.

The camera, newly circulating in China (as it was worldwide) as a cutting-edge gadget, was purportedly able to capture truth or provide a realistic depiction of reality through mechanical reproduction. As photography circulated, photographic portraiture was increasingly deemed superior to painting portraiture and verisimilitude, a concept previously not important in Chinese art criticism but gaining currency in contemporary discourses on visuality (Yi Gu 2013, 120, 127). Given this context, Chen's casting of doubt on the camera's ability to grasp or convey visual truth stands out. In the last two lines, the poem notes how photography, referred to via the synecdoche "moon mirror," or the camera lens, falls short. It accuses the "hazy moon mirror," photography, of delivering merely the person's image, not his or her true spirit.

The final compound in the last line, *chuanshen*, "deliver the spirit," is yet another multilayered pun. First, it refers to the immortal—Zhen Zhen—coming out of the painting in the Tang tale. Second, it evokes the long-standing aesthetic principle in elite portraiture of grasping and conveying the true essence of a person.[48] Finally, Chen seems to suggest that, like traditional portraiture painting, bamboo-branch poetry, with its multiple puns and playful wit, better captures the real and the genuine more effectively than any new media technology. In the factory-girl poem, we saw how both Chen and Lumière were drawn to the moment when factory girls pour out of a factory and capture that moment to bring attention to industrial production and the publicness of new working women. Yet whereas Lumière did this with his iconic short film, a quintessential new technology of mechanical reproduction, Chen did it just as confidently with poetry, a decidedly long-standing genre that obliquely addresses and playfully puns rather than literally portrays its subject matter. Chen's reference to *chuanshen* in "Bright Moon Mirror Photography"—a traditional Chinese aesthetic that seeks not to convey the realistic but to grasp the essential—suggests that he is making a similar claim about poetry.

Chen was never one to diminish the power of new media technologies and was wholly appreciative of new gadgets. Later in his career, he was extremely appreciative, for example, of the potential of mass advertising's ability to convey a seemingly "genuine" bond between product and consumer, which, although ultimately illusory, nonetheless helped distinguish the Butterfly brand from all other similar brands. And at this point Chen was likely already taken with photography, despite the slightly skeptical tone about it in his poem "Bright Moon Mirror Photography." Photography and the camera were at the heart of a culture of "play" that was extremely fashionable in courtesan and literati circles of Jiangnan at the time and that informed Chen's literary practices and his fascination with new technologies. This culture drew inspiration from *The Dream of the Red Chamber* (*Hongloumeng*). This eighteenth-century romance novel by Cao Xueqin (1715 or 1724–1763/1764) had come to gain cult status in China's emerging urban playgrounds such as Shanghai, which were alternative spaces for disenfranchised young men alienated from politics. At the core of the novel is the theme of blurring the boundary between reality and illusion. Practitioners of this culture of play— local courtesans and their suitors—explored this boundary between the real and the illusory by readily enacting in their flirtatious exchanges scenes from the novel and assuming the personae of the novel's passionate characters. They assumed the sentimental voices of the novel's effete heroes to elide what was the cold fact of a commercial exchange at the heart of courtesan–client relationships (C. Yeh 2006, 116). As new-style technologies that literally blurred that boundary in their ability to produce the likeness of a real person, photography and mirrors also became emblematic of this craze. Courtesans, for example, liked to use cameras to record their staging of personae from *The Dream*. As another gadget that blurred the real person and an illusion of the person, the mirror also appeared frequently in courtesan photographs and residences, just as it does in the novel (Yeh 2006, 146–153).

This contemporary craze for cameras and mirrors begs the question why in his poem Chen struck a tone of skepticism about the "hazy moon mirror" and the camera's capacity to deliver mere imagery rather than the authentic spirit. Perhaps he was expressing differing views of technologies in different forums. Ever mindful of the potential skepticism toward the newfangled among his peers, he might have been using his poetry as a means to establish his credentials with this audience by assuming an ironic, disinterested stance. The author's slight ironic distance from the object featured tended to characterize bamboo poetry. Accordingly, an allusion to the Tang tale in "Bright Moon Mirror Photography" would have appealed to Chen's fellow readers as learned and clever. And if his tone conveyed a slight degree of suspicion or disappointment toward the camera's hazy lens, the poem nonetheless still functioned to introduce the new gadget, which was certainly characteristic of Chen's more general agenda to promote new technologies.

Indeed, perhaps because bamboo-branch poetry was a familiar and relatively accessible genre, Chen found it to be a powerful means to shed light on the local terrain and daily life of turn-of-the-century Hangzhou. The genre provided Chen with the means to assume a posture of noncommittal dalliance while commenting on a range of topics, including new forms of technologies. His observations were not completely neutral, and he employed this long-standing poetic genre to discipline the potentially disruptive nature of the people, practices, institutions, and customs featured, especially those that were appearing newly in Hangzhou. Each poem always included ironic distancing in the final lines, which served to contain, neutralize, or question with a witticism the custom, technology, or institution featured in the poem.

LETTERED EXPERIMENTATION WITH MONEY

By the time Chen opened his appliance store in Hangzhou, he already understood that the deliberate attempt to make money could generate considerable social anxiety. He grappled directly with the issue of money in his fiction writing at the same time, including in his novel *The Money Demon (Huangjin sui)*.[49] The novel was published serially in Shanghai's major daily *Shanghai News (Shenbao,* formally transliterated as *Shunpao*; hereafter, *Shenbao*) from June to October 1913, after he arrived at the cosmopolitan center, though he had written it earlier in Hangzhou. It was then published as a book in 1914. It was one of several novels that established his reputation as a brand author in Shanghai's competitive fiction market. Resembling Western coming-of-age novels, *The Money Demon* has been seen as an account based on Chen's youth, concerned with events in his own life between 1894 and 1901 in his hometown. As the literary scholar Patrick Hanan notes, the characters are based on real people, and the narration of events is generally accurate (1999, 6–9).[50] Protagonist Shan, author Chen's alter ego, is a relatively well-to-do young man who matures over time through myriad escapades in love and business.

The Money Demon falls under the category of the so-called butterfly fiction. In her genealogical study of sentiment in modern Chinese literature, Haiyan Lee describes such fiction as populated by men and women of sentiment who "without exception . . . are talented, handsome, and sensitive. . . . They weep a great deal; their tears drench their pillows and love letters. All in all, they live and die for *qing* [passion], the one word that encapsulates their entire existence" (2007b, 100). Shan is one such figure. The novel specifically recounts Shan's gradual maturation from a frivolous and hopeless romantic to someone who can assume financial responsibility and come to terms with money. Serial installment after serial installment traces Shan's complicated love relationship and heart-wrenching struggles with a girl named Koto as well as with the pull of money on him from his childhood until he is twenty-two. Although he experiences numerous other infatuations over the years and has an arranged marriage to Susu, a woman he comes to care for, his true love for Koto always holds center stage. At one point, when Shan returns home to his wife and divulges that he had been to visit Koto, the intimacy that arises from the revelation of his secret results in physical love making, which he describes in the following terms: "My rapturous soul and hers were magically transformed into a pair of butterflies flying together into oblivion" (Chen 1999, 209).[51] Shan's intense passions are neatly encapsulated in the image of the magical butterfly, which transcends any vulgar physicality in this passage.

Early in the novel Shan's love for Koto is idealized; it becomes even more so when he realizes that her mother is forcing her to marry for money. Shan heroically offers to make her his concubine so she can escape her cruel fate, but Koto rejects his offer. She states that if they cannot be in a monogamous relationship, she would rather sacrifice the possibility of consummating their love and instead establish her own financial autonomy and freedom. It is at this point that his lurking doubts about her being possessed by the money demon emerge. As his own feeling toward money changes, however, his view of Koto's situation changes, too. This shift in attitude is enabled by his other key love relationship, the one with his wife. With his family in financial decline, his devoted wife starts pawning her jewelry to enable him to continue to lead the life of a lettered gentleman. As a result of her sacrifice, he is shamed into maturing and taking responsibility. He pursues—somewhat unsuccessfully—business opportunities that are still fairly unconventional for upper-class men (including establishing a newspaper and opening up a tea-and-bamboo dealership, two enterprises Chen pursued in real life) and comes to respect Koto and to sympathize with her circumstances.

The gendering of money is striking in the novel. As a man of feeling, Shan comes across as fickle, irresponsible, and for much of the novel primarily unconcerned with financial matters. Women—from his mother to his wife and even his housemaid, Little Tan—manage the finances in the family, though engagement with money always presents a perilous course for women in terms of their virtue. Indeed, the story ends on a note of ambivalence. Shan discovers that his beloved has once again married for money, and Koto explains that she has done so to kill Shan's love for her because its unattainability was bedeviling her. Shan protests: "'No! No!' I cried bitterly. 'How could love possibly bedevil you . . . ? To my mind, that man you're marrying is nothing more than the money demon, the money demon!'" (Chen 1999, 277). This final passage, in which the impact of money once again confounds their love, reflects the author's own continued sense of ambivalence toward money.

The novel is useful to explore how money and the pursuit of profit were issues that Chen and his peers were wrestling with in Hangzhou and would have to come to terms with as some of them relocated to Shanghai. Like other butterfly novels, *The Money Demon* provided a window for readers to view the life of a privileged young man at the turn of the century, the late-imperial Chinese family structure, notions of marriage and love in that period, and how a household was run and finances were managed. Given the decline of secure ways to reproduce China's grand families, the topic of the Chen family's plight—social and financial—could well have struck a chord with readers.[52] The shifting family financial strategies of this period shaped intellectuals and writers and were often at the basis of their self-conscious concern with money, commerce, and industry. Chen turned to writing for profit (first in Hangzhou and then in Shanghai) and to writing romance novels in large part due to his family circumstances, in which his mother, who was a concubine and not the first wife, had to fend for her immediate family when his father died early. Furthermore, with the dismantling of the civil-service exam system, many urban elites like Chen were transitioning from an idealized understanding of the literati who transcended mundane matters such as subsistence to new ways of being that revolved more centrally around the open pursuit of profit. Yet a long history of Confucian distrust of profit did not disappear entirely, and the rush to capitalism in treaty ports engendered anxiety even as it generated opportunity. The Shan storyline seems to reflect Chen's real-life grappling with the transition to commercial activity, even as he profited by it.

By embellishing this reality, *The Money Demon* allowed readers to sympathize with Shan, grow with him, and likewise change their attitude toward money. That the novel could mediate readers' real-life concerns is particularly evident when one considers how *The Money Demon* was part of the turn-of-the-century cultural craze surrounding the eighteenth-century novel *The Dream of the Red Chamber*. The sensitive man-of-feeling protagonist in *The Dream*, Jia Baoyu, is the embodiment of authentic sentiment (*zhenqing*), which made him the model of the alienated rebel and romantic hero for disaffected young men at the turn of the twentieth century (C. Yeh 2006, 139). Young men and their courtesan lovers would play-act the novel in their interactions. By engaging in elaborate rituals of play, courtesans seemed to promise genuine love, and their disaffected male lovers could then feel as if they were escaping from their arranged marriages and other ritually sanctioned familial and political obligations and duties. The rituals of play found in courtesan circles in urban China also took place in print. The fad of reenacting *The Dream* also generated numerous sequels of the novel. They were meant to be formulaic and derivative. Readers, authors, elite men, and courtesans assumed the personae of Jia Baoyu and other characters through their repeated production and consumption of these emulative stories.

Chen's literary and cultural production was informed by this *Dream* craze. His early novels, including *The Money Demon*, were modeled not after Western romance novels but after *The Dream*. By hewing closely to *The Dream*, they explored the theme of sentiment vis-à-vis Confucian ritual propriety and played with the boundary between reality and illusion, just as *The Dream* does. In discussing the serialized novel *Teardrop Destiny*, published in 1900, Chen's daughter recounted,

> This is a story that alludes to the old days of the Chen family, self-narrating [Chen's] life story and featuring the appreciation of poetry, drinking games, medicine, divination, astrology and face reading, as well as music. [Chen] wields his pen with intention and writes

the romance fiction along the lines of *The Dream of the Red Chamber*. After the Grand View [Publishing House] printed a special edition of five thousand copies, [Chen] appended a poem [about the novel] that reads: "Half illusion, half reality, combined, the affairs of five years ago [covered by the novel] still cause anguish; others say it resembles *The Dream of the Red Chamber*; I say that I *am* from *The Dream of the Red Chamber*."
(Chen Xiaocui, Fan, and Zhou 1982, 210–211)

As if to disarm any charges that his novel overly resembled the eighteenth-century novel, Chen embraced the performative cult of sentiment in this poem. He claimed that the novel he wrote, based half on reality and half on illusion, nonetheless captured the essence and the feeling from the affairs of five years earlier in his life, upon which the novel is based. As a result, not only does the novel resemble *The Dream*, a story about the blurring of reality and illusion, but also in his writing of the novel he is enacting the principle of blurring reality and illusion that is so central to *The Dream*. Chen assumed a Zhuangziesque stance by evoking the parable of dreaming about the butterfly to preempt any critique that the novel was merely derivative.

In an increasingly commercial world of urban decay and materialism, novels like *The Money Demon* presented a fictional world of sincere feelings and romance. Just as the role of sentiment in courtesan quarters papered over the fact that the courtesan–client relationship turned on the heartless exchange of cash, these sentimental novels claimed authenticity in the moving narratives and drew visceral reader response, even while they were a product of mass reproduction, serialized and reproduced endlessly for innumerable mass readers. Chen's readers were to play-act alongside him, pretending to relive the lives of the characters of his novel and thereby grapple with the issue of money with him and ultimately sympathize with his choice to pursue profit. Chen was thus creating a seamless amalgamation of myth and man that depended on his readers pretending to be Shan, who was in turn Chen himself. The readers' empathy for him in his plight as a genuine man of sentiment was something that he then capitalized on. Fans became devoted to the protagonist and by extension to Tianxuwosheng, the novel's author. It was in this way that Chen was able to elicit powerful reader sympathy and fan fervor even as he engaged in the anxiety-provoking endeavor of writing for money.

CONCLUSION: PLAYFUL ENTREPRENEURISM AND ENGAGEMENT WITH THE NEWFANGLED

Lettered men affiliated with societies and associations located around the West Lake in Hangzhou were immersed in a culture of playful connoisseurship and broad learning. Yet it was that very culture of whimsical dabbling in an array of topics that allowed for experimentation with new-style pursuits and entrepreneurial efforts. Some groups were quite radical and engaged in Western learning. Chen, too, expressed curiosity for and engagement with Western learning, new technologies, and emerging institutions within the context of the safely tasteful gatherings of elegant men and through familiar literary genres. His bamboo-branch poetry featured new forms of technology circulating into Hangzhou and helped domesticate them even as they held these technologies somewhat at arms' length through satire, bemusement, and even sly skepticism. Chen made the opening up of a scientific-appliance shop more readily acceptable to his peers by attaching a reading room to it, even if in the end neither the store nor the room stayed open for long. He also relied upon fresh genres, such as the serialized novel, to examine new if confounding themes such as money. And as a brand author, he worked to cultivate a reputation of sincerity as a singular man of feeling in order to legitimate commercial pursuits, even as he capitalized upon them handsomely. With his novels, he was to earn enough money to launch his enterprise the Association for Household Industries in 1918. The strategic deployment of networks of intimacy that was achieved through face-to-face meetings as well as imagined connections forged via poetry and literature would help Chen endorse science, industry, and profit.

Chen Diexian offers us an excellent vantage point from which to see how elites at the turn of the twentieth century turned to new kinds of activities. Cultural entrepreneurs were emerging in China's urban centers at the time, following interests that spanned education, print, commerce and industry, and other spheres (Rea and Volland 2015). They increasingly did so for the explicit purpose of making a profit, even as this goal earned the wrath and disgust of reformist intellectuals such as those associated with the New Culture Movement, who scorned the explicit act of producing culture for pay. Where Chen Diexian might stand out among this group of new-style actors is in his strategies of self-branding. He turned out to be exceptionally skillful in self-branding, a practice he had already started when he was in Hangzhou. The pen names that he chose, the networks of elegant gatherings he deployed, the poems he composed—all helped Chen establish himself as a Zhuangziesque eccentric who dabbled tastefully even in things considered déclassé or suspicious in their newness. Chen sought to establish legitimacy for himself even as he promoted new forms of knowledge and carried out somewhat questionable commercial activities and manufacturing. This strategy became a core part of his approach to the mass production of things, words, and images and was important for his success as a serial author, pharmaceutical industrialist, and brand marketer in Shanghai.

PART TWO

Manufacturing Knowledge, 1914–1927

INTELLECTUAL LABOR IN
EARLY-TWENTIETH-CENTURY SHANGHAI

With his move to Shanghai in 1913, Chen Diexian joined others migrating from the late empire's culture centers to find new occupations in the thriving print markets of major treaty ports. There, he engaged in new and newly commodified forms of literary production. He would also launch manufacturing endeavors, which are explored in more depth in part III. In both the world of letters and the world of manufacturing in Shanghai, he continued what he had started in Hangzhou: to draw from his resources in the cultural arena to legitimate his for-profit activities, both lettered and industrial. Unlike his imperial literati predecessors, Chen and other writers of his generation built a literary reputation explicitly for money and in new media forms, such as newspapers, serialized fiction, and even mass advertising and marketing.[1] This for-profit cultural activity and the new media forms in which it occurred generated considerable anxiety, however. Aware of this social ambivalence, Chen sought to assuage some of the concern by cultivating his reputation as a *genuine* man of feeling and as a brand author of sentimental fiction.

When Chen arrived in Shanghai, he entered a vibrant and commercially oriented print and entertainment milieu that intermingled the legacy of late-imperial connoisseur culture with Shanghai's new print capitalism (see, e.g., Reed 2004; Meng 2006). The Shanghai print world was booming not simply in terms of diversity of new genres and products but also in terms of the variety of information being featured and presented. The increasingly competitive and commercial print economy was also remaking the contours of intellectual work. To meet the demands of a thriving commercial market for print, new forms of knowledge production and intellectual labor were starting to emerge. In presses such as the Commercial Press (Shangwu yinshuguan), the work of editors and compilers was reorganized to maximize efficiency and minimize expense to allow the ceaseless production of an increasing number and variety of texts (Culp 2016). The need to produce for as large a readership as possible at as low a cost as possible also meant that content was often treated as fungible and easily repackaged. Texts or parts of texts were treated as products with interchangeable parts, and material and content were easily transferred, copied, and adapted. Robert Culp (2016) has characterized this form of knowledge production as "industrial" and notes that it often invited an assembly-line production of text and knowledge, which was precisely how Chen engaged in translation work (see chapter 4). This approach would guarantee ever-greater profits for the publishing companies and the ability to mass-produce cultural commodities that would ensure the widespread circulation of new forms of knowledge in the twentieth-century.

It was in this context that Chen became a pen for hire, a newspaperman, an editor, and a writer of installment fiction. With the appearance especially of new installment fiction in commercial newspapers and the rise of brand-name authors such as Chen, the trope of the professional writer emerged. Alexander Des Forges (2009) cites the novel *New Shanghai* (*Xin Shanghai*, 1909) by Lu Shi'e (1878–1944) as an example of a fictional exploration and satirical delineation of the professional writer, or *yeji*. The term *yeji*—literally meaning "wild chicken"—was also the compound used for streetwalkers. This was not a coincidence. According to the more highbrow cultural arbiters, just as the streetwalker prostituted her body for money, the pen for hire was seen as prostituting his (such writers were usually male) literary skills for profit.

Regardless of the disdain cast upon them by highbrow critics, these professional writers often proved successful in making money through their writing. Because their work as writers often overlapped with their work as newspaper columnists, reporters, editors, and even publishers, the aesthetics of their novels was often shaped by newspaper aesthetics (Des Forges 2009, 42 n. 8). Presented in short snippets, serial novels would offer brief gratification each day, thereby forcing the reader to come back for more and causing them to become quite literally addicted to the text. With readers increasingly desiring never-ending narratives, a professional author's ability to acquire a reputation or brand name proved important. Installment fiction was an ongoing enterprise, with authors and, by extension, columnists and essayists for newspapers paid for their prose on a daily or weekly basis. For installment novelists, this arrangement meant that if they had a hit on their hands, they could levy considerable power over their publishers, who were dependent on them to produce the next installment. Such authors were able to negotiate the terms of their compensation with publishers and with that compensation had the means to initiate other projects.

Chen was a real-life example of the professional writer satirized in *New Shanghai.* He flourished in an era when there was an explosive growth in original fiction and the standardization of payment by word for fiction manuscripts. He successfully forged a following for his serialized fiction and established himself as a popular brand author. In Hangzhou, Chen had proved remarkably prolific and wide ranging in his literary production, writing novels, plays, poetry, and treatises on a variety of subjects. Much of his literary output found its way into the newspaper he coedited, the *Grand View.* In Shanghai, Chen built on the literary production he had already started in Hangzhou to gain quick renown in the city's fiction circles. Wang Dungen, the influential editor of the *Shenbao* literary supplement *Free Talk* (*Ziyoutan*), commissioned Chen's novels for publication in daily installments, including *Money Demon* and its sister novel *Teardrop Destiny*, which he had penned and published earlier in his hometown. After the resounding commercial success of these novels, newspaper after newspaper sought his manuscripts. Other Chen novels appeared in famous editor Bao Tianxiao's *Illustrated Newspaper of Fiction* (*Xiaoshuo huabao*), the *New Hunan Newspaper* (*Xiangzhong xinbao*), and the *Pastime* (*Youxi zazhi*), a journal

Bao coedited with Wang Dungen (Chen Xiaocui, Fan, and Zhou 1982, 211–212). New Culture intellectuals derided these romantic fabulations as hopeless entertainment and escapist literature, but these "old-style" novels proved politically and socially salient, and ordinary readers flocked to them. Chen capitalized on this thirst and crafted his persona into a more romantically inclined symbol with his writing of butterfly fiction. He was able to turn himself—under the pen name "Tianxuwosheng"—into a literary brand.

It is important to note that in this commercial context Chen's intellectual labor did not center solely on original authorship but also included editorial work, translation, and skilled copying. For Chen and others in his generation, such labor was hardly anachronistic. Transmission of knowledge through compilation and editing (*bianji*) rather than through original authorship or singular creation had a long and virtuous history. Confucius fashioned himself as only one of a series of authorities, stating that virtue lay in transmitting the Dao and not in creating (*shu er buzuo*). Imperial China's book history saw the institutionalization of this classical ideal in literary habits, state-sponsored book projects, and a vibrant commercial printing industry, where an emphasis was placed on ordering, cataloging, and thus effectively transmitting virtuous knowledge.[2] In this context, late-imperial literati considered activities such as editing and compilation to be just as noble as original authorship. By the latter part of the nineteenth century, as China sought to access new forms of scientific and technological knowledge during the Self-Strengthening Movement, translation (*bianyi*) joined compilation as a powerful form of intellectual work. Both compilation and translation were seen as crucial in legitimating and transmitting new forms of knowledge.[3]

Chen was steeped in these forms of intellectual labor that while remaining respected forms of work also became increasingly profitable in Shanghai's sophisticated print market. In addition to his authoring of novels, verse novels (*tanci*), poetry, and plays, much of his cultural work turned on translation, compilation, and adaptation. His serial novels were reworkings of familiar formulas from various Chinese classics. He worked with colleagues to translate and adapt legal tracts, chemical formulas, and fiction, often from Japanese. He was well known, for example, for a translation of all the Sherlock Holmes stories. Once he established himself as a brand author, he then leveraged this success to engage in further lettered work to become an important entrepreneurial figure in Shanghai's lettered circles more generally. His endeavors were almost always for profit and included opening up a five-person translation bureau. He also assumed an array of editorships. From 1913 to 1915, he coedited the *Pastime* with his patron Wang Dungen. His role was to obtain submissions for a variety of columns, including humorous essays, translations, discussions of drama, and teaching materials for theater studies (Chen Xiaocui, Fan, and Zhou 1982, 212). From December 1914 to mid-1915, he edited a women's magazine, discussed in chapter 2. On Wang Dungen's recommendation, he then edited the literary supplement *Free Talk* from the spring of 1916 to the fall of 1918. In 1918, he took over the column "Common Knowledge for the Household" published in *Free Talk* until 1928, discussed in chapter 3. He compiled and edited plays for the Civilization Theater Group (Wenmingxi shetuan), which were performed in Shanghai. He also wrote three film scripts (Chen Xiaocui, Fan, and Zhou 1982, 212).

The significance of compilation for Chen is particularly evident with his establishment of the Xuyuan Compilation Agency (Xuyuan bianjishe), in 1917 (*Tianxuwosheng jinian kan* 1940, 3; Chen Xiaocui, Fan, and Zhou 1982, 214–215). One of the agency's main purposes was to compile works for publication. Important compilations included the legal publications *Supreme Court Verdicts in Civil and Criminal Cases* (*Daliyuan minxingshi panjue li*) and *A Compilation of Laws* (*Falü huibian*). The agency also provided the curious service of composing courtesy letters (*yingchou wen*) for others. According to one account, Chen decided to make available what had long been a practice of having a lettered person write for someone who was not or to have someone famous compose a letter on someone else's behalf in order to impart greater status on the sender of the letter. Another service the agency provided was teaching creative writing by mail. At the time, young writers and lettered elites were increasingly interested in writing serialized fiction. Given Chen's reputation, many aspiring writers sought him out for advice or asked him to touch up or edit their manuscripts. To manage the requests, he gave advice and taught writing via correspondence. In the latter classes, he had more than two hundred participants from cities and provinces around the country (Chen Xiaocui, Fan and Zhou 1982, 214–215). Students, people who loved classical literature, and even industrial workers paid a monthly fee for four classes over four months. Aspiring writers sent in their essays, poems, and fiction for his revision and feedback. Chen fielded literature questions and featured student work that was of high quality in a literary journal that he edited. He published both the original draft submitted by the student and his revised version and placed them next to each other for readers to compare. Chen later pulled out some of this material to compile a publication on teaching materials for correspondence schools.

It was in this context of Shanghai's thriving print culture, where new forms of intellectual labor and knowledge work were emerging, that we can better understand Chen's production of knowledge on manufacturing. The chapters in part II turn to this knowledge production as part of Chen's vernacular industrialism and show how textual strategies of masterful adaptation and innovative transmission extended to his knowledge work on the industrial arts. Chen compiled, translated, and often recycled or repurposed recipes and knowledge on *xiao gongyi* for different audiences and occasions and often for a price. This knowledge work sought to legitimate light industry for his readers, to guarantee his expertise in and "ownership" of the information, and to lay the ground for his own and others' actual engagement in industrial and commercial work.

CHAPTER TWO

One Part Cow Fat, Two Parts Soda

Recipes for the Inner Chambers, 1914–1915

In December 1914, Chen Diexian, using his sobriquet "Tianxuwosheng," launched the Shanghai-based journal *Women's World* (*Nüzi shijie*) (1914–1915). During its brief run, the journal featured the section "Industrial Arts" ("Gongyi"), which included a curious column titled "The Warehouse for Cosmetic Production" ("Huazhuangpin zhizao ku"). Chen both edited and contributed to this column. There, he ran highly detailed articles on how to manufacture soap, hair tonic, perfume, rouge, and other products. What makes this column particularly notable is how it deemed this manufacturing information as appropriate for genteel women (*guixiu*) to apply in their inner chambers. A typical example of such gendered and class-specific domestic manufacturing can be found in the first two runs of the column. In the February 1915 issue, Chen wrote that the article published in January, "An Exquisite Method for Manufacturing Hair Oil," had elicited much interest and that a reader named Mme. Xi Meng had sent in a request asking him to divulge more tips (Chen Diexian 1915, vol. 2 [February], 3).[1] In the February issue, Chen provided specific information on how to produce at home some of the basic ingredients in the hair tonic, including the essence of roses.

The complete list of ingredients for the hair tonic was fairly lengthy. It was in Chinese, of course, but also provided Western-language glosses for several of the ingredients:

純粹硫酸	Acidum Sulphruicum [*sic*]
檸檬油	Oleum Limonis
精製植物油即前節製原料法中自製之油[2]	
玫瑰精	Spiritus Rosae
硼砂	Borax
橙花水	Aqua Aurantii Florum
洋紅細粉亦須自製酒精[3]	Spiritus
丁香油	Nelkeuöl [*sic*]
肉桂油	Oleum Cinnamomi
橙皮油	Oleum Aurantii Corticis
屈里設林	Glycerin
白米澱粉即本節製法中自製之水磨粉[4]	
白檀油	Oleum Santali

(Chen Diexian 1915, vol. 2 [February], 4)

Most items were glossed in Latin. In English, they are sulfuric acid, oil of lemon, the essence of roses (i.e., the scent of roses), borax or hydrated sodium borate, orange-flower water, alcohol, oil of cinnamon, oil of orange peel, sugar alcohol, and oil of sandalwood. Oil of cloves, or *dingxiangyou*, was glossed as "Nelkeuöl," a misprinted or misspelled version of the German term *Nelkenöl*. *Glycerin* was the English term for *qulishelin*. A few of the ingredients did not have a foreign-language gloss (my translations of these ingredients are provided in notes 2–4). Some of these items, including oil of cinnamon and oil of orange peel, were not traditionally found in late-imperial recipes for cosmetics.[5] Several were imports at the time. The column noted explicitly that the ingredients could be purchased in Shanghai's pharmacies, including the German KOFA Dispensary, Koelkel & Schroeder Ltd., and the Anglo-Chinese Dispensary. However, because *spiritus rosae* was particularly expensive, Chen wanted to make the recipe for it available. His instructions for manufacturing this ingredient were: "Extract the fragrance of fresh flowers, and attach it onto something solid, so that it lasts and does not disappear. There are many ways of doing this. One can use the method for suction, the method for squeezing, the method for steaming, the method for soaking. None of these is as ideal as the method for absorption. To make *spiritus rosae*, use the method for absorption" (Chen Diexian 1915, vol. 2 [February], 6). A detailed technical description of how to achieve the method for absorption followed.

The column was to continue for the duration of the journal, about half a year. As these excerpts from the first two entries reveal, the articles in the column struck a balance between presenting technical detail and assuming practical how-to sensibility where tacit knowledge was crucial. Notably, there was an effort to mark the cosmopolitan nature of the recipes. The foreign-language rendering of several of the ingredients helped establish that sense of cosmopolitanism. The column also conveyed a sense that its offerings were meant to help domesticate imported practices of manufacturing. The exorbitant cost of store-bought imported ingredients was mentioned explicitly as a reason for sharing recipes. Household manufacturing and production were elevated over the consumption of imports from new-style pharmacies. Experimentation, chemical lab work, and sensorial, tactile involvement with materials were promoted as appropriate for the home. Finally, Chen Diexian and fellow contributors seemed driven by a mission to unveil heretofore secret or unavailable recipes in the new urban press.

Chen was not alone in featuring recipes to manufacture daily-use items at home. The Commercial Press *New Student Journal* (*Xuesheng xinza*) had similar industrial arts columns that included a variety of technological digests (Chou 2005, 126). But what was interesting about "The Warehouse" column was that it promoted a form of production suitable specifically for respectable ladies to pursue in their inner chambers (*guifang*).[6] Another publication portrayed household production in this manner as well. In 1915, the *Ladies' Journal* (*Funü zazhi*), one of Republican China's longest-running women's journals, featured a series of articles on household manufacturing of cosmetics and toiletries for women in its "Knowledge and Skills" ("Xueyi") section.[7] The article "A Brief Explanation on Methods for Making Cosmetics" appeared in the January issue, "Method for Making Rouge" in the March issue, and "Method for Producing Cosmetics" in the May issue.[8] Like Chen's column, these articles emphasized the making of things (*zhizuo* or *zhizao*), demanded physical engagement with material objects, and exhorted experimentation and experiential knowledge. They espoused the manufacturing of recipes as well as knowledge of chemistry and physics. Finally, they, too, presented these recipes as something genteel women of the inner quarters could leisurely do.

By examining Chen's column and these how-to pieces in the *Ladies' Journal*, this chapter investigates the politics behind these pieces and inquires why this manufacturing know-how was being conveyed as appropriate for genteel women to apply leisurely at home. Why was Chen invested in publishing these recipes, and what kind of community of readers and users emerged around his column and others like it? With China's increasing integration into a new form of global capitalism and the emergence of an increasingly commodified world of mass-manufactured daily-use items, how did Chen and his community of readers and practitioners use these recipes to manage, organize, and give meaning to a highly materialistic and commercialized milieu? In an era when knowledge was also becoming commodified, did the mass-printed recipes also provide Chen with a means to establish his brand of expertise in new ways of knowing and to articulate a new urban lifestyle?

Finally, the question remains whether the recipes in these columns were regularly applied in practice. The treatment of leisurely manufacturing as something suitable for respectable women was on one level prescriptive. Yet on another level readers may well have applied the recipes. If so, was the targeted producer, the genteel woman, always the actual practitioner? Given that cosmetic production had long taken place within the domestic realm, the question needs to be raised seriously whether female producers who had long made cosmetics at home would have turned to articles that formally and publically codified how-to knowledge they had long embodied. If female household producers were putting these recipes to use, how and where did they get the ingredients? If female producers were not the likely practitioners, for whom and for what other purposes might such knowledge have been compiled and printed? In an era when science was not yet formalized, how might these pieces have encouraged forms of amateur science even while they provided tips for actual would-be manufacturers?

RECIPES AS A SOURCE, WOMEN'S MAGAZINES AS A GENRE

To grapple with these questions, this chapter shows how on one level these texts were prescriptive and ideological and were appreciated as such and yet on another level were recipes in action, used for practical purposes, and applied. To do this, the chapter draws from recent scholarship in recipes studies that pays close attention to the generic nature and material form of the recipe.[9] Such works explore the compilation process behind the making of the recipe, where and why the recipe was collected, and, if it was printed, where it was published and for whom. They do not take for granted the formal characteristics of the recipe and raise questions about the order of ingredients, whether such an order was stable, and what the logic of such ordering might be. Neither the recipe compiler's authorial form nor what the readers-users knew, including what tools to use in preparing the recipes, nor what quantities of the listed ingredients were required are taken for granted. By adopting such an approach, these scholars are better able to consider how recipes from the past might have been used and applied, who their users might have been, and how they functioned to constitute authority and knowledge on the part of both the compiler and the practitioner.

The how-to recipes discussed here were published in women's magazines. "The Warehouse" column appeared in *Women's World*, the periodical that Chen founded and edited starting in December 1914. Literary scholar Perry Link estimates that three thousand copies of each issue of *Women's World* were published, and copies were then shared or read collectively, with an estimated ten thousand readers per issue.[10] These recipes therefore reached a more anonymous reading public than would recipes that circulated in manuscript cultures.[11] Mechanical printing replaced the handwritten, and the publicization of the recipes had the explicit goal of standardizing production processes (even if this goal was not always met). Yet the readership of Chen's column and others like it, even if relatively anonymous, was nonetheless limited to those with the expertise, literacy, curiosity, and resources to read and possibly apply the recipes in practice.

It is important to note that the women's press was a particularly lively space in early-twentieth-century China. It was highly progressive and experimental in terms of its genre, the information featured, and the readership catered to.[12] Furthermore, despite being known as women's journals, these titles offered an unprecedented editorial space where *both* male and female writers and readers could explore new ideas.[13] To be sure, male editors of such journals (most editors were men) were sincerely committed to targeting women readers and writers, and as a result women authors and readers were increasing their participation in the public literary realm. Famous editor Wang Dungen—who played a key role in luring Chen to Shanghai, edited the literary journal *Saturday* (*Libailiu*), which featured butterfly fiction on a regular basis, and coedited the *Shenbao* literary supplement *Free Talk* (*Ziyoutan*) with Chen for a couple of years—noted that Chen had hundreds of female disciples who read his journal and wrote letters to him (Pan Jianguo 2003, 236). Bao Tianxiao, the editor of the *Women's Eastern Times* (*Funü shibao*), an influential woman's journal during this period that, like Chen's journal, was committed to vernacularizing knowledge, cited in his memoirs that women contributed at least 20 to 30 percent of the journal's content (Judge 2015, 68). Furthermore, women's total contributions to these journals in the form of hidden female labor likely superseded the contributions from them that their male editors publicly acknowledged. In the case of *Women's World*, the production of the journal was critically dependent on unrecognized female and family labor. Chen's wife, Zhu Shu, never received a by-line but essentially coedited the journal and contributed to its regular features. Their children, son Dingshan and daughter Xiaocui, helped with translations (Hanan 1999, 4). Yet Chen always took primary credit.

However, characterizing these journals as *primarily* by and for women or consumed by "bourgeois housewives" overstates women's participation in them.[14] Men remained active as editors, contributors, *and* consumers of women's journals (Mittler 2004, 310). Male students and intellectuals were interested in the journals, and some read the pieces along with their wives (Chou 2005, 126). We also cannot take authorial claims of female authorship literally in every single instance. Lesser-known or unknown male writers or even major male writers and editors often assumed female monikers when contributing to journals such as the *Ladies' Journal* (Nivard 1984, 46–49). In the *Ladies' Journal*, most of the contributors who were writing sections on common scientific knowledge (*kexue xiao changshi*) and on knowledge in chemistry and physics were probably men (Chou 2005, 126). Just as Chen used the man-of-feeling persona in his fiction as a vehicle to legitimize new endeavors and pursuits, including the making of money, in journals he employed a female voice by targeting the *guixiu* as the ideal practitioner of his manufacturing recipes.[15]

In addition to the gendered nature of contributors and readers, we also need to pay attention to the concrete practices of translation and compilation in these publications. Articles and recipes on light industry, *xiao gongyi*, in publications and newspapers of the day often included sections that were direct, if unattributed, translations of pieces from Western and Japanese-language sources. In her discussion of the early-Republican title the *Women's Eastern Times*, Joan Judge discusses how the journal tapped into a "global reservoir of texts and images," with Japanese sources being the primary conduit. Authors and editors of urban presses subjected these global texts, images, and templates to China's specific cultural grammar as well as to each journal's respective agenda. They drew from their publishers' libraries for sources and engaged in the importation of images, passages, and recipes from a host of different sources, which they would then paste together when compiling articles.[16] Pieces were often the composite results of translated modules of texts, recipes, and images, and producing an article would frequently involve cutting and pasting blocks of text with imported images. Editors would add introductory remarks or commentary on the images to give the article a sense of cohesiveness.

Chen Diexian approached the compilation of pieces in *Women's World* column in this manner. A retrospective account notes how Chen and his wife, Zhu Shu, often drew from texts on the manufacturing of industrial objects that originated from the large cache of books on industry and manufacturing that Chen had received from his Japanese tutor in Hangzhou (Chen Xiaocui, Fan, and Zhou 1982, 212). This cache of books may well have included Japanese translations of Western-language recipes. It is likely that the recipe to make *spiritus rosae* that starts this chapter was compiled in a cut-and-paste manner, with translated parts possibly coming from this cache. The name of the purported female reader who wrote to Chen, "Mme. Xi Meng," sounds very much like a transliteration of a Western name (Simone?).[17] There is also no mention of the exact amount of ingredients to use, which suggests the recipe's piecemeal production.

Translated and compiled, these pieces were hardly transparent conduits or fixed conveyers of stable information. The ingredient list for the hair-tonic recipe is worth our attention because it illustrates the composite nature of the compilation process and the porous nature and instability of translation. The list featured several languages. All items were first given in Chinese. Western-language glosses were provided for the majority of items; most glosses were in Latin. The Latin terms were well-accepted terms for pharmaceutical ingredients by 1915. *Acidum sulphuricum, spiritus, oleum limonis, oleum cinnamomi,* and so on were standardized names that appeared as early as 1898 in the *British Pharmacopoeia* (General Medical Council 1898), one of the most authoritative pharmaceutical reference books in the British Empire at the time. They also appeared in *A Manual of Therapeutics and Pharmacy in the Chinese Language* (*Wanguo yaofang,* literally, "Prescriptions of the World" [Hunter 1915]), which built on the *British Pharmacopoeia.*[18] Chen may very well have consulted the *Manual of Therapeutics* for the compilation of this recipe. There is also the possibility that he retrieved the terms from the foreign dispensaries in Shanghai that he frequented for ingredients. He did not provide the Latin term *oleum caryophylli* for oil of cloves but used instead the German word *Nelkenöl* (though it was misspelled or misprinted as "Nelkeuöl," which might have been due to flipping the *n* and the *u* in the typesetting process). He may have acquired the German term from the German KOFA Dispensary. The term *glycerin* appears in English. The English and Latin terms were possibly from the Anglo-Chinese Dispensary.

In addition to its linguistic hybridity, the list of ingredients is riddled with errors. With the use of multiple languages in global chemistry at this time, scientific-knowledge production in Europe was littered with examples of "language friction"—instances in the scientific text where misspellings or mistakes expose or make visible the imperfect acts of translation and crossings of linguistic barriers that had characterized scientific communication and practice in the West for centuries (Gordin 2015). Such "linguistic friction" is evident in this hair-tonic recipe printed in a Chinese journal in 1915, which is peppered with spelling errors. In addition to the misspelling or misprinting "Nelkenöl," the first ingredient, sulfuric acid, is glossed and spelled incorrectly as "Acidum Sulphruicum." Such mistakes were indicative of the unstable command Chen and other compilers had of foreign languages and speak to the complex nature of the translation process lurking behind the presentation of this how-to knowledge as well as to the diverse linguistic circuits these recipes traversed.

The material production of these articles thus poses interesting challenges and opportunities for the historian. Although we cannot assume there is any "original" authorial voice behind these pieces per se, they are fascinating precisely because of how Chen rendered the modular texts or images compatible and linked them together to make a compelling "read" for readers. Appropriation and adaptation rather than original authorship of these recipes need to be central to our analysis. From this perspective, we can see how Chen's introductions, prefaces, and editorial touches reveal the logic of compilation. Chen had a strong sense of how to adapt the oft-translated recipes to address the tastes and interests of their community of readers and practitioners. His mention of specific Shanghai pharmacies in his recipes was a clear intervention on his part. So, too, was the framing of the recipe as something suitable to the genteel female reader, an ideal reader who resonated powerfully and held symbolic significance in the urban China of the 1910s.

"THE WAREHOUSE"

Chen's column "The Warehouse" appeared in the "Industrial Arts" ("Gongyi") section of *Women's World*, the woman's periodical that he started editing in 1914. The front sections of the journal were devoted to poetry and fiction, long-familiar categories of proper knowledge for elite women. The back included the "Household" ("Jiating"), "Fine Arts" ("Meishu"), "Hygiene" ("Weisheng"), and "Industrial Arts" sections, all of which featured newer categories of knowledge.[19] "Industrial Arts" included not only "The Warehouse" but also a regular column dealing with new food recipes and articles on the tailoring of clothes. It showcased forms of knowledge and practices involving the use of original ingredients to make something new, often with chemical processes.[20] Articles on how to make dye and on manufacturing cosmetics illustrate this emphasis.

According to "The Warehouse," matters of the "industrial arts" were to occur in the well-to-do space of the genteel inner chambers. The respectable, educated woman, or *guixiu*, the denizen of that space, could speak in the name of the featured knowledge. In the May 1915 contribution to "The Warehouse" column, Chen Diexian, writing under the pen name "Xuyuan" (Garden of Vitality), depicted appropriate pursuits for the female quarters in the following manner:

Use [the method for absorption] to make gifts for your companions in the inner chambers (*guiyou*). It is quite enjoyable. You can use seasonal flowers and make different kinds of solid fragrances; you are not restricted to using rose essence [the only fragrance available on the market]. The chemical method of absorption (*xishou fa*) has become the strategy of experimentation (*shiyan ji*) in the inner chambers. All you need to do is obtain some simple tools and make [fragrances] according to the [instructions below].
(Chen Diexian 1915, vol. 5 [May], 1)

"Some simple tools" included a glass jar and a copper sheet (which would be made into a thin tube), petroleum jelly, glycerin, and flower petals. Flower petals were conceivably readily available in upper-class households. Glycerin, however, was not an everyday household item and had to be purchased at specialty import stores. Nor was a copper sheet a likely item to have at home. The earliest domestic manufacturer of ingredients such as caustic soda and sulfuric acid was probably China Acid and Alkali Co., Ltd. (Zhongguo suan chang gufen youxian gongsi), founded in 1919 (*Handbook of Chinese Manufacturers* 1949, 221–224), after "The Warehouse" articles were published. None existed in 1915 to help Chen's readers, so he pointed practitioners to Western pharmacies—including the KOFA Dispensary and the Anglo-Chinese Dispensary—for the ingredients and tools that were more difficult to procure.[21]

The column portrayed the inner chambers not as the quarters of modest homes or as the parlors of modern treaty-port houses but as the refined inner chambers of elite households. References to gift exchange among genteel women, the seemingly disinterested act of "enjoyment," and the emphasis on "friendship" among like-minded people managed to evoke the image of literati cultivation that had been long associated with such spaces. Yet although the chambers referred to were still clearly the inner chambers, they had been updated. They did not resemble the traditional male literatus's study, where reflective moral contemplation took place through the study of texts.[22] Nor were they a space for talented women to embroider, exchange poetry, paint, or make rouge with natural ingredients in a separate, genteel "women's culture." They also diverged considerably from imperial-period households engaged in textile production and weaving, long encapsulated in the imperial-era slogan "men till and women weave," which identified female production of cloth as the core of a productive empire. By the time *Women's World* was issued, the inner chambers had become a modern site where things were manufactured through chemical means, where experiments abounded, and where chemistry-based production practices could be enjoyed. They were also a newly publicized space featured in journals and connected to some of China's new-style pharmacies and import shops.

These inner chambers were, moreover, strongly characterized by the sensibility of refinement and focus on playful leisure. The space was not a site of work for subsistence, and these recipes were not aiming to improve productivity for the sake of productivity. These recipes portrayed the activity of producing substances as something genteel women were meant to find leisurely delight in pursuing. The attitude by which genteel women had long exchanged poetry was the approach they were meant to take when distilling a liquid. Such an approach coincided with the larger culture of play in the early republic that emphasized playful engagement with gadgets just as one would with literary works (Rea 2015a, 40).[23] This emphasis on whimsically engaging with objects is explicit in Chen's recipes. A section on bending the glassware necessary for the hair-tonic recipe included a line in parenthesis that states, "This [glass bending] method is very delightful (*you quwei*) as it allows you to use the glass tube, bend them at your will, and render the glass into a plaything (*wanju*)" (Chen Diexian 1915, vol. 2 [February], 5). This activity was presented not as an efficient means to manufacture a necessity or as a marker of the most pioneering scientific process. Bending glass was enchanting, an activity that invited toying around with the material process. This playful approach echoed lettered approaches toward knowing the natural world and experimenting with technology that turned on their capacity to delight rather than to do something for practicality alone.

Sensorial engagement was also central to the recipes. Tactile involvement in the process facilitated a grasp of physics and allowed one to showcase one's taste through the act of production. In "The Warehouse" entry for May 15, 1915, on manufacturing solid fragrances, Chen Diexian, writing as Xuyuan, narrated the exact steps by which to calibrate the strength of fragrances with different kinds of flower petals. He stressed, "Fragrance is like color. If a color is too strong, it appears murky and dark. If a scent is too strong, it causes unpleasant olfactory sensations. If you use less, the scent will unfold and be alluringly fragrant. Those making scents must thus understand the physics (*wuli*) [behind the process]" (Chen Diexian 1915, vol. 5 [May], 2–3). Sensorial ways of knowing were crucial, too, in making China's products competitive vis-à-vis Western commodities. In "The Warehouse" entry on hair tonic published in January 1915, Chen described Western imports in the following manner: "Even if one does not smell [the tonic's] fragrance, [the visual quality] draws one's eyes to it and elicits desire [for it]" (Chen Diexian 1915, vol. 1 [January], 6). He then commented critically on how domestic hair tonics on the market used poor ingredients, resulting in their impure or unclean appearance. He went on to provide tips on how to improve the products by relying on the senses in the process of making them. Together, these pieces portray the inner chambers as a place where women were to deploy their senses tastefully. They present the technical information—the physics behind the recipe—as knowable not solely through erudite book learning but also through refined yet sensorial ways of knowing.

Even as Chen's column prescribed hands-on activity for these spaces, it nonetheless ultimately asserted that it was to guide the activities textually. Chen instructed in fairly precise detail lest his readers would tinker too wildly. The article on manufacturing fragrances, for example, prescribed the exact kind of jar to use at home, provided instructions on how to turn a copper sheet into a thin tube and how to place it in the jar, and gave the precise distance the tube needed to be from the sides of the jar. Direction for how to sterilize the jar without cracking the glass and how to use Vaseline and scents to make solid perfumes were also carefully provided. The skill and know-how presented here was not in the tradition of craft knowledge, where transmission took place face-to-face, from masters to apprentices, who were to extract information through hard bodily work and years of loyalty. This skill instead rested on instruction through a published text.

These pieces also allowed readers to grapple, if obliquely, with the larger contexts of the material world, including untrustworthy markets. In the May 1915 entry on fragrance production, Chen heralded household production as superior to market consumption:

> Now, in the inner chambers, it is a common practice to use hair tonic. That which is sold on the market is called hair gel and uses

fat. It is sold in small glass bottles or stored in small porcelain boxes. Its weight is no more than an English tael, and its selling price is regularly higher than a silver yuan and two jiao. If you buy the original ingredients and make it yourself, it is far less expensive. Try what is explained [below]. . . . You can use it whenever you like, and it hardly differs from what you can buy on the market. [Furthermore,] . . . [the kind sold] on the market is rose scented. . . . [At home], if you like other scents, you can use . . . other kinds of perfumes and add it into the mixture.
(Chen Diexian 1915, vol. 5 [May], 1)

In the passage, Chen legitimated a do-it-yourself approach and promoted the homemade version as the same if not better in quality as the store-bought type and far less expensive. He stressed how home manufacturing allowed for more flexibility and the production of more scents. He warned that store-bought fragrances ran the risk of being "infected with dirt" because they were mixed with different kinds of inferior fat.

These pieces purposefully contrasted the productive domain of the inner chambers with the crass market, where manufactured yet potentially adulterated versions of these items could be procured. In doing so, they appealed to readers anxious about the impact of capitalism as well as to those seeking to demarcate their social standing through the consumption of manufacturing know-how rather than through the purchasing of finished commodities. Lurking behind these pieces is the idea that marketplace goods are potentially tainted, whereas homemade ones are pure.[24] This idea tapped into a growing anxiety about impure goods in an era when standardization and testing were not yet institutionalized in China (or around the world).[25] Frugality was also promoted as a virtue to demarcate standing. A tasteful gentleman of the High Qing, for example, would not have discussed matters as prosaic as saving money, but in the 1910s, when money was very much on the mind of his readers, Chen promoted the virtuous household as one that pursued frugality in contradistinction to the wasteful and distrustful ways of the market.

Even though "The Warehouse" inveighed against the consumption of store-bought cosmetic items and other toiletries with its promotion of home-based production, many of those items were on sale. In the hair-tonic entry, Chen railed against the hair tonic sold commercially at one silver yuan and two jiao. Yet he also instructed producers to buy Vaseline (whose price was around five jiao) for making the tonic. Although Vaseline was much less expensive than the finished product, Chen was nonetheless still prescribing consumption of basic ingredients. Readers imagined as women were also instructed to buy lab equipment for their home laboratory.[26] The mention of specific pharmacies had the feel of "product placement." Chen Diexian founded Household Industries a few years after the publication of these pieces. The articles' promotion of *domestic* manufacturing and their explicit critique of consumption of finished commodities in the stores thus might seem to go against Chen's immediate commercial interest. Yet their more general effect was to create consumer desire for ingredients and products that Chen and others like him were eventually to manufacture. Identifying Chen's potential commercial interests in these writings is not meant to suggest that his commitment to spread science and modern production know-how to his compatriots was somehow less than genuine. Far from it: as we will see, these articles were inextricably linked to his commitment to encourage patriotic and nativist manufacturing.

Finally, what was ultimately available for purchase was the knowledge itself. Published in a commercially produced woman's journal, "The Warehouse" notably aspired to create a sense of familiarity between the entry contributors and the readers, and this sense of intimacy served to entice readers to come back for more. To secure their authority as mediators of taste and expertise, Chen and his contributors presented the column's know-how with an intimate tone rather than an impersonal, disembodied narratorial style. The persona of a chatty writer sharing tips with the reader in a familiar manner was volubly present. Take, for example, "Method for Making High-Quality Soap" in "The Warehouse" column of the March 1915 issue (Kuang 1915, vol. 3 [March]). The entry is clearly pedagogical. It provides the English gloss for new ingredients, a rhetorical gesture that was at once instructional and meant to evoke the authority of scientific knowledge from the West. The Chinese term for caustic soda is followed in parenthesis by the English term, though it is misspelled as "caustc soda."[27] At the same time, the article struck a strong personal tone, imparting practical pointers and urging hands-on experimentation as the means to find the best method. Toward the end of the entry, a long section beginning with "Things that I noticed" was included, consisting of things the contributor, Kuang Yu, personally discovered in his own trials with making soap, such as the best kind of cow fat to use and the suggestion to use it when dry. Kuang Yu dispensed advice on how not to use caustic soda with sulfates because when cooked in an iron pot, this type of soda would generate black sulfurized iron. Detailed counsel was furthermore dispensed on how best to dissolve the caustic soda into water and create the ideal thickness of the mixture: 8 parts caustic soda to 96 parts water for the initial mixing of soda and water, 11 parts caustic soda to 89 parts water for the second mixing, and 14 parts soda to 86 parts water for the third.

The column's serialized format lent itself to the creation of a sense of intimacy—even if that intimacy was ultimately illusory—between the contributors and their (female) readers. The regular appearance of the column generated what appeared to be an ongoing conversation, and contributors would reference past entries to reinforce that feeling. In the entry quoted at the beginning of the chapter, Chen explicitly mentioned how a reader's letter referenced the column from the previous month. He thus acknowledged his regular set of readers, literally identifying a community among readers willing to accept his and his fellow contributors' expertise. In April 1915, Kuang Yu referred back to the column's first entry on hair tonic written by Chen and similarly addressed readers as if they were regulars. In addressing their targeted female readers, such as "Mme. Xi Meng," in this manner, these male contributors established a new form of male authority–female disciple relationship.[28] Just as he did with his brand reputation as a fiction writer, Chen used this familiarity to build a regular audience. The commodified nature of this knowledge—its dissemination turning on the sales of his journal—demanded his ability to brand and sell himself as available to all.

POLITICS OF MANUFACTURING AND THE *LADIES' JOURNAL*

Similar recipes appeared in the women's periodical the *Ladies' Journal*, first published in 1915. These recipes are worth looking at in detail because they make evident the moral, political, and national implications lurking in the more leisurely stance of Chen's "Warehouse" column. Unlike the brief life span of *Women's World*, the *Ladies' Journal* was one of the longest-running women's journals of the Republican period and had a considerable geographic reach.[29] *Ladies' Journal* writers often identified themselves explicitly as modern female students writing to like-minded female readers, including teachers, fellow female students, and educated women from better-off urban families. Writers claimed that they were women by using the title *nüshi*, "Lady" or "Mme.," in front of their names, by identifying themselves as female students at a particular school, and by referring explicitly to their targeted (female) readers as "comrades in the women's world."

Just as Chen's column presented knowledge considered ideal for its imagined female readers to pursue, so, too, did the *Ladies' Journal*. This knowledge included geometry, applied chemistry, and personal hygiene, along with the traditional appreciation of poetry and literature. After an initial set of illustrations and photographs (often of respectable modern women), the leading section of the journal featured opinion essays, including women-related pieces that dealt with topics such as education for women as well as pieces that were not specifically related to "women's issues" (an article on the "current situation in the Pacific" [March 5, 1915] is one such example). The back part of the journal included sections on home economics (*jiazheng*), fiction and other literary selections (literally "a garden of literature," *wenyuan*), the arts, and other miscellaneous areas.[30] Articles on how to make cosmetics and toiletries were included in the *xueyi* section, a term that might be glossed in English as "knowledge and skill," especially those associated with the industrial arts and science.[31] This section covered a range of topics from domestic production of soap to simple cures for common maladies to the chessboard. Article titles included "A Brief Discussion of Daily Physics and Chemistry," "Method to Eliminate Stains from Cloth," "The Way to Measure Chinese Weights," "Animals' Self-Defense," and "The Consciousness of Plants."

The *Ladies' Journal* articles on manufacturing toiletry items are similar to Chen Diexian's pieces in "The Warehouse" column. Both identified the feminized inner chambers as the spatial site of scientific activity and sought to depict production activity as virtuous and politically relevant to the new age. Written in an accessible form of classical Chinese, the article "A Brief Explanation on Methods for Making Cosmetics" published in the January 1915 issue of the *Ladies' Journal* was typical. The author, Ling Ruizhu, identified herself as a third-year student at the

Number 2 Girls School of Jiangsu. The article offered instructions on how to make several different kinds of daily-use items, including soap:

> [*Shijian*] is commonly referred to as *feizao*. When it provides a cosmetic function, it is called *xiangzao*. There is more than one kind. There is cassia-scented soap, *zhulan*-scented soap,[32] sandalwood soap, etc. For ingredients, one must collect [caustic] soda and cow's fat, pig's fat, or coconut oil, etc. Then add perfume. Its quality depends on the expensiveness of the perfume and doesn't have anything to do with the difficulty of making it. . . . When you use it, first dissolve the soap in water, and the soda will slightly float apart. Then, you lather it in water and use it to clean your skin or body hair of filth. Its efficacy is remarkable.
> (Ling 1915, 17–18)

Information is imparted in a straightforward prescriptive tone. The entry reveals the various names used to identify soap, the necessary ingredients, steps in manufacturing the item, and how to use the manufactured material. It assures the reader that the product is not difficult to make. Other entries detailed information on making toothpowder, hair oil, and perfume.

These *Ladies' Journal* writings—like those in "The Warehouse"—notably framed the knowledge they were promoting in terms that evoked the modern disciplines of chemistry and physics as well as the cosmopolitanism of that knowledge. The article "Method for Making Rouge" (March 1915) provided the following explanation:

> Rouge is made from the flower petals of the red flower (*Carthamus tinctorius L.*) and is one of the important items among cosmetics. [This] flower is part of the chrysanthemum family. . . . Its height is around 2–3 *chi*. Its flower petals contain red and yellow pigment. The red pigment named Karthamin ($C_{14}H_{16}O_7$) is the main component of rouge. The yellow pigment[33] has miscellaneous elements in it that need to be expelled, or else the quality of the rouge will deteriorate. . . . When [the petal pigment] comes into contact with an acid, it precipitates into sedimentation.
> (Hui 1915, 15)

In explaining the ingredients of rouge, this passage explicitly uses scientific terms. *Carthamus tinctorius L.* is the Latin name for safflower in the Linnean taxonomic system, referring to the flower needed to make the dye for rouge. In the article, this name is written in the romanized alphabet and stands out sharply in the otherwise primarily Chinese text.[34] The Latin term for red dye, *Karthamin*, is similarly romanized, as is the chemical compound $C_{14}H_{16}O_7$. The text also employs the discourse of modern chemistry in describing the rouge-making process. Sodium carbonate (sodium salt of carbonic acid) is specified as the preferred acid type for precipitating the petal's pigment into sedimentation.

Like the entries in "The Warehouse," these writings in the *Ladies' Journal* emphasized experimentation, sensory know-how, and bodily engagement with the process of making things, while also presenting the author as expert. "A Brief Explanation on Methods for Making Cosmetics" was typical in that it featured a high degree of prescriptive technical knowledge while at the same time reading like a practical pointer. The author, Ling Ruizhu, not only displayed expertise in chemistry and manufacturing but also served as a practical adviser whose "tips" resulted from her own hands-on experience in the making of and experimenting with things. Ling advised readers that the best way to tell whether the soap is high quality is through one's senses. "With the tip of the tongue, taste it. If there is no peppery, acrid taste, then it is a quality commodity (*shangpin*)." This advice, although terse, nonetheless spoke volumes by alluding to a way of knowing that included relying upon one's sense of taste through the tip of one's own tongue and by promoting ingenuity and inventiveness as virtues.

What these *Ladies' Journal* pieces did well—perhaps even more so than Chen's column—was lift out the moral and political imperative behind domestic production in the inner chambers. Several pieces presented the imagined domestic site of production in ways that resonated powerfully with both long-standing discourses on household management and recent ones on personal hygiene and national strength that had gained currency in the late nineteenth century. "The Method for Producing Cosmetics," an article written by a Mme. Shen Ruiqing, declared that women's knowledge about how to make cosmetics and thus the ability to know their nature was at the crux of improving the state of the household. She began with a warning: "Cosmetics are products (*pin*) that women need. Their price is rather expensive. When women are being thrifty, cosmetics count as a kind of expendable item. Is it better, then, not to use them?" (Shen Ruiqing 1915, 18). To answer the question, Mme. Shen invoked the traditional belief that women's proper appearance and deportment form one of four womanly virtues. "Having balding hair and not treating it, and having teeth plaque and not cleaning it, all obstruct the hygienic welfare of the household (*jiating weisheng*). . . . [I]f we use [cosmetics] without knowing their nature (*pinxing*), this is lacking in household knowledge (*jiating zhishi*)" (18). By placing such a premium on household order, Mme. Shen evoked the classical neo-Confucian (*lixue*) discourse that linked the harmony of the domestic feminized realm (*nei*) with the moral harmony of the masculinized outer realm (*wai*) of political cosmology. Family relations had metaphorical implications for political relations; wifely chastity and filial piety were metaphors for political loyalty. Women's work in the household was deemed crucial for the productive state of affairs beyond the domestic domain.

For Mme. Shen, the full grasp of *women's* objects was crucial. Cosmetics and intimate items of the woman's boudoir had a long history in Chinese culture of being seen as morally fraught objects. In Chinese literary history, the peddling of such items was often depicted as threatening because they were seen as symbols of seduction, luring innocent women out of their inner chambers to the improper domain of the public streets. In Mme. Shen's piece, a similar ambivalence persisted. Vanishing face cream and hair grease were at once necessary and potentially destabilizing. They helped women uphold the virtue of appearance and deportment and yet were fraught with potential danger. If their nature were not understood properly, they could lead women and by extension the household to dissolute, wasteful consumption. The rest of the piece provided a prescription against such a scenario by detailing production know-how and the proper understanding of the nature of such things. It recounted the chemical makeup of different cosmetic items and how to manufacture and properly use them. Readers also learned how to make hair dye, face powder, l'eau de toilette, liquid rose rouge, face lotion, perfume glycerin, toilet powder, lavender water, hair tonic, pimple caustic, rose-scented hair grease, lavender-scented hair tonic, camphor toothpowder, and Hazeline Snow vanishing face cream.[35] Supplementary notes included a warning about how to handle the glycerine properly when making lotion that expelled freckles.[36]

In identifying the production of women's *things* to be the crux of household harmony and in emphasizing greater knowledge of the nature of things through their production (and through the consumption of the journal's text), the *Ladies' Journal* article resonated strongly with the tradition of *gewu zhizhi*, the "investigation of things." Since the Song dynasty, the philosophical discourse on *gewu* had identified the examination of the external nature of a thing (*wu*) as a means for one to obtain an understanding of that thing's true principle (*li*) and as central to grasping the moral truth of the Way (Dao). As the subject of broad learning (*bowu*), the concept of things was defined expansively to include not just material objects but also events and mental phenomena. All were to be known or decoded primarily through the words and language of philosophers and connoisseurs rather than through an actual engagement with material objects, with the express goal of probing universal principles and seeking moral harmony with the larger sociopolitical cosmos.[37]

What was unprecedented, however, was the subtext behind the interest in the material nature of "women's things" in 1915. No longer at the head of a cosmopolitan empire that ideologically subscribed to a Confucian cosmology, China had become a republican nation-state—one of many—competing in an international capitalist arena. A palpable concern emerged regarding China's competitive strength in the global market and the biopolitics stemming from a distinctly modern discourse that posited a close relationship between the health of the individual and the health of the nation. The rise of global capitalism in the nineteenth century had resulted in Chinese markets being flooded with foreign commodities, ranging from opium to industrial goods. The humiliating military defeats meted out to China by Western powers and Japan seemed only to confirm China's technological and material inferiority. This anxiety ensured that materiality loomed large in these journal articles and notably often in a language that arose from the context of international commerce.[38] Knowing thoroughly the constituency of key commodities and how to produce them was linked to national strength.

As Mme. Shen's reference to the need for the household's hygienic welfare suggests, the international discourse of China's deficiency in hygiene and health conditions, which had gained currency by the latter part of the nineteenth century, cast a large shadow in these pieces. Inextricably linked to the perception that China's weakened state resulted in increasingly aggressive and violent imperialist subjugation, this discourse had become internalized by Chinese intellectuals, reformists, and administrators. The need to modernize the "sick man of Asia" implied that the Chinese body had to be made clean and healthy. Reformists and intellectuals were thus actively promoting new regimes of hygiene and corporeality in the reformist press, through antifootbinding associations, and in the creation of physical-education curricula and institutions. The *Ladies' Journal* pieces and Chen's column "The Warehouse" allied themselves to the reformist cause by calling for good hygiene welfare in the household. They recommended concrete methods to manufacture high-quality cosmetics. The focus on the production of these objects served to transform cosmetics from a potentially dangerous consumerist attraction into something homemade that would strengthen the nation.[39]

COSMETIC CHANGES: HOME PRODUCTION AND THE PLACE OF RECIPES

Prescriptive in tone, these pieces could very well have been applied in practice. Did women of the inner chambers actually follow the recipes given? Would domestic producers who had long produced rouge and lipstick at home and had the tacit knowledge and embodied skill to make cosmetics turn to these articles to procure more how-to knowledge? If they did, was it to save labor and make home work more efficient? If they did not, what was the purpose of having this knowledge in print, framed in the context of modern chemistry and circulated so widely? Did other practitioners turn to the recipes? To answer these questions, we need to consider first what practices of cosmetic production already existed and what might be new about these journal pieces. Indeed, even as these articles professed a cutting-edge sensibility—for instance, with images of modern chemical glassware—some of the production knowledge presented in these recipes would have been highly familiar to those long used to making cosmetics at home.

Ming–Qing China had a rich history of household healers, male and female, relying on recipes to produce medicine and make cosmetics in late-imperial homes.[40] Many of the products featured in these early-twentieth-century journal recipes (and the cosmetic and hygienic practices for which they were meant to be used), although new in form, had earlier precedents. Toothpowder and toothpaste were new to the twentieth century, but there had been a long history of caring for one's teeth and mouth. Using one end of a willow stick that had been frayed by incisions to brush one's teeth with salt was a custom brought to China from India with the introduction of Buddhism more than a millennium earlier (Dikötter 2007, 209).[41] Soap, too, was not part of the indigenous domestic production repertoire. Methods using chemicals such as sodium carbonate to saponify a substance into soap were not imported until the nineteenth century, and bars of soap rendered through this saponification process were initially considered *yanghuo*, foreign goods.[42] That said, there was a long history of recognizing the functionality of fat and oils to help lather and clean clothing and skin, including using oily plant pods to launder and clean.[43] Given this history, it is not surprising that the Mandarin compound *feizao* came to be used to refer to saponified soap. It had referred to the existing organic matter and technologies, but the earlier usage of the term *fei* simply meant the thickness of the oily pods used to launder clothing, whereas the modern usage connoted the process of rendering fat into soap.

Much of the late-imperial production knowledge about manufacturing cosmetics and toiletry items was embodied, tacit, and transmitted through practice rather than recorded in text. Thus, it is difficult for historians to retrieve and document the history of cosmetic production, though literary sources are helpful. In the eighteenth-century novel *The Dream of the Red Chamber*, discussed in chapter 1, author Cao Xueqin lavishly explores the goings-on of an upper-class Chinese family and includes homemade cosmetics as a powerful trope by which the romantic protagonist, Jia Baoyu, navigates the household. Rouge, in particular, functions to enable Jia to flirt (often indecently) with female characters, including maids and Lin Daiyu, his well-educated, intelligent, and beautiful female romantic partner (who also happens to be his cousin), as well as to establish his own feminine, sentimental nature. Passages describe him "eating" the rouge on the lips of women (and women often tease him by putting rouge on their lips to be eaten) (chapters 19 and 24), and at one point Baoyu has to be stopped from bringing a pot of rouge to his own mouth (chapter 21).[44] In chapter 19, Baoyu admits to Daiyu that he had made rouge with the maids: "Daiyu noticed that there was a blood-spot about the size of a small button on Baoyu's left cheek.... Baoyu lay back to avoid her scrutiny and laughed. 'It isn't a scratch. I've just been helping the [maids] make rouge. A little of it must have splashed on to my face.' ... Daiyu wiped it off with her own [handkerchief], clicking her tongue censoriously as she did so. 'So you're up to *those* tricks again?'" (Cao 1977, 204).

For these passages to work, the author, Cao Xueqin, focused on the domestic production of rouge, an activity that would have been common in upper-class Qing households. The novel describes in detail how cosmetics are to be made, and this information coincides with encyclopedias from the period that include such manufacturing know-how. In chapter 44, Baoyu comforts the character Patience after she is caught in a lovers' squabble between her mistress, her mistress's husband, and his lover. Although innocent and not directly involved in the love triangle, Patience has borne the brunt of her mistress's and the husband's anger. To console her, Baoyu offers to make up her face. He insists on using the best makeup available in the residence and on sitting her at a dressing table, and he explains how the various powders are made in order to demonstrate their purity and quality.

> Pinching off one of these novel powder-containers, [Baoyu] handed it to Patience.
>
> "There you are. This isn't ceruse, it's a powder made by crushing the seeds of garden-jalap and mixing them with perfume."
>
> Patience emptied the contents of the tiny phial on to her palm. All the qualities required by the most expert perfumers were there: lightness, whiteness with just the faintest tinge of rosiness, and fragrance. It spread smoothly and cleanly on the skin, imparting to it a soft bloom that was quite unlike the harsh and somewhat livid whiteness associated with lead-based powders....
>
> "This is made from safflower, the same as ordinary rouge," Baoyu explained to her, "only the stuff they sell in the shops is impure and its color is inferior. This is made by squeezing the juice from the best quality safflower, carefully extracting all the impurities, mixing it with rose water, and then further purifying it by

distillation. It's so concentrated that you need only a dab of it on the end of hairpin to do your lips with and still have enough left over to dilute with water in the palms of your hands for using on your cheeks."
(Cao 1977, 376)

This account of how to use safflower for rouge production is similar to a description of manufacturing safflower cakes for making rouge in a seventeenth-century compendium on industrial technologies titled *The Works of Heaven and the Inception of Things* (*Tiangong kaiwu*, 1637).[45] As part of a larger trend in the late Ming where knowledge was compiled in encyclopedias and sold on the booming print market, *Works of Heaven* covered technologies that required large-scale investment, including mining, making salt, producing ceramic, casting weaponry, and producing jade and pearls. Its description of safflower-cake production, which was part of its dyes section, was also for large-scale production and called for using high-quality safflower and purifying the cakes through processes of distillation, just as Baoyu does at a more intimate register in the inner chambers to comfort Patience. In another Chinese novel, *The Plum in the Golden Vase* (*Jin Ping Mei cihua*, c. 1610), the author incorporated snippets and passages from everyday encyclopedia and compendia from the late-Ming marketplace of books (as noted in Shang 2006). Cao probably did the same in *The Dream*, procuring knowledge on rouge making from *The Works of Heaven* and other sources where descriptions of cosmetic making were preserved, ranging from medical books to household encyclopedias.[46]

By 1915, readers in urban settings were experiencing new trajectories of commodification that increasingly rendered home production less vital and more inefficient. As people moved to thriving treaty ports such as Shanghai, homes literally became smaller and served less as sites of production. Time also became configured differently as people left the home for work and had little time for producing goods. In other words, the publication of these recipes for manufacturing was taking place in a society where city dwellers had the means and leisure to consume not only these journals but also ready-made toiletries and cosmetics, which were fast becoming popular commodities in China.[47] Ads for pharmacy and medicine stores started to appear in the same women's journals that ran these articles and are indicative of this new political economy. They often featured items specific to the women's quarters. Sai Sei Do, a Japanese pharmacy, sold beauty products, medicines, medical tools, and glass containers for medicine. The ad for the Great Five Continents Drugstore (Wuzhou da yaofang) featured the African Tree Bark Pill, the Wonder Pill of the Woman's World, and an assortment of other types of famous drugs and ointments. Another Shanghai establishment, the Watson's Pharmacy (Quchenshi da yaofang), specifically sold cosmetic and adornment items for women's quarters:[48] different types of face powder, varied and marvelous scented soaps, toothpaste, liquid rose rouge, creams for smooth skin, hair tonics, scented salts, water to supplement one's body, fragrant hair oils, tonic for a peaceful night's sleep, and all kinds of candy. For those who had the resources and time to read these journals, purchasing the cosmetics and soap advertised in the journals in local pharmacies was also often within their means.

There thus seems to be little reason for those who had long produced cosmetics at home and for whom the making of cosmetics had become embodied or tacit knowledge to turn to these journals to acquire basic production know-how. As urban consumption of makeup and toiletry items grew, manufacturing such items at home would also seem less pressing. Thus, to understand why these pieces appeared when they did and who was consuming them and why, it is worthwhile to consider what might have been unprecedented and newly attractive about them. What perhaps drew readers was the epistemological frame within which the knowledge was presented (chemistry and physics) and the material accoutrement (lab equipment and modern glassware) stipulated as necessary. The means of transmission may also have been an attraction: the knowledge was distributed in the mass media, and columns like Chen's made certain skills public, presented them in new terms for new purposes, and made them readily available for a far greater reading and practicing audience. From these factors, we can surmise that those who likely turned to these recipes were individuals curious about the new methods and explanations of chemistry and the modern lab equipment featured. They would also be people who had ready access to these journals as well as to the ingredients featured in the recipes.

These recipes appeared in an era before the professionalization of industry and science started to occur. Science was not yet associated primarily with formal sites such as the university, the science lab, or the modern factory. It was also a time when modern chemical education varied enormously over time, place, and level of instruction. At the university level, the development of science departments, labs, and qualified instructors varied from place to place.[49] Science flourished mostly in missionary schools. The Rockefeller Foundation, which was committed to bringing modern medical education and the attendant fields of biology, chemistry, and physics to China, played a crucial role. The Peking Union Medical College was the centerpiece of the foundation's efforts, but its funds also reached Chinese colleges and universities through grants specifically targeting the development of the study of science.

For women, the target audience for these recipes, access to modern education was not common, though modern chemistry and other sciences with a domestic orientation did start to appear in progressive curricula as early as the late Qing (Bi 2010, 69). Such curricula drew in part from the "good wives and wise mothers" discourse from Japan, where female educators often argued that for talented women to be mothers of citizens, the education of girls and women needed to include science (Bi 2010, 67–71). Textbooks translated from Japanese included titles such as the *Physics for Women Textbook* (*Nüzi wuli jiaokeshu*) and the *Chemistry for Women Textbook* (*Nüzi huaxue jiaokeshu*) (Bi 2010, 68). By the 1920s, some women started to take advantage of newly institutionalized chemistry education at the higher levels. In the article "A Chemist in China" (1972), missionary W. G. Sewell discusses how chemistry was introduced to the West China Union in Chengdu, one of thirteen missionary universities in China at the time, and the arrival of female students in 1924: "There were eight of newly admitted women. The experiment was so novel that they had to be chaperoned. One such pioneering woman taking chemistry, graduated in medicine and after working in Toronto, returned as a professor of obstetrics and gynecology" (531).

Given the sporadic institutionalization of chemistry education by 1915, when these recipes appeared, the recipes could have easily served as a source for chemical knowledge for amateur chemists and would-be manufacturers. A closer examination of the recipes sheds light on how potential learners could have gleaned knowledge from them. Even if some of the information conveyed in them might have been familiar to readers, the mode of presentation was often new. In Mme. Shen Ruiqing's article "Method for Manufacturing Cosmetics" (Shen Ruiqing 1915), for example, the ingredients listed in the section on manufacturing lotion to expel freckles were glossed in English (often misspelled) and presented as formal chemical compounds. They included "potass cyanic" (potassium cyanide), "acid salicylate" (salicylic acid), "glycerine" (glycerin), and "tinct cantharidis" (a tincture or solution of the chemical compound $C_{10}H_{12}O_4$ in an alcohol solvent). These ingredients were to be mixed together with a glass stick in a "fo-lan-si-ke" (佛蘭斯竒), the transliteration of the term *flask*.[50] Then two ounces, or two "English taels," of lavender spirit—which is first transliterated as "le-wen-da" alcohol, or 勒文達 alcohol, followed by the misspelled English gloss "Sprite Lavendur"—had to be added (Shen Ruiqing 1915, 21).[51] As noted earlier, the unstable spelling and the transliteration of new terms suggest how much of the information was being freshly (and irregularly) translated.

The application of these recipes would have required considerable investment in resources and time. The directions required practitioners to undertake what were not uncomplicated steps. The instructions to manufacture a basic ingredient for hair oil, for example, were quite lengthy and required an impressive array of lab equipment: "Alcohol Burner—1; Alcohol—2 lbs.; Glass tube of 2 centimeter diameter—½ stem; Long-necked glass funnel—1; Double-opening bottle—1; Washing 'gas' bottle—1; Wide-mouth bottle that holds 1 lb.—1; Wide-mouth bottle that holds 5 lbs.—1; Marble—5 lbs.; Hydrochloric acid—1 lb." (Chen Diexian 1915, vol. 2 [February], 4).

Given the nascent state of the glassware industry, chemical apparatuses were imports and available for purchase at a cost at scientific-appliance stores such as the China Educational Supply Association.[52] According to a store inventory in 1917, a shopper could purchase an alcohol burner, one of the items needed to manufacture the hair oil, for 5 yuan and 40 jiao ("Shanghai Kexue yiqiguan zizhipin mulu" 1917, 9).[53] In the recipe, Chen specifically mentioned this enterprise as a place for his readers to procure lab tools. For readers who did not live in Shanghai, the store had branches in Hankou, Xinxiang in Henan, and Xi'an. One could also order materials by mail. However, those with the wherewithal to know and access the store and afford its merchandise were not large in number. Even if the store was no longer a hub for revolutionary politics by 1915, it remained quite exclusive.

Once producers procured the ingredients and equipment, they had to follow the detailed instructions: "How to Bend Glass Tubes," "The Installation Method," "How to Apply," and, finally, most coveted, "Method for Absorption." Each method demanded substantial hands-on work. Practitioners would have to drill holes into stoppers that were to plug the glass bottles (drills to drill the holes were available at the China Educational Supply Association). The holes had to be large enough for a glass tube and funnel to be inserted. The glass tube then had to be bent. To help readers, Chen provided detailed instructions on how exactly to use an alcohol burner to heat the glass and mold it to the appropriate shape. The installation method for the lab devices was particularly lengthy and complicated. A long textual insert guided the readers through the elaborate process:

> Start by taking the stopper of the double-opening bottle and drill a hole into it; insert a funnel and place the end or "foot" of the funnel down to approximately one inch from the bottom of the glass. Insert the short end of the three-bend glass tube (A) flat against the bottom hole of the rubber stopper. Then, take (2) the washing bottle and its stopper and drill two holes. Take the long end of the glass tube with the three bends that is attached to the double-opening bottle and insert it into the left hole; the [insertion] depth should be like the funnel. In the right hole, insert the short end of the three-bend glass tube (B) just as you did with the short end of A. Then take the wide-opening bottle that holds 5 lbs., arrange it as in (3) above, and add a soft wooden stopper. Drill two holes. Insert the long end of tube B in the left hole; insert the short end of tube C in the right. The depth should be the same as above. Then, with the 1 lb. wide-opening bottle, arrange it as (4) is above, and, as with the previous method, take the long end of tube C and insert it into the left hole. With the end of the D tube, insert it into the right

hole. The horizontal part of the tube should face right. Everything is now ready for assembly.

(Chen Diexian 1915, vol. 2 [February], 4–5)

An accompanying visual was provided to show where to insert the bent glass and how to assemble tubes, the stoppers, the funnel, and the bottles (see figure 2.1).

Clearly, these recipes required considerable commitment. A practitioner had to procure the necessary lab equipment and have the leisure time to set up a laboratory. In the case of the hair-oil entry, household producers had to be physically adept enough to fire glass and shape it appropriately. Another entry was equally if not more challenging. "Manufacturing Method for Raven-Black Hair Tonic" instructed readers how to secure the silver necessary for the silver nitrate, a key ingredient, from silver coins and ingots. The piece acknowledged the challenge of such a procedure but then provided step-by-step instructions. An adventurous

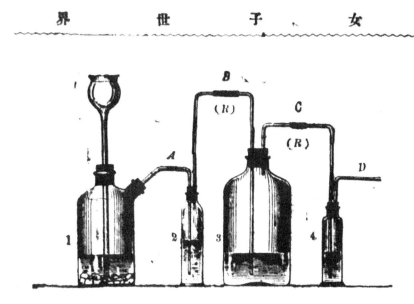

FIGURE 2.1 Visual included in the section "How to Bend Glass Tubes" in an entry in "The Warehouse" column in *Women's World* (*Nüzi shijie*) on how to manufacture *spiritus rosae*, an ingredient for hair oil, at home. Source: Chen Diexian 1915, vol. 2 (February): 5.

type seeking to put the recipe into practice had to acquire equipment such as glass beakers (whose gloss was misspelled "glass deaker"), hydrochloric acid, a glass rod, a funnel, filter paper, and a wash bottle (Kuang 1915, vol. 4 [April], 8–9).

The promises of flexibility, convenience, and frugality in such articles have led scholars to portray them as domestic hints or recipes that functioned to encourage efficiency in the domestic labor of "bourgeois" housewives (e.g., Orliski 2003, 53). Yet, given that these recipes required a considerable amount of investment, women producers at home who were seeking labor-saving tips were probably unlikely reader-practitioners. Those able to apply these recipes would have needed the leisure time, resources, and motivation other than the saving of labor and cost. It was entirely possible that others beyond the targeted audience read the piece—would-be manufacturers or emerging industrialists, for example. In fact, Hong Kong industrialist H. C. Ting (1903–1976) has written about how Chen Diexian's writings inspired him when he was a young and emerging manufacturer of batteries. In his recollections, he notes admiringly that Chen was both a noted columnist and among China's early "pioneers who ran . . . early factories . . . with single-minded determination despite the lack of public awareness of the importance of industrial production" (Ting 1974, 18).[54] His mention of the lack of public awareness points to the promotional role Chen's writings served, and although Ting doesn't state explicitly that he read this column and put its recipes to use in his home, the comment does suggest a familiarity with Chen's publications.

Another example of someone who might represent a constituency that read and applied Chen's recipes is Fang Yexian (1893–1940), the cofounder of what became a highly successful light-chemical-industry company. Born in Shanghai in 1893 into a business family (the family had banking houses, pawn shops, jewelry shops, and sundry-goods stores), Fang was sent to the Anglo-Chinese College (Zhong-Xi shuyuan), a missionary educational facility founded in 1882 in Shanghai, where he developed a particular interest in chemistry. According to biographical accounts, his interests were further developed in turn-of-the-century missionary-related networks of public science and reading rooms. Along with specialized books, he consumed journalistic writings featuring chemistry—much like those discussed here—in order to create a house-hold laboratory, engage in experiments, and make daily-use items such as cosmetics. Building on such activities, Fang Yexian founded China Chemical Industries Company (Zhongguo huaxue gongyeshe) with his mother's support in 1912 (his father was against the enterprise).[55] It started with a few individuals and disciplines but in twenty years became the leading Chinese manufacturer of toothpowder, one of its most popular items being the Sanxing brand of toothpowder.

In addition to emerging manufacturers, dabblers of science may have also consumed Chen's column or writings similar to it. Take, for example, Daoist practitioner Chen Yingning (1880–1969). Chen Yingning engaged in chemical experimentation with his well-educated friends and collaborators in pursuit of the Daoist goal of longevity (X. Liu 2009, 70–72). His domestic experiments were a team effort. His wife, a modern gynecologist, and four other fellow practitioners of alchemic self-cultivation, financed the endeavor. Chen set aside two rooms in his urban home, located near the entertainment center of the Yu Garden in Shanghai, for alchemical experiments, most of which involved smelting metals in attempts to test the veracity of secret formulas in ancient alchemical recipes. His laboratory was stocked with key alchemical minerals such as cinnabar, mercury, silver, and lead and elaborately equipped with heating furnaces and refining crucibles. He would invite friends over, perform experiments in front of them, and discuss for hours into the night various formulas and their efficacy. According to Xun Liu's study of modern Daoism in Republican Shanghai, practicing Daoists—many of them doctors, scientists, and scholars educated either abroad or in modern universities in China—were exposed to popular-science journals such as the ones under consideration here, and their alchemical experiments, although following ancient recipes, were nonetheless informed by modern chemistry (2009, 71).

Daoists pursuing immortality may be among the more colorful examples of those who turned to Chen's column or to writings similar to it, but other, more familiar types of "amateur chemists" did so as well. Among the latter were hobby photographers at the turn of the century into the Republican period. Du Jiutian (1876–?), an early Republican proponent of photography and a cousin of Du Yaquan (1873–1933), the editor in chief of the *Eastern Miscellany* (*Dongfang zazhi*), experimented with chemicals to develop photos. Like many others in his generation, Du had taught himself mathematics and chemistry with missionary publications, Japanese translations, and publications like Chen's. He then relied on this knowledge to develop photos and conduct scientific experiments, often suffering chemical burns in his inadequately equipped makeshift darkroom (Yi Gu 2013, 129). His lab work was another example of the ad hoc experimentation that dotted the Republican-era cultural landscape.

The Fang Yexians, H. C. Tings, and Chen Yingnings of the world provide profiles of male reader-practitioners, but it is entirely possible that industrious women with the right resources also read these how-to writings and put the knowledge they acquired into practice. Specific female readers are hard to identify, but a look at Wu Yizhu (1882–1945), Chen Yingning's wife, can give us a potential profile. Wu was one of several new-style women who, along with their male counterparts, took advantage of the array of new ideas and opportunities increasingly available in treaty ports. She was a well-educated female who traveled in the circles of these new urban elites. In addition to having been trained at the Sino-Occidental Medical College (Zhong-Xi yixueyuan) and becoming a successful modern gynecologist, she was also an active participant in building modern Daoist communities and supporting, if not actively engaging in, the chemical experimentation integral to these communities' pursuits of self-cultivation.[56] Chen Yingning and Wu Yizhu were not alone. Other Daoist couples joined them, including Huang Chanhua (1885–1972) and his wife, in carrying out longevity-oriented alchemical experiments (Liu 2009, 199).

In addition to the evidence given in biographies of individuals' manufacturing products in their "home labs," the recipes provide clues of how they would have appealed to practitioners. The article "Method for Making Rouge," published in the *Ladies' Journal* in March 1915, offered concrete suggestions for how to improve China's manufacturing techniques and called for patriotic manufacturing, which could very well have appealed to aspiring industrialists during the NPM. Author Hui Xia (a distinctly feminine moniker) asserted that China had long had the technological knowledge to manufacture cosmetics and toiletries, but she decried indigenous technologies for failing to strengthen the nation.

Our country's rouge has been long famous. Yet as a beauty product of the [traditional] inner chambers, it was not related to the plans of the nation and the lives of citizens. But if we acquire the [proper] method to manufacture [rouge], we can grasp the technique to become rich. Recent imports include the so-called foreign rouge, whose color is fresh and quality beautiful. If [foreign powers] did not have quality manufacturing techniques, how could they have taken by force our economic rights? I . . . offer [the method for manufacturing] to my comrades in the women's world for all to examine and study! With this technique, we can obtain true mastery! (Hui 1915, 15)

Calling upon the "women's world" to jump to action, the article directly tied the nation's potential richness to the manufacturing techniques of the inner chambers and the proper knowledge of how to produce rouge.

The piece then proceeded to differentiate foreign rouge production and domestic technologies. The entry stipulated that China had long had technology similar to modern chemistry-based technologies of production but needed to update them and render them more scientific through an adaptation of chemical procedures. It outlined two methods of manufacturing rouge, the "normal kind" of rouge and the foreign rouge. For the "normal kind" of rouge,

gather red flowers into a bucket, and carefully add water; . . . use your foot and stomp on their petals until they have become a soft and yielding yellow-colored liquid. Move them into a linen bag, and apply the high-pressure extract method to squeeze out the yellow liquid. Spread [the flowers] out on a mat; add some water, and in approximately a day add some more water, and then squeeze to extract the liquid. Go through this process a few times. At this point, all the yellow liquid in the flower petals will be extracted, and the red flowers will have become a paste. Then use round- or square-shaped molds to pattern them and dry them. . . .

When making the rouge, soak the red cakes in water for three days. Once they soften, pound them to pieces in a bag. Knead the pieces in water. Extract the yellow pigment by taking the bag and adding lye; the red pigment will gradually dissolve, and the liquid

will appear red in color. Sprinkle in a little plum vinegar. . . . The red pigment will then form into sediment. Add in more lye to dissolve the red pigment. Once it dissolves, add in plum vinegar and form the mixture into a sediment yet again. . . . Place the sediment into a cloth bag, add pressure to extract the liquid, refine [the sediment], and you have rouge.
(Hui 1915, 16)

It is worthwhile to compare this passage with the one on making rouge in the section on dyes in *Works of Heaven* (1637):

Pick the safflower blossoms while they are still moistened with dew and thoroughly pound them. Place the pounded mass into a cloth sack and add water [for a certain time]. Squeeze it to remove the yellow juice. Pound the solid residue and further purify it [by decomposing its yellow coloring] with soured millet or rice juice. First place [the mass] back into a sack, and soak it in water, and, finally, squeeze to remove any decomposed yellow matter. Cover this solid residue for a night with [branches of] [the *qinghao* plant][57] and then shape [it] into cakes, dry in the shade, and store.[58]

The processes described are what we now understand in modern chemical terms as acid-induced sedimentation, where acidic liquids (in this case soured millet or rice juice) are used to extract yellow matter from the solid red-residue core that will serve as the safflower cakes. Dregs of these safflower cakes constituted the material for making rouge.

By placing the *Works of Heaven* entry alongside the modern passage, we find considerable overlap. Both explain the process by which acid causes the petal's pigment to precipitate into sedimentation, necessary in making rouge. Both provide the step-by-step instructions on exactly what ingredients have to be gathered; on how to mix, squeeze, and extract the material needed; and on the various stages of the production process. Whereas the early-modern text identifies soured millet or rice juice as the means to alter material states, the *Ladies' Journal* passage points to lye and vinegar. Both texts demand physical engagement. The *Ladies' Journal* article informed its reader to use her foot to stomp on the petals and called for squeezing, extracting, and pounding. Water had to be splashed and molds used to pattern and shape the rouge cakes. Readers were to roll up their sleeves and get their hands (and in this case feet) dirty.

The *Ladies' Journal* article proceeded to identify the "normal method" as less desirable than the method used to manufacture "foreign rouge," or *yanghong*:

> [*Yanghong*] . . . is called European rouge. Take red flowers and throw them into a diluted solution of sodium carbonate. Let the red pigment dissolve and throw in a cotton cloth to absorb [any liquid]. Add in diluted acidic liquid. The red pigment will turn into sediment. Then take the cloth and soak it in diluted sodium carbonate. The red pigment will again dissolve. Add more diluted acidic liquid, and the red pigment will once again turn into sediment. Do this a few times. (Hui 1915, 16)

This method forwent the pounding and physical engagement called for in the "normal method" and the *Works of Heaven* recipe, promoting instead stronger chemical solutions to achieve the same effect. It was the use of these chemicals that constituted "quality manufacturing techniques." Yet even as the article urged the need for methods of manufacturing products such as "foreign rouge," it did not cede absolute superiority to Western manufacturing methods. It noted that although the manufacturing methods for the "normal" indigenous method and the "foreign rouge" differed, the principle underlying their manufacturing was still the same. By making this argument, the author could more easily legitimate and pitch the need for manufacturers and others to adopt foreign methods of manufacturing to render "Western goods" such as soap and rouge into something that Chinese producers could legitimately domesticate and produce.

For those who sought information on how to appropriate foreign technologies and manufacture locally, actual tips on large-scale production were included in some articles. In "Method for the Refined Production of Cosmetic Soap," a contribution to "The Warehouse" column in *Women's World*, author Kuang Yu wrote,

> Today our countrymen establish factories to manufacture soap and attend to its production. One reason is that the ingredients are

inferior. Another reason is that the manufacturing method is not ideal. We cannot be surprised that the soap used in our inner chambers cannot compete with imported products. Trace the cause of this . . . not to a thorough enjoyment of using foreign products [per se], but to the fact that in our country there are no good products. (Kuang 1915, vol. 3 [March], 3)

Included in a column dedicated primarily to pushing for domestic production, this frank comment underscored the substandard quality of ingredients used in manufacturing Chinese products. The article asserted that for China to compete internationally, it had to start with better-quality ingredients. "The basic ingredients for soap include high-quality cow fat, or olive oil, and high-quality caustic soda. For its scent, use musk fragrance, cinnamon bark oil, Mountain Pepper Oil, Orange Peel oil, fennel seed oil, clove oil, and the essence of roses." The piece then guided the reader step by step in the production process:

> To make this, you first need to take 1,000 *liang* of high-quality cow fat (you can also use the highest-quality olive oil), throw it into a cauldron, and melt it until the fat is completely dissolved. Then, take 150 *liang* of high-quality caustic soda and dissolve it into clear water until it becomes a thin liquid. . . . After [being cooked] to the point of boiling for approximately 4 hours, the caustic soda and the cow fat will have thoroughly combined. That which floats on top is the pure white, fine, and delicate soap paste. The sediment on the bottom can then become brown soap paste. When [the concoction] stops boiling, take out the top layer and add different types of coloring agents . . . and then choose the best kind of fragrance . . . and add it in. Thoroughly mix. After you let [the mix] sit for a few days, pour it into a mold, and form it into a beautiful shape; an exquisitely fragrant colored soap is the result.

The mention of "1,000 *liang* of high-quality cow fat," which is around 83.33 pounds of cow fat, is noticeable and would produce a considerable amount of soap.[59] Small-scale or domestic users could have adjusted the recipe and the proportions to fit their particular needs, but the large sum of fat suggests that those interested in producing a more prodigious amount for large-scale production could just as readily rely on these instructions.

Finally, because cosmetics were fairly easy to manufacture and required relatively little overhead, the small-scale cosmetic production of toiletry items with chemical methods spread rapidly, even among people with limited means. As Janet Chen notes, a vocational-education movement had already been launched during the New Policies reforms, which lasted into the Republican era (2012, 19–20). A centerpiece of this movement was the establishment of handicraft and industrial-training centers (*gongyiju*). With the goal to create a more productive workforce, these institutions and their organizers could very well have tapped into the articles written for *Women's World* and the *Ladies' Journal*. These institutions proliferated during the Republican era, when some of the more efficient and better-run workhouses for the poor trained their residents in the production of toiletry items. The Beijing-based Capital Vagrant Workhouse (Jingshi youmin xiyisuo) was one of the major workhouses for the indigent and ran workshops to manufacture cosmetics using chemical methods. Whereas the music department trained China's poor to perform as music entertainers, the workhouse's chemical workshop trained the poor in "pure and exquisite chemical manufacturing processes" to produce soap, ink, toothpowder, and vanishing cream.[60] The individuals who ran these more modest workshops could conceivably have turned to the journal articles and recipes for ideas.

In spite of the rhetorical claims of being written to improve daily convenience, efficiency, and frugality, these pieces were hardly mere "practical tips." They were recipes in action. They assumed multiple purposes. To start, the texts were prescriptive. But they were also being put to use for a variety of reasons, often not exactly in the ways intended. Leisurely readers and connoisseurs of technological knowledge with no intention of applying these recipes in practice appreciated these texts tastefully and consumed the recipes' production techniques as an expression of their own social distinction and cosmopolitanism. Featuring the know-how with which readers could engage in forms of production that were singular, done at home, and not machine based or mass in nature, these pieces allowed readers the means to demarcate themselves from new and aspiring consumers (and, in principle, from producers) of mass-produced items, whether they put these recipes into practice or not.

These recipes could have been put into practice. Those who had long produced cosmetics in domestic quarters may not have had much need to turn to these articles, and the articles were hardly practical hints to simplify production processes. However, those curious about the chemistry or the modern glassware and lab equipment featured or those seeking to update their domestic practices of production could have read the printed pieces and in their homes applied the production techniques outlined. Indeed, the articles' appeal lay in their packaging of production know-how in terms of modern chemistry and physics, in their promotion of modern chemical glassware and tools as something necessary for the manufacturing process, and in their featuring of new exotic ingredients that were not part of the existing repertoire. For would-be manufacturers, leisurely connoisseurs of technology, and young amateur tinkerers and experimenters, both male and female, it was precisely the professed modernity of these recipes that proved appealing. Dabblers in science could have thus used the recipes to experiment and get their hands dirty. So, too, might have budding industrialists, who scoured them for tips to pursue commercial manufacturing efforts.

CONCLUSION: THE *GUIXIU*, PLAY, AND VOICE IN THE 1910S

These recipes published in 1915 were following in the tradition of neo-Confucian household-management texts written by Ming–Qing male gentry (*shidaifu*) that had long prescribed proper comportment in the household, including in the realm of production. Female gentry had long been identified as domestic managers who ran corporate households, instructing staff and monitoring domestic production. In such a context, a gendered distribution of elite skills in the late empire emerged in terms of the concept of *qiao* (craft, cunning, skill). Manual *qiao* was an attainment to which educated men or even farmers never really aspired. It instead was pursued primarily by male artisans. For elite women, *qiao* was not a problem. Associated with "womanly work," especially in textile production, *qiao* functioned to denote a relation to the material world through which women crafted a path to virtue. The imperial-era slogan "men till and women weave (*nangeng nüzhi*)" speaks to this gendering of skill: virtuous skills among men resided in the agricultural arena, whereas skills among women involved manufacturing (Bray 1997). Confucian ideologues and the *shidaifu* thus authored household-management texts to teach women proper production practice, even as they themselves often dabbled in production work, if (at least in principle) only on the side.

Given this history, it is not surprising that the preface to the first issue of the *Ladies' Journal* explicitly cited the canonical Han dynasty prescriptive text *Lessons for Women* (*Nü jie*) by Ban Zhao (c. 45–c. 116). Like Ban Zhao's classic, written in the first century CE to instruct her daughter on navigating entry into her husband's household, the twentieth-century journal similarly sought to prescribe proper female behavior in the inner chambers and to define the virtuous female producer for the greater good of the republic. Yet even as these articles' gendered orientation drew from a long tradition, it assumed new meaning. With China's lettered class in crisis during the fragile years of the early Republic, the trope of the "woman" had become politicized as a site for the articulation of modernity. Female identities such as the new female student, the modern bourgeois housewife, and the *guixiu* (genteel woman) became powerful rhetorical tropes by which editors and experts could convey new information and prescribe new ways of being.

However, the *guixiu*'s ability to serve as an emblem of modernity has generally been overlooked in the field because scholars have tended to focus on the New Woman (Xin nüxing) trope, an icon of the later iconoclastic period of the New Culture and May Fourth Movements. In fact, to promote their ideal of the politically engaged male modern intellectual (*zhishi fenzi*) and his female icon, the New Woman, reformist intellectuals of these movements vilified genteel women, the *guixiu*, as footbound, oppressed in the inner quarters, and—like their male counterparts, the *jiu wenren*, or "traditional literati"—engaged in impossibly retrograde, nonproductive, and non–politically relevant practices. These high-minded intellectuals moreover denigrated as trivial and frivolous the women's periodicals featuring such "Republican ladies" (Judge 2015, 46–48). By extension, this New Culture/May Fourth critique has led to our contemporary underestimation of the willingness of the so-called traditional literati class to experiment with new ideas and ways of being as well our tendency to overlook the symbolic potential of the *guixiu* for exploring the modern.

In these publications, the *guixiu* was hardly an outdated or retro-grade symbol. Rather, she was engaged in experimentation with new knowledge and assumed progressive social roles. She, along with new female professionals and students, fit the category of Republican ladies who graced the journal *Women's Eastern Times* (Judge 2015). Some new-style Republican ladies differentiated themselves from the *guixiu* in their pursuit of the new Republican ideal of civic publicness, which included volunteering, becoming a professional, attending schools, and writing for journals (Judge 2015, 49–51). Chen Diexian's genteel women were determined to remain in the inner chambers, even if to remake the home into a site of manufacturing. And yet their inner chambers were being publicized to an unprecedented degree. Chen and other compilers publicized the newly remade boudoir far and wide. The *guixiu* figure was quite literally the face of Chen's periodical *Women's World*, as the cover illustration shown in figure 2.2 depicts.[61] Inside the journal, Chen's portrayal of technical knowledge and material experi-mentation as suitable for the *guixiu* at home served as a compelling way to carve out ways of knowing, to domesticate technical know-how and chemical knowledge, and to imbue the agenda of production with moral and political urgency, if in a strong register of leisure and play.

With a large part of the May Fourth critique of China's traditional culture turning on the latter's alleged apolitical, dilettantish nature, what also gets overlooked is the possibility of the politics of play. The culture of play informing the world of entertainment in turn-of-the-century Jiangnan saw its participants delight in experimentation in both literary forms and technological gadgets. Chen was a central participant in such play. The title of his earlier journal the *Pastime* (*Youxi zazhi*) speaks directly to his investment in the movement.[62] The politics of play also informed "The Warehouse" column in *Women's World* and related pieces in the *Ladies' Journal*. Written in the more commercially viable new-style classical Chinese rather than in the new national vernacular, these writ-ings rendered the seemingly unproductive sites of leisure as a locale for manufacturing. They located chemical experimentation and the making of cosmetics as forms of tasteful activities suitable for the domestic quarters of elite households. The genteel lady of the house was undeni-ably modern and embodied the ideal of leisurely innovation and new forms of knowing. She proved to be a model for the new social personae

FIGURE 2.2 The cover of the January 1915 issue of *Women's World*. The cover visually evokes the inner chambers of the *guixiu* by featuring a well-groomed, respectable woman posing demurely in a graceful sitting position. On other covers, the woman of the inner chambers is framed by a doorframe or wall and accompanied in some cases by a cat or a teakettle, items of the household domain. Source: Chinese Collection of the Harvard-Yenching Library, Cambridge, Mass.

of the day, including actual female producers of cosmetics, lettered connoisseurs of technology, amateur scientists, and patriotic would-be manufacturers.

These pieces were thus part of the arsenal of strategies available for readers navigating their new cosmopolitan identities in a post-civil-service-examination arena of urban playgrounds and industrial centers.

By appreciating these pieces with a sense of refined curiosity or in a posture of playful leisure, readers—male and female—could define their sense of exclusivity based on notions of production that were tasteful and authentic in terms of their scientific, domestic, and noncommercial nature. Followers of "The Warehouse" could share each issue's entries literally, exchanging the newly discovered knowledge of modern productive technologies over tea and in genteel social circles. Others did so virtually, communing with fellow readers as part of an imagined community of readers. Either way, readers could demarcate themselves from the gawking masses, who not only increasingly consumed mass-produced commodities but also consumed spectacular depictions of science and technology in China's variegated urban press.[63] Readers consumed (and applied) these recipes to establish their standing and good bearing distinguished from a nascent if fast-growing society of mass consumers.

The ideal portrait of the woman of the inner chambers leisurely embodying new forms of knowledge and experimentation projected a utopian order that was lacking in the outer world of politics, which was riddled with paralyzing machinations of all stripes. Distinct from the state agenda of the Self-Strengthening past and from the Republican Beiyang politics of the present, this woman's production knowledge was attractive precisely because it was positioned within the domestic everyday realm as a counterpoint to "public" political knowledge. The domestic realm as a site of production moreover served as a metaphor for the larger marketplace in treaty ports, a place that was outside of the reach of the state, where scientific, commercial, and manufacturing knowledge increasingly displaced moral knowledge and statecraft as the preferred epistemological foundations for a competitive nation. The concept of leisure, or *xiuxian*, once seen as the means of literati cultivation, could now serve as a platform for cultivating an orientation toward manufacturing and productivity. The recipes "cleansed" the manual work of production and enjoined a readership of disenfranchised elites to explore industry, capitalism, and manufacturing for profit, pursuits once deemed unseemly for the lettered class.

Just a few years later, however, a strong reaction rose against presenting chemical experimentation and manufacturing as a dilettantish endeavor appropriate for genteel women. With the May Fourth Movement,

Sai Xiansheng, "Mr. Science," would emerge as part of the slogan "Mr. Science and Mr. Democracy," core aspects of the foundation of a powerful nation. The term *xiansheng*, which is conventionally translated into English as "Mr.," is actually more gender neutral in Chinese and a polite way to address either men or women. Yet the masculine pronoun in the English translation captures what was primarily an elite male agenda of cosmopolitan intellectuals associated with the New Culture Movement and was in distinct contrast to the presentation of manufacturing and chemistry in Chen's journal.[64] Chen's strategy for presenting manufacturing as something suitable for genteel women of the inner chambers notably disappeared in his post–May Fourth publications. His later writings were to advocate for a far more gender-neutral presentation of the industrial arts to be located not in the inner chambers but in the updated arena of the modern household (*jiating*).

CHAPTER THREE

An Enterprise of Common Knowledge

Fire Extinguishers, 1916–1935

During the Lantern Festival banquet, tables were set near the beds . . . ; carpets were on the floor, and cups and plates were placed on the table. . . . Host and guests ate and drank merrily. . . . The waiter served the hot pot[1] and . . . unexpectedly, . . . dropped the pot, and the wine caught fire. . . . The brandy in the broken cups made it worse. As the [burning] brandy flowed to the ground, the carpet, bed, and bed nets burned. Great danger ensued. . . . On the chest, I saw a long tube of toothpowder, and it dawned on me that magnesium carbonate extinguishes fire. I scattered the powder everywhere, and wherever the powder came into contact with the fire, the flames were extinguished. One large site of chaos luckily did not become an even greater disaster. . . . Afterwards, we reviewed the debris and discussed the matter. The amount of toothpowder we used to buy was not much, but after this incident we bought large amounts and put tubes in each room. . . . Among Butterfly Toothpowder's usages, this one was discovered accidently. . . . Ultimately, however, . . . one should really buy powder that specifically extinguishes fire or purchase a chemical-based foam fire extinguisher (*yao shuilong*).

—*SHENBAO*, AUGUST 8, 1930

Chen Diexian submitted the description of a banquet fire to "New Knowledge for the Household" ("Jiating xinshi"), a column that was part of the *Shenbao* literary supplement *Free Talk* (*Ziyoutan*). Appearing on August 8, 1930, this entry described the eruption of a small blaze in a celebratory banquet setting and provided useful information on how to put out a fire. It shared the clever tip to use toothpowder and informed readers about toothpowder's unique ability to quench a blaze due to its main ingredient, magnesium carbonate, of which Chen's Household Industries had become the largest domestic manufacturer. The entry featured a fire extinguisher, a device Chen was also manufacturing. It even managed to work in a plug for Butterfly Toothpowder. The account suggests an accidental "discovery" when Chen realized the potential of his toothpowder to put out fires. However, the actual "discovery" was hardly serendipitous. Chen had invested in and tinkered with the foam fire extinguisher for years before he wrote this entry and had no doubt long been aware that magnesium-carbonate-based toothpowder could function to stamp out a blaze. The account was embellished. It was informational and clearly promotional.

In this chapter, we follow Chen's life-long pursuit of manufacturing the foam fire extinguisher to explore why in the late 1910s and 1920s, when new ways of carving out legitimacy, expertise, and authority were starting to emerge, Chen presented the manufacturing knowledge behind the extinguisher as *changshi*, "common knowledge." His experimentation with the fire extinguisher had started earlier in Hangzhou. His interest in developing the gadget persisted with his move to Shanghai. By 1925, Household Industries started to manufacture the Butterfly Fire Extinguisher (Wudipai yao shuilong), and by 1928 the company sought—if unsuccessfully—to secure a patent for the device.[2] From a contemporary perspective, Chen's desire to share manufacturing knowledge on the extinguisher as "common knowledge" and his goal to seek exclusive ownership over the knowledge via a patent appear contradictory. For Chen, however, they were complimentary. Both were part of a set of strategies he pursued to lay claim over the know-how in the manufacturing of fire extinguishers (and much more) in a period when credentials to establish expertise and the means to "own" ideas and things were still up in the air.

One of the most effective ways by which Chen promoted his authority and expertise regarding the manufacturing of the fire extinguisher was through textual production. He systematically attempted to pitch and share information on both the production and use of the fire extinguisher in not just the "New Knowledge for the Household" column but also through at least two other publications in the 1920s: the *Shenbao* column "Common Knowledge for the Household" ("Jiating changshi," 1916–1927) and the publication *Model Correspondence on Industry and Commerce* (*Gongshangye chidu ou'cun*, 1928). Both publications featured multiple entries on the fire extinguisher but also covered much more. It was through these texts that Chen ended up presenting himself as both a generalist committed to spreading "common knowledge"— including how to make and use the fire extinguisher to help build a modern lifestyle—*and* an emerging specialist, or someone who was becoming a new-style industrialist (*shiyejia*). In the latter capacity, he was interested in sharing with other budding industrialists his experiences and expertise in manufacturing and industry. Finally, in his capacity as a professional editor and compiler, he was also invested in outmaneuvering competing publications that were seeking to lay claim over presenting so-called common knowledge as the basis of their authority.

CHEN'S FOAM FIRE EXTINGUISHER

The chemical-based foam fire extinguisher occupied a special place for Chen Diexian in his career. In recounting his father's life-long commitment to developing the extinguisher, Chen's son Dingshan writes,

> When I was seven or eight years old, I saw my father inventing the chemical-based foam fire extinguisher.[3] He went to Chenghuang mountain and built a grass shack. He mobilized people to watch him, [set the shack ablaze, and then proceeded to] douse the fire with the extinguisher. He failed that time, but he never stopped experimenting. By 1925, he invented the Butterfly Fire Extinguisher, though as with any invention by him, he never applied for a patent. On the contrary, he shared with others the detailed process or experience by which he invented the item in order to allow others to emulate (*fangzao*) [his findings].
> (Chen Dingshan [1955] 1967, 192)

This passage celebrates Chen's lifelong investment in manufacturing a chemical-based foam fire extinguisher. It recounts how he mobilized the people of Hangzhou in testing out his product and his persistence in research even after the initial failure. It describes how after years of work he finally met with success. In a retrospective account, Chen's daughter,

Chen Xiaocui, echoed her brother and recalled how Chen spent twenty years manufacturing the extinguisher and that it took four revisions to produce something that he felt was comparable to the French fire extinguisher available on the Chinese market (Chen Xiaocui, Fan, and Zhou 1982, 221).

Chen's fascination with the foam fire extinguisher is indicative of his being an inveterate tinkerer throughout his life. He was not alone in that pursuit. It was an age when tinkerers and innovators sought to create all sorts of gadgets and machines worldwide. In a study of the Chinese typewriter, Thomas Mullaney (2017) identifies linguists, engineers, and clerks, Chinese and foreign, who tinkered and experimented with tray beds and keyboards necessary to manufacture a Chinese typewriter. Like these typewriter experimenters, Chen was fascinated with newfangled things. He expended considerable time and energy conducting research and test manufacturing a variety of devices. These devices included the hand-held photocopier, the flat offset mechanized press, and the bottle-cap-affixing machine, among others (Chen Xiaocui, Fan, and Zhou 1982, 221–222). Chen's choice of gadgets and machines to tinker with was hardly ever random and was linked to larger industrial and manufacturing trends. His interest in the offset press, for example, coincided with the developments in the manufacturing of printing machines from the 1910s to the 1930s. With the rise of Chinese cigarette manufacturers in particular, there was a need for offset machines to print advertising images, and Chinese machinery shops rose to the occasion, especially during the 1920s (Reed 2004, 141–143).

Chen's commitment to manufacturing a chemical-based foam fire extinguisher was similarly strategic and timely. Fighting fires had become a central and pressing concern worldwide by the nineteenth century. In China, urban fires were a menace by the tenth century, and systems of firefighting involving manned watchtowers were established (Gernet 1962, 34–38). With the rise of dense cities in other parts of the world by the seventeenth century, devastation wrought by urban conflagration spurred investment in technologies to fight fire and minimize the potential destruction it could bring (Bankoff, Lübken, and Sand 2012, 6–7). In addition to the professionalization of the fireman and the policeman, investment poured into developing increasingly fire-retardant buildings and effective extinguishing technologies.[4] In Hankou, China, at the end of the eighteenth century, the hand-drawn fire engine, or *shuilong* (literally, "water dragon"), was introduced, and a "revolution took place in the technology of fire-fighting" (Rowe 1992, 164). Throughout the nineteenth century, far-reaching interest in these technologies grew. Published by Protestant missionary John Fryer (1839–1928) and affiliated with Shanghai Polytechnic, a missionary organization and reading room dedicated to promoting Western manufacturing practices and scientific knowledge to Chinese readers, the monthly missionary publication *Chinese Scientific and Industrial Magazine* (*Gezhi huibian*) translated articles into Chinese and featured ads in Chinese on the extinguisher.[5] The article "An Explanation on How to Use the Fire Extinguisher" appeared in 1876, and "An Account of the Fire Extinguisher" was published almost a year later.[6] Both featured the same visual of a fire extinguisher that is operated by hand (figure 3.1). The visual was taken from a foreign source. Its foreign provenance and its double appearance speak to the worldwide circulation and frequent sharing of such material.

By this time, the fire extinguisher was also increasingly familiar as an actual commodity. In the *Chinese Scientific and Industrial Magazine*, an advertisement for the China and Japan Trading Company peddled the foam extinguisher among an array of other imported *yanghuo*, "foreign goods."[7] An American company with branches in Shanghai, London, and several cities in Japan, the China and Japan Trading Company, specifically sold materials related to the needs of steam engines and steamships: kerosene burners, lampwicks, switch sockets, glass containers and utensils (of all sizes), cases of rosin oil, sodium borate, cotton and linen sails, steel anchors, rope, steel and copper nails, clocks (striking and chiming ones), files, saws, soap, matches, and steel and copper items for docks. The chemical-based fire extinguisher was featured most prominently in the ad, which included a prominent visual of the extinguisher (see figure 3.2) and dedicated a full passage to the device.[8] The copy assured potential consumers that the chemical would not harm humans. It suggested that the extinguisher, although not useful for large fires, could contain fires that might occur on ships. The visual included two parts: a drawing of a cylindrical extinguisher and one of a man wearing this extinguisher in a halter on his back, holding it as if in miduse.

FIGURE 3.1 Image of a fire extinguisher accompanying articles in the *Chinese Scientific and Industrial Magazine* (*Gezhi huibian*). Source: "Shiyong shuilong shuo" 1876, 7. C. V. Starr East Asian Library, Columbia University, New York.

By the early republic, Chinese manufacturers such as the Aurora Company (Zhendan jiqi tie gongchang, est. 1918) were producing fire extinguishers, water meters, and pumping machines.[9] Household Industries, too, became invested in manufacturing fire extinguishers domestically and sought to innovate and manufacture a device that could compete with devices produced by both import and domestic companies (Chen Xiaocui, Fan, and Zhou 1982, 221). Part of Chen's strategy for the company to compete on the market was to share knowledge about how to use and manufacture fire extinguishers in a variety of columns and publications. Chen's son Dingshan claims that rather than apply for a patent to own the knowledge exclusively, his father willingly shared his findings with others so they could emulate his findings and manufacture the gadgets (Chen Dingshan [1955] 1967, 192). This claim was blatantly false. Chen had sought a patent in 1928 for the Butterfly Fire Extinguisher,

FIGURE 3.2 Image of portable fire extinguisher in a China and Japan Trading Company advertisement that appears in the *Chinese Scientific and Industrial Magazine (Gezhi huibian)*, 1876–1877. Source: C. V. Starr East Asian Library, Columbia University, New York.

although unsuccessfully. However, the general point—that Chen was committed to sharing the discovery more broadly for others to emulate and learn from—was true and characteristic of Chen's vernacular industrialism.

"COMMON KNOWLEDGE FOR THE HOUSEHOLD"

On November 21, 1926, the *Shenbao* column "Common Knowledge for the Household" featured an entry on the fire extinguisher titled "The Plan for a Fire Brigade's Use of the Fire Extinguisher."[10] The piece presented the foam-based fire extinguisher as something that should be found in all communities. It instructed readers point by point on how best to use the extinguisher. Advising fire brigades, the entry recommended that they spray water directly on the burning object and try to extinguish the root of the fire. "If you shoot in the air, you will not succeed." It warned not to mix the chemical solution with the powder too early so as to avoid a premature reaction. And, finally, instructing villages and cities that were seeking to organize fire brigades, it detailed,

> If you have two brigades . . . , the money you need to buy the equipment is no more than one hundred dollars. You need to have ten people. . . . Each team installs an extinguisher and needs to prepare a siren or gong. Whenever there is an accident, you can hit the gong to report it, and the firefighting team can then arrive immediately. . . . For every 25 homes, install an extinguisher in the front and back, left and right; and in this way, you can cover more than 125 homes. Each family spends several cents, and this can be organized [locally].
> (*Shenbao*, November 21, 1926, 17)

The fire extinguisher functions here to help articulate the social organization of a community that is quite similar to the late-imperial *baojia* system, a collective neighborhood by which the government was able to maintain order and control through all levels of society, while employing relatively few officials. The entry echoes the chapter epigraph, which is from a contribution to "New Knowledge for the Household," the column that followed "Common Knowledge" in the *Free Talk* supplement. Both promoted the fire extinguisher as "common knowledge" and pushed for tubes of toothpowder and the extinguisher to become an integral part of everyday life. This vision of modern daily life would include toothpowder and extinguishers in every room, home, and community.

Chen contributed to the column "Common Knowledge for the Household" (hereafter, "Common Knowledge") starting as early as 1917 and served as its editor from 1918 to 1927. He was editor of *Free Talk* from 1916 to 1918, at which point he stepped down and assumed the editorship of the column only. As one of his most influential columns, "Common Knowledge" allowed Chen to promote himself as a learned amateur in an era of growing specialization for China's new citizen-readers. Covering an array of topics from hygiene to medicine and from the industrial arts to local lore, the information in the column was described as "common knowledge" and was presented in easily digestible entries available for a general if fairly sophisticated reading public.

A typical set of entries in "Common Knowledge" was published on April 13, 1917, and exemplifies the wide range of knowledge included in the column. This range in turn suggests readers who were broad in their knowledge and curious about a variety of topics. The set started with an item on how to manufacture a spray bottle:

> *Penwuqi* (a sprayer) is commonly referred to as *xiangshui chui* (perfume sprayer). Nowadays, barbers use sprayers. But they are expensive and break easily. To make one, go to a scientific appliance store or a Western pharmacy and buy the thinnest glass tubing; use a small file and file the four sides until it is very narrow and can snap apart. Take a one-foot long tube, heat it with an alcohol lamp (while heating, twirl). When it is softened to the point that it can be stretched, pull the middle part to be as thin as a lamp filament and then remove it from the heat and snap it into two. The ends are open. . . . Take one of the [halves] of the conical-shaped tube. Use the left hand and prop it up vertically in the bottle (with the pointed part pointing upward). Use the right hand to grab the other bamboo pipe-shaped tube and lay it horizontally toward the sharp end of the other tube. Use force and blow with one's mouth and water can be sucked in. When the water is sucked up, it can then be sprayed out as a mist.[11] If you use a couple of wires to tie [the two] together into the shape of a carpenter's square, it is easier to use. (Tianxuwosheng)
>
> (*Shenbao*, April 13, 1917, 14)

Several shorter entries followed:

> • Red Nose (*chibi*): There are many ways to cure it, but they all are inelegant. The easiest method is as follows: everyday when you wash, rub salt on [your nose]. Use fine salt, not coarse salt. After two months, [the redness] will disappear. When you rub it, it might hurt a bit. . . .

• Sometimes clothing will mold. Take the loquat pit, grind it into powder, and use it to wash the clothes to get rid of mold.

• Bean paste: when it is hot, worms will grow in the bean paste. If you use mustard seeds or Sichuan peppers, grind them finely and place them in the paste. Worms will not appear.

• When playing musical instruments, if one's fingernails are not thick enough, the sound will not be clear and crisp. . . . If you burn dead silkworm, smoke your fingernails and they will thicken. Give it a try, musicians.

• When flower trees have bug holes, use sulfur powder to stuff the holes. As for salted meats, if they have an odor, when you cook them, use ten walnuts, and poke holes in the shell and cook with the meat, and the odor will disappear. (Yang Xinghua)[12]

• When there appears a bump on your skin, as long as it is not an open sore, use rosin (*songxiang*) powder, mix [the powder] with wine, and apply it to the bump, no matter where it is. It will disappear in twenty-four hours. One kind of sore is known as a "chestnut sore." As long as it is not an open sore, you can apply this method too. I had one under my armpit (on the left side) and used iodine to no avail. After one month, it was still red and swollen, and after a while I could not even move my left arm. Then an elder gave me this method to try, and it worked. Others also tried it and found that this worked.

(*Shenbao*, April 13, 1917, 14)

From this selection, one gets a sense of the column's tone and the range of topics it covered. Entries tended to be short. The sprayer entry is an example of a longer one. Some were practical and could be used as tips for household application. Others were playful and whimsical, conveying clever if not absolutely necessary information. Most provided tips that were quite straightforward to follow and execute. To get rid of a red nose, a simple and regular application of fine salt was all that was needed. To treat a boil, rosin powder and wine—both household items—would do. Many of these entries were similar to the ones found in late-imperial daily encyclopedias or offered tidbits of knowledge that had long circulated in oral communities.

Other entries included fresh information and required more substantial investment. The first tip on how to manufacture a sprayer was similar in kind to entries in Chen's "The Warehouse" column on cosmetic manufacturing in 1915 insofar as it focused on technical know-how and on manufacturing something. As Chen did in the earlier column, he assumed a know-it-all persona, and the entry assumed a knowing, capable audience. The reader was expected to understand Chen's reference to a carpenter square, arguably a household instrument or tool but certainly one that was far from universal in Chinese homes. He or she was also presumed to have access to scientific-appliance stores and Western pharmacies. Like some of the entries in "The Warehouse," entries in "Common Knowledge" required practitioners to use their hands and mouths to engage in a bodily manner in the manufacture of something and to have enough skill and dexterity to heat and bend glass tubes with an alcohol lamp, for which step-by-step instructions were provided. At the time, the perfume sprayer was seen as a modern object of hygiene and "everyday modernity," worthy of display and promotion. It was featured, along with a host of other hygiene products, at the Haircutters Association Booth in the Hygiene Hall at the Taipei Police Exhibition in 1925, for example, and served as a material embodiment of the hygienic modernity that the Japanese colonial regime was invested in establishing in Taiwan (Tsai 2014, 21–23). Notably, whereas the *penwuqi* was displayed intact at expos, in Chen's column the object was dissected and "reverse-engineered" insofar as it was the instructions on how to manufacture one rather than simply the opportunity to consume one that were on display.

Chen's column was informed by both the new Republican-era epistemology and an emphasis on science but retained a broad nonsystematized topical range and considerable epistemological pluralism. Scholars have described the emergence of a new Republican-era epistemology that privileged experience, empiricism, and, in the context of the periodical press, the quotidian as the basis of a modern nation-state (Judge 2015). Others have noticed how science or claims to science could be found in columns dedicated to common or general knowledge (*changshi*) during the period. In the early twentieth century, Cantonese newspapers, for example, featured new sections on the "general knowledge of society" ("shehui changshi"), which sought to introduce scientific changes in everyday life by featuring new, scientifically proven ways of consuming food that were deemed the opposite of previously wasteful, extravagant, and unhygienic ways of consumption (S. Lee 2011, 121). Entries in "Common Knowledge," especially those focused on light industry, certainly drew their authority from fields of modern science.

However, the overall characteristic of the column was epistemological pluralism. Years later, in 1933–1941, Chen Diexian compiled entries in the original column and organized them into sections: clothes and tools, food and drink, body, animal, and plants. Topics covered by the clothes and tools entries included precious curios, metals, clothing, dyes, glass, lights and optics/lenses, wooden tools, magnetic tools, stationary and literary goods, and miscellaneous. Entries on the body included useful knowledge on the head, eyes, ears and nose, mouth and teeth, throat and larynx, hands and feet, intestines and digestive tract, skin, gynecology and pediatrics, and emergency prescriptions. During its actual run, however, "Common Knowledge" was not organized in any formal manner, and topics would appear without apparent or obvious order. Chemical knowledge sat comfortably next to entries that drew from Chinese materia medica traditions. Information on household hygiene followed tips on manufacturing. Entries on how to care for a sore on one's body that privileged an elder's prescription to use rosin powder over iodine were listed alongside entries that explicitly invoked the laws of physics. Some entries were collected from indigenous sources, including daily encyclopedias or native compendia on herbs. Some were miscellaneous forms of knowledge, tidbits of local wisdom circulated to contributors by word of mouth or sent in via letters to the editor. Unlike what you might find in the era's new-style textbooks, entries containing chemical or industrial knowledge translated from abroad were not set in opposition to or as better than any form of "local" or "indigenous" knowledge. Rather, "Western" and "local" were irrelevant, and knowledge hierarchies collapsed. Translated industrial know-how ran alongside folk knowledge, which nuzzled up against the materia medica of classical Chinese pharmacology. Local conditions, practice, epistemological pluralism, and seeming randomness dictated the reformulation and revaluation of knowledge. For the reader, this arrangement offered a veritable feast of parcels of knowledge from which to choose.

The variegated sensibility of "Common Knowledge" was, in fact, similar to the larger *Free Talk* supplement of which it was a part. Meng Yue

(1994) has discussed how *Free Talk* was characterized by a highly literary and lettered sensibility that invoked playfulness and connoisseurship even while working at a more serious and political level. Such a tone suggests a fairly exclusive audience that encompassed lettered urbanites, including merchants, intellectuals, and new industrialists. The term *free* in the title, notes Meng, did not connote freedom in a liberal, democratic sense but pointed more to the playfulness and leisure by which readers could move among different registers (1994, 14). The supplement was known not only for its literary content, including poetry, but also for the couplets, songs, local opera commentary, regulations and edicts, legal contracts and plaints, diplomatic letters and telegraphic dispatches, travel notes, advertisements, and puzzles it published. The variegated content meant that the supplement could be read seriously *and* consumed playfully. It could engage people politically even while serving as entertainment. In this way, it followed in the tradition of play associated with late-Qing *Playful Magazine* (*Youxi Bao*, 1897–1910), to which Chen had once contributed (Meng 1994, 11), and with *Women's World*, discussed in chapter 2.

It is notable that the title of the *Shenbao* column—"Jiating changshi"—features the compound *changshi*, "common knowledge," and pairs it explicitly with the term for the modern household, *jiating*. In Chen's "The Warehouse" column, the featured domestic domain was distinctly genteel. In the "Common Knowledge" column, which started only a year after the end of "The Warehouse" run, Chen shifted away from a strategy of presenting the knowledge featured as something suitable for the ladies of the inner chambers and emphasized instead the new, gender-neutral, if not masculine domestic space of the *jiating*. This shift was most likely made in part because the space of the inner chambers had increasingly been targeted as a retrograde feminine space. Male reformists associated with the New Culture Movement (1915–1919) attacked the ideal of the grand household as a sign of traditional Confucianism's hold on China and promoted instead the nuclear household (*xiao jiating*), "new" styles of marriage, free love, and women's liberation.[13] The *jiating* was to be a site of reform crucial to the modernization of the nation. Even profit-seeking entrepreneurs such as milk entrepreneur You Huaigao (1889–?) were committed to securing profit by selling to the nuclear family/

household and to reforming the domestic arena by disseminating modern commodities to China's modern homes (Glosser 2003, 134–166). Chen similarly treated *jiating* as both a site of reform and a site to be marketed to. No longer gendered specifically as a feminine space of cosmetic manufacturing and virtuous production, it represented a space whose parameters were characterized by learned if not professional pursuits and by the consumption of an eclectic array of knowledge and practices. This *Shenbao* column was to help build this new domain by providing to China's new (implicitly male) citizen reader and denizens of the modern household with tips on healing oneself and others, keeping foodstuff fresh, maintaining proper hygiene, and manufacturing things.

On the surface, one might see the "common knowledge" of Chen's column as a form of amateurism. In English, the etymology of the term *amateur* can be traced to French, where it refers to "someone who has the taste for something" or is a "lover of something," which is reflected in the word's root, the past participle of *amare*, "to love." The term gained added significance with the postindustrial rise of modern leisure when it came to be contrasted to productive or professional endeavors. In early-twentieth-century Japan, for example, with the rise of mass consumerism and a middle class, salaried employees found themselves with the time and money to become amateur photographers and engage in photography as a pastime or hobby (Ross 2015). Yet such a description does not fully capture the complexity of the politics of this term for early-twentieth-century China. Nor does it capture the indigenous tradition of *bowu*, "broad learning." By the Qing dynasty, the tradition of broad learning became the basis of claims over distinct forms of knowledge. In the world of female reproductive health, broad learning and a grasp of correlative cosmology marked the moral cultivation of the learned position of amateurs who sought to distinguish themselves from the rising influence of physicians, whom they portrayed to be venally occupation oriented and crassly professional (Y. Wu 2010).

It was only in a post-civil-service examination era that new credentials to legitimate occupation and professional identity were emerging, and the idea of specialization was becoming increasingly legitimate. In this context of emerging specialization, the column "Common

Knowledge," although often playful in tone, was not simply about pure connoisseurship or amateurism. It functioned to hone expert knowledge even while maintaining a generalist, whimsical tone. It featured knowledge related to industry, manufacturing, and modern disciplines of science, alongside other bits of useful information that could address a host of concerns particular both to lettered and leisurely Chinese readers *and* to new-style specialists, household practitioners, and China's modern citizens. It was entirely possible that those interested in the application of "common knowledge" in industrial settings or those seeking literal household application, both out of practical purposes and for purposes of cultivating taste, consumed the column. Some entries, such as the one on thickening one's fingernails with the smoke of dead silkworms to enhance the playing of one's musical instruments, might have easily resonated with cultured readers. At the same time, there is considerable evidence that the column also attracted budding specialists and industrialists. One digest addressed how to enlarge the size of one's written characters: "To enlarge the size of one's characters, first write the character on a piece of glass. At night . . . cast a light on the glass and reflect the character onto a wall, and you can trace the character to whatever size you need" (*Shenbao*, June 23, 1917, 14). Such a "tip" would appeal to a reader who was invested in calligraphy as much as he or she was in appreciating the basic physics of casting light onto glass to enlarge an image. It might also appeal to someone interested in making a shop sign.

Entries informed by chemistry and physics as well as by techniques for manufacturing were featured throughout the column's run. For example, there was the entry on the "method to tighten an iron hoop":

Daily-use wooden equipment, such as wooden tubs and basins, all use iron hoops. Once the wood dries, the hoops become too loose. If you want to re-loop the hoop and tighten it, heat the hoop in fire until it is reddish, then [tighten it] and place it [back] on. When it cools, it'll shrink and therefore, tightly grasp the wooden frame. This kind of metal has the quality of expanding when hot and shrinking when cold. With railroad tracks, there is the need to leave space at each juncture point, as the metal will heat up (and expand) when trains drive over the tracks and cause friction. Use algebra and physics to calculate how much the metal will expand. (*Shenbao*, June 23, 1917, 14)

Here, information on how to tighten an iron ring is shared. So, too, is knowledge about how metal expands and contracts depending on its temperature. The reference to railroad tracks and the need to leave space at different points because the tracks expand when the friction of the train causes the metal to heat up was followed by a reference to the modern disciplines of algebra and physics to calculate the exact amount by which the metal will expand (or shrink). Basic physics was presented and mobilized as a source of authority. Households might have housed such barrels, and household managers might have needed this information to ensure that their barrels' hoops stayed firmly secure, but such knowledge was quite easily transferred to an industrial or manufacturing setting and situation, including the many that were based in homes. By moving from a concrete domestic object—metal hoops—to more abstract physics principle of metal expanding and shrinking, the entry illustrated the principle with something of national significance and obvious modern allure, railroads. It ended by asserting the forms of knowledge that would allow for the calculation of the expansion or constriction of the domestic item, metal hoops for barrels. The concrete and abstract, foreign and domestic, household and national were inextricably bound together in the column, much like the tightly wound hoops.

Chen and his contributors also mobilized new forms of expertise to promote common knowledge on light manufacturing. Consider the inclusion of a portion of a letter from a reader at the end of the run on December 27, 1918:

I [editor Tianxuwosheng] attach this letter about our [earlier entry on] December 23: "You published Li Hongjun's [entry,] where he described a testing method (*shiyan fa*)—but actually, his was groundless talk that was unreliable. . . . I specialize in botany at the University of California in the United States and especially in germs. I contributed the article 'Method for Distinguishing Germs' to China's *Science Magazine* (*Kexue zazhi*), volume 1, issue 8. This piece is based on the article . . . and is, as a result, authoritative. I report this to you briefly here and urge the 'Common Knowledge' editor not to include Li Hongjun's entries, as what is at stake is the public's well being." [Signed] Hu Guangsu, University of California botany graduate. Nanjing Higher-Level Teachers College, horticulture teacher.

(*Shenbao*, December 27, 1918, 14)

By including Hu Guangsu's letter to the editor, Chen created a sense that there was the possibility for a back-and-forth exchange among readers and the editor and reinforced the sense that readers were enmeshed in a semipersonal network of learned readers. In the letter, Hu requested Chen as the editor not to include Li Hongjun's "groundless talk." To challenge the earlier entry by Li Hongjun, Hu forwarded as authoritative his own credentials, which were earned at the University of California, a foreign university not in Japan, where earlier generations of intellectuals had attended university, but in the United States, a country from which a more current generation of intellectuals were returning. He also referenced his current job as a horticulture teacher at the Nanjing Teachers College and an earlier publication of his. Hu Guangsu was an example of someone who could define worthy "common knowledge'" because of his expertise. His credentials included foreign schooling, publications, and the ability to engage directly with the editor.

These entries earned the column an overall reputation for emphasizing *xiao gongyi*, light industry. Chen Xiaocui, Chen's daughter, remarked that the column featured techniques for manufacturing everyday items and that such knowledge became Chen's signature style in the journals of the day (Chen Xiaocui, Fan, and Zhou 1982, 217). Similarly, Chen's son claimed that this column was part of his father's agenda to promote the common knowledge of China's citizens, which should be noted in particular for its contribution to bolstering China's industrial arts and chemistry (*gongyi huaxue*). Indeed, *xiao gongyi* digests in the column promoted dusting clockwork and watches with kerosene and instructed readers on how to develop photographic images on platinum-plated paper in alcohol (*Shenbao*, December 27, 1918, 14). Articles with titles such as "Method for Manufacturing Matches," "Method for Bleaching," "Method for Gilding Gold," "Method for Manufacturing Camphor," "Method for Manufacturing Soy Sauce" seemed to cater directly to manufacturers (Chen Dingshan [1955] 1967, 182). Those engaged in small businesses might have consumed "The Method to Carve/Engrave Copper Plates," "The Method to Weld Together Aluminum," or "The Method for Taking Color Photographs" for helpful tips.

Chen also directly addressed his reputation as a promoter of *xiao gongyi*. He claimed to want to publish *xiao gongyi* information as "common knowledge" in order to reverse purportedly long-standing practices in China's manufacturing world of hoarding recipes about manufacturing and science as secrets and to make such information public and less exclusive. On several occasions, he wrote how sharing manufacturing knowledge to both budding and established Chinese industrialists would bolster China's native industrial sector. In the preface to *The Peppermint Industry* (*Bohe gongye*), the translation of a Japanese manual that he published in 1933, Chen credited Mr. Xiao, a Household Industries shareholder, for China's flourishing peppermint industry: "As for the proper method to select the ideal variety [of mint] and to extract mint essence, [Mr. Xiao] put great effort into disseminating the information, rendering [such knowledge] into common knowledge (*changshi*). . . . [As a result,] not only is there no possibility for Japanese mint to penetrate our hinterland market, [but] we can also export ours and compete with Europe and America" (Chen Diexian 1933, 2). The success of China's nativist industry on the global market, Chen asserted unequivocally, was crucially dependent on generating knowledge that is transmitted and circulated far and wide—ideally through Chen's own commodified publications.

Although identifying *xiao gongyi* as "common knowledge," the column ultimately struck the tone of a learned yet lay viewpoint. As the editor, Chen was far more of an eclectic mixer than the editors of industry-related or specialist journals. The knowledge in this column was expansive and variegated. He exalted the practical and the commonsensical (often achieved through experiential know-how) and, as we saw in the hoops example, co-opted the abstract, the theoretical, and the specialized into the home and into spheres of commerce and mass media. The recipes could serve as objects of taste that could be leisurely consumed, read with a playful sense of appreciation, but the *xiao gongyi* entries were portrayed as crucial to national industrial power. Chen's common knowledge and his overall approach toward industry were animated *both* by the tradition of literati versatility and broad learning *and* by trends toward specialization. In certain respects, Chen's publications were similar to earlier Qing manuals used by learned amateurs that assumed that any scholar-gentleman possessed fundamental qualifications for practicing medicine as long as he had the right access to medical literature (Y. Wu 2010). His publications constituted a form of gentlemanly expertise, which remained distinct from the occupationalism promoted by more specialized industry journals and modern textbooks that were appearing more frequently (as competing print commodities) in the print market of the day. Yet the "common knowledge" of Chen's publications had clearly been updated to meet the needs of the modern reader-citizen, for whom such knowledge was relevant to the making of a strong nation. His son, Dingshan, notes in a biographical account that Chen's "learning [was] broad, and yet that practice must be specialized and refined" (Chen Dingshan [1955] 1967, 14). Dingshan goes on to state that his father was hardly an outdated connoisseur of an array of useless knowledge, but rather his broad learning was relevant and modern insofar as it exhibited the ability to specialize and focus on useful knowledge for a variety of purposes, including developing Chinese industry.

MODEL CORRESPONDENCE AND GENTLEMANLY EXPERTISE

By the late 1920s, Chen Diexian continued to publish "common knowledge" but did so beyond the generalist yet lettered columns such as "Common Knowledge." He also sought to reach out to aspiring industrialists and young students by repackaging and deepening (making more technical) the kind of *xiao gongyi* information featured in earlier columns, and so he put together the compilation *Model Correspondence on Industry and Commerce* (*Gongshangye chidu ou'cun*, 1928). Not a new-style industry journal or a modern textbook, this publication followed a long-standing genre, the *chidu*, the gathered letters of an upright individual. It collected the business correspondence that Chen had drafted while at the helm of Household Industries. The coverage was fairly expansive and included an array of matters that Chen had encountered in building

Household Industries. Manufacturing toothpowder, making peppermint, using brine to manufacture magnesium, assessing the state of China's raw materials, manufacturing packaging, preparing shop signs, and fighting counterfeit trademarks were covered. Other topics were raw materials in the production of cosmetics, cosmetic bottles, counterfeited man-made silk, methods for manufacturing perfume, improved packaging, ferrotyping printed material, and methods to expel unwanted smells from scented soaps.

The publication included letters that Chen had specifically drafted about the manufacture of foam fire extinguishers. See, for example, the letter titled "The Matter of Testing a Fire Extinguisher" from 1922:

> The foam-based fire extinguisher is based on physical and chemical principles. When it is hot, the extinguisher dissolves the steam and expels the oxygen [from a fire], so that the fire will slowly be extinguished. This does not require water. When the fire starts, its core is not very large, and at that point, you can use water to extinguish it. Last time the Shuanglun Toothbrush factory caught fire, the blaze burned from downstairs through the floors and shot out through the roof. . . . When the chemical foam was applied [to the fire's core], the conflagration was extinguished immediately. . . . Each room should have a canister. . . .
>
> Two years ago, our very own Association [for Household Industries] experienced a fire; alcohol ignited, and there was fire in the room, and our bedding started to burn. We relied on a canister of foam [to extinguish the fire]. . . .
>
> [Household Industries] produces this kind of foam. Since we sell it widely, our price is not egregious. We . . . welcome your help in its promotion and are attaching an instruction booklet and price list. We also have the fire-extinguishing canister, which is known as the *yao shuilong*. This is specifically designed to spray tall buildings. . . . Horizontally, it can reach around 30 feet. Vertically, it can reach approximately 15 feet, and one person can manage it. Each one is twenty-four yuan without the discount. It is expensive to produce, so we have to sell at full price. But, for special contracts, we can grant a discount of 5 percent.
> (Chen Diexian 1928, vol. *renxu*:24–25)

The rest of the letter informed the recipient, probably a potential wholesale dealer, that each case packed ten-dozen canisters and that if he was willing to distribute canisters, he simply needed to put down a five-hundred-yuan deposit, and Household Industries would immediately ship out twenty cases. Those canisters that the recipient failed to sell could be returned, though the fire extinguisher itself could not.

Like the chapter epigraph, this letter cited examples of fires that Chen had ostensibly experienced (and from which his authority partially stemmed). It suggested that fires were regular occurrences in factories and industrial sites, homes and banquet settings. Whereas in the "New Household Knowledge" entry Chen claimed he had used tubes of tooth-powder containing magnesium carbonate to douse the flame, here he described how he used the fire-extinguishing foam that Household Industries manufactured to extinguish the conflagration that erupted in his own company. This letter furthermore sounded like a promotion, describing how many canisters would be necessary for the buyer's intended purpose and providing what it claimed to be a discount. By the time *Model Correspondence* was issued in 1928, the specific business deal laid out was clearly no longer available. Yet as an exemplary model, the letter showcased how Chen made smart business deals and how he was savvy in his goal of both disseminating information and making a profit.

Published by Household Industries' in-house press and under his pen name "Tianxuwosheng," *Model Correspondence* was not generalist in its orientation but explicitly sought to provide model letters for workers and young students and to allow Chen to share his insights in manufacturing and commerce. In a biography, Chen's son Dingshan reminisces about his father's general dedication to helping new and small industrialists:

> [Father] was [constantly in action], waking up every day at 5:30 am working and running the company until 11:30 pm. . . . [O]utside his office there were always people waiting to see him for advice. My father . . . designed their industry according to their needs, suggesting, for example, that they do a small-scale soap factory or small-scale mechanical workshop, start-ups that did not require a lot of capital and would be easy to establish. If they lacked capital, he helped them out. He never sought profit himself. (Chen Dingshan [1955] 1967, 186)

Model Correspondence would have been part of this larger commitment to helping start-ups and young industrialists.

Chen stated his dedication to helping out young industry in the preface to *Model Correspondence*:

> Ever since I established Household Industries in 1918, I have collected all my correspondence in a file. . . . Model correspondence compilations found in street stalls are mostly fabricated and have little to do with reality. [In contrast,] what I wrote [in these letters] is grounded in the facts of the time; I use paper and pen to represent my voice. There is absolutely no gilded discourse, and all is written down straightforwardly. Even though it is written in classical Chinese, it is no different from the vernacular. . . . As for manufacturing methods, I keep no secrets. I divulge all to allow people to get results . . . I select those that can serve as reference material for students of industry and commerce, and workers. . . . These letters are the crystallization of my sweat and tears over the past ten years. . . . This [compilation] benefits [China's] youth even more than *Zeng Wenzheng's Family Letters*. To serve society, the young must have diverse experiences, and where best to get this experience but from reading and practicing?
> (Chen Diexian 1928, n.p.)

Here, Chen guaranteed the authority of his compilation in several ways. First, he differentiated his publication from common, vulgar ones sold in street stalls. His was a quality product. Then he positioned the text vis-à-vis more highbrow publications that might be associated with the New Culture and May Fourth Movements. Pointing to anxiety about "gilded words" or classical Chinese, he nonetheless defended his choice to write in classical Chinese by stating that there was actually no difference between his linguistic register and the new national vernacular ("sui xi wenyan wu yi baihua"). Finally, unlike others who hoard information, his was an altruistic act of transparency. For China's youth to succeed, he argued, diverse experiences were needed, and to accomplish this diversity, reading and engaging in the practice of industry were crucial. The implication was clear: one needed to read this compilation in particular to ensure productivity—he was selling it at a reasonable price, it was written in the new-style classical Chinese, and it functioned to render the knowledge accessible or "common."

The content of these letters included considerable technical information that would have appealed to the targeted audience of *Model Correspondence*: would-be manufacturers and young workers. One epistle from 1924, titled "Reasons Why Magnesium Carbonate Extinguishes Fire," detailed the chemical properties of magnesium carbonate and introduced the physics behind how the magnesium carbonate fire extinguisher worked:

> Magnesium can extinguish fires; this everyone knows. Ordinary fire extinguishers mix sodium carbonate in water, and add sulfuric acid or hydrochloric acid and turn it into sodium sulfate or sodium chloride [*sic*]. Carbon dioxide is released. Use the pressure from the steam to squeeze out the water. [The extinguisher] can spray very high. Once it encounters heat, the carbonic acid and water separate, so that you can douse the burning oxygen at the heart of the fire. This is the basic principle. In an ordinary school experiment, one puts sodium carbonate into a glass bottle and adds hydrochloric acid, which results in the release of carbon dioxide. If you put fire near the opening of the bottle, the fire will immediately be snuffed out. . . . This principle is identical to the one above.
>
> Now use magnesium carbonate and mix it with hydrochloric acid or sulfuric acid to produce magnesium sulfate . . . and release the carbonic acid. The effect is the same . . . but magnesium carbonate has a very special characteristic, which is not shared by the above ingredients. If you place magnesium carbonate into a metal container and heat it up, while the container becomes red hot, if you touch the bottom, you will find that that is not hot as [magnesium carbonate] does not conduct heat.
> (Chen Diexian 1928, vol. *jiazi*:46–47)

The technical information is not surprising given that the original letter was addressed to the foreign pharmaceutical company Schloten, H. (Xueludun yaohang). The letter proceeded to list more reasons why magnesium carbonate could be used to such great effect and explained why it had far more capacity to douse a conflagration than other carbonates. Explicitly characterizing the level of technical knowledge needed as comparable to that of high school students, the letter nonetheless still conveyed considerably more technical detail, chemical knowledge, and physics than comparable entries in "Common Knowledge."[14]

Distributed during a period when publications dedicated to the dissemination of industrial and manufacturing knowledge were multiplying, *Model Correspondence* was notable for being gathered letters, a *chidu*.[16] Publishing a *chidu* was common from the late-imperial period to the Republican era, and epistolary collections ranged from letters sent to the family (*jiashu*) to love letters (*qingshu*).[15] Lettered men and women saw letter writing as an art form meant for public display, so they often crafted their letters with the expectation that they would be published (Chen Pingyuan 2010, 181–194). Chen's self-conscious choice to publish manufacturing advice and expert knowledge in the form of a compilation of model epistles indicates that he may have composed his letters from the start with publication in mind.

In the preface, Chen referred to the longer history of this genre by mentioning the late-nineteenth-century publication *Zeng Wenzheng's Letters Home*. "Zeng Wenzheng" was a posthumous name for the famous late-Qing statesman Zeng Guofan (1811–1872), and *Zeng Wenzheng's Letters Home* was a collection of letters he wrote to his family that was compiled after he died. In a period when the Qing Empire was in crisis, gathered letters by Zeng, a famous general who had played a role in putting the empire back together after the Taiping Uprising, were compelling. Readers could learn not just how Zeng reigned over his family through these letters but also by extension how he could reign over a fragmented empire. The letters served to exhibit Zeng's exemplary moral rule. Though hardly as famous or influential as Zeng, Chen was clearly seeking to forge a genealogical link between himself and the late-Qing statesman and was fashioning himself (rather audaciously) as someone similarly authoritative on matters—in his case, industry and commerce—and with comparable moral standing. His commodified classicism drew from long-standing genres that middling-level readers, familiar with if not nostalgic for the late-imperial lettered culture, would appreciate and potentially purchase. And yet while explicitly evoking a late-imperial sensibility in the reference to Zeng, *Model Correspondence* was ultimately meant to serve distinctly modern purposes. The *chidu* was updated to function as an easy manual for how to do business and build industry.[17]

At first glance, *Model Correspondence* might seem at odds with the "Common Knowledge" column. "Common Knowledge" presented manufacturing knowledge not as occupation-specific know-how for the specialist but as eclectic generalist information for the learned urban citizen-reader to appreciate tastefully. Its "common knowledge" was not to be the basis of any exclusive domain or discipline. Yet those who may not have been demarcating professional boundaries but were nonetheless invested in industry and manufacturing pursuits could have appreciated the entries related to the "minor industrial arts." This potential to provide know-how to young students and new industrialists emerged even more prominently in *Model Correspondence*. Its publication was indicative of a shift in Chen's persona. He had become a seasoned captain of industry by the time he published his *chidu* and wanted to share his wisdom through a compilation of his business correspondence and thereby serve as an exemplar for upcoming industrialists and youthful entrepreneurs. Ultimately, however, even as *Model Correspondence* was explicit in its goal of helping young manufacturers, because it followed the genre of collected model epistles, it was infused with an air of gentlemanly learnedness rather than with explicit occupational specialization. In this way, it remained distinct from competing publications on the market, such as specialized industry periodicals and textbooks.

Years later, in 1982, Chen's daughter, Xiaocui, noted that "aside from being busy tinkering [with things] (*shiyan*) and emulating (*fangzhi*) [manufacturing technologies] on a daily basis, Chen also spent a lot of time responding to the letters of industry workers and young students . . . These [letters] . . . were . . . published as the four-volume *Model Correspondence*; these [letters] were the ones that fell specifically under the category of *xiao gongyi*" (Chen Xiaocui, Fan, and Zhou 1982, 222). In this quote, Xiaocui articulates how knowledge work such as epistolary replies to workers and students, tinkering, and emulative manufacturing (the latter two elements discussed in chapter 4) were important facets of Chen's vernacular industrialism. *Model Correspondence*, along with "Common Knowledge," furthermore helped produce the dream of industrialism. Much like the examination system, these *xiao gongyi* pieces introduced new forms of social ambition and helped turn chemistry, physics, and the manufacturing enterprise into a motivating ambition. The two titles might thus have shared an overlapping set of readers. Some of the dilettante dabblers in chemistry and cosmetic manufacturing who had consumed Chen's "The Warehouse" column in 1915 were likely lured out of their home laboratories and intimate social networks of like-minded practitioners to pursue their interests in newly emerging academic settings or in the realm of modern industry by the 1920s. At the same time, some could have continued to appreciate Chen's newer publications, reading "Common Knowledge" for more leisurely enjoyment and *Model Correspondence* for concrete insight and information.

CHANGSHI AND COMPETING CLAIMS OF EXPERTISE

In the era of emerging specialization and industry formation, new-style industry publications and professional journals were appearing in China's print market. Notably, some of these specialized publications included articles that identified knowledge on specific and even branded manufacturing processes as "common knowledge." While presenting manufacturing information as "common knowledge," these specialist journals diverged from both "Common Knowledge" and *Model Correspondence* in how they presented such knowledge as primarily specific to the production of formal, specialist, or expert knowledge on science and industry. The *Chemical Industry Journal* (*Huaxue gongyi*), published by the Shanghai School of Chemical Industries (Shanghai huaxue gongyi zhuanmen xuexiao), is one such journal that presented "common knowledge" on chemistry and industry as the basis of emerging expert knowledge. The school was an example of vocational education starting to appear in large cities such as Shanghai that was focused on industry and commerce and was to train and educate lower-middle-class youths (W. Yeh 2007, 36–40). The periodical noted that the institution's express goals were to promote the chemical industry and to educate future industrialists. One needed only one or two years of high school and a strong academic background to enroll. For more specialized electives, students had to have at least a high school diploma.[18] Basic coursework included "The Complete Studies of Cosmetics," "The Method for Manufacturing Ingredients," and "Daily Hygiene Items." Although the journal was published by the school and was intended for students, it was also meant to be available to a general audience. Three thousand copies of each issue were distributed gratis to industrial institutions, schools, factories, drug stores, and all major newspaper agencies. Articles articulated new occupational identities, such as the modern chemist (*huaxuejia*). They also offered a different way of becoming a technical expert. One was no longer apprenticed as part of an artisan workshop or lineage but instead educated in a distinctly modern manner wherein the training of students included the more anonymous style of consuming journals.

The *Chemical Industry Journal* featured articles on chemical and manufacturing knowledge that was characterized as "common knowledge." This knowledge was meant to function as a kind of capital that students could develop to shore up their professional credentials. The article "Common Knowledge Chemists Should Possess" (Yu Ziming 1923), claiming to be a translated piece from the U.S. journal *Scientific American*, detailed exactly what "common knowledge" entailed.[19] Serving the same purpose was "Common Knowledge One Needs to Use Cosmetics" (Lü 1922), a piece describing the basic knowledge in cosmetics production that a student needed to acquire, including how to manufacture soap, vanishing cream, toothpowder, scented powders, hair tonic, and perfumes. The acquisition of such knowledge was directly related to investing in the infrastructure of China's chemical and industrial future. In "Urging My Countrymen to Establish a Chemical Research Institute," Fa Chang made a direct link between chemistry and industrial and commercial development, writing, "Chemistry is the Mother of Industry" (1922, 5).

In the *Chemical Industry Journal*, there appears to be little sense of exclusive ownership over the manufacturing knowledge or specific formulas and recipes presented as "common knowledge." The publication freely printed articles on large-scale manufacturing processes, surveys and reports on factories and companies, as well as pieces on chemical research, some of which included specific information about the production processes used by famous brands and companies. Each issue included a full section devoted to reviewing manufacturing methods. Typical titles were "The Method to Make Foreign Candles," "Common Knowledge in Testing Soap," and "The General State of Guangxi's Manufacturing of Cinnamon Oil." Others were "The Relationship Between

Hygiene and the Chemical Industry," and "The Industry of Oils and Fats." In an era before trademark and patent protection, some pieces described how to manufacture famous brands of cosmetic items and described the workings of well-known factories. One student report reviewed the ingredients and provided step-by-step instructions on how to make Xiangmao Soap, a popular British soap known as Honey Soap in English (Fang 1922).[20] It was followed by "Is the Wintergreen Oil by the China-British Pharmacy a Natural Product or a Man-Made Product?," which meticulously detailed the oil's chemical ingredients (Guo Shangbao 1922). A review of a visit to the Great Five Continents Drugstore's soap factory described in detail the kind of machinery being used, including the filter press, the automatic soap dryer, milling machines, and the compressor machine.[21]

Notably, one piece was a detailed survey of Household Industries, Chen Diexian's then young cosmetics company. In the report, readers learned about the ten factories owned by Household Industries, strategies of management utilized by the company, and the exact allocation of its shareholding interests. Also divulged were the exact steps it used in mixing manufacturing magnesium carbonate:

There are two methods: use magnesite . . . (whose quality is not pure, so it cannot be used to make toothpowder). Crush the magnesite into powder and add sulfuric acid. [The magnesite] will decompose and turn into magnesium sulfate, which is soluble in water. Filter it and add sodium carbonate into the filtered solution and mix together. It will become a white colored sediment. Dry the sediment and it will become magnesium carbonate (*qing meitan yang* 輕鎂炭養 [*sic*]). See its reaction sequence below:

1. $MgCO_3 + H_2SO_4 = MgSO_4 + CO_2 + H_2O$
2. $4MgSO_4 + 4Na_2CO_3 + XH_2O = (3MgCO_3 + Mg[OH]_2 + XH_2O) + CO_2 + 2Na_2SO_4$ [*sic*]

The second method: Take the waste product from manufacturing salt and use it as a raw material. Sodium chloride (*lühuana* 綠化鈉 [*sic*]) is in abundance in seawater; this is the ordinary salt we eat. There is also magnesium chloride ($MgCl_2$). By evaporating seawater, sodium chloride crystallizes. The magnesium chloride remains in the solution, and if you add sodium carbonate into the solution, you can extract the insoluble salt of magnesium carbonate. . . . See the reaction below:

$$4MgCl_2 + 4Na_2CO_3 + XH_2O = [3MgCO_3 + Mg(OH)_2 + XH_2O] + CO_2 + 8NaCl \; [sic].$$

(*Huaxue gongyi* 1 [2] [October 1922], 42–43)

The report treated the reactions and formulas not as manufacturing secrets exclusive to Chen's young company but rather as common knowledge to be shared broadly and for the purposes of developing national industry.

The presentation of the knowledge in this passage asserted authority differently from the presentation of chemical manufacturing knowledge found in the recipes of "The Warehouse" column discussed in chapter 2. Although domesticated in the inner chambers, the know-how in the earlier column was still being presented as a foreign wonder, and the strategic inclusion of Western translations of the names of ingredients helped create that effect. Here, however, the manufacturing recipes moved away from wonder and assumed a certainty beyond the earlier pieces by treating the chemical notation as if it were fixed and authoritative. No Western-language glosses were given, and the reactions and chemical notation were treated as self-explanatory. Yet there was still considerable lack of standardization at this point, and this lack can be seen in the Chinese characters chosen to represent chemical compounds in this passage.[22] Chinese characters eventually used to connote *gas* were increasingly those with the radical 气 (*qi*), and at least by 1936 the standard method of writing the term *sodium chloride* was 氯化鈉 (*lühuana*). Here, however, *sodium chloride* is written as 綠化鈉 (*lühuana*), where the first character is 綠 *lü* and not the homophone 氯 *lü*, which would become the standard later.[23] Similarly, the term *magnesium carbonate*, written here as 輕鎂炭養 (*qing meitan yang*), would become 氫鎂炭氧 (*qing meitan yang*), where the 輕 (*qing*) was replaced with 氫 (*qing*), a homophone used with the gas radical 气 (*qi*), and the final character 養 (*yang*) was replaced with 氧 (*yang*). Thus, in 1922, when this passage was written, chemical notation was not yet fixed in China (or, arguably, around the world).[24] Despite this looseness of terminology, there was little indication of doubt in this article. An authoritative tone was adopted to present the information, which would have echoed how the information would have been appearing in new-style textbooks popular during the day. This was no longer the purposeful portrayal of science as a foreign wonder but rather a formal, sober presentation of the method of manufacturing along with chemical formulas for readers to master.

The "common knowledge" in the *Chemical Industry Journal* was for students and specialists in the making and included manufacturing formulas, detailed accounts of factory sites, and information about both Chinese and foreign pharmaceutical companies and their brands. The appearance of "common knowledge" here might suggest a tension between the journal's professional aspiration and the student body it served, on the one hand, and the emphasis on "commonly" shared knowledge for a general population, on the other hand. Yet the identification of "common knowledge" as useful for the formation of expertise might not have been contradictory at all. Rather, to help Chinese industry the journal sought to disseminate as widely as possible the knowledge and research needed to sow the grounds for the growth of native industry. Furthermore, the direct association of these industrial recipes with successful brands and companies—both Western (e.g., Wintergreen) and Chinese (e.g., Household Industries)—was not considered a violation of intellectual-property rights for the editors or readers but served to facilitate the sharing of "common knowledge" for Chinese industry.

For Chen Diexian, however, it was precisely the authority by which journals such the *Chemical Industry Journal* circulated his and other manufacturing processes that he sought to challenge with his own common-knowledge publications. Although the legal concept of intellectual-property rights might have been inchoate and rarely resorted to at the time in China, players in the manufacturing game were nonetheless still invested in claiming ownership over certain forms of knowledge to distinguish their own authority and expertise. In response to the widespread circulation of manufacturing formulas, including those created by his own company, Chen's decision to publish manufacturing formulas and information as "common knowledge" in "Common Knowledge" and related publications might be characterized as an act of fuller transparency. In the print market, his position was that of generalist lay knowledge and gentlemanly expertise, which contrasted to the more narrow professional occupationalism of industry publications. By making manufacturing processes "common" beyond the narrow expert readers to whom competing journals were catering, he sought to outmaneuver competing specialist publications to lay claim over the know-how as well as to control the sales of both the publications of "common knowledge" and objects made from such manufacturing know-how. He sought to preempt others from rendering knowledge common by doing it more effectively. His publications on "common knowledge" were thus to bolster his own reputation and undercut that of the competition.

CONCLUSION: POLITICS OF COMMON KNOWLEDGE IN THE CHINA OF THE 1920s

The 1920s were a period when heterogeneous practices of manufacturing and knowledge production coexisted and multiple claims were being made over what "industry" exactly was and who exactly owned, produced, and authorized industry-related knowledge. By the turn of the twentieth century, educational reform had led to the rise of related academic fields, from chemistry to physics. Located in missionary schools and Chinese universities as well as eventually in modern-style middle schools and high schools, these fields came to accredit expertise through training and degrees, and the approach toward broad learning taken by late-imperial literati was quickly rendered obsolete. In the Republican era, the professional boundaries of medicine, law, and journalism were being erected and defined through organizations such as the Shanghai bar and journalist associations that separated professionals by occupation (X. Xu 2000). These changes engendered the rise of the new-style professional, who emerged in distinction to the late-imperial ideal of the gentlemanly nonspecialist whose classical education marked social standing and was the basis of success on the civil-service exam. Expertise was no longer located in the bodies of bureaucrats who learned their expert knowledge while serving office. New occupational identities such as the industrialist (shiyejia) and chemist (huaxuejia) were being carved out and validated in university departments, factories, emerging industrial corporations, and professional associations. Because much of this professionalizing and defining of occupations occurred during a period of considerable central-state weakness, efforts to establish formal lines of expertise were often incubated and fostered by regional networks run by elites. In an article on the Shanghai Industrial Arts Expo in 1924, author Wu Chengluo's overview of the state of China's chemical manufacturing described this trend by noting how private companies were taking the lead in developing native production and how industrialists of the day had to be self-promoters because the state had been weakened by ceaseless internecine warfare (1924, 7).

Yet even as specialized publishing and formal occupations were beginning to emerge, often under the purview of regional elites, participation in industrial production and science by self-proclaimed nonspecialists persisted. In the realm of practice, "informal" production of light-manufactured goods regularly occurred outside of factory walls, even as more and more mechanized industrial sites were being built. British American Tobacco imported its factories and mechanized manufacturing methods to China to produce rolled cigarettes, but at the same time handicraft workshops popped up and recycled tobacco and hand-rolled cigarettes for sale on a second-tier market (Benedict 2011). It was also not until the 1930s and 1940s that modern laboratories sponsored by corporations or the GMD state started to be built. In the 1920s, chemical experimentation occurred in a host of spaces, from makeshift darkrooms for the development of photographs to home labs and literati reading circles.[25] In the realm of knowledge, even though there was a discernible trend toward the formalization of scientific disciplines, "science" was hardly the exclusive domain of specialized academics. New science disciplines were being established at Beijing University. Yet New Culture intellectuals promoted scientific knowledge (or, more specifically, the slogan "Mr. Science,") in journals such as *New Youth* and in newly established science societies as something to be pursued more broadly by cosmopolitan intellectuals and concerned citizens regardless of their profession.

If the term *changshi* is often rendered today as "common sense," something that is innately embodied by all, in the 1920s it was a neologism from Japan that gained significance during a period when lines of expertise and specialization were not yet indelibly fixed.[26] Occupational expertise and professional membership were only starting to be established through academic and formal credentials, but not always consistently. As a result, different actors jostled over demarcating and defining "common knowledge." For the legal medical profession in the early twentieth century, for example, legal officials sought to acquire "common knowledge" in medicine through fiction, journal articles, didactic primers on legal medicine, and Q&A columns in science journals so that they had enough knowledge to employ forensic experts and specialists (Asen 2016). *Changshi* was nonspecialist knowledge, yet the jurists pursued such knowledge to bolster their professional credentials.

Chen's *changshi* was similarly a form of ordinary, vernacular know-how that was to be learned and disseminated widely via the mass media for China's emerging citizen-readers to consume and apply in practice, even as emerging experts also tapped into such resources. Chen's column "Common Knowledge" made *changshi* broadly available to citizen-readers and lettered urbanites in the form of general lay knowledge that could serve to carve out taste and social distinction and to shape China's modern citizenry. His collection *Model Correspondence* repackaged and repurposed much of the same information as the basis of his own gentlemanly expertise and reputation in industry as well as that of his experts-to-be readers. Both publications thus ultimately exemplified a hybrid approach toward industry and science. They conveyed a stubborn insistence on Chen's part that although engagement with manufacturing and industrial knowledge could function to carve out his and his readers' expertise, this knowledge was not to fall solely under the purview of narrow professionalism or of state-sponsored industrial efforts. Chen's publications implied that access to "common knowledge" on industry would allow the learned reader, cultivated citizen, and emerging specialist of the early twentieth century to establish a progressive, modern daily life. Such common knowledge might have also been used for self-fashioning in the urban playgrounds of Shanghai or for cultivating citizenry in the new Republican nation. It was definitely distinct from yet coexisted with and, indeed, gained significance vis-à-vis newly developing domains of professional knowledge. Finally, its contours were sharpened in contradistinction to emerging trends of specialization with the growth of formal factory-based manufacturing and new academic disciplines.

The sensibility of tasteful lay knowledge in the column "Common Knowledge" and the gentlemanly expertise that characterizes the tone of *Model Correspondence* furthermore served commercial purposes. It was to be public, textual knowledge available for a price; and it was through the purchase of Chen's authoritative printed commodities that this knowledge was to be rendered "common." In this respect, Chen diverged sharply from New Culture writers who also promoted nonspecialist cosmopolitan investment in science and the new family. He linked the reform of the household through industrial knowledge not just to the larger issue of national salvation but also to the pursuit of profit. An undeniable commercial undercurrent ran through his two publications. These publications furthermore functioned to advertise Chen's devices, to peddle raw ingredients (many of which Household Industries manufactured), and to sell commodities. The writings showcased Chen's personal projects, including the foam fire extinguisher, as well as ingredients such as magnesium carbonate that his pharmaceutical company manufactured.[27] They divulged manufacturing secrets and techniques even as they produced knowledge and engendered desire for the products and devices that Chen sold. Finally, the knowledge itself was for purchase. *Model Correspondence*, for example, was packaged cleverly in the genre of the *chidu*, compiled business epistles, which smacked of nostalgia and literati nonprofessionalism. It was thus decidedly distinct from the modern specialist manuals, new-style textbooks, and industry journals peppering China's print market at the time.

To illustrate concretely how these publications helped facilitate commercial pursuits and, indeed, restructure daily life, let us return to Chen's promotion of the fire extinguisher. By the 1930s, Chen Diexian remained committed to practicing what he had long been preaching in his columns—namely, integrating the Butterfly Fire Extinguisher and other objects featured in publications of "common knowledge" into the realm of the everyday. In 1935, Household Industries was sending representatives to schools and other places to demonstrate in what was a rather spectacular fashion the efficacy and necessity of the perfected Butterfly Fire Extinguisher.[28] The training institute for the political personnel of Jiangxi Province, for example, hosted a Household Industries representative, who revealed in the institute entryway's courtyard how the Butterfly Fire Extinguisher worked. The head of education at the institute ordered students and instructors to make a circle around the representative, who set a metal basin filled with kerosene ablaze and then used the extinguisher to put out the billowing flames in mere seconds. News-worthy, the spectacle was reported in the institute's weekly publication ("Jiating gongyeshe biaoyan miehuoji" 1935). As the account noted, the institute held this demonstration so that all students could obtain the basic knowledge (*changshi*) of putting out a fire. It also purchased two fire extinguishers to guard against future fires. This demonstration and Household Industries' success in selling its extinguishers and dissemi-nating its *changshi* showed how far Chen Diexian had come from 1905, when he had first mobilized a group of friends to climb a hill in Hang-zhou to see his unsuccessful attempt to use the fire extinguisher he had been tinkering with to douse a blazing grass hut. Chen's position as a leading manufacturer of the foam fire extinguisher in 1935 was the result of years of hard work. Popularizing light-manufacturing information as "common knowledge" and presenting business acumen in the kinds of publications discussed here played a key role and were emblematic of Chen's vernacular industrialism. So, too, were other traits. Tinkering and experimenting, translating and adapting, improving upon existing technologies, as well as honing fierce marketing strategies were addi-tional attributes crucial in Chen's becoming a leading captain of industry in China.

PART THREE

Manufacturing Objects, 1913–1942

With the emergence of treaty ports and the rise of light industry in the latter part of the nineteenth century and the early twentieth century, China's material landscape saw not only the proliferation of mass-produced modern commodities but also the emergence of multiple tiers of markets and kinds of good. Mass-produced goods, both domestic and foreign manufactured, permeated all spheres of life, formal and daily, urban and rural. Commercial markets and consumer cultures became increasingly complex, and different tiers of objects and commercial exchange emerged (Dikötter 2007; Benedict 2011). With this proliferation of goods and multiplication of things for sale, different ways of classifying daily-use items appeared. Some were deemed domestic in opposition to imported goods. Others were brand-name commodities or "counterfeit" goods or in between recycled and repurposed goods. These categories also changed over time and among different groups of producers and consumers. Fervent debates about what exactly formed an "authentic" versus a "fake" or a "native" (*guohuo*) versus an "enemy" (*dihuo*) good were constantly taking place, with much at stake in those shifting definitions. It was in this context that Chen and other manufacturers like him were invested in identifying their products as authentically native-branded goods in contradistinction to fraudulent enemy products or fakes and counterfeits (chapter 6).

Related to this increasingly complex consumer culture was the reconfiguration of forms of manufacturing and production. Whereas the early part of the Self-Strengthening Movement had focused on heavy industry and the building of arsenals, its later phases in the 1880s to 1890s witnessed a shift in state-sponsored initiatives to key light industries, such as textiles and drugs. In the second part of the movement, there was furthermore a particular interest in encouraging joint government and private merchant enterprises. With the turn of the century into the early republic, political chaos and internecine warfare ensured that any truly substantial state investment was to come to a halt. To be sure, modest state investment in growing China's light industry continued when in 1915 the Ministry of Agriculture and Commerce established the Bureau of Industrial Research, which was dedicated to the analysis of native products, including cosmetics and dyes. But because the weak state could not pour resources into developing heavy industry, this period saw a definitive turn toward light industry, which did not require big capital investment, overhead, deep expertise, or large facilities. It furthermore witnessed a shift away from government-sponsored enterprises to privately owned and managed enterprises (Köll 2003, 36). A few large-scale industrial mass-manufacturing enterprises were present, including foreign multinationals, such as British American Tobacco, as well as domestic regional behemoths, such as Dasheng Number One Spinning Mill (Dasheng diyi shachang) (Köll 2003; Benedict 2011). The majority of factory-based enterprises in the light-industry sector were, however, small-scale, moderately mechanized, and oftentimes family-based firms. There were also innumerable handicraft workshops. Very much part of the Chinese modern industrial landscape after the turn of the century, these workshops often engaged in acts of recycling and repurposing objects for a lower-level tier of consumers who could not afford brand-name items (Benedict 2011).

It was in this complex, changing environment that Chen Diexian exhibited an awareness of the evolving social ambivalence about the new materiality and China's industrial modernity. As a man of letters in Hangzhou and then a writer-editor in Shanghai, Chen had deployed a variety of textual strategies and engaged in knowledge production to domesticate imported goods and new technologies and to neutralize any perceived threat these new material phenomena might pose to social order and cultural sensibility. As he matured as an industrialist, he continued to be cognizant of the shifting anxieties about industrial materiality in China. Much of this anxiety was the direct result of mass production—mass commodities blurred together, and a sea of counterfeits and fakes threatened to undercut the market advantage of brand companies. The influx of foreign goods also generated considerable distress and spurred the emergence of the NPM, whose merchant-leaders sought to redefine products that had been seen as foreign products, or *yanghuo* (literally, "ocean products"), in the latter part of the nineteenth-century into quintessential "national products," or *guohuo*, during the Republican period. Chen was one of those merchant-activists. By examining the building of his National Products factory and the marketing of his goods, this part shows how Chen sought to manage new challenges and anxieties about industrial modernity, even as he capitalized on them.

From the time Chen founded Household Industries, he grasped the need to present it as small scale and local despite the reality of its establishment being dependant on global circuits of information and materials and the fact that the company eventually became an industrial powerhouse. He always touted the company's roots in tinkering and as a family-run enterprise and in this way distinguished it from the investment-intensive research and development commonly associated with state-sponsored heavy-industry initiatives or corporate powerhouses emerging around the world. Chen's initial industrial efforts were indeed decidedly modest. Just as he copied and pasted, compiled and adapted in his editorial and lettered work, he also engaged in the "copy-and-paste" style of innovation in the material world. The technologies he used to produce cosmetics and daily-use items tended to turn on relatively straightforward skills of assembly and mixing. He did not invent his manufacturing formulas from whole cloth but rather translated and adapted recipes from abroad. By the early 1920s, Household Industries quickly scaled up to become a vertically integrated complex corporation. And yet even as the company became a manufacturer of both raw materials (e.g., magnesium carbonate) and finished commodities (e.g., tooth-powder and other pharmaceutical and daily-use items) and emerged as a spry competitor among global brands in the Chinese and Southeast Asian markets, Chen's reputation of self-reliant nativism and the ability to make a virtue out of necessity remained invaluable. In an era of ardent economic patriotism, that reputation became a powerful marketing tool (chapter 4).

In addition to conferring legitimacy to his company, Chen was furthermore aware of the need to guarantee the quality of his commodities in a competitive market. He used a variety of methods to verify that his products were genuinely "native" and trustworthy in a period when fakes, counterfeits, and fraudulent "enemy" products were in abundance. To achieve these goals, he tapped into global legal structures of ownership and commercial strategies of marketing that were emerging and evolving in response to widespread industrial-based mass production. Chen readily translated and compiled the relevant commercial and legal knowledge on the regulation and practice of selling and owning objects, often including such texts in his *xiao gongyi* publications. These texts offered commercial know-how on how to run a joint limited company and how best to choose a trademark, among other things. He also translated and published legal treatises, allowing himself and fellow Chinese manufacturers to draw quickly and selectively from the most up-to-date legal information and a newly emerging global trademark legal regime.

By the 1930s, economic anxiety in general and concern about the abundance of goods—both domestic and foreign—had reached new heights. Cultural producers articulated concern about the rampant capitalism and alienating industrialization that characterized life in large cities such as Shanghai. Leftist writer Mao Dun (1896–1981) levied a critique of Shanghai's crass materialism in his novel *Midnight* (*Ziye*, 1933). Right-wing ideologues, including GMD leaders such as Dai Jitao (1891–1949), promoted militaristic discipline and aesthetic and spiritual transcendence to counter urban decay, greed, and corruption. Fear of fakes and counterfeits was evident in all sorts of advertisements, which warned consumers of the danger of buying an inauthentic item. After World War I, the growing concern over material overabundance was also in part generated by doubts about the promise of industrialization and ongoing economic imperialist pressure. Finally, the larger global context of economic depression affected China in multiple ways, including the reduction of viable markets for its exports abroad. NPM advocates issued dire warnings about buying enemy products.

It was in this context that Chen proved particularly astute in marketing and branding his goods and company. Just as he had drawn from lettered naming practices to establish a Zhuangzi-esque persona when starting his experimentation with new things in Hangzhou, as a mature entrepreneur he executed cutting-edge branding and advertising strategies to distinguish the quality of his company's goods among a sea of mass-produced cosmetics (chapter 5). He leveraged, for example, his reputation as an author of butterfly fiction to justify his industrial and capitalist endeavors, including reinforcing the Butterfly trademark. Household Industries and its overseas subsidiaries in Southeast Asia readily adapted pioneering ad campaigns launched by multinational companies such as Unilever, even while pitching Butterfly goods as National Products to Chinese diaspora communities. Extremely appreciative of the value of the brand and mark, Chen was furthermore ruthless in targeting local copycats and trademark infringers. He utilized a range of methods to discourage the ripping off of the Butterfly brand. He intimidated alleged copycats in court and humiliated companies and stores that sold counterfeit Butterfly products by naming them in the press. Finally, Chen continued to compile and compose textual work on *xiao gongyi* in the final decade of his career. He published several collectanea in the 1930s that were meant to help readers navigate this period of dense and overwhelming materiality. Ever the marketer, he employed sophisticated strategies of authenticating native products—including his own—in an era of penetrative economic imperialism.

CHAPTER FOUR

Chinese Cuttlefish and Global Circuits

The Association of Household Industries

One of the most prominent anecdotes in the biographical literature on Chen Diexian's industrial endeavors can be found in a memoir penned by his son, Chen Dingshan (1897–1989). Published in Taiwan in 1955 and then reprinted in 1967, the biography features a story of Chen Diexian in 1913—then a county government official, part-time novel writer, and dabbler in chemistry—figuring out that cuttlefish bones could serve as the source of a key ingredient to manufacture toothpowder (182–183.)[1] The account suggests that realizing this connection was crucial in Chen Diexian's founding of the Association for Household Industries Co., Ltd. (Jiating gongyeshe gufen lianhe gongsi),[2] which would manufacture and sell Butterfly Toothpowder (Wudipai yafen) for years to come with tremendous success. The anecdote starts with Chen visiting He Gongdan, a former Hangzhou colleague who was serving as the county magistrate (*zhishi*) of Cixi, a county in Ningbo prefecture in Zhejiang Province, next to Zhenhai, where Chen was posted. The two passed the time by sitting in the literary hall behind the magistrate's office, drinking wine, composing poetry, and enjoying a view of the seacoast. It was at that point that Chen noticed how the beach that stretched before him was white. He Gongdan informed him that with the start of the winter and the falling tide, seawater smashed cuttlefish onto the beach. Once the fish's flesh rotted away, all that remained were white cuttlefish bones. The bones went on for miles. Upon hearing this tidbit, the story goes, Chen realized that he had found at his disposal an abundant, natural, and, most importantly, local source of calcium carbonate. Calcium carbonate is not only a main component of the shells and bones of many marine organisms but also a key ingredient often used in the production of toothpowder and other powder-based toiletries.

Zhenhai, the coastal area where Chen came upon the beach full of bones, was indeed cuttlefish territory. Micah Muscolino has written on the fisheries on the Zhoushan Islands, located across from Zhenhai, and notes how the environmental landscape of the Zhoushan archipelago and the coast where Zhenhai is located creates an ideal ecosystem where a mix of water systems can support a diverse array of marine life, including what was one of China's most important cuttlefish populations (2009, 15–16). Chen's impression of natural abundance when he happened upon the shore full of cuttlefish shells actually belied what was a period of crisis. By the twentieth century, this area's fish population was already under considerable distress. As Muscalino demonstrates, despite the relatively successful regulation of human usage aimed at reducing conflict among competing fishermen during the late-imperial period, such human intervention did not address sustainability issues, and permanent damage to the environment resulted, with the depletion of the area's natural fish population by the modern era.

Regardless of the actual environmental situation, from Chen's vantage point a Chinese seacoast full of cuttlefish shells seemed to promise an autarkic method of securing raw materials for producing his toothpowder. Cuttlefish bones had long been important in China's traditional materia medica.[3] This connection would not have been lost on Chen, who had been exposed to Chinese pharmacology from an early age, when he voraciously read his father's materia medica reference texts.[4] For son Chen Dingshan, this account of stumbling across cuttlefish bones was appealing because it helped illustrate his father's heroic self-reliance and ability to innovate for purposes of building Chinese industry. Not surprisingly, he used the anecdote to start his father's biography. In the biography, he underscores his father's commitment to locally sourcing original ingredients and establishing China's industrial autonomy by quoting him as saying:

If we want China's industry to develop, we cannot yet talk of the machine. The biggest issue is original ingredients. If we don't solve the original-ingredient problem, we can't solve the capital issue. . . . If we are to defeat the Japanese Lion [Shizipai] brand [of toothpowder], we need to be self-sufficient with our ingredients. . . . Don't think you can succeed simply by propagating patriotic native goods; you also have to manufacture quality products at a fair cost [through the production of one's own raw materials].
(quoted in Chen Dingshan [1955] 1967, 188)

The cuttlefish epiphany turned out to be rather useless in the end. As Chen Diexian noted in the preface to his translation of the Japanese book *Peppermint Industry* (Chen Diexian 1933a), although he did indeed originally plan to use cuttlefish in the manufacturing of toothpowder, he realized almost immediately that the fish's output of calcium carbonate was too low, and so he rather quickly turned instead to the chemical production of magnesium carbonate.[5] Given that cuttlefish bones were never a significant source of calcium carbonate, it is noteworthy that the "discovery" of cuttlefish nonetheless looms so large in retrospective accounts. The outsize emphasis on this discovery speaks more to its role in perpetuating a particular image of Chen. It was meant to be emblematic of Chen's commitment to developing a domestic industry in China that would be autarkic and not reliant upon foreign ingredients for manufacturing, a reputation he was already cultivating for himself in the 1920s and 1930s as an NPM leader.

Yet even if the cuttlefish account was to an extent apocryphal, Chen certainly did engage in locally sourcing key ingredients and became *the* leading manufacturer of magnesium in China. He was, moreover, intent on building nativist industry and establishing unequivocally that his goods were not foreign-style goods (*yanghuo*), but native products (*guohuo*) down to their domestically produced raw ingredients. The question remains, therefore, to what extent was Chen truly autarkic and homegrown in his industrial endeavors? By the time he died, he had forty-two factories (Link 1981, 158–59). Over the course of his career, he manufactured high-end cosmetics and household items, including different flavors of children's toothpaste, whitening toothpaste, "snow" toothpowder, red-colored tooth-cleansing liquid, indigo-boxed and yellow-boxed face powder, milk powder, perfumed powder, Western-style cold cream, Western-style cosmetic oils, Daughter Oil (Nü'er you), Butterfly oil, Lubricant Hair Oil, l'eau de toilette, Ten Drops (Shidishui, a popular medicine for summer ailments), grape juice, wine, and other items (Chen Xiaocui, Fan, and Zhou 1982, 222–223). The extent of this empire begs the question of whether it really was built mostly on nativist ingenuity and local resourcefulness, as the cuttlefish bones story so romantically implies. Did Chen tap into global circuits of chemical knowledge, machinery, and technology and eventually into marketing and legal resources even as he cultivated a reputation of "vernacular industrialism"? If so, how? Were there also points when he failed in his career?

To answer these questions, this chapter draws in part from biographies, including the one written by his son Chen Dingshan that includes the cuttlefish bones story, as well as from a People's Republic of China *wenshi ziliao* (literary and historical materials) account, based in part on an oral interview with Chen's daughter, Chen Xiaocui. I am cognizant of the challenges that such memoirs and retrospective biographies pose as sources. In both the son's memoir and the *wenshi ziliao* account, Chen is presented in sympathetic, virtuous, and even heroic terms that emphasize his patriotic motivations, "home-grown" sensibility, wily resourcefulness, and ability to innovate and manufacture as a pioneer independently without foreign or state assistance. They weave a typical founder's narrative in which a young Chen is depicted to be someone with little means beyond a pioneering idea—the cuttlefish bones as a source for calcium carbonate—but nonetheless goes on to build an industrial empire out of sheer determination and ingenuity. The son's account, moreover, celebrates his father as a "native products recluse" (*guohuo zhi yinzhe*). It recalls how Chen's ivory seal had those very words inscribed on it and quotes Xie Zhuchen (1897–1971), a former vice minister of the judiciary who had chosen the moniker, saying, "Promoting National Products was everyone's responsibility, but to be a recluse is not easily achieved" (quoted in Chen Dingshan [1955] 1967, 179). This characterization unabashedly evoked the image of late-imperial-era "recluses" who would remove themselves from officialdom to lead virtuous, if secluded, Daoist-inspired lives. And the message was unambiguous. Just like the earlier recluses, Chen was being promoted for his dedicated building of industry in the face of minimal or weak state support—not for profit, fame, or recognition, but out of more genuine and lofty ideals. This image coincided with Chen's own romantic evocations in his choice of pen names and sobriquets that emphasized Daoist ideals of transcending the prosaic matters of the political and commercial world.

Although these biographical sources are easily characterized as subjective and often overtly hagiographical, I am nonetheless hesitant to dismiss out of hand their value as historical materials. Despite the obvious biases, biographical accounts still provide information on how Chen came to found his company and manufacture his products. By moving beyond the rhetorical flourishes, one can still retrieve a great deal of information from them. In addition to paying attention to the minor details (rather than to the overall arc), I supplement the information from the memoirs with other kinds of materials: an internal Household Industries handwritten history of the company produced in 1957; *Peppermint Industry* (Chen Diexian 1933a), Chen's translation of the Japanese book on producing peppermint essence; a survey and report on Household Industries done in 1923; as well as industry bulletins and contemporary articles on the company. It should be noted that these other accounts strive to portray the company and Chen in a certain way, although they are less overtly hagiographical. By juxtaposing these sources while keeping in mind the social function and political agenda behind each type of source, it is possible to identify what information is reliable and useful for our purposes.

Taken together, these sources allow us to explore how Chen moved from experimenting and tinkering with cuttlefish bones on the Zhenhai seacoast to the founding of his company, Household Industries. His tinkering entailed conducting research, adapting and emulating (*fangzhi*) foreign technologies, and testing (*shiyan*) and experimenting to improve (*gailiang*) the original technologies in order to adapt them to local conditions. This approach of emulating and improving (rather than inventing anew) a commodity or line of industry would inform how Chen Diexian and others understood his particular success in industry. It also came to frame more generally the means by which people perceived how Chinese industry might succeed vis-à-vis foreign powers. Finally, although this approach of gradual and modest improvement and local adaptation of technologies was a key factor behind Household Industries becoming a pharmaceutical powerhouse, Chen also shrewdly branded these attributes, turning them into the basis of a carefully cultivated reputation of humble nativism and vernacular industry. Such a reputation coincided with the virtues of self-reliance and, by extension, industrial autarky that were being celebrated more generally in China of the 1920s and 1930s. Emerging in response to the flood of foreign goods on Chinese soil, the NPM, with its boycotts and slogans "Buy Chinese" and "Resist Foreign Goods," had as its primary purpose the desire to make Chinese manufacturing and by extension the nation self-sufficient and strong. It was in this context that the reputation Chen was cultivating proved able to go a long way. That reputation would also help paper over aspects of his career that were marked by failure and frustration.

THE COMPANY: THE ASSOCIATION FOR HOUSEHOLD INDUSTRIES

In the first decade of the Republican era, a cosmetics and daily-goods industry started to flourish in China. Chinese and foreign companies started to open up factories that produced commodities such as soap and cosmetics. European companies were not only moving into the East Asian markets at this time but also producing locally. Lever Brothers of Britain, known in Chinese as Lihua youxian gongsi, initially looked to Japan for an eastern base, opening up the Rība Manufacturing Soap Warehouse in Japan to promote sales of soap in the Far East (Wilson 1954, 140–141, 192). In 1911, the company also opened up the Chinese Soap Stock Company, Ltd. (Zhongguo feizao gufen youxian gongsi) in Hong Kong. The outbreak of World War I in Europe, however, delayed the formation of Lever's in China proper, though Lever was able to open a branch in Shanghai by 1923.[6] With the weakening presence of European companies and growing demands for daily necessities prompting prices to spiral, unprecedented opportunities for East Asian manufacturers emerged. For aspiring imperialist powers such as Japan, China became an increasingly attractive and important market, and commerce there quickly became entangled with Japanese imperialist ambitions. Japanese pharmaceutical manufacturers increased production from 19.9 million yen in 1914 to 51.2 million yen by 1920 (T. Yang 2013, 168), and many of these companies moved aggressively into markets in China while European manufacturers were distracted by the war at home.

The sudden influx of Western and especially Japanese goods spurred a deep sense of patriotism among Chinese domestic manufacturers, including Chen. As foreign goods flooded China's markets in the 1910s, Chinese merchants and industrialists started to focus on developing domestic light manufacturing, especially in the textile industry. Toothpowder did not initially draw as much attention despite the fact that its production process was extremely simple (Chen Xiaocui, Fan, and Zhou 1982, 217–218).[7] Only a few Chinese companies were producing cosmetics or soap. An early soap factory, the Nanyang Soap and Candle Factory (Nanyang zhuzao chang) in Jiangsu Province was established in 1910.[8] China Chemical Industries Co. followed in 1911, also in the Jiangsu area. It was in this relative vacuum that the Japanese quickly came to dominate the toothpowder market of the 1910s with the Lion (Shizipai) brand and the Diamond (Jingangshi) brand, outmaneuvering many Western products (Link 1981, 158–59).

It was around this time that Chen Diexian decided to turn to the manufacturing of toothpowder specifically and cosmetics more generally. One biographical account noted that Chen turned to building Chinese industry specifically in response to how the Chinese president Yuan Shikai was forced to accept the humiliating set of twenty-one demands from Japan in 1915 (Chen Xiaocui, Fan, and Zhou 1982, 217). Whether that was indeed the case, by May 1918 Chen formally listed the pharmaceutical and household-goods company Household Industries as a joint-stock, limited-liability corporation.[9] He founded the company with funds he had earned from his fiction and editing work (Hanan 1999, 4).[10] Household Industries was to become one of China's most successful cosmetics and household-goods companies, its products selling far and wide throughout China and Southeast Asia.[11] By 1933, the *China Industrial Handbooks Kiangsu*, compiled and published by the Ministry of Industry Bureau of Foreign Trade, identified Household Industries as one of China's most notable cosmetics companies (508). Aware that he could capitalize on the growing sense of anti-imperialism, Chen presented Household Industries as an NPM company and his goods as National Products, claiming boldly that they would stave off the economic incursion of Japanese and Western brands. Over time, the company manufactured several hundred types of consumer products. In addition to the dual-functioning Butterfly Toothpowder, they included paper and daily-use chemicals and goods, such as mosquito repellant and peppermint oil ("Jiating gongyeshe" 1935, 115).

In the beginning, however, Household Industries was a typical small-scale venture. It started off as an intimate family and home-based operation centered on manual production.[12] An account of the corporation's history handwritten in 1957 recounts how at the point of its formal founding Household Industries employed a mere ten workers beyond family members and increased to thirty in the first few years (Shanghai shi tongjibu 1957, 134–136). During the initial start-up period, almost all of the manufacturing was done by hand, with the use of only a few simple manufacturing tools. In the *wenshi ziliao* account put together in 1982, his daughter, Xiaocui, reinforced this account, describing how Chen and his family started off producing at home in a sideline occupation, much as they had worked together as a family on his editorial and translation efforts (Chen Xiaocui, Fan, and Zhou 1982, 217). His wife was in charge of producing the fragrance of the company's initial products, including the dental powder and vanishing cream, and his daughter vetted the quality of the powder (*Tianxuwosheng jinian kan* 1940, 3).

Almost immediately, Household Industries saw its profits soar and the scale of its enterprise start to compound. According to a short history of the cosmetics industry in the *Handbook of Chinese Manufacturers* published by the Foreign Trade Association of China in 1949, Household Industries took advantage of the May Fourth Movement and the attendant rise in patriotism to present NPM dental powder as superior to the powder produced by Japanese competitors (57). The only area of the country that the toothpowder was not able to break through Japanese dominance was the northeastern provinces, where the Japanese imperialist presence was strong and Japanese merchants dominated (Chen Xiaocui, Fan, and Zhou 1982, 221). With its quick ascent, the company also began to mechanize as early as 1920, when it raised more capital, and built China's Number One Magnesium Factory (Zhongguo diyi zhimei chang), the first of its kind in China (Ye 1923, 46). By 1921, the company rented more property to expand its production facilities, which allowed it to mechanize further, with additions including self-designed powder-sifting machines and mixing machines obtained from a local Shanghai factory.

Although at this point there were large industrial complexes in China (primarily in Manchuria and in the Yangzi region, including the large arsenals mentioned earlier), most Chinese industry was on a small scale in the early twentieth century. By the 1930s, these small-scale factories were concentrated predominantly in Shanghai, Nanjing, Guangzhou, Ningbo, and other cities and included match factories, soap and candle factories, knitting mills, cigarette factories, chemical works, paper mills, silk mills, water works, woolen factories, and so on.[13] As Frank Dikötter notes, the majority of such factories employed no more than thirty workers. They tended to carry out only one stage of the manufacturing process, and each worker would produce a standardized part, which would then be added to the assembled whole. Dikötter notes, too, that modest types of machinery were everywhere (2007, 115–21). Most factories used small machines for small-scale, labor-intensive work. These small machines included relatively cheap hand machines such as sewing machines and spinning machinery. More complicated machines included dyeing equipment and cotton gins. Finally, as modest mechanization became the norm, locally produced machinery increasingly started to replace imports.

In this context, Household Industries qualified as a medium-size firm already by 1923. By that point, the company had moved beyond a family-members-only production to employ 80 men and 280 women for a total of 360 workers (Ye 1923, 45). In the toothpowder factory, most workers were women, which was typical of most of the light-manufacturing factories at the time, especially in the textile industry. A female manager was in charge, which was also typical. Male workers were used in the toothbrush factory and glass factory. According to one survey of the company, having men was more important in the glass factory, where more strength was required for glass blowing and cutting (Ye 1923, 43–44). Wages totaled around 3,000 yuan a month, expenditures for advertising the factory were around 4,000 yuan, and total capital was 20,000.

The company was able to achieve a considerable degree of vertical integration relatively quickly.[14] By alkanizing brine (*kulu*), Chen manufactured the key raw material of magnesium and established China's Number One Magnesium Factory in 1921. He quickly opened up several other factories. By 1923, they included the Butterfly Peppermint Factory (Wudipai bohe chang) in Taicang, a talcum powder factory in Yingkou, a household-use paper factory in Wuxi, the Household Box Factory (Jiating zhihe chang), a printing press, a toothbrush factory, and, of course, the toothpowder factory (Ye 1923, 46). He also had related factories, including the Hui Springs Soda Water Factory (Huiquan qishui chang) and a textile factory in Hangzhou, where he manufactured Butterfly stockings.[15] He founded a glass factory in 1924, and a paper mill in 1926 (*Tianxuwosheng jinian kan* 1940, 4). The factories allowed Chen to gain control over almost all points of production, and Household Industries quickly expanded far beyond the initial product it manufactured, Butterfly Toothpowder, to produce ten different kinds of dental powders, a slew of other cosmetics and medical goods, as well as toothbrushes. It also ensured that its products were sold widely. By 1923, Household Industries products appeared in markets in Shanghai, Hankou, Zhenjiang, Nanjing, Changsha, Tianjin, and Chengdu and penetrated markets as far as Singapore, Malaysia, and the Philippines (Ye 1923, 43).[16]

By the late 1920s, Household Industries was clearly no longer a modest, family company. It had grown into a major force, becoming the third most important domestic cosmetic company until it faced problems during World War II. With much of the basic industrial facilities completed by 1923, the late 1920s was mostly spent expanding the company (Shanghai shi tongjibu 1957, 134–135). At this point, Chen divided the company into two arms. One was focused on powder products, and the other on cosmetics. Household Industries also mechanized further and purchased machines from abroad. It acquired box-making and glass-bottle-sorting machines for packaging purposes, a trademark-printing machine for marketing, and, by 1929, printing equipment to establish its in-house press for publications, including a dual-color rubber printing machine purchased from a foreign merchant in China (Shanghai shi tongjibu 1957, 135). The talcum-powder factory housed grinding machines; the peppermint factory had two self-manufactured double-steamer boilers; and the printing machines used printing ink from a U.S. company and paper from Sweden (Ye 1923, 45).

In the 1930s, the company's growth into a substantial company could be seen in its new headquarters in Shanghai and its movement into new, if related, industries. Its success resulted in the purchase in 1930 of a Western-style building in the Chinese section of the town on Train Station Road (which would later be changed to National Products Road) to be the site of its headquarters. Chen then purchased the lot next door, on which he built yet another toothpowder factory and a factory to manufacture boxes and opened up his in-house press with the imported press equipment. Household Industries was also branching out to related industries. It used the waste product of magnesium production—the released still water—to manufacture soda water. Then, from the soda water it moved to making wine, brandy, whiskey, and even Butterfly Shaoxing rice wine (Chen Dingshan [1955] 1967, 190). Finally, the company experimented with producing pulp to manufacture paper and tried to move into the paper-products industry, though it proved far less successful on this front.

In 1934, the employee pool at Household Industries ballooned to a peak of 420 people (Shanghai shi tongjibu 1957, 136). Its gross annual output value that year was one of its best at 2,438,706 yuan. [17] At its height, Household Industries was the second-largest cosmetics and daily-goods manufacturer in China, after China Chemical Industries Co. It was also *the* manufacturer among those that manufactured toothpaste, toothpowder, face powder, and vanishing cream and was celebrated as a leading national products company in the cosmetics industry.[18] In the mid-1930s, however, the company's volume of production started to plateau, especially for popular items such as the original Butterfly Toothpowder and Butterfly Cream (Dieshuang), a vanishing cream. From 1935 to 1937, on the eve of war, Household Industries sought to reduce expenses and maintain a stable operation by being more selective in the products it produced.[19] It was able to add some machinery and open new branches in Guangzhou, Chongqing, and Nanchang, but World War II brought growth to a grinding halt, despite attempts to move factory production inland. Various branches were subjected to bombing and destruction ("Jiating gongyeshe qianhui?" 1942, 70). Although the company survived into the post-1949 period and continued to produce until the mid-1950s, it never again reached the height it had achieved in the mid-1930s (Shanghai shi tongjibu 1957, 138).

Although Household Industries became a considerable force in China's pharmaceutical industry during the Republican period, it was notably committed from the start to presenting itself as a small-scale, humble, and modestly mechanized company with an autarkic orientation. Given the tax exemptions the company received from the state, which recognized it as a considerable manufacturer of machine-produced foreign-style goods, this portrait might be somewhat surprising. Yet it makes more sense if one considers the deepening NPM discourse that celebrated nativist manual work over mechanized production, wherein the latter was increasingly associated with the foreign (Fernsebner 2003). It was on this context that Chen promoted what was turning out to be a brand of vernacular industrialism in an era of growing enthusiasm for nativist manufacturing.

The Republican state's understanding of Household Industries was notably at odds with Chen's portrait of a modest, family-run company. Invested in building a modern, mechanized industrial sector, the early Republican state provided tax exemption to companies that machine-produced foreign-style goods. Chen Diexian's Butterfly brand products qualified for this tax exemption very early on. In the *Jiangsu Provincial Bulletin* (*Jiangsu sheng gongbao*) in 1919, provincial official Hu Xianglin noted that he concurred with the Ministry of Agriculture and Commerce and the tax bureau that the Butterfly brand qualified as a foreign-style good produced with modern machinery that needed to be taxed only once:

> We regulate all foreign-style machine-made goods to be taxed as exports . . . pursuant to [this] new tax policy . . . [and] after our thorough examination, Household Industries' tooth powder is produced as a foreign-style good and should be handled accordingly. . . . The tooth powder gets taxed at the first station, receives a transfer ticket . . . [and] at following ports they pass through, as long as one verifies that the product matches the ticket; there is no case of tax avoidance, and the product can be passed through without taxation.[20]

By the end of 1919, the same policy was applied to Household Industries' magnesium carbonate and by 1922 to its Meili Face Cream (Meili shuang).[21] The state clearly saw Household Industries as a modern, machine-based company that produced foreign-style goods.

Perhaps to counter the state's view of the company as a mechanized manufacturer of foreign-style goods in an era of nativist manufacturing, Household Industries worked to cultivate its reputation as a homegrown, modest, and self-sufficient company. Take, for example, a published survey and report of Household Industries that appeared in 1923 in the journal *Economy Report* (*Jingji huibao*). The account characterized the company as relatively small in scale and modest in appearance, if with impressive and hygienic facilities (except for the dust that inevitably flew in the production of powder) (Ye 1923, 43–44). The company's facilities, described the report, employed some new, up-to-date machinery, including a powder-grinding machine that ran on electricity, a paper-layering machine dependent on manpower, and, finally, an electricity-run machine for piercing holes in toothbrushes. Yet the survey also made a point to mention that these machines, although copied from machines produced abroad, were made domestically in China or even in-house (Ye 1923, 47). The powder-grinding machine was made in Shanghai, but the paper-layering machine and the machine to pierce toothbrushes were manufactured in-house. The report also noted that many of the tools in the factories were adapted and self-manufactured.[22]

It was likely that Chen's actions influenced the compilation of the report, and the survey provides us with a sense of how this occurred. To prepare this report, the compiler, Ye Mingdong, visited three Household Industries factories, including its toothpowder factory, toothbrush factory, and glass factory. He also met with Chen Diexian personally. It was in the face-to-face meeting that Chen clearly left an impression. Ye concluded the report by expressing considerable admiration for Chen Diexian's charm and personal touch. He noted that Chen "personally received guests and explained things in great detail. [As a visitor], one can see the trouble that was taken. . . . [Chen] is a patriot . . . and a man of refinement, who unexpectedly threw himself into industry with great energy, invented [his own] methods of manufacturing, and has become a model for his countrymen" (Ye 1923, 44). From this rather rapturous description of Chen, one can imagine how by being personally received and given a tour by Chen, the factory's owner, Ye was charmed and persuaded by Chen's presentation of the factory as family oriented and moderately mechanized.

There were times, however, when the company was portrayed as an icon of modernity. By the 1930s, as the company became a leading domestic manufacturer, the English-language Shanghai newspaper the *China Press* featured the article "Association for Domestic Industry Startles Shanghai with Modernity" (October 10, 1933, B57), which stressed the modernity of the corporation, the purity of its products, and the trustworthiness of its trademark. In its description of the new headquarters for the company on Nankang Road in Shanghai, the article noted, "Everything about the building is up-to-the-minute in modernity." After recounting the array of products from cosmetics for women to alcoholic beverages for male consumers, the piece commended that the Butterfly trademark was "a guarantee of purity and quality." It described how every commodity underwent a "severe laboratory test" so that the "word Butterfly is synonymous with superiority." Butterfly Toothpowder in particular was noted for how its chief ingredients were "made with chemicals and the mechanical process." The author was especially impressed by how the magnesium carbonate produced had been analyzed and certified by a Mr. L. W. Dupre of the Shanghai Chemical Laboratory as "the purest of its kind," and he cited the fact that the company had received awards from the government "as a proof of the superiority of this dentrifice." The entire emphasis in the piece—focusing on the chemical purity of the product tested in laboratories, the mechanical superiority of the company's production process, and its formal recognition by the state—diverged from the emphasis of the report written in 1923. To be sure, both stressed the company's modernity but did so in different ways. If the earlier article highlighted its modest scale and self-made machines, the later article underscored how the firms' products were unadulterated and confirmed by laboratory testing. The presentation of the later article, published as it was in an English-language periodical, was likely catering to a cosmopolitan audience that would have valued such modernity rather than any purported small-scale, nativist qualities.

Clearly, the portrait of Household Industries was somewhat pliable and depended on who the imagined viewer might be. However, there is evidence that the reputation of modesty and humble mechanization found in the initial accounts of the young company continued over time as a viable characterization for Chinese audiences. Later biographical accounts, for example, still presented Household Industries as a modest venture. Chen Dingshan's biography explicitly dwelled on his father's ambivalence toward mechanization. Dingshan writes with pride that because Butterfly Toothpowder had initially been made by hand, it had for a while *not* been tax exempt under state policy (though, as the earlier discussion shows, this claim was false). He also quotes his father as saying, "It is not because we do not know how to make machines [that we don't use them]; it is because I do not want machines to replace our workers and render them unemployed, especially at Household Industries, where, for the past twenty years, every worker has family and children, and their parents and children all work in our facilities" (quoted in Chen Dingshan [1955] 1967, 187). However, again, we know that this statement provides an unlikely portrait if we take into consideration the report from 1923, which described the factory's considerable mechanization. Finally, Chen Dingshan acknowledges later in this same account that his father was eventually granted tax exemption by the GMD state, which sought to bolster factory production, but notes almost apologetically that his father did so only with self-manufactured machines.[23]

Published in postwar Taiwan, son Dingshan's somewhat inaccurate emphasis on the small-scale and homegrown status of the company and portrayal of Chen's reputation for being committed to manual labor over mechanization notably resonate with Yan'an notions of self-reliance and Maoist descriptions of ideal industry in China in the late 1950s.[24] In particular, the point about human labor serving as China's strength and resource maps onto Mao Zedong's now infamous statements about China's population being the country's greatest resource when defending the autarkic path and industrialization undertaken during the Great Leap Forward (1958–1962). Because Chen Dingshan's biography was a Republic of China rather than a People's Republic of China publication, it was likely that his audience was not invested in a Maoist orientation toward self-sufficiency and manual labor per se. The emphasis on modest, homegrown industry instead resonated more with the Republic of China's sponsorship of small-scale manufacturing movements, such as the "living rooms as factories" campaign that relied heavily on female labor (which was often underappreciated and undercompensated), movements that were being identified as the foundation for the country's postwar economic development.[25] Yet even if this account did not directly link up to Maoist ideals of self-reliance, both the account and Maoist ideals were reflective of postcolonial trends in different parts of postwar Asia in which nativist industrial participation among ordinary citizens was being mobilized. Furthermore, this shared emphasis on autarkic industry in both postwar Taiwan and Maoist China can be traced back to an orientation already evident in the National Product Movement. The self-branding and political-cultural cache of Chen's vernacular industrialism in the earlier period thus might be seen as presaging later approaches.

AN ENTERPRISE IN TINKERING: MAGNESIUM CARBONATE AND COASTAL BRINE

If modest and homemade mechanization was important in establishing the nativist reputation of Household Industries, so, too, was the company's dedication to sourcing raw ingredients locally. Although the cuttlefish bones story was in large part apocryphal, we should nonetheless not underestimate the degree to which Chen was committed to securing materials domestically or how resourceful he was in terms of procuring the means to accomplish this. Again, without taking the hagiographical accounts of Chen as a self-reliant pioneer at face value, it is possible to recognize that Chen exhibited considerable ingenuity to achieve as much as he did in raw-material production in what were the relatively inhospitable conditions of the 1920s. Specifically, he was able to leverage skills that he had started to hone as a new type of man of letters in the changing cultural worlds of turn-of-the-century Hangzhou and early-twentieth-century Shanghai into industrial endeavors. Chen also exhibited resourcefulness and willingness to tinker with manufacturing processes and adapt them to local conditions and challenges. As a result, he was able to move from the point where his cuttlefish bones experiment ended in disappointment to a point where he became *the* leading domestic producer of magnesium carbonate, successfully locally sourcing key ingredients for cosmetic production.

In 1918, when Chen founded Household Industries, industry was barely formalized in China. Institutions shaping commerce and capitalism were in flux; ingredients, raw materials, machines, and basic facilities of industrial production were erratically available or prohibitively expensive, and imperialist manufacturers dominated manufacturing inside (as well as outside) China. As noted in chapter 1, when Chen (and others) started tinkering with chemistry in the early 1900s, the only places where one could acquire chemical ingredients were Western pharmacies and exclusive stores such as the China Educational Supply Association in Shanghai. Many of the items sold at these stores were imported from Japan and were exceedingly expensive. As a result, Chinese factories started to produce some of these items domestically. The China Educational Supply Association opened an in-house factory by 1929. It manufactured chemistry and physics supplies, natural-history specimens and replicas, as well as musical instruments, stationary, and drugs and chemical goods, and at far more reasonable prices one could purchase magnesium carbonate, calcium carbonate, and an array of chemical ingredients needed to produce cosmetics. A bottle of calcium carbonate cost seven jiao, a bottle of magnesium carbonate five jiao, a bottle of borax five jiao, and a bottle of sulfuric acid four jiao.[26]

Household Industries also started to manufacture some of its own raw materials and came to play a central role in locally sourcing raw materials for the cosmetic industry. This effort included the manufacturing and selling of talcum powder, peppermint oil, artificial musk, calcium carbonate, and some perfume essences. Most notably, it became *the* manufacturer and supplier of magnesium and magnesium carbonate, operating several factories in Shanghai, Wuxi, and Jinjiang (*China Industrial Handbooks* 1933, 512). It was not alone, though. Other Chinese factories produced key ingredients for cosmetic production as well. China Chemical Works (Zhongguo huaxue gongyeshe) manufactured magnesium carbonate and starch. The Shunchang Stone Pulverizing Works (Shunchang jizhi shifen chang), established in 1924, joined Household Industries to produce the bulk of talcum powder used by China's cosmetic industry (*Handbook of Chinese Manufacturers* 1949, 237). Small factories around Jiangsu, where the peppermint plant was readily available, made peppermint oil, and Nanyang Soap and Candle Factory and the Great Five Continents Drugstore produced a limited amount of glycerin. By the 1930s, only a few key ingredients had to be obtained from abroad including musk and borax.

Chen's efforts illuminate how Chinese manufacturers grabbed the opportunity and initiative (often in ad hoc ways) to build local factories for manufacturing raw materials in the first quarter of the twentieth century. For example, in the biographical accounts we get a glimpse of his resourceful strategies for producing magnesium from local brine. According to his son's memoir, Chen experimented with the discarded brine found in the fields and beaches near Ningbo and the Daishan area to extract magnesium to produce magnesium carbonate. He initially approached local salt merchants to purchase their "waste" materials, which he then converted into the raw material to source the magnesium. To do this, he built a small-scale "factory" onboard a steamboat to extract the magnesium from the brine, using the boat's steam heater as a baking urn. When local merchants started to catch wind of his plans and raised the price for their waste product, Chen went to neighboring Zhoushan, Caiqiao, Xiashi, where he found smaller merchants scattered on the coastline and convinced them to turn over their discarded brine. In return, he provided Butterfly Toothpowder for them at wholesale, which the merchants then sold for profit in neighboring villages. This mutually lucrative arrangement could not be sustained, however, when local competitors allegedly began buying up all the locally produced magnesium in an effort to undermine Chen. As a result of this shift in buying opportunities, in 1921 Chen moved to procure a license for transporting the brine to Wuxi, where he built China's Number One Magnesium Factory, which used a motorized boiler and coal to dry the magnesium (Chen Dingshan [1955] 1967, 190).

Such a telling resonates with the cuttlefish story in its celebration of Chen's resourcefulness in finding a local solution, his commitment to helping the small merchants and local business, his innovation in using a boat's steam heater as a baking urn to produce the magnesium, and his determination to succeed despite challenges and setbacks. As if aware of the rhetorical significance and hagiographical implication of his narration, son Chen Dingshan states explicitly that this detailing of the production of magnesium was meant to demonstrate his father's dedication and determination to succeed:

> I had mentioned before, we needed to supply our own ingredients, but this was not simply a slogan. Why do we start from manufacturing magnesium to manufacturing paper and then from manufacturing paper to self-manufacturing pulp? Here we are talking

about twenty years of struggling: we failed, we succeeded, we succeeded, and we failed. Success and failure affect each other. . . .
Next, I relate to you this experience of manufacturing magnesium
carbonate so that you will know how difficult it was to succeed in
business.
(Chen Dingshan [1955] 1967, 188)

Even if we put aside the hagiographical portrait of Chen Diexian selflessly
helping the local economy and ingeniously innovating with his boat's
heater, the details of the account remain reasonable insofar as they provide us with a sense of the possible conditions under which Chen initially tried to produce magnesium. Chen Diexian and local merchants
could indeed have extracted magnesium on his boat. Magnesium is a
commonly dissolved mineral in seawater, and traditional sources of magnesium are mineral deposits in the ocean. Brine wells are commonly
used to extract magnesium from seawater. One can do this by mixing
seawater with its suspended salts and calcium oxide or lime to alkanize
the solution and produce slurry. The slurry is left to sit so that the solids
settle to the bottom and the water rises to the top. The solids are removed,
filtered, and then washed to remove residual chlorides. The end result is
a loosely packed "cake" of material that, when calcined in a kiln, becomes
magnesium.

To be sure, these memoir accounts are also open to an alternative
reading. For example, they allude to how Chen's actions might have been
brutally opportunistic. If read between the lines, Chen Dingshan's biography hints at how once local salt merchants were able to organize and
rally to raise the prices of the salt "waste" by-product that Chen was seeking to secure, Chen was forced to head farther inland to bypass these
local upstarts and move his industry to cheaper, less-enlightened places,
where smaller merchants could be exploited. The later *wenshi ziliao*
account that Chen Diexian's daughter helped produce notes how his ability to tap into local saltworks included driving down the price for salt
brine, which enabled him to produce magnesium carbonate and ultimately his toothpowder at a far lower price than his competitors. This
in turn resulted in an outstanding return in profit (Chen Xiaocui, Fan,
and Zhou 1982, 219). Such accounts might be read for evidence of how
Chen engaged ruthlessly with local salt merchants, getting the cheapest

possible goods for the lowest possible price and with little commitment to building the local economy. Thus, even as these readings against the grain generate evidence that Chen produced a competitive toothpowder through tinkering and practices of adaptation, they also suggest that his behavior was not as noble as his offspring's memoirs claim.

Ultimately, Chen's tinkering with brine—unlike the failed cuttlefish experimentation—generated concrete results. He opened China's first domestic factory to produce magnesium and eventually came to dominate the domestic production of magnesium carbonate for China's burgeoning cosmetics industry. The memoir that his daughter helped compile claims that magnesium carbonate played a key role in making his toothpowder competitive if not superior to foreign brands (Chen Xiaocui, Fan and Zhou 1982, 218). Echoing Chen's son's memoir, her account similarly describes the process by which he got to this point: how he experienced multiple failures but finally succeeded in using salt brine and alkali, added the process of evaporation, and manufactured the magnesium (219–220). Chen's success in manufacturing magnesium and magnesium carbonate also stemmed in part from his being more than willing to share his knowledge about manufacturing and using magnesium carbonate for toothpowder. For example, he published his formula for making dental powder in his "Warehouse" column (see Kuang 1915, vol. 3 [March], 1–2). The know-how helped advertise not just the end product, the dental powder, but also the ingredients, including magnesium, which Chen not so coincidentally was the leading manufacturer of in China. His commitment to producing raw materials furthermore proved to be not only a smart commercial move but also effective in reinforcing the vernacular reputation he was seeking to cultivate. By the late 1920s, efforts to draft the National Products Standards took place amid debates raging over what standards should be used to determine what exactly constituted an NPM product.[27] Questions arose over whether a Chinese-made item using, for example, Japanese cloth could constitute an NPM good or whether the materials and ingredients had to be domestically made as well. For Chen, using domestic ingredients and materials as much as possible for his end products would guarantee that his commodities, which in its tax assessments the state had identified as being foreign-style goods, could be presented as genuine NPM goods.

Finally, recent chemical analysis of Chen's toothpowder confirms that he did in fact use magnesium carbonate as an important component of the cosmetics he manufactured. Infrared spectography performed by Excel Laboratory Services on the residual content of one of Chen's toothpowder containers (the container featured on the cover of this book) determined that the dental powder's major components were magnesium carbonate, calcium carbonate, and talc (magnesium silicate).[28] Though we may question the motives ascribed to Chen in sourcing these ingredients locally and doubt the hagiographic narratives that later writers spun to explain his choices, it is clear that as far as the actual ingredients used for producing his products go, Chen was remarkably up front about his recipes: magnesium carbonate was indeed the major component used.

AN ENTERPRISE IN TRANSLATION: CHINESE PHARMACOPOEIA AND GLOBAL KNOWLEDGE

Chen's initial ability to secure knowledge on how to produce magnesium and magnesium carbonate and to engage in nativist production of materials and ingredients more broadly was predicated upon accessing both local knowledge of the Chinese pharmacopoeia and global circuits of knowledge. Chen translated foreign technologies and recipes for manufacturing raw materials but adapted them to local conditions, often by improvising with local resources using practices of medicine and pharmacopoeia (including assembling and mixing medical concoctions) that he had been exposed to as a young boy growing up in a household where medicine was practiced. Tapping foreign materials and exotica has a long history in Chinese pharmacological practice.[29] In the early twentieth century, Chen secured foreign knowledge and adapted recipes from abroad. He did so smartly and with a lifetime of pharmacological and chemical knowledge, acquired through both translation and hands-on trial experimentation and testing. To accomplish this, he drew from skills, resources, and knowledge that he had honed as a professional writer, translator, and editor. He literally applied his skills in translation and compilation to transmit the information. But he also did more. He intervened in the translation to adjust and adapt recipes to suit local conditions and to achieve local sourcing and domestic autarky in the production of raw materials. When Chen realized he could not locally source calcium carbonate, he turned to magnesium carbonate as a substitute and ensured that he had the local ingredients to generate the needed magnesium. Just as he translated fiction and other genres in a way that would appeal to a Chinese audience, he fiddled with recipes, added prefaces to compiled recipes, and framed the presentation of them in a manner that made the imported knowledge more appealing to local tastes and concerns.

Chen's proactive approach toward the translation of manufacturing recipes was part of a larger turn-of-the-century culture in China in which translation was a form of intellectual labor that was hardly secondary to original authorship. Starting with the Self-Strengthening Movement, translation was seen as integral to building China and its industrial and technological realms as well as to ensuring its cultural and intellectual vibrancy. Scholars who have written about the Jiangnan Arsenal, the Fuzhou shipyards, and other arsenals have long noted the importance of Chinese intellectuals such as Yan Fu (1854–1921), Western missionaries such as John Fryer, and Chinese converts to Christianity in the translation of technical, legal, and scientific texts for the purposes of building Chinese armaments and the Qing navy and more generally recapturing China's wealth and power (Meng 1999; Elman 2005). By the late Qing, translation continued to be a significant form of intellectual labor, a central means by which to participate in literary and cultural life, and was both a source of considerable profit and enlightenment. In a recent study of Fujianese translator Lin Shu, Michael G. Hill (2013) illuminates how in the burgeoning cultural market of turn-of-the-century Shanghai, Lin not only commodified classical knowledge but also put a premium on translation work. Lin engaged in translation with an entire team of translators, undertaking collective practices such as "tandem translation" (duiyi). He used classical language and ancient-style prose to translate modern foreign fiction to confer authority both to the fiction being translated and to his own reputation as a leading cultural figure. As Hill demonstrates, Lin's robust tactics of translation also served as a means for him to critique the very forms of "Western learning" he was translating.[30]

Chen Diexian was part of this generation of lettered men who saw translation as a powerful literary tool and a valued and legitimate act of intellectual labor. Like Lin Shu, whom he briefly worked for during his early years in Shanghai, Chen did not know a single foreign language.[31] Yet he obviously did not see this as a problem because in 1913 he founded a five-person translation bureau in Shanghai.[32] Lasting until 1918, the bureau translated seventy-three long and short texts, around thirty million words, all into classical Chinese. These texts included English, American, and French publications and were in multiple genres, including society pieces, romantic and detective fiction, as well as household, education, history, and science works. Chen saw the work of translation as inherently collaborative in nature and his lack of knowledge of foreign languages as not problematic. The bureau included his friend Li Chuangjue as well as another colleague, Wu Juemi. Also on board were his then eighteen-year-old elder son, Chen Dingshan, and thirteen-year-old daughter, Chen Xiaocui.

Chen's approach to translation turned on virtues of efficiency and intervention. In an retrospective account, daughter Chen Xiaocui referred to their method of translation as an "assembly line" (more literally, "flowing-water operations," *liushui zuoye*) (Chen Xiaocui, Zhou, and Fan 1982, 213). Such an assembly-line approach entailed the following division of labor: Li Chuangjue—the only one on the team who knew foreign languages—would choose the book or text to be translated and translated it orally into vernacular Chinese, while one of the other three transcribed his translation. Once Li finished one text, he moved on to the next with a second transcriber. In the meantime, the first transcriber focused on rendering the transcribed vernacular version into classical Chinese. Li would then follow the same series of steps with a third text and a third transcriber. The team then started the process over again, with Li working with the first transcriber. Verbal translation by Li was continuous, as was the recording, so the overall process was fluid and fast, like flowing water. Once a text was transcribed and rendered into classical Chinese, Chen Diexian revised, touched up, and polished it.[33] The polished translation would then be sent out for publication. Chen's name would be first on the masthead, and he frequently used the pen name "Taichangxiandie," "Immortal Butterfly of Taichang."[34]

A key assumption behind Chen's translation theory was that translation was a form of mental labor where fidelity to the original could be eschewed as the main goal in favor of active intervention in the act of translation. According to his daughter, Chen Diexian described his translation activity as "translating with intention (*yiyi*)." His aims were to absorb the technique of the writing found in Western literature and adapt it to China's lifestyle and Chinese readers' emotional tastes. To achieve these goals, Chen was more than willing to tinker with the text by taking out whole sections and adding commentary to express his thinking. Chen Xiaocui explained that the goal was not to produce a document identical to the original author's text but to tell the story in a way that would be familiar and compelling to Chinese readers (Chen Xiaocui, Zhou and Fan 1982, 213).

It was with this practice of intervention in translation as well as with the inherited traditions of improvising and adjusting in medical treatment that Chen had been exposed to as a young boy that he approached the procurement of manufacturing knowledge and recipes from abroad. As an editor, Chen was committed to publishing columns on the industrial arts, so translated sources on chemistry, pharmaceuticals, and manufacturing provided content for his columns. He also relied considerably on state-sponsored publications in his industrial and commercial pursuits, and many of these texts were also translated by the state. In the 1910s, state-sponsored journals on industry that sought to disseminate knowledge on manufacturing and industry started to appear as a resource for would-be manufacturers and burgeoning industrialists like Chen. The Ministry of Agriculture and Commerce's publication *Industry in Laymen's Terms* (*Shiye qianshuo*), published from 1915 to 1925, was a source that Chen regularly turned to.[35] The publication featured a range of articles, including ones on the merits of a joint- stock, limited-liability organization (which Household Industries became); how to name a company; how to manufacture toothpowder; and how to copy foreign things but not counterfeit them. Provincial-level publications were also dedicated to spreading knowledge on industry, such as the *Anhui Industrial Journal* (*Anhui shiye zazhi*), which printed manufacturing and commercial tips for all to share.

For Chen, however, translation was not merely a conduit for transferring knowledge but also a site of innovation and improvement.[36] We can see this understanding at the level of the translated recipe: Chen was very willing to intervene and adjust manufacturing formulas that he translated from abroad. This willingness to adjust and interpret recipes and prescriptions had long been central to medical practice in China. As early as the Song dynasty (960–1279), there emerged the persona of the literatus-physician, or *ruyi*, who was celebrated for the virtuous ability to improvise in his evaluation of ways to heal the patient and provide individualized approaches to treatment rather than merely to follow standardized prescription.[37] Such learned improvisation also informed the mixing and assembling of herbal and powder-based medicines and concoctions as well as the adjusting of textual prescriptions to the patient's specific situation. With a father who was a *ruyi*, Chen had grown up in a household where knowledge about the Chinese pharmacopoeia was abundant and the willingness to adapt to situations to heal was a virtue. Chen took the Chinese pharmacological tradition seriously. One biographical account notes that he memorized his family's collections of medical books, including the classic *The Compendium of Materia Medica* (*Bencao gangmu*, c. 1578), and could diagnose and write prescriptions with such facility that he was known for writing "prescriptions just as quickly as he composed poetry verses" (Chen Xiaocui, Fan, and Zhou 1982, 210).[38] In his columns and publications, he promoted knowledge from the Chinese pharmacopoeia as "common knowledge" that was on par with translated industrial and manufacturing knowledge. With this prescription-writing background and his skills more generally as a craftsman of words, Chen proved comfortable with adjusting manufacturing industrial processes to suit local conditions and resources (as in his manufacturing of toothpowder), just as he recombined and adjusted texts in his lettered acts of translation and compilation.

Chen was not alone in engaging in interventionist strategies of translation to secure manufacturing and chemical knowledge from abroad. Students of chemistry throughout China were forced to engage in interpretive acts of translation, drawing from preexisting knowledge and local conditions to make faulty or poor translations legible and applicable. In the article "A Chemist in China," the missionary W. G. Sewell relates how chemistry textbooks were a problem in formal chemical education, given students' language skills, and that the only available texts were Chinese editions of Japanese translations of British and American texts. Such editions were riddled with mistranslations and ineffective transliterations. Chemical terms were mostly incomprehensible, so Chinese students found that they had to write in Chinese their own texts on inorganic,

organic, analytical, and physical chemistry, along with laboratory manuals and technical handbooks on dyeing and leather manufacture. Sewell notes that the supplementing of translated texts did not take place in a vacuum: "We were involved with ancient industries, such as paper manufacture, silk dyeing, natural gas and the preparation of salt, all known in Szechwan before the Christian era, as well as with the newer ones, such as the manufacture of alkalis, sulphuric acid (Chamber process), cement, ammonium sulphate, suphur dyes and tanning, in addition to everyday requirements like ink and silk" (1972, 531).[39] The students' adaptation of foreign texts relied on long-standing knowledge of processes that resonated with and overlapped with modern chemistry.

For Chen, just as important as the act of translation were the application and research that ensued once a recipe was translated. These steps included a willingness to embrace mistakes and learn through trial and error. According to son Chen Dingshan, "[my father] did not know English or any other foreign language, but through research he could grasp from the side and become aware of [things]" ([1955] 1967, 182). Chen's modus operandi was to translate foreign recipes and manufacturing processes via collaboration, play around with local ingredients, and engage in test after test to refine the process of production. The last step included learning from failure—as the experimentation with cuttlefish illustrates. This multifaceted approach of translation, tinkering, and testing can be seen specifically in how Chen approached manufacturing ingredients for his toothpowder. After realizing that using local cuttlefish was not going to work out, Chen turned to Japanese reference books, which he had his team translate, and then engaged in repeated tests to manufacture and refine magnesium carbonate (Chen Xiaocui, Fan, and Zhou 1982, 219). To secure peppermint, another key ingredient for toothpowder, Chen had initially sought to purchase domestic peppermint from local producers but found the peppermint too ripe and the flavor not sharp enough. He thus decided to open his own peppermint factory in Taicang in 1919, and to perfect his product he relied heavily on his team's translation of a book about Japan's peppermint industry.

Chen's preface to *Peppermint Industry*, the translation of the Japanese reference book, points directly to the tightly bound relationship between translation and industrial production, and the tinkering needed to adapt and emulate foreign techniques in a domestic setting. There he wrote,

> In the first year of the Republic, we planned to use cuttlefish bones to make toothpowder. After some initial trials, we discovered that the output [of calcium carbonate] is low, so we used brine and pure alkali to produce magnesium carbonate successfully. The remaining item we needed to secure [for toothpowder] was peppermint, but it was taking time. We tried to buy the oil from two places, Taichang and Ji'an, and refine the essence of peppermint ourselves, but the results were not satisfactory. We then went to Japan, got hold of a specialist book, and translated it to use as a reference. (Chen Diexian 1933a, 1).

The preface describes how Household Industries went on to establish a mint factory in-house but also how in the ensuing ten years China's mint factories grew in number, making Household Industries' own specialty factory obsolete. By 1949, China had several successful peppermint- and peppermint-oil-producing companies, including the Dah Fong Peppermint Factory (Dafeng bohe gongsi) and the New China Peppermint Co., Ltd. (Xinhua bohe chang gufen youxian gongsi).[40] This success in building China's peppermint industry was no doubt also helped by the fact that Chen shared the information as "common knowledge" by publishing the translation of *Peppermint Industry.*

The recipes and industrial manuals that Chen relied upon were often from Japan, and those Japanese texts were in turn most likely translations of recipes and books from America or Germany, which could also very well have been translated from another source. Chapter 2 discusses the recipe for manufacturing hair tonic that appeared in Chen's column "The Warehouse for Manufacturing Cosmetics" in *Women's World* (*Nüzi shijie*). As noted, its list of ingredients included Latin, German, and English glosses for the ingredients alongside the Chinese, so it is likely that the recipe (or parts of the recipe) was translated from abroad. Although I have not been able to trace the original source of this particular recipe, one can nonetheless identify similar kinds of recipes with similar ingredients in the Western-language pharmaceutical gazettes and digests circulating globally in the latter part of the nineteenth century and into the twentieth. On June 1, 1886, *Pharmaceutical Record and Weekly Market Review*, a semimonthly journal of "pharmacy, chemistry, materia medica, and the allied sciences," selected recipes for cosmetics to be used to take care of one's hair and mustache from Eugene Dietrichs's *The New Pharmaceutical Manual*. These included ingredients such as "spiritus," "aquae rosae," "olei rosae"' (if not "spiritus rosae"), and glycerin—ingredients also found in the "Warehouse" recipe.[41] Other similar journal titles were the *American Druggist and Pharmaceutical Record*, a turn-of-the-century illustrated journal of "practical pharmacy" also published in New York. Chen's failure to identify the absolute "original" of a recipe should thus not be seen as an obstacle to our analysis and may be precisely the point. There was no "original." Instead, these pieces circulated and crossed linguistic, geographical, and epistemological borders, and as they did, constant alteration and innovation occurred in them. The key issue, therefore, is that innovation and adjustment take place at the point of translation.

Notably, some of the fictional texts that Chen's translation bureau translated may have helped to reinforce the ideals of tinkering and empirical work that were so valuable for Chen's industrial innovation as well as to bolster his curiosity in science. Specifically, the bureau translated and compiled *The Complete Series of Sherlock Holmes Cases* (*Fu'ermosi zhentan'an quanji*). This was a smart commercial choice. Detective novels and British crime fiction were extremely popular at the time (Kinkley 2000, 26–28).[42] New magazines with names such as *Detective World* (*Zhentan shijie*) and *Detective Monthly* (*Zhentan yuekan*) were wholly dedicated to the genre (Hung 1998, 74). Foreign crime novels overlapped considerably with the late-imperial Chinese genre "court case literature" (*gong'an xiaoshuo*), especially those works featuring the famous, virtuous, and clever hero Judge Bao. But, beyond the Judge Bao novels, the Sherlock Holmes stories also introduced an appreciation for science and, in the mythic figure of Holmes, a celebration of uncanny powers of observation and the ability to deduce, reason, and draw conclusions based on empirical clues. Chinese author-translators appreciated the Sherlock Holmes stories as educational material, and some of them, including celebrated poet Liu Bannong (1891–1934), claimed that Sir Arthur Conan Doyle's mission in writing these stories was to instruct nascent detectives in the art of the trade (Hung 1998, 74). Authors noted in prefaces to the translations that the scientific method of detection deserved praise, suggesting how Chinese author-translators appreciated the pedagogical potential of the Holmes stories and of crime fiction more generally. As one of the key translators of the Sherlock Holmes series in early-twentieth-century China, Chen Diexian no doubt admired Holmes's and sidekick Watson's ability to deploy forensic science and chemistry with great aplomb to solve their cases. Although there is no evidence that he read these stories as a sort of do-it-yourself manual, Holmes and Watson certainly exemplified the self-sufficient tinkering and experimentation that Chen came to embody and promote.

IMPROVEMENT AND EMULATION: A MASTER OF CHEMICAL EXPERIMENTATION

Chen's daughter, Xiaocui, noted retrospectively how Chen believed it was far better to revamp smaller-scale manufacturing, especially of practical products, than to build from scratch (Chen Xiaocui, Fan, and Zhou 1982, 221). According to her description, his approach was multifaceted. Chen would start by studying chemistry intensively and experiment; he came to refer to himself literally as a "master of chemical experimentation (*huayanshi*)" (Chen Xiaocui, Fan, and Zhou 1982, 219). With this basis, Chen then sought to improve a product, technology, or small-scale industry rather than radically discover or invent anew. This approach was often predicated on copying and studying an often foreign manufacturing process or gadget, tinkering with it to improve it to the point of real innovation and, arguably, invention (*faming*). It was an approach that turned on emulation, adaptation, and improvement.

This same approach toward innovation that turned on tinkering and improvement informed how other actors in East Asia at the time understood their actions. Colonial-era Korean self-made inventors who emerged in the mid-1920s, for example, engaged in "research," the long process of trial and error, to improve a gadget or to come up with modest inventions that were not necessarily grounded in formal "science" but nonetheless were submitted to the Imperial Patent Office in Tokyo for patents. Jung Lee (2013) characterizes these patented inventions as "inventions without science" to underscore that the notion of invention in colonial Korea was quite different from the conventional conceit that has long dominated the history of technology literature: the individual genius whose inventions lead to scientific breakthroughs. The notion of invention in colonial Korea was instead far more modest, not located in large science laboratories but rather done at the small-scale and everyday level. It was also the basis for small-time inventors to gain respect and acknowledgment for their activities and improve their economic and political standing.

Like these Korean "inventors without science," Chen, too, seemed to recognize the capaciousness of what it meant to innovate. The term *faming* was included on the trademarked logo that Chen used to market Butterfly Toothpowder (see figure 4.1 or, for the full container, see

FIGURE 4.1 Butterfly Toothpowder, color logo. Source: Photograph by Yanjie Huang.

the book cover).[43] The logo consists of a tennis racquet surrounded by flowers and a butterfly. On the head of the racquet are larger red Chinese characters for "face and toothpowder" (*camian yafen*). "Butterfly (Wudipai)" is written in smaller font above these characters. To the left is "Manufactured by Household Industries (Jiating gongyeshe zhi)" and to the right "Invented by Tianxuwosheng (Tianxuwosheng faming)." (The literal translation of "Wudipai" is "Butterfly brand," but the trademarked English name was "Butterfly," as discussed in chapter 5.) In modern Chinese, the term *faming* means "invent." However, Chen "invented" the toothpowder by adapting foreign recipes, adjusting the procedure to local materials, and tinkering until he produced a much-improved product. His Butterfly Toothpowder cum powder was thus an "invention" along the same lines of improvement and modest innovation that Lee discusses.[44] For Chen and the Korean inventors, practices of copying, adapting through tinkering, and improving a product were the same thing as innovation. Innovation and invention were thus not distinct from copying and adapting but crucially dependent on them.

As Chen sought to move beyond toothpowder into higher-end cosmetics, he continued emulating and improving products from abroad. When the Household Industries' product Daughter Cold Cream (Nü'er shuang) was not selling well, for example, Chen promptly stopped its production and had Household Industries pour its resources into emulating the successful Three Flowers Vanishing Cream (see figure 4.2), a product initially created by Richard Hudnot (1855–1928), one of America's earliest druggists and perfumers to find international success.[45] Three Flowers had been dominating the Chinese vanishing-cream market under the Chinese name "Sanhuapai xuehuagao." Chen proved able to master the production formula for Three Flowers, play around with the ingredients, and then generate his own improved version, Butterfly Cream (Dieshuang) (see figure 4.3), which went on to become one of Household Industries' highest-selling products.[46] He was meticulous in his efforts. The first ten thousand bottles manufactured by Household Industries proved shoddy in quality and were not well received (Chen Xiaocui, Fan, and Zhou 1982, 223), so Chen sought to improve the product, including its packaging, by ordering thirty thousand glass bottles manufactured by a Japanese glass factory that were affordable and yet

FIGURE 4.2 Three Flowers Vanishing Cream, c. 1920s. Source: Power of One Designs website, https://www.powerofonedesigns.com/.

FIGURE 4.3 Butterfly Cream, package c. 1920s. Source: Darmon 2004, 71.

exquisite and spotlessly white. He studied and researched these bottles, and in three years Household Industries was able to move to manufacturing their own. The company thus achieved a "natively" produced National Product as a result, and in terms of color, scent, and exterior appearance the finished product closely resembled Three Flowers and yet was sold at half the price of the American brand.[47] At this lower price, Butterfly Cream was able to undercut Three Flowers in the Chinese market (Zuo 2016, 169).

There is no evidence that Chen ever had access to the original Three Flowers recipe. It is more likely that he studied the actual cream and reverse-engineered the product to come up with a version that Household Industries could manufacture. The practice of studying or researching the actual foreign product and playing with the ingredients to figure out how to manufacture the item domestically appeared to be a well-accepted practice in China. The *Ladies' Journal*, discussed in chapter 2, included a manufacturing tip on how to produce Burroughs Wellcome & Co.'s (BW&C) internationally popular Hazeline Snow vanishing cream. The article, "The Method for Producing Cosmetics," featured an entry on manufacturing vanishing creams that were readily available on the Chinese market. Two were Chinese brands, the Three Star Brand (Sanxing) and Shuangmeimo, and the third was Hazeline Snow (Xiashilian) (see figure 4.4). The entry explained:

> They all are different in their characteristics. The Three Star Brand is known for its short shelf life and cannot be stored long. Hazeline Snow melts and turns into a liquid easily.[48] Shuangmeimo, although not really so, is thought to be too greasy to apply to the face, and since it causes a glow, it is not as good as the above two. Although Hazeline Snow does not have these problems, its quality has not been as good as it once was. Yet, recently, people are researching Hazeline to study what it contains. In the end, it only requires the simple mixing of the following ingredients, Hazeline, Stearic Acid, Glycerine, Sodium bicarbonate and soda water *to manufacture*. . . . Because the procedure is slightly complicated, and difficult to understand, it has not been well understood.
> (Shen Ruiqing 1915, 24–25, emphasis added)

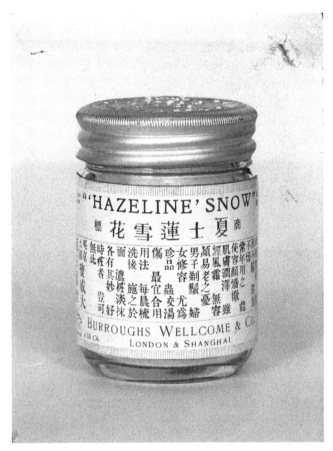

FIGURE 4.4 An "authentic" BW&C Hazeline Snow pot sold on the Chinese market around 1923–1924. Source: Wellcome Collection, London.

The passage notes how careful research had been undertaken domestically to identify the ingredients of Hazeline Snow. The journal was also comfortable with sharing those ingredients widely. The familiar ingredients were listed first in Chinese, and then a Western language gloss was offered for the less-familiar ingredients. The English name "Hazeline" was printed after the Chinese compound for the name, Haishiling. Stearic acid was listed first in Chinese as *fangsuan* and then followed by "Stearic Adib [*sic*]."[49] "Sodii Bicarb [*sic*]" followed the Chinese gloss for "sodium bicarbonate."[50] The piece demonstrates well how the practice of studying and researching brand items for the sake of approximating them was quite acceptable. Finally, it is worth noting that in this quote I have translated the Chinese term *faming*, which means "to invent" in modern Chinese, as "to *manufacture*," which I have emphasized with italics. The conventional rendering of the term as "to invent" is not appropriate here, and "to manufacture" reflects the flexible connotation of *faming* at the time.

Chinese journals were not the only ones seeking to identify and share the ingredients and recipe of Hazeline Snow and other popular commodities. By the late nineteenth century, as brand commodities spread worldwide, so too did recipes, trade secrets, and formulas for manufacturing. Emerging manufacturers around the world sought access to manufacturing processes of successful brand-name items, but those companies that were manufacturing successfully became increasingly wary of the spread of their brand formulas and the possibility of what we might today call industrial espionage. In 1892, BW&C introduced Hazeline Snow as the first commercial stearate cream. By the 1910s, Hazeline Snow had become one of the most popular vanishing creams worldwide. It was also one of the most copied creams.[51]

With the emergence of modern intellectual-property law in the late nineteenth century, simpler manufacturing processes, including those behind daily commodities such as vanishing cream and other cosmetics, were usually *not* subjected to patent protection. By the 1880s, for example, U.S. courts made a distinction between mere recipes or simple formulas where ingredients retained their discrete characters despite assemblage with other ingredients and formulas for a specific product that included the production of something new through assemblage. Patents were granted only to the latter.[52] Large pharmaceutical companies such as BW&C thus had to rely on using trademark law to stake a legal claim over its manufacturing processes and to halt their widespread circulation. Such tactics could prove effective. The St. Louis–based journal *National Druggist* shared an entry on Hazeline Snow and its formula in the August issue of 1907 ("Hazeline Snow, a Toilet Cream" 1907, 272). Translated from the French *Journal de Phamacie d'Anvers*, the entry itself was indicative of the global reach and movement of such information. By the December issue, however, the *National Druggist* published the article "Hazeline Snow a Trade-Mark, and Name Not Public Property," in which it cited the August issue's inclusion of the extract from the *Journal de Phamacie d'Anvers*. Essentially a retraction and apology, the announcement stated:

> Our attention has been called to fact that the title Hazeline Snow is the trademark of Burroughs Wellcome & Co and, hence, being their exclusive property can not [*sic*] be employed by any other person or firm. We take pleasure in publishing this notice, and we will ask our readers to take care not to use this title to designate any preparation of their own or anybody else's besides that of Burroughs Wellcome & Co in order that they may avoid the imputation of trademark infringement and a possible suit for injunction and damages.
>
> ("Hazeline Snow a Trade-Mark" 1907, 411)

BW&C had learned of the earlier publication of its recipe, intervened with the threat of legal action, and forced the *National Druggist* to publish this notice.[53] With the global circulation of manufacturing information of specific brand-name products, large pharmaceutical companies were starting to crack down on the free movement of such knowledge and to promote practices of corporate ownership over ideas, practices that were to buttress what was an emerging industrial-property regime.[54]

Although BW&C had cracked down in the United States already by 1905, the entry on Hazeline Snow in the *Ladies' Journal* shows that manufacturing knowledge of brand products—procured either through translating foreign sources or from domestic testing and research (or both)—was still being shared in print in China as late as 1915 because China's print markets were perhaps harder for BW&C to police. What this also suggests is that Chinese translators and compilers such as Chen were participating in what was a global network of circulating manufacturing information about brand products and that their adaptation of foreign recipes was not considered particularly egregious. Instead, as we see next, such adaptation was the basis of improvement and industry building in China and came to be celebrated by NPM leaders and the Nationalist state as a key element of innovation in the Republican period.

TOYING WITH GADGETS: SERIAL TINKERING, INNOVATION, AND BETTERING NATIVIST INDUSTRY

Chen proved to be a serial tinkerer. He was not content with merely fiddling with cosmetic and chemical recipes but also toyed with an array of gadgets, some for fun and some to manufacture. The process by which he did so paralleled the steps he took to adapt foreign recipes, to test and experiment with local ingredients, and, ultimately, to manufacture domestically. Take, for example, his experimentation with manufacturing a copy machine (Chen Xiaocui, Fan, and Zhou 1982, 221). To pursue his goal of producing a copier, Chen first found a French-made copier that was light and convenient. By playing around with the French copier, he improved it. He figured out how to add a sifting screen of fine silk that he originally used to manufacture toothpowder to "sift" the ink and make multiple copies without damaging the original document. When he dabbled in the flat offset machine-based printing, he borrowed an American-manufactured offset printing press from Shanghai's Commercial Bank.[55] To copy the machine, he carefully examined the parts. He calculated how much the rollers and ink cost (they were imported from Britain) and how often they had to be changed and then sought to source these parts locally and less expensively. After tinkering with the machine again and again, he produced ink that was able to withstand greater temperature than the imported ink. With the superior ink, his machine could print more sheets. He also improved the flat-surface roller, which in the original tended to break easily because of its sticky surface. He worked to improve the quality of the roller and manufactured an improved and cheaper domestic machine, which he called the Butterfly Flat Offset Printing Press (Wudipai pingmian jiaoyinji). He followed the same process in fiddling with the cap-affixing machine to manufacture the cap on soda bottles as part of his foray into the soda-water industry. Characteristically, Chen started by purchasing a foreign machine and then reverse-engineered it. In copying the machine, he found that he could improve it and then manufacture it at a much lower cost. The foreign machine required the machinist to use his or her feet to motor the machine, but it proved clunky and inconvenient to use. Chen thus redesigned it as a hand-cranked machine. He also refined the machine to manufacture both big and small bottle caps and to be able to change a used cap into a new shape and thereby potentially to recycle caps (Chen Xiaocui, Fan, and Zhou 1982, 221–222).

Chen's proclivity for experimenting with domestic and imported technologies and manufacturing processes was at the heart of his ability to build and innovate his company more generally. After finding success with manufacturing magnesium and refining peppermint essence, Chen went on to experiment with manufacturing soda water. By 1921, he opened up the Hui Springs Soda Water Factory and planned to take on the English company Watson's monopoly over the soda-water market. He also moved into paper production and tinkered with white mulberry, hemp, bamboo, and a variety of grasses to improve the production of white paper. He established a National Product factory to manufacture nativist paper and participated in the boycott of foreign-manufactured white paper. He did the same with the production of mosquito repellant and incense.

To be sure, not all of Chen's endeavors met with success. His experiments in pulp and paper manufacturing and mosquito repellant failed to replicate the success he found with toothpowder and cosmetics (Chen Xiaocui, Fan, and Zhou 1982, 220). Furthermore, this nativist approach of adapting foreign technologies and producing them at lower cost, although a hallmark of the NPM, did not always guarantee consumers. Chinese consumers consistently doubted the quality of NPM products even if those products were available at a lower price.[56] Chen's daughter noted that Chen was frustrated with the entrenched belief that domestically produced goods were inferior to foreign brands and imports. She quoted him complaining bitterly, "Society has no faith in domestically produced goods. How can they be cheaper yet better? . . . It is this kind of thinking that impoverishes our nation" (quoted in Chen Xiaocui, Fan, and Zhou 1982, 222).

Yet, regardless of some setbacks, Chen's approach toward innovation was increasingly recognized as a legitimate means to build China's industry. Emerging at this time was a larger discourse on improving (*gailiang*) manufacturing technologies rather than attempting original invention or discovery. In the 1910s, the Ministry of Agriculture and Commerce publication *Industry in Layman's Terms* (*Shiye qianshuo*, 01915–1925), a text with which Chen was intimately familiar and was later to recompile for publication, included the entry "To Improve Native

Products, It Is Fitting to Start with Ordinary Everyday Items." The piece addressed the need to focus on everyday items such as toothpowder as the key to improving Chinese manufacturing and noted: "There is no need to focus on expensive items. First, start with improving everyday items, including the above listed toothpowder, perfume, and the like. China itself can manufacture these items. . . . [T]hose who use these [products] are many, and [so] it is naturally easy to sell [them]. The path to profit is thus broad and National Products can naturally flourish . . . so to improve National Products everyday items are crucial" (*Shiye qianshuo* 1915–1925, 11:12). Chen's building of Household Industries, as we have seen, embodied both this emphasis on improvement and the focus on daily items.

Chen's approach toward evolving manufacturing techniques as the basis for success was to receive both state endorsement and regulation over the years. A Ministry of Industry account in 1936 explicitly praised Chen's efforts in tinkering and testing to improve raw materials and manufacturing techniques. More than twenty years after the quoted entry from *Industry in Laymen's Terms* was published in 1915, the article "Shanghai Merchant Chen Diexian Improves Raw Ingredients for Manufacturing Paper" appeared in the *Monthly Bulletin of the Ministry of Industry* (*Shiyebu yuekan*) ("Hu shang Chen Diexian jihua gailiang zao zhi yuanliao" 1936). It described and praised Chen's activities at an industrial exposition that was aimed at producing competitive domestically manufactured paper. During this time, Chen was the planning commissioner of paper reform in the Construction Bureau of Zhejiang's provincial government and helped establish the Provincial Reformed Paper Mill (Shengli gailiang zaozhi chang) in Zhejiang ("Zhe sheng gailiang zhiliao" 1937, 48). Some of his initiatives at this mill included using cheaper ingredients such as star or ryegrass rather than bamboo or mulberry as raw materials in paper production. The piece "Shanghai Merchant Chen Diexian" framed his contribution in terms of how he employed chemical experimentation and tinkering to improve and refine these raw materials, which were concerns that had shaped his entry into industry as early as 1918.

> Zhejiang and Jiangxi . . . are holding a Joint Exhibition for Local Specialty Products in May. . . . It is now known that this

city's Chen Diexian of Household Industries, who manufactures a great amount of paper each year for Zhejiang province, will participate. . . . [Manufacturers] are stuck in a rut and are being attacked from abroad by foreign industrial nations to the point that the handicraft industry has suffered setbacks that impact rural industry. Yet all is not lost, and [Chen] devised this exhibit as an opportunity. . . . He has collected the raw materials from around the province. [They] include young bamboo, tree bark, and the chaff of wheat [all of which can be used] to make pulp [for paper]. . . . [Chen] chemically experiments (*huayan*) to purify the raw ingredients and uses a scientific method to improve the manufactured product and provides [this method] for each factory to adopt (*caiyong*). . . . The Specialty Products Exhibition thinks this is very important and . . . will reap great benefit.

("Hu shang Chen Diexian" 1936, 107)

The passage dwelled in particular on the chemical experimenting and scientific methods used to refine the raw ingredients and improve the final product, pulp. These contributions were on display and available for adoption by other nativist factories and paper mills. Published in a publication by the Ministry of Industry, Chen and his approach of experimenting and improving a product had now become endorsed by the state.

However, if the state encouraged industrial tinkering and chemical experimentation to improve Chinese industry, it also sought to regulate these processes. As industry started to grow in the first few decades of the twentieth century, civic, provincial, and national bureaus and testing centers sought, often in the name of hygienic modernity (*weisheng*), to regulate and discipline a variety of industrial practices, including the experimentation with chemicals and raw ingredients in the making of manufactured goods. When Household Industries tinkered with new products—especially those involving chemical experimentation—it would submit prototypes to industrial testing bureaus (*gongye shiyansuo*) for approval. When the company chemically manufactured a wild-grass and flower-based pill to help smokers quit smoking, it submitted its prototype in 1929 to the Central Hygiene Experimentation Institute (Zhongyang weisheng shiyansuo) for approval.[57] In 1933, the company submitted an improved table salt refined through chemical experimentation to

Hebei Province's Industrial Testing Institute (Hebei sheng gongye shi-yansuo).[58] Both were granted approval.

State commendation of a company's efforts at improving technologies enabled manufacturers like Chen to lay claim to certain technologies. The Ministry of Industry and Commerce publication *Industry and Commerce Report* announced in 1930 that Kong Xiangxi, the ministry's head, had approved that seven yuan be paid and a plaque issued to "Chen Xuyuan" (another of Chen's sobriquets) for his "improved tool for printing characters (*gailiang yinzi qi*)," the Butterfly Pen, to recognize his efforts to improve the technology.[59] An *Industry Journal* (*Shiye zazhi*) article discussing the making of the writing implement similarly described how Chen and his disciple, Lin Lübin, remade the body of an ordinary pen by piercing a hole into the side in order to insert the Butterfly brand dual-tone ink ("Wudibi" 1935). The result, the piece boasted, was that the pen could write up to three thousand more Chinese words. The process of improving the pen's body is described in detail: "On the side of the body of the pen, [Chen Diexian] pierced a small hole without compromising the aesthetics. He proceeded to refine it by filling up the hole to make it into a thumbtack prick. He also improved the body of the pen, turning it into a 'double-style pen.' . . . [Chen] applied for a patent with the Ministry of Industry . . . and fixed the name, Butterfly Economical Pen [Wudipai jingji bi], which was shortened simply to 'Butterfly Pen'" ("Wudibi" 1935, 20). This passage literally outlines the steps in Chen's adjustments that allowed him to change an ordinary pen into a new-style pen. These improvements were the grounds upon which he sought to apply for a patent and to trademark the object. Tinkering to improve served as the basis for claiming formal intellectual-property rights.

CONCLUSION: BRINE + PEPPERMINT + TINKERING = IMPROVED TOOTHPOWDER

In an era when resources were scarce and state support relatively meager, Chen Diexian proved to be resourceful in building his empire, although not quite in as unremittingly an inspiring manner as hagiographically portrayed by his biographers. Chen's success in commerce and industry was dependent on a willingness to experiment in informal spaces and ways as well as on the ability to draw from an array of nonindustrial practices, such as translating, editing, and adapting technologies and knowledge about production from abroad. His approach to tinkering with manufacturing technologies resonated with the goal of "improving" technologies and products stressed by the NPM and endorsed and regulated by the Republican state in the 1930s. The virtues he promoted and sought to put into practice—including the focus on improving industrial goods and treating improvement as a site for innovation—were central virtues praised and rewarded by the state.

At the same time, we have seen how even though the founding of Household Industries was dependent on Chen's ability to tap into global circuits, in the presentation of the company's brand an emphasis was placed on the need to "go local" (e.g., to source locally) and to establish a reputation of autarky and vernacular industrialism. This chapter has mined biographical sources for information on Chen's manufacturing practices but has also been deeply interested in the subjective nature of these sources to figure out how their biased portrayals functioned to help secure Chen Diexian's reputation and success, both contemporaneously and retrospectively. In other words, rather than merely dismiss these biographical accounts' hagiographic flourishes as mere rhetoric, the chapter thinks critically about those rhetorical strategies, asking why the sources portrayed Chen and the company in the way that they do.[60] A presentation of Chen as dedicated to building "homegrown" nativist industry emerged almost as soon as Household Industries was established and was to appear later in retrospective memoirs. Such a portrayal helped legitimate a form of vernacular industrialism, an ethos informed by a DIY sensibility that included practices of tinkering and adaptation as well as by a deep investment in nativist manufacturing that was ostensibly free from being reliant upon foreign materials and overt state assistance. These characteristics, some of which Chen sought to put into practice and all of which he promoted in writing, allowed him—so the narrative goes—to battle substantial obstacles, ranging from resource scarcity to inhospitable political conditions created by imperialist manufacturers and a discernible lack of state support if not outright state obstruction. Ultimately, these same characteristics helped establish Household Industries as a National Products company.

And although these narratives of vernacular industrialism have presented Chen's endeavors as constituting a form of autarkism, it is undeniable that central to the process of industry building for Chen was the ability to adapt foreign technologies and recipes. Neither a process of direct "technology transfer" nor a diffusionist model in which Chen served as a mere conduit, his practices of adaptation and translation involved several layers of mediation. Historians of science have recently started to pay specific attention to the key role translators served as brokers and go-betweens and the role that translation played in technology transfer.[61] Chen provides us with a fascinating angle on go-betweens. He was an individual in a semicolonial (rather than directly colonial) situation who did not speak a single foreign language and yet proved able to gain access to global circuits of science and chemistry, adapting and translating circulating knowledge already mediated through translation from Western sources into Japanese as well as testing and playing around with foreign products to manufacture native products. He was an active broker and go-between, but he was also more—an innovating practitioner of the technology, seeking to create through the process of translation, reverse-engineering, and improvement in order to build Chinese industry and manufacturing.

Finally, Chen's practices in tinkering allow us to focus on the processes of mediation and innovation that occurred in technology transfer at the level of *both* text and things. At the material level, he tinkered with the manufacturing recipes, adapting both the translated recipes and the manufacturing practices to local conditions to accomplish his goal of local sourcing. At the textual level, relying on collaborators to translate, he rendered Japanese translations of Western-language recipes into classical Chinese. Yet his mediation did not simply stop with the translation and adaptation of recipes of manufacturing from abroad. As chapter 3 discusses, Chen sought to make this adapted knowledge accessible to a wider reading public by presenting the knowledge in a tasteful manner in columns on "common knowledge." It was in the various layers of mediation that creative intervention occurred. This intervention included the production of knowledge, the building of industry, and the creation of new identities, whether a national Chinese identity or occupational identities, such as the patriotic new-style industrialist, which Chen then was able to brand and market to great success.

CHAPTER FIVE

What's in a Name?

From Studio Appellation to Commercial Trademark

> The [Butterfly or Wudipai] trademark is harmonious and easy to pronounce. It is meaningful and brings prosperity. A trademark should be beautiful, meaningful, and accessible. This trademark has all of these characteristics. Readers, if you need a model, consider this one.
>
> —WANG TAIJUN, *JOURNAL OF INDUSTRY AND COMMERCE*, 1924

In the epigraph, commentator Wang Taijun lauds the famous Wudipai trademark. The literal translation of "Wudipai" is "Peerless brand," but it is more commonly known in English and in dialect as "Butterfly" brand. He specifically notes how the trademark was easy to pronounce yet meaningful, accessible yet beautiful. It promises, he adds, to bring prosperity and serves as a model. The Butterfly trademark—or, more accurately, trademarks—was crucial not just in the selling of Household Industries' cosmetics but also in establishing Chen Diexian's persona as a genuine businessman and in legitimating his commercial endeavors. Indeed, ever mindful of the importance of both name and brand, Chen Diexian artfully combined elements of the literati culture of studio names and his reputation as a man-of-feeling brand author with legally protected trademarks to sell his products. In Hangzhou, he had used carefully curated names, several of which revolved around the butterfly theme, to establish a Zhuangziesque reputation. When he moved to Shanghai to become a pen for hire and a new-style industrialist, the butterfly motif continued to prove useful. He initially capitalized on his Hangzhou reputation but also developed a new persona as a man of authentic feeling (*qing*) who penned sentimental fiction for urban readers. This authorial brand as a *genuine* man of feeling in turn provided him cover for the selling of both words and things for money.

The reputation that arose from Chen's literary endeavors also proved useful in portraying his commercial and industrial persona as sincere. The butterfly appears in Chen's sobriquet or public name "Diexian," "Butterfly Immortal," and is a symbol of the "Mandarin duck and butterfly fiction" that he authored so prolifically. It was also the motif and image at the heart of the trademarks. This was no accident, and the motif functioned to merge Chen's persona as man of feeling that he had established so well through his literary production with the reputation of his company's commodities. Just as readers of his fiction were meant to experience the seemingly authentic feelings of protagonist Shan in *The Money Demon* and brand author Tianxuwosheng, the marketing strategies adopted by Household Industries were created with the goal of establishing its customers' genuine attachment to the brand. In the end, the mutually constitutive branding between his literary brand and his commercial brand, between the making of a persona and the making of an industry, led to considerable success. Household Industries utilized a host of methods to guarantee the reputation and name of its products as well as Chen's cultivated persona. These strategies included pushing for the institutionalization of trademark enforcement in industry journals, using courts of law to squash copiers, allying with movie star Butterfly Wu to forge a cultural association with the name "Butterfly," and, finally, promoting in writing the pursuit of counterfeiters as basic "common knowledge" that all patriotic citizens should know. At the crux of the company's approach was the realization that one needed to forge a sense of genuine attachment between the consumer and the brand in a new era of mass production.

BUTTERFLY AS TRADEMARK

In China, the promotion of the trademark as something that could guarantee a company's reputation, ensure profit, and thus be deserving of legal protection by the state emerged under the auspices of imperialism and global capitalism. The Qing's thriving tradition of customary state protection of commercial names and marks as well as guild mechanisms to protect a brand had previously applied only to domestic merchants.[1] Foreign traders entering the Chinese market in the nineteenth century saw their products quickly counterfeited by Chinese manufacturers and had little to no legal recourse. To remain competitive, foreign merchants worked with their governments to press for reform in China's commercial law (Alford 1995, 34–35). Britain led the charge and put pressure on successive Chinese governments in the late nineteenth and early twentieth centuries to draft regulations to police trademarks. To justify the need to establish formal trademark law, previous practices of customary state protection of name brands (which were notably similar to what Western powers were seeking from modern China through law) were discredited. Chinese legal reformers were under pressure to codify trademark infringement and establish a sense of legal equivalence with the newly superior West. The first registered marks were with the Imperial Maritime Customs, but because the Customs was unable to enforce these registrations, the British Foreign Office pressed the matter during negotiations over the Boxer Uprising protocols. A series of commercial treaties seeking to deal with protection of foreign marks followed at the turn of the twentieth century.[2] By 1904, the Qing government promulgated a set of provisional regulations in accordance to British demand, titled "Experimental Regulations for the Registration of Trademarks" (Heuser 1975).[3] These regulations were to be the foundation of future trademark code, which British and other imperialist powers pushed for in the Republican period. China's first complete Trademark Law was drafted in 1923 and served as the basis of the Nationalist government's law until 1930, when the Nationalists offered their revision of it.[4]

Despite reform at the level of code, the application of the law and the institutionalization of mechanisms to enforce the law were often nominal. Vibrant copying persisted and generated considerable anxiety for supporters of disciplining trademark infringement, whether Chinese or foreign. In this context, where trademark regulation was nascent and irregular, on the one hand, and trademarks were increasingly crucial in marketing mass-produced goods, on the other hand, Chen and his company, Household Industries, poured an inordinate amount of energy and resources into crafting the Butterfly brand name and trademark(s) and then went to great lengths to establish an ownership over them that would be as exclusive as possible.

As early as 1924, the young Household Industries purchased from abroad a trademark-printing machine with which to print its trademarks in-house (Shanghai shi tongjibu 1957, 134). The company employed designers for hire in Shanghai's growing advertising and commercial art world. Utilizing these resources, it crafted a brand name that was multilingual and employed several levels of linguistic play. In doing so, it helped turn the name "Wudipai" in Chinese and "Butterfly" in English into a wildly popular brand. The literal meaning of the Chinese characters for the brand name "Wudipai" is "the brand without enemy" or "Peerless brand." The militaristic phrase "without enemy" evoked the passionate call to arms of the NPM, in which Chen was a leading participant. The iconic logo on the brand's toothpowder carton was featured in chapter 4 (figure 4.1) and can be seen here in an ad for Butterfly Toothpowder in 1947 (figure 5.1).[5] The logo alluded not too subtly to this politicized context by featuring a tennis racquet, which was meant to represent the means by which Household Industries could smash the Japanese sun, in the form of a tennis ball. The sun, in turn, symbolized

FIGURE 5.1 Butterfly Toothpowder, carton and logo. Source: Shanghai jizhi guohuo gongchang lianhehui 1947, 44.

Japanese goods, especially the popular Japanese Diamond (Jingangshi) and Lion (Shizipai) brands (toothpowders) in the Chinese market.[6] In figure 5.1, the packaging seems to have become a logo, with the carton appearing more important than the actual product, which is not even shown. Four characters appeared on the packaging: *zhong, hua, guo, chan*, which together meant "Chinese National Products." With the additional four characters for "the marvelous tooth-protecting product" (*hu chi sheng pin*) at the top and the characters for "Butterfly Toothpowder" (Wudi yafen) on the right-hand side, the entire visual could have circulated for advertising purposes. In figure 5.1, the front panel of the package is enlarged—again emphasizing the importance of the logo—and a tennis racquet (though here without a ball) is featured prominently, with the words "face and toothpowder (*camian yafen*)" written across the racquet head.

The strident patriotic connotation comes across in Mandarin, but the name "Wudipai" becomes far wittier and more whimsical in dialect. Specifically, the Mandarin pronunciation for the characters *wudi* in "Wudipai" is homophonic with the Shanghaiese pronunciation of *wudipai*, "butterfly."[7] The trademark for Wudipai registered with the Trademark Bureau in 1917 included not simply the Chinese characters, 無 (*wu*), 敵 (*di*), and 牌 (*pai*), but also the English name "BUTTERFLY" in capital letters. The efficacy of the trademark thus lay in large part in the homophonic interplay between regional dialect and Mandarin Chinese. With the meaning of the name as "peerless" or "without enemy," Wudipai was an effective trademark for the national audience, one increasingly aware of the economic warfare against enemy products in the NPM. But it was also a compelling brand name for a local Shanghai audience, which could grasp the aural pun between *wudi* in Mandarin and *hudie* in dialect. With its English name, "Butterfly," it could also cultivate a more global appeal. (I hereafter use the brand's English name, "Butterfly," unless I am making a specific point about its literal translation as "Peerless.")

Beyond its whimsicality, the aural pun in Chen Diexian's Butterfly trademark name is indicative of the cosmopolitan modernity of the southeastern and southern region of China at the time, a modernity characterized by the seamless integration of international, national, and regional inflections. In her discussion of Shanghai's film and entertainment culture, Zhen Zhang discusses the term *yangjingbang*, which might be roughly translated as "pidgin." The term originally referred to a canal where East met West and where compradors, flower girls, and Westerners intermingled. At the linguistic level, *yangjingbang* was the creative if at times irreverent grammar—with its mixture of English, Chinese, and regional dialects—that was used at the site. For Zhang, the term is extended to connote more expansively Shanghai's vernacular yet cosmopolitan entertainment culture (2005, 44–52). For our purposes, both the linguistic register and the metaphorical meaning of *yangjingbang* are significant. The wittiness involved in the term can be applied to our understanding of the aural and regional wordplay in the Butterfly trademark. In addition to the dialect pun of the Chinese name "Wudipai," which directly appeals to the regional audience, and the national and patriotic appeal of the Mandarin pronunciation of that name, the English name "Butterfly" suggests the global or cosmopolitan register of the mark. Thus, like the area's film and entertainment culture as well as Shanghai's vibrant commercial, consumer, and visual/aural cultures, the Butterfly trademark was cosmopolitan and marked by both vernacular and national meaning.

Although the homophonic pun was critical, the Butterfly trademarks (over time, multiple visual trademarks were used for the brand) mixed visual and linguistic elements as well, conflating the idea of the butterfly with the word and the image. The butterfly, the heart of the brand's concept, was the central visual image of the trademark. As such, Household Industries made sure that the image of a butterfly, under which the characters for the name "Household Industries," 家 (*jia*), 庭 (*ting*), 工 (*gong*), 業 (*ye*), 社 (*she*), are placed, was registered as an independent trademark (see figure 5.2).[8] The company's various logos would expand upon the butterfly motif. In the colored logo of the brand (figure 4.1), one sees how Household Industries included romantic images of violets, roses, and butterflies alongside the tennis racquet. Zheng Mantuo (1885–1959), a famous Chinese artist and man-about-town at the time, regularly painted artworks for Chen Diexian and was known for his romantic imagery and painting style.[9] Zheng most likely created this particular combination of flowers and the butterfly for the toothpowder logo, which became so iconic that copycats almost immediately borrowed the imagery for their products.[10]

FIGURE 5.2 Butterfly brand registered trademark. Source: Photograph by Yanjie Huang.

The most effective Butterfly trademark included a visual pun that merged the image of the butterfly and characters to make a powerful logo. Registered in 1933, this trademark also sought to evoke the renewed authority of classical culture in the market.[11] As seen in figure 5.3, seal script was chosen for the characters of the name "Household Industries," which are arranged into a butterfly image. The butterfly's upper-right wing is a seal-script character for *jia* 家.[12] The bottom-right wing is the character for *ting* 庭, and together they constitute the compound *jiating* 家庭, "household." The characters that constitute the butterfly's antenna and body are *gong* 工 and *ye* 業, and as a compound *gongye* 工業 means "industries." The characters making up the left wing are *hui* 會 and "*she* 社, which constitute the compound *huishe* 會社, a neologism from Japan that meant "association" or "corporation." Together, the six characters spell out "Jiating gongye huishe," Association for Household Industries. The choice to use seal script in a commercial trademark is hardly accidental. This script evokes a long history and the rich literati culture of

"BUTTERFLY"

FIGURE 5.3 Butterfly Brand, registered trademark c. 1933. Source: *Zhongguo guo-huo diaocha ce* 1934–1937, 300.

carving, collecting, and using seals, so the seal script imbued Chen's com-modities with a whiff of learnedness and classical culture—something that Chen, his literary products, and manufactured items all sought to embody. Far from being retrograde, this commercial classicism helped secure handsome profit for the company.[13]

Contemporaries appreciated the efficacy of the Butterfly trademark. In the article "The Question of Trademarks" written for the *Journal of Industry and Commerce (Gongshang xuebao)*, author Wang Taijun made a strong case for the use of trademarks: trademarks are less easily coun-terfeited than shop names; in Chinese society, which has such a low lit-eracy rate, trademarks are recognizable, even for those who cannot read characters; and a trademark guarantees a shop's reputation. For Wang, an effective trademark is one that relates to the product being sold, has artistic imagery, and makes proper and balanced use of characters and pictures. Strong trademarks are simple in design. The simpler they are, the easier for the customer to remember. He also made the perhaps counterintuitive argument that simple trademarks are actually more difficult to imitate; in other words, a simple and catchy trademark ensures a stronger association with a particular product and is thus harder to copy. Finally, Wang presented examples of famous and effective trademarks, starting with the trademark for Chen's Butterfly Toothpowder. This trademark is effective, he contended, because of the homophonic substitution of the name in Shanghainese; the image of roses and violets to indicate the fragrant nature of the product; and the combination of flowers with the butterfly motif, which he felt to be particularly clever and appropriate. Not surprisingly, Wang concluded with the statement used for this chapter's epigraph: "The Butterfly trademark is harmonious and easy to pronounce. It is meaningful and brings prosperity. A trademark should be beautiful, meaningful and accessible. This trademark has all of these characteristics. Readers, if you need a model, consider this one" (Wang Taijun 1924, 18).

The attention that Household Industries paid to its trademarks was extended to the packaging of its products. Take, for example, the container used for Butterfly Toothpowder. A photo of an original Butterfly Toothpowder container is featured on this book's cover. There is no definitive date for the container, but there are clues. The toothpowder logo with the tennis racquet and roses and butterfly imagery on the top of the lid (see figure 4.1) was trademarked by 1917, and the logo of the butterfly consisting of the Chinese characters (figure 5.3) was registered circa 1933. Both logos are featured on the container, so it is likely that the container was used for Butterfly Toothpowder in the early to mid-1930s. The online auction house from which the container was purchased notes that a Shandong-based store posted the container on the website.[14] Round and about ten centimeters in diameter and three centimeters tall, the container is made out of a wood pulp or paper (i.e., is cellulose based). It is exquisitely decorated. The colored logo of figure 4.1 graces the top of the lid. The side lip of the top lid has a ribbon of characters that reads "Butterfly Brand Dental and Face Powder" (Wudipai camian yafen), followed by the characters for "Association for Household Industries product" (Jiating gongyeshe chupin). It includes in smaller but clear print the three English words "MADE IN CHINA." Each Chinese character is encircled in a light-yellow disk and spaced from the other characters by overlapping pale-blue and pale-pink disks, colors that pick up the faded colors of the logo on the top of the lid. The bottom part of the container also has the same ribbon of characters wrapping around its lip. The delicate inclusion of beautifully written characters on the side of both the top lid and the bottom of the container serves to emphasize the lettered sensibility of the product and brand. The inside of the lid includes not only the trademark with the Chinese characters but also considerable text set against a faded scene of clouds and pavilions populated with elegant men and women that is reminiscent of classical Chinese painting (figure 5.4). The text describes the amazing, indeed near miraculous, capacities of the powder. It promises that in addition to serving as face and dental powder, the white powder can treat skin afflicted by a puncture wound by an ordinary knife, a damp and ticklish foot, and underarm odor. That containers like this one have survived for almost a century suggests that they were considered keepsakes in part because of the appealing packaging and trademark logos.[15]

FIGURE 5.4 The inside of the lid of a Butterfly Toothpowder container, circa mid-1930s. Source: Photograph by Ariana King.

Given the success of the Butterfly trademark, Chen and Household Industries were driven to protect Chen's name and the company's brand and to stake as exclusive a claim over the butterfly motif as possible. Copycats abounded, and alleged counterfeiters were increasingly perceived as threats who would sully the reputation of "genuine" Butterfly products. Carol Benedict (2011) has discussed the widespread hand-rolled imitations of British American Tobacco and other manufactured cigarettes. Much of the production of copied cigarettes took place in handicraft environs and small workshops in and around Beijing and Shanghai rather than in large mechanized factories. Sales of "fake" cigarettes soared in the early 1930s, occupying almost a 25 percent share of the Chinese cigarette market. Similar trends existed in the pharmaceutical market, with Chinese copiers of cosmetics proving able to imitate with great success both international and domestic brand-name cosmetics. The success and wiliness of copiers prompted British and transnational companies, such as Unilever and BW&C, to work with the British government to place diplomatic pressure on the Nationalist government to crack down on Chinese counterfeiting and trademark infringement (Lean 2018). Yet, as Benedict rightfully notes, although foreign companies and their governments were infuriated and taking action, the large companies were often ironically responsible for spurring the copying. The hand-rolled cigarette workshops that sprouted left and right in the 1920s and 1930s were not simply a holdover from the preindustrial artisanal past but new models of handicraft production that resulted directly in response to the rise of industrial production. The large manufacturers' mass marketing, meant to spur desire for their own brands, also generated, if unwittingly, considerable desire for cheap imitations of their brands that lower-end consumers could buy.

In face of this vibrant imitation culture, nonstate domestic entities often had to promote trademark enforcement on their own. This was a period when a formal, institutional apparatus to fight purported counterfeiters had barely begun to materialize and certainly not at the pace that either large Western or domestic companies wanted. Trademark legislation was imperfect, and the central state was distracted with other concerns. In this context, domestic corporations such as Household Industries took on the fight. By the late 1910s and early 1920s, the newly established Household Industries was fending off alleged copycats counterfeiting its Butterfly trademark and started pushing for enforcement of trademarks, especially at local levels. Without systematic institutional and legal support, the company proved resourceful in its efforts and pursued a variety of strategies to fend off copiers and to own the Butterfly name and mark as exclusively as possible.

One approach Chen took was to take advantage of his access to the world of print to expose alleged copiers and to put pressure on local authorities to take action against fraudulent behavior. In 1921, Zhang Yi'ou, the head of the Jiangsu Industrial Bureau, posted a public notice of trademark-infringement cases involving the Butterfly trademark in the Industrial Bureau bulletin the *Jiangsu Industrial Monthly* (*Jiangsu shiye yuekan*).[16] The notice (Zhang Yi'ou 1921) stated that Chen Xuyuan, one of Chen's alternate names, had brought to the bureau's attention that the Wuchang Heji Company (Wuchang heji gongsi) of Hubei Province had been plagiarizing the Butterfly Toothpowder trademark by copying its unique visual combination of butterfly, roses, and violets to sell its own product, the Evolution (Jinhua) brand toothpowder. The notice sought to achieve multiple goals. First, it served as the central-state and provincial-level state agencies', including Jiangsu's and Hubei's, declaration to institutionalize trademark enforcement. The text described for readers the new institutional apparatus for policing trademark ownership and explains how Shanghai's Household Industries had officially requested the Ministry of Agriculture and Industry to investigate the infringement and prohibit further offense. In turn, it noted how the Ministry of Agriculture and Industry had ordered the Hubei Industrial Agency to investigate and decide on the matter. This agency then submitted a report that declared that the Jinhua trademark used by the Wuchang Heji Company was identical in color and style to the Household Industries trademark; the agency thus ordered the Wuchang district magistrate to prohibit such counterfeiting. According to the district magistrate's report, an officer had been sent to the company to instruct it not to use the trademark, and the company had agreed to change its mark. This notification's careful listing of the offices involved in the enforcement of trademark use was aimed specifically at legitimating and promoting official efforts to institutionalize trademark legislation. It concluded, "[This notification] shows that our government ministry and agency have the best and most sincere intentions in protecting the trademark" (Zhang Yi'ou 1921, 45).

The notification also reveals how Household Industries sought to mobilize and cajole reluctant bureaucrats and officials to act and enforce trademark ownership. It mentioned another purported case of counterfeiting the Butterfly trademark submitted by Chen, which makes evident the considerable degree of foot-dragging among local officials as well as the potential of police fraud. In this case, Household Industries accused Meida Chemical Industry (Meida huaxue gongyeshe) of the Changshu District of using Butterfly Toothpowder's trademarked imagery of the butterfly, roses, and violets in selling its Flower Ball (Huaqiu) brand toothpowder. Household Industries understood the protection of its trademark to be the responsibility of the industrial office of the district government and thus prepared a letter requesting the Changshu magistrate's office to investigate the alleged infringement. Three months after the request, however, there had still been no news, and another company, the Hengchangchou foreign-goods store, meanwhile started to distribute its Superior (Dingshang) brand face and toothpowder using the butterfly, rose, and violet imagery. Household Industries felt that the Hengchangchou store was deceiving customers in claiming that this imagery constituted an original trademark. The notice stated that Household Industries intended to request the Tai County magistrate to investigate and prohibit such actions but was afraid that, like the Changshu magistrate's office, the Tai County office would simply ignore the request. The printing of this notice, therefore, served to identify in print those offices Chen saw as uncooperative. By treating the provincial-level agency as the agent with the power and responsibility to enforce trademark regulations, the notice was intended to put pressure on that agency as well.

These notices offer us evidence that Chen was pushing for trademark enforcement as early as the first half of the 1920s. They also provide a glimpse of what must have been local officials' considerable reluctance to make the effort to enforce trademark legislation. This reluctance stemmed in part from the fact that policing trademark abuses was still unchartered territory; another factor was that new industrialists such as Chen might have faced opposition from local interests at the provincial level. Third, the fact that Zhang Yi'ou, the head of the Jiangsu Industrial Bureau, posted this notice, presumably acting on Chen's request, speaks to how Zhang sought to present his provincial-level bureaucratic office as "modern" and invested in promoting the idea and institutionalization of singular corporate trademark ownership while pointing out how other provincial-level enforcers had failed. Both Chen and Zhang were clearly well aware of the power of the press and were willing to mobilize that bully pulpit to assert the idea of corporate ownership of trademarks. Indeed, the published announcement specifically noted how Chen had requested the agency to announce this case of infringement in public in the newspapers so as to prevent others from plagiarizing his mark and to emphasize that such an action would be for the public good.

Chen was to continue fighting counterfeits through other publications during this period when legal enforcement remained inconsistent. In 1928, in his in-house press publication of business correspondence for Household Industries, *Model Correspondence*, he proudly showcased how Household Industries was at the forefront of pursuing counterfeiters and included letters that documented its fight against counterfeiters and dedication to protecting its products. Several of the published letters shed light on exactly how Chen employed a variety of means to pursue and discourage copiers. One letter commented, for example, on the case of the Xicheng printing company that had printed counterfeit Butterfly Toothpowder bags:

> Recently, counterfeits of our brand have been discovered around Changzhou. We have learned that the Xicheng printing company near your place printed [counterfeit] paper bags. . . . I am familiar with that company and . . . know that the manager, a Mr. Wu, is [upright], and there could not have been any willful intent on his part to do anything [wrong]. But this paper bag is indeed the exclusive property of our brand. No matter whether it is a branch or retail store that carries our brand, they have no right to produce our bags. Perhaps Mr. Wu does not understand this and misunderstood what was expected when he accepted the printing job. If that is the case, . . . we won't blame him. But who was the person who requested this? What is his name and address? . . . Since you live nearby, . . . may I ask you to check on this for me? We will not make any difficulties for the printing company. When we get the person who commissioned the counterfeit, we will sue him directly. . . . We hope to

find a fair way of resolving the situation. . . . We have asked officers and detectives to investigate the evidence of the case and based on our humble and sincere intentions, we have also sent a letter directly to Mr. Wu. Because we worry about the possibility of a misunderstanding, we are asking you to follow up.
(Chen Diexian 1928, vol. *wuwu*:19–20)

From the letter, we can see how Household Industries not only pursued more official means, including the threat of legal recourse, to deal with the counterfeiting but also used personal connections and social persuasion. It hired detectives to investigate the case in question; it also relied on personal connections—Mr. Zhong He—to follow up and ensure that Mr. Wu, the owner of the printing shop stopped the printing of copycat bags. Household Industries promised that nothing would happen to the printing company and Mr. Wu, a man whose reputation was known to be upright. It seemed to grant Mr. Wu the benefit of the doubt, stating that he probably acted on behalf of his customer, the real culprit, without realizing what was at stake. Yet, despite the polite tone, there was to be no mistake: these bags were the exclusive property of Household Industries, and Mr. Wu had to halt his printing immediately—even if it had not been done with deceit.

A follow-up letter on this case details how Chen further pursued the perpetrators:

I went this past week to Xishan to investigate this case . . . and just got back last night. . . . The counterfeit item is manufactured in Wuxi and distributed in Changzhou area. It . . . was produced by Changzhou's Nanyang pharmacy, [packaged in a bag] printed by Wuxi's Xicheng company, and sold by the Yifeng general store. I am suing them all. The matter should be handled in the courts of law, but the [main] perpetrator is on the run. Nanyang pharmacy has shut down, and [its owner] is gone. There is only Yifeng and Xicheng who remain to take the blame. The [local] newspapers . . . *Xinbao* and *Shenbao* have reported on the case. This might have some effect on others who want to counterfeit.
(Chen Diexian 1928, vol. *wuwu*:19–20)

Through his own investigation, Chen confirmed where the counterfeits were made, where they were distributed, and which parties were involved. In addition to Mr. Wu's printing company, which had printed the counterfeited paper bags, these parties included the Nanyang pharmacy, the actual perpetrator of the counterfeited product, and the Yifeng general store that had carried the offending item. Whereas the earlier letter assured that Mr. Wu would not be legally targeted, here it is noted that all parties would be sued. Because the original perpetrator, the Nanyang pharmacy, was on the run, the ones who would bear the brunt of any legal action would be the general store and Mr. Wu's printing company. The mention of major newspapers running the news on the case suggests that transmitting the news to a general reading public was a deterrent of further counterfeiting by these companies.

These letters also sought to mobilize support for the fight against counterfeiting by appealing to patriotic merchants and identified National Product merchants in particular as ones who would oppose unpatriotic acts of copying. Another letter focused on counterfeit toothpowder and how to discourage copiers:

I recently received your letter where you informed me of a packet of fake tooth powder. I could feel that you were very earnest. Our country's industry is weak . . . because of immoral merchants who cheat the public; they are our real public enemies. According to national law, they violate criminal law by committing fraud. No matter what, citizens can intervene. . . . But, unfortunately, enthusiastic people are few, and those who are patriotic and promote National Products even fewer. Most think things have nothing to do with them. . . . Alas, this is a shame. We should request the police to investigate and prohibit [such behavior]. But only if the buyer more actively interferes [by not buying fraudulent items] will stores not dare cheat people. . . . In addition to publicizing this matter in the newspapers and alerting the police, I am shipping you a carton of our tooth powder, which contains 600 packets; please share these with friends to allow them to distinguish [the real ones] from the fakes.

(Chen Diexian 1928, vol. *bingyin*:5–6)

This letter appealed to both producers and consumers and presented both the pursuit of counterfeits and the refusal to buy counterfeits as moral and patriotic acts. In an era when trademark-infringement regulation was inchoate, Chen pursued multiple strategies to discourage fraud, including publicizing illicit activity in newspapers, notifying the police, and shipping out six hundred packets of the genuine article against which fakes could be distinguished. He also sought to share his own experiences in *Model Correspondence* as concrete tips for others to suppress counterfeiting.

BUTTERFLY WU: AN ENDORSEMENT AND A TRIAL

Chen Diexian also adopted high-profile methods to stake a claim over the Butterfly brand name, including forging a public association with Hu Die (1907–1989), "Butterfly Wu," one of the most famous movie stars of the Republican period. Chen was no doubt appreciative of the punning quality of her name. In Chinese, the name "Butterfly Wu" is based on an aural pun: "Hu Die" is a homophone to the compound *hudie*, "butterfly." The surname "Hu" is a different character from the *hu* in *hudie*, but they are pronounced the same. Her name is also a homophone to the word for "butterfly" in dialect. The "Hu" in "Hu Die" is pronounced *wu* in dialect, hence the English name "Butterfly Wu." And the dialect pronunciation of her surname is also a homophone to the *hu* character (pronounced *wu*) of *hudie* in dialect.[17] Both Chen and Butterfly Wu were tapping into the popularity of the butterfly as a motif for the culture of sentimentalism in the Republican era. Chen's brand-author reputation as a sincere man of feeling was forged in sentimental fiction that frequently featured the romantic motif of butterflies, and Butterfly Wu's reputation as a genuine actress was established in similarly melodramatic films.[18]

In certain respects, the mass-media mechanisms by which movie star Butterfly Wu and commercial and cultural persona Chen branded themselves and lent their reputations and names for product endorsement were quite similar. Yet key differences existed. Though Chen gained a reputation as a writer and later as an industrialist and civic leader, Butterfly Wu's fame as a movie star beginning in the 1920s was substantially more far-reaching. Whereas Chen was branding his own products, Butterfly Wu was endorsing other people's goods. Tapping into the popular-film industry for product endorsements and having film stars appear at commercial events were common marketing practices in China, as they were around the world. There was also a gendered component. As Butterfly Wu became one of China's most famous starlets, companies vied to use her name and face for purposes of representation and endorsement.

Seeking to benefit from a public association with Butterfly Wu, Chen Diexian had the film star lend her endorsement and quite literally her name to one of his side endeavors. In 1930, Chen and his son decided to open a hotel, which they named the Butterfly Lodge (Dielai, literally "Hither, Butterfly"). After the Hangzhou Expo of 1929, at which Chen had exhibited his Butterfly-brand products, they realized that Hangzhou and the West Lake had become a popular tourist destination and emblems of cultural authenticity. They decided to open the lodge behind what had been the expo site near the Xiling Bridge.[19] Chen invited Butterfly Wu and Xu Lai (1909–1973), two of China's most popular film stars at the time, to attend the groundbreaking ceremony in 1934 (Gu Ying 2009, 3).[20] He sought to mobilize their star power specifically because of their given names, "Die" and "Lai." When put together, these two names formed the compound "Dielai," the name of the hotel. Like the wit on display in the Butterfly trademark, here, too, wordplay was central in the name of Chen's hotel.

That the butterfly motif was valuable is evident in several trademark-infringement court cases in the 1930s, which ensnared both Household Industries and Butterfly Wu. One of the most fraught and extended disputes featured the Hua'nan Chemical Industry Company (Hua'nan huaxue gongyeshe). This case started when Household Industries discovered in the early 1930s that Hua'nan's mark for its cosmetic line included the name "Butterfly." Household Industries thus filed a complaint with the Trademark Bureau, accusing Hua'nan of counterfeiting. Agreeing with Household Industries, the bureau objected to Hua'nan's trademark. In response, Hua'nan appealed the bureau's decision and demanded a retrial. The bureau retried the case but upheld its original decision that Hua'nan was in violation. Hua'nan then filed an appeal with the Ministry of Industry, though again to no avail. On November 4, 1933, the ministry denied Hua'nan's appeal and agreed with the Trademark Bureau's decision in favor of Household Industries.[21] Hua'nan finally caught a break in 1936, when Household Industries filed a suit against the Ministry of Judicial Administration for not prosecuting Hua'nan for its continued use of the allegedly fraudulent trademark. In this decision, the ministry denied the Household Industries suit, presenting two primary rationales. First, it argued that to determine whether a trademark is identical or similar enough to merit fraudulent use requires that both the characters and the images have to overlap and not simply one of the two, which was the case here. Second, it stipulated that the special right to claim a trademark must be limited to the mark's name and image at the time of registration. Other names included in the explanation and/or practice of the trademark at the point of the submission of the mark for consideration of registration could not be advocated for exclusive use of the trademark. The Ministry of Judicial Administration ruled that neither requirement was met in this case.[22]

The seemingly hapless Hua'nan Chemical Industry Company was also embroiled in a legal dispute with Butterfly Wu, who was the company's purported spokesperson by the early 1930s. Notably, in the course of this dispute Hua'nan cited the legal ferocity with which Household Industries pursued alleged copiers. Described by one reporter as causing a stir in society and standing out in China's trademark history, the suit was initiated by Butterfly Wu in 1934 when she sought to dissolve her contract with Hua'nan (Yao Jiayu 1934, 25). In 1932, Butterfly Wu had agreed to associate her name exclusively with Hua'nan's cosmetic, signing a contract with its owner, Xu Gongming, that granted him the right to use the name "Hu Die," a homophone to *hudie*, the compound for "butterfly," as well as to use her image as Hua'nan's trademark for its line of cosmetic goods, including cold cream, powder, perfume, toothpowder, and toothpaste. The characters for Butterfly Wu's name were officially registered with the Shanghai Trademark Bureau as Hua'nan's trademark. In return, the contract stipulated that Butterfly Wu would earn a guaranteed one percent of total sales per year or no less than 1,500 yuan ("Sinian yilai wei huo" 1936, 824).

However, by 1934 Butterfly Wu had not received any compensation for the two years that the company had been using her name. This was because of the company's flat sales, accused the star's lawyers. Soon after she had signed the original contract, Hu Die Toothpowder by Hua'nan appeared on the market. The company projected to launch several more cosmetic products that would use the star's name as endorsement. It was at this point that the company's earnings started to fall and rumors started to emerge that it would go out of business. On July 6, 1934, Butterfly Wu's lawyers claimed that she had no choice but to bring the case to the Shanghai district court and sue Hua'nan for violating the contract. At the crux of her lawyers' argument was that Hua'nan had been established for a considerable amount of time but had produced only one kind of toothpowder and thus had not fulfilled its end of the contractual agreement to produce an array of cosmetic products ("Sinian yilai wei huo" 1936, 824).

From Hua'nan's perspective, however, the flat sales were due to the actress's lack of appeal ("Sinian yilai wei huo" 1936, 824). Notable for us here is the fact that the defense also claimed that its sales had been substantially harmed because Chen Diexian's company Household Industries was seeking to monopolize the Butterfly brand name and had requested the Shanghai Trademark Bureau to withdraw its approval of Hua'nan's use of the film star's name "Hu Die" as a trademark, as discussed earlier (Yao Jiayu 1934, 25). Despite Hua'nan's objections that the image of the film star it featured was not at all like the Household Industries trademark, Household Industries pushed forward with the case. Hua'nan also faced problems on the business front because of all the legal wrangling. One article noted that because Hua'nan had been enmeshed in the legal conflict with Household Industries for years, it had delayed the production and sales of more of its products (Shi 1934, 238). Hua'nan claimed, however, that despite the inhospitable environment created by Household Industries' bullying tactics, it had tried its best to manufacture Hu Die toothpowder to sell competitively and that, according to the contract, as long as there was a product, there was no violation.

In the end, the legal court agreed with Hua'nan's defense and decided against the movie actress. It upheld the original contract. In response to the failure at the district level, the star's lawyers appealed the lower court's decision to the Jiangsu Superior Court, Branch Three. But this court, too, decided to deny her appeal. The skepticism regarding Butterfly Wu's motives was not limited to the court. One journalist surmised that the actress's real motivation to sue Hua'nan stemmed from her success in the film *Twin Sisters* (*Zimei hua*, 1934). Her reputation and value had increased considerably, and, as a result, it was claimed, she was eager to terminate what turned out to be a restrictive contract with Hua'nan and offer her name and image to those who could afford a higher remuneration (Shi 1934, 238). The close timing of Household Industries' case against Hua'nan and Butterfly Wu's attempt to disentangle herself from Hua'nan suggests, too, that Household Industries and Butterfly Wu may well have been working together to reclaim the name "Butterfly."

More generally, the case sheds light on the complexity of defining trademarks and claims over trademarks using Chinese characters. For Household Industries, the claim to ownership of the butterfly motif as a trademark was quite expansive and not restricted to the literal characters for the term *hudie*, "butterfly." It extended to the ability of names to evoke "butterfly" aurally or otherwise, and the aural puns rested not simply with *wudi*, "peerless," sounding like *hudie*, "butterfly," in dialect, but also with Butterfly Wu's name, a homophone of *hudie*, the compound for "butterfly." The Butterfly Wu versus Hua'nan case illustrates the extent to which Household Industries sought to crush competitors who it felt were using the Butterfly mark fraudulently. Hua'nan felt that the pressure from Household Industries was so formidable that it was worth citing as a legitimate argument in Hua'nan's line of defense in the star's suit against it. From a certain perspective, the aggressiveness with which Household Industries pursued complete ownership over the butterfly motif was simply smart business. Hua'nan was manufacturing the same kinds of items—cosmetics, toothpowder, and so on—and using a similar marketing name. And with the rise of a new legal regime of trademark ownership both domestically and globally, Household Industries did not shy from using an array of legal and economic tools to stake its claim over its trademark to guarantee the company's reputation and by extension to ensure its monopoly over the Butterfly mark and to profit in the toiletries market.

Household Industries was among the earliest generation of Chinese companies to push for the institutionalization of trademark enforcement in China. It did so by exposing copycats in print, using the courts, and pursuing copiers through early trademark law. And Chen continued to use the media pulpit to promote trademark regulation into the 1930s. In 1934, using his pen name "Tianxuwosheng," Chen penned an article in a special column titled "Bulletin on the Trademark Question" (Chen Diexian 1934) for the *Machinery Association Journal* (*Jilianhui kan*), a journal he edited, to contend how the trademark legal code needed to be strengthened even further.[23] Much of the fervor behind the company's claim over the Butterfly name most certainly turned on the consideration of profit, but the Butterfly trademark was also an important extension of Chen's personal reputation and brand. Chen had emerged from a lettered culture where one's name was tied to one's personhood, so not only was his reputation at stake, but his persona was too. Indeed, it is easy to imagine how the personal association of Chen Diexian, the man with the name "Butterfly," factored significantly into Household Industries' assertiveness in securing exclusive and expansive legal and cultural ownership over the popular mark.

GLOBAL BUTTERFLY

Household Industries also realized the important role of advertisements in promoting its brand and quickly became aggressive in its marketing campaigns throughout China and beyond. The rise of modern advertising in the late nineteenth century occurred around the world in conjunction with the emergence of mass-manufactured commodities such as patent medicine, pharmaceuticals, personal-hygiene items, and cosmetics. In Chinese newspapers, cosmetic advertisements appeared as early as the 1870s in *Shenbao*, Shanghai's daily newspaper. By the 1920s and 1930s, cosmetic and toiletry items competed with patent medicines for domination in the pages of urban dailies, many of them becoming increasingly glossy with the inclusion of more visuals.[24] Western and Japanese firms as well as local and overseas Chinese merchants peddled and advertised a range of toiletry and cosmetic products, including soap, cold cream, toothpaste and toothpowder, deodorant, nail polish, and lipstick. It was in this context that Household Industries competed for a market niche and did so with considerable success.

At the heart of the company's marketing success was its grasp of what was a basic principle governing advertising at the time—namely, the need to find marketing techniques that fostered a sentimental attachment or consumer loyalty to products. This basic principle was conveyed quite literally in some of its ads. Take, for example, an ad for Butterfly Cream that appeared on October 3, 1932, in the daily *Shenbao* (figure 5.5): "The superior Butterfly Cream. SHE NEEDS IT. SHE ADORES IT." In a

FIGURE 5.5 Newspaper ad for Butterfly Cream. Source: *Shenbao*, October 3, 1932.

separate block of copy, the ad elaborates, "She desperately needs a superior National Product beauty item. The market is filled with other products, but none of those are satisfactory. Only Butterfly brand guarantees a charming complexion: BUTTERFLY CREAM." Accompanying the text is an image of a modern, glamorous woman in profile, extending her hand as if reaching for the characters for "Dieshuang," the product's name. The ad assures consumers that this National Product is sold in all department stores throughout China and is easily available for purchase. It presents the commodity as something to adore (literally, "to deeply love"). The product itself is completely absent in the advertisement. Instead, what is vividly illustrated with the woman's outstretched hand is the female desire for the product—that crucial if at times elusive target for all marketers. By featuring the sentimentalized relationship between the subject (the female mass consumer) and object (the particular brand of a mass commodity), the ad conveys the idea that the buyer's individual fulfillment was to be accomplished through the consumption of a particular make of cosmetic item. Although familiar to us today, this method of presenting a woman's sentimental bond to commodities was hardly universal or natural in 1932. Earlier ads in late-imperial China, for example, did not emphasize an affective relationship between the potential buyer and the commodity. It was only in an era when markets were flooded with a profusion of near-identical industrially produced goods that advertisers around the world started to present their products as something that consumers—especially women—not only needed but also could form an affective attachment with and, indeed, even love.[25]

Perhaps one of the most effective ways that Chen's company generated sentimental attachment to its products was by drawing from the vibrant film culture emerging worldwide. To be sure, companies and advertisers of an array of commodities tapped into a perceived sense of intimacy between fan and star that existed in China and the region's thriving domestic film culture to sell their goods. Calendar poster advertisements frequently featured stars promoting products ranging from cigarettes to Indanthrene color cloth (see, e.g., Laing 2004, figure 7.20 and plate 24). State NPM campaigns employed stars to promote the movement's ideals of nationalistic consumption (Gerth 2004). Many cosmetics and daily-use product companies were also adopting this strategy. The British–Dutch cosmetics conglomerate Unilever, for example, was one of the world's leading cosmetics companies to grasp this approach and applied it aggressively and powerfully around the world wherever its products were sold. In the United States, Unilever took advantage of the U.S. star system and featured Hollywood stars to sell its laundry soap. In 1933, Jean Harlow advised readers of the film journal *Modern Screen* to use Lux Soap to wash their stockings. In an advertisement in 1934, Mae West recommended Lux Toilet Soap to potential buyers. In the ad, she is having a conversation with Cupid and is quoted as coquettishly stating, "We get our men, all right. But then we've been using Lux Toilet Soap for years. A luscious skin gets them every time."[26] By winning screen stars' endorsements, Unilever sought to channel fan fervor for that star into brand loyalty to its product.

China turned out to be another important place where Unilever engaged in a marketing blitz for Lux Soap and detergent, blanketing its market with ads featuring movie stars. Unilever—or, more accurately, the British company Lever Brothers, the predecessor to Unilever—had been one of the earliest foreign companies to peddle soap in East Asia.[27] To secure its foothold in the increasingly competitive cosmetics market in China, the international conglomerate relied on international advertising agencies that had set up shop in Chinese cities such as Shanghai.[28] It even had its own in-house agency, Lintas, an acronym for Lever International Advertising Services. In 1932, this in-house advertising shop launched an competition in Chinese cities that called upon (female) readers-consumers to choose the best face for Lux Soap, one of Unilever's most popular products, from among more than twenty Chinese movie stars.[29]

The campaign stretched out for more than three months, with ads for Lux Soap featured every day in at least two major urban dailies, *Shenbao* in Shanghai and *L'Impartial* (*Dagongbao*) in Tianjin. From May to August 1932, ads rotated a different movie star each day to peddle Lux Soap. The ads were extremely large, ranging from a sixth to half of the page, standing out among a sea of advertisements in both papers. They even frequently were on the front page, making the campaign difficult for any reader to miss. As Unilever sought to dominate the East Asian market, it adjusted its global campaign to specific conditions in China by using film stars from Shanghai's vibrant film world.[30] Some of China's biggest stars were featured, including Ruan Lingyu (1910–1935), Li Lili (1915–2005), Wang Renmei (1914–1987), and Butterfly Wu. Each ad included a signed photograph of a female Chinese screen star and handwritten testimony professing why the actress enjoyed using Lux Soap. Consumers of the campaign and, ideally, consumers of Lux Soap were expected to choose the genuine face of Lux Soap by mailing in their vote. At the end of the campaign, the results of the competition were announced: Butterfly Wu was in first place, Ruan Lingyu in second.

In China of the 1930s, the female movie star had replaced the courtesan of late-Qing society to become the famed female personality of urban mass society (M. Chang 1999). Whereas the courtesan had been an object of elite adoration among turn-of-the-century urban literati, the Republican-era female entertainer emerged as a product and symbol of mass society and of China's connection with a larger global cinematic culture.[31] The female movie star of the 1930s was thus subjected to the desiring gaze of a much larger urban audience. She was embedded in an entirely new urban mass culture that consisted of other new subjectivities, including the fan, the critic, and "industry insiders," as well as in a range of new urban practices such as going to the movies, reading fan magazines, writing fan letters, circulating and collecting personally autographed photographs, writing movie criticism, and ranking stars in contests (M. Chang 1999, 132). The Lux campaign inserted itself into China's rich fan culture. Fans and readers who might have otherwise skipped the ads in their perusal of newspapers could check out a daily ad to see which star was being featured. The marketers hoped that at the same time these fans would become regular buyers of their brand.

As supposed experts in beauty, stars were in an ideal position to help fight material and physical decay, the express goal of the cosmetics and toiletry items being pitched for sale. The introduction of filmic and photographic technologies actually called for stars to participate in an extensive hygiene regimen in which soap was claimed to be indispensable in its ability to enable unblemished, cleansed, and beautiful skin. Like photography, the technology behind film exposes the face in close-up. But, unlike the photograph, the filmic image is blown up even more when it is projected onto a screen. Film actresses, far more so than their live-theater counterparts, had their faces (and bodies) subjected to extreme scrutiny under such a technologically mediated gaze. Not only did they embody the modern form of beauty, but their livelihoods also depended on achieving perfect skin.

These ads furthermore treated the female movie star as a commodity alongside the cosmetic item. It was her splendor that was attainable through consumption. The "mass" screen actress was someone whom everyone could not only dream of but also dream of becoming. Once this desire of becoming just like a screen star was articulated, the promise of acquiring the same exquisite skin as that of a screen star through the regular consumption of Lux Soap was imaginable. As the quintessential entertainment figure of a new mass society, the female movie star was effective in defining face cream or soap as a quintessential mass commodity.[32] Both representative of the masses and yet standing above the rest, the star was a powerful spokesperson and could lead potential consumers to think about the commodities they consumed as both an everyday toiletry item and yet something special that could transcend the quotidian by bringing exclusive beauty to them. The advertisements thus often visually featured the two commodities—the star and the cosmetic item—in a similar manner (see figure 5.6). They included drawn images of Lux Soap that were equal or near equal in size to the photo of the female movie star. The commodified beauty of the movie star was quite literally available for purchase along with a bar of the soap.

At the crux of generating attachment to an object lay the ever-elusive chase for the genuine in an era of mass production. Unilever's campaign aimed to close the gap in that chase. In the campaign, the headshot, the handwritten testimony, and the signature were particularly powerful mechanisms to foster a sense of genuine attachment to the movie star and the mass-produced item even though this attachment was ultimately a form of mediated authenticity. As close-ups, headshots suggested that they could reveal the star's true self, and they were a medium through which the actress was rendered at once identifiable as the commodity individuated from all other stars and in this manner seemingly authentic (Gunning 1995). Yet the generic headshot emerged in a regime of authentication associated with Hollywood's global cinematic culture

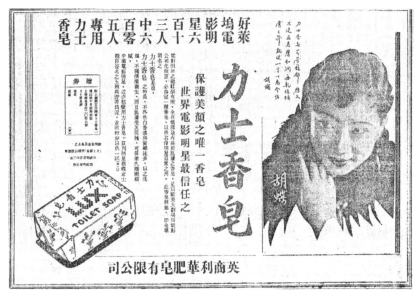

FIGURE 5.6 Newspaper ad for Lux Soap featuring screen star Hu Die. Source: *Shenbao*, May 6, 1932.

and became something so reproducible that to render it unique fans had to seek the star's "personal touch" by securing her autograph.[33] Yet the signature's ostensible "personal touch" was, of course, also mass-produced. In the campaign for Lux Soap, the headshots, all nearly identical, and the purportedly "personal" signature were reproduced through lithography for mass consumption.[34] The telegraphic female hand authenticated a photograph of the star (rather than the star herself), and both the autograph and the photograph were then mediated one more time in the advertisement, which was lithographically produced and distributed in the newspaper. This, in turn, multiplied the image to countless of readers. Through these mediated layers, the anonymous reader-consumer captured a glimpse of intimacy, though one that was constantly deferred. Yet it was precisely due to this deferral that the desire to consume in hopes of achieving real intimacy was elicited.

In the Unilever campaign for Lux Soap, this (deferred) intimacy was furthermore cultivated with the inclusion of handwritten testimony purportedly by the screen star about the product being pitched. This testimony, too, was meant to enhance the sense that the viewer could obtain a bit of the actress and to convey a sense of the star's allegedly personal voice. The ads featured bold claims ostensibly by the stars. In an ad appearing on June 9, 1932, Butterfly Wu penned, "Lux Soap, sweet smelling and fragrant. The scent lasts and will not fade away. Your skin will be moist and never dry. . . . Let me share this [product] with you." Her signature was meant to authenticate the sentiment and the promise of permanent beauty. Yet this testimonial, although seemingly expressing the actress's personal sentiment, reads as a variation of the same theme when placed next to similar ads. The film star Ruan Lingyu wrote: "Lux Soap uses high-quality material, sells at midlevel prices, and I am happy to endorse it" (*Shenbao*, June 29, 1932, 1). Liang Saizhen testified that "Lux Soap's fragrance is surprising; it cleans and expels dirt, moisturizes one's skin. . . . A rare wonder" (*Dagongbao*, June 13, 1932, 9). And Li Lili claimed, "Lux is so clean and white and so easy to love. It makes one's skin soft and smooth. I love using it" (*Shenbao*, May 9, 1932, 6 and *Dagongbao*, June 13, 1932).

The campaign's use of stars was indicative of how new media technologies and their materiality informed new ways of making guarantees in the commercial arena of the early twentieth century. There was an explicit awareness in some ads of the influence of media technology in making guarantees. Take, for example, a serial advertisement for Lux Soap that ran in almost every issue of volume 5 of the *Young Companion* (*Lianhua huabao*) in 1935 (figure 5.7). This series echoed Unilever's earlier pitch in 1932 by featuring a different yet interchangeable film star in each advertisement. The image in figure 5.7 features Li Lili. If the star changed, what remained the same in every ad was what happened in the audience

FIGURE 5.7 Ad for Lux Soap featured regularly in *Young Companion* (*Lianhua huabao*) over the course of 1935. Source: Paul Fonoroff Collection, University of California, Berkeley, Library.

pictured. There, a woman turns to her male companion and asks, "Why is it that the stars' skin is so fine?" The man replies, "It's because they use Lux every day to wash themselves." At the bottom of some ads were two smaller numbered inserts: in the first panel, the female fan is depicted at a shop buying Lux Soap, and in the second one she is in front of a wash basin, her hands raised, declaring triumphantly, "Lux Soap makes my skin so fresh. I am so happy." The act of consumption—both the purchase of the soap and its use—is literally narrated. So, too, is the affective impact of consuming Lux. To reinforce this message, the ad had whichever star share a personal handwritten testimonial, also found in the ads of the main campaign in the daily papers, *Shenbao* and *L'Impartial*, which is superimposed on the projection light of the screen. Personal fulfillment and the ability to achieve happiness for both the man and woman were possible through both the love of Lux Soap *and* the act of consuming it. The emotive message was meant to cement the reader's brand loyalty.

The advertisement is fascinating, moreover, in how it plays with multiple forms of media technology and addresses directly the question of what was genuine in this new era of mediated viewing. The ad did not draw the star's face directly as the image projected onto the theater movie screen at the top-right corner of the ad. It instead superimposed a photograph of her face—her professional headshot—on the silver screen. The multiple layers of media are thus literally piled on top of each other: the photograph of Li Lili (or of Chen Yanyan [1916–1999] or of Ruan Lingyu) is used in lieu of a drawn image of the star on the theater movie screen; the movie screen and the photograph are then transmitted both to viewers in the picture itself (i.e., the audience members gazing at the featured star's flawless and magnified skin) and to the consumers of the advertisement, which was lithographically produced and mechanically reproduced in the newspaper. This layered presentation and purposeful juxtaposition of different forms of media brought to the viewer's immediate attention the issue of the materiality and technologies of different forms of mass media. The ad showcased explicitly the relevance of these forms of mass media for strategies of verification in an era of mass reproduction, where mediated layers were utilized to engender a sense of the authentic.

The Unilever campaign to sell Lux Soap by utilizing local Chinese movie stars became the gold standard of such ad campaigns. Chinese companies quickly adopted this template to peddle their products, and the commodity being sold in advertisements was often just as interchangeable as the stars were in the Lux campaign. For example, an ad issued by the China Chemical Industries Co. selling its Gem Toothpaste and its Sanxing mosquito-repellent incense features Xu Qinfang (1907–1985), one of China's major screen stars (figure 5.8). It includes her headshot, handwritten testimony, and signature. Receiving Xu's endorsement meant that China Chemical could tap into fan support for her and direct it into brand support for its products, whether soap or hair tonic or incense.

Household Industries was not to be left behind in this marketing trend. It, too, utilized screen stars to sell its wares and did so not only in China's domestic markets but also in international ones. The early 1930s saw a renewed effort by the company to pitch the Butterfly brand as a global one. On October 10, 1933, a flurry of articles, for example, appeared

FIGURE 5.8 China Chemical Industry ad promoting Gem Toothpaste and Sanxing mosquito-repellant incense on the inner cover of *Overview of the National Exhibit of Handicraft Goods* (*Quanguo shougongyi pin zhanlanhui gailan*), 1937. Source: Quanguo shougongyi pin zhanlanhui bianjizu 1937. Chinese Collection of the Harvard-Yenching Library, Cambridge, Mass.

in the English-language newspaper the *China Press*. These pieces stressed the modernity of Household Industries and the chemical purity of the Butterfly products. One article ran the headline "Association for Domestic Industry Startles Shanghai with Modernity." Another read, "Butterfly Cream Perfect Aid for Keeping Skin Fresh," and yet another was titled "Care of Teeth Is Important Daily Routine: Butterfly Is Called 'Nature's Greatest Gift to Dental Hygiene.'" Finally, part of the page included pictures of the company and products under the heading "Butterfly Products and Their Home Are Creating Sensation" (*China Press* [Shanghai], October 10, 1933, B57).

Household Industries sought not only to raise its profile among English speakers in China but also to bolster its overseas reputation. Butterfly products were already being sold in Singapore and Malaysia as early as 1923 (Ye 1923, 43). But one of the company's more sustained campaigns featuring movie stars was pitched to its Southeast Asian markets in 1934. In pitching its goods abroad, Household Industries functioned as a franchise system, contracting out the production and marketing of its product to affiliates abroad while maintaining oversight over the general strategy.[35] The local company that launched Household Industries' products in Singapore was the Overseas Prosperity Company (Qiaoxing gongsi), whose name made clear that it was serving the overseas Chinese, or *huaqiao*, communities.[36] Through an affiliate, Household Industries aggressively pitched the Butterfly brand as a National Product to the ethnic Chinese community in Singapore. In addition to touting the efficacy and hygienic modernity of Butterfly products, Butterfly ads in Singapore's papers promoted the superior quality of the Butterfly brand over that of imports, or "enemy" products. Household Industries' decision to keep the nativist pitch strong in the Southeast Asian markets suggests that the NPM was transnational in reach and resonated among ethnic Chinese diaspora networks.

One of the more sustained campaigns for Butterfly products appeared in 1934 in the *New Union Times* (*Zonghui xinbao*) in Singapore. This particular campaign took a page from Unilever's playbook by essentially adapting the latter's advertising campaign for Lux Soap in 1932. The Singapore campaign included a series of ads featuring some of China's most popular stars from March to April 1934. First published in 1906 as the *Union Times* (*Zonghui bao*) and named the *New Union Times* (*Zonghui xinbao*) by 1929, this newspaper was one of Singapore's most widely read periodicals and reached a circulation of up to fifteen thousand per day by the 1930s (Kenley 2014, 587).[37] In Singapore's multiethnic, multilanguage print market, the daily was a Chinese-language paper and among Singapore's Chinese dailies was second in popularity only to the *New People's Daily* (*Sin kok min jit po* or *Xin guomin ribao*). Unlike the *New People's Daily*, which was affiliated with China's Nationalist Party, the *New Union Times* had the reputation of being politically independent. In the 1930s, it was a thriving commercial paper. Ads for foreign (i.e., Western and Japanese) products often sat side by side with ads for Chinese products with which the Chinese overseas readership in Singapore would have been familiar, reflecting the cosmopolitan commercial culture of Singapore.

For the campaign in 1934, ads selling either Butterfly toothpowder or toothpaste or face cream were rotated on an almost daily basis. Each ad would feature the photograph of a movie star. Li Lili pitched Butterfly Toothpaste and Butterfly Cream; Wang Renmei also promoted those two products; and Xu Lai endorsed either Butterfly Toothpowder or Butterfly Cream in separate ads featuring different photos of her. Bold promises about the products were made. The ad featuring Li Lili promised that Butterfly Toothpaste and Butterfly Cream both embodied the technique of modern beauty and employed the method of scientific hygiene.[38] One with Xu Lai claimed that Butterfly Toothpowder could expel freckles and clean yellow teeth and guaranteed results that would surpass those of the best imported products.[39] The photograph of the star, which was always set prominently next to the image of the featured Butterfly product, served to imply that the movie star endorsed such a claim and, of course, the product (see figure 5.9).

The use of Chinese film stars to endorse one's product in Singapore was an effective approach because Southeast Asia, also known as the South Seas, or Nanyang, was the biggest market for Chinese films outside of China at the time (Z. Zhang 2005, 116, 212). Major film studios in China expanded from Shanghai as the epicenter toward both the inland and south into Southeast Asia. They competed with local Southeast Asian producers, including the famous Shaw brothers, who also produced Chinese-language films. It was in this vibrant market that Singapore's ethnic Chinese communities consumed Chinese-language

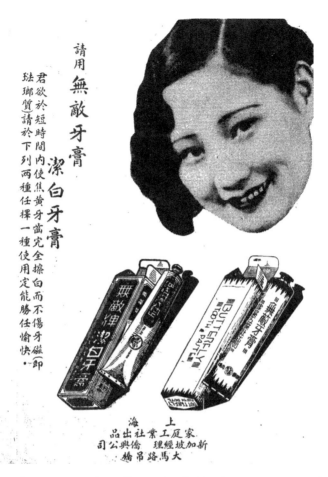

FIGURE 5.9 Screen star Xu Lai selling Butterfly Toothpaste in Singapore's *Union Times* (*Zonghui xinbao*). Source: *Zonghui xinbao*, April 18, 1934. National University of Singapore Libraries.

films avidly and came to know Chinese film stars through a lively fan culture. Singapore was at this time a multiracial, multiethnic, cosmopolitan colonial port city, where English was the lingua franca. There were a considerable number of non-Chinese-speaking Singaporeans—Indians, Malays, and the English. Most of these groups would not have been consumers of these films. "Straits Chinese," who were of Chinese descent but were traditionally more oriented toward English and Anglophone culture and had far more tenuous links to China politically and culturally, were starting to become increasingly bilingual in the 1930s (learning Chinese often for commercial opportunities if not also out of cultural interest) and could have been a potential audience.[40] But the primary audience of these films would have been *huaqiao*, or the overseas Chinese community, the dominant ethnic group in Singapore, comprising three-quarters of the population. They tended to be influential prominent businessmen, the middle class, and the well educated. They would also have been heavily courted by the Nationalist regime, linked to the Chinese nation legally by blood and race with Chinese Nationalist law based on jus sanguinis.

Chinese entrepreneurs outside of the film industry had also long been aware of the potential consuming potential of the overseas Chinese in Southeast Asia. Middlebrow Chinese entrepreneurs with transnational aspirations had been expanding their companies and exporting their wares into Southeast Asia since as early as the 1880s.[41] Some were expanding from China. Others were overseas ethnic Chinese, such as Aw Boon-haw (1881–1954), the producer of Tiger Balm, who tapped into these transnational networks that reached to and from China to launch their empires from Southeast Asia. These merchants have been categorized as intermediaries who played a role in "appropriating" a host of business practices from the West and adapting them at each node of the "local" (from Shanghai to the smallest village, from China's domestic markets to the overseas Chinese markets in Southeast Asia). By relying upon strategic alliances with governments in China and Southeast Asia and by localizing marketing strategies and employing the print media of Southeast Asia to their advantage, they were often able to outmaneuver Western and Japanese competitors (see, e.g., the discussion of Chinese medicine men in Cochran 2006). To be sure, this view of Chinese business practices has complicated the very notion of the "local," showing how nodes of the local in these transnational networks spanned from villages in China to cosmopolitan entrepôts in Southeast Asia. Pioneering as this interpretive approach has been, the question remains, however, whether it rests on an overdetermined analytical binary of the local (China and overseas Chinese in Southeast Asia) and of the West as the implicit "global."[42] A related issue is whether it is entirely apt to perceive the South Seas market as merely part of the greater China region. Recent global histories have instead started to characterize the Chinese diaspora in Southeast Asia and elsewhere not simply as an extension of the Chinese nation but as transnational by definition (McKeown 2001). According to this more recent approach, the marking of China and Greater China as the "local" and the West as necessarily "global" becomes increasingly untenable. A global approach also insists upon seeing Chinese "overseas" as part of the Southeast Asian entrepreneurial circles and on their own terms, but with transnational connections to China, an approach that thereby avoids what scholars of Southeast Asia are increasingly taking exception to—namely, adopting a national framework that treats Southeast Asia as part of Greater China.[43]

The approach adopted here takes its cue from this turn toward a more global approach to understanding the overseas Chinese communities in Southeast Asia. Specifically, it sees Household Industries' foray into the Nanyang market for cosmetics as not merely an extension of Chinese national history, even as the company strategically branded its products as National Products. Nor does it see it as a "local" market vis-à-vis the global West. Commercial practices adopted by Household Industries were part of transnational diasporic flows, and the company's deployment of patriotism in its advertising campaigns for National Products assumed connotations that were distinct from the nationalism emerging within China proper. Indeed, the overseas Chinese during this time were fiercely patriotic precisely because of their dislocation from the homeland, a characteristic common among diaspora communities, and their need to demarcate their sense of community in a multinational polity. It was in this context that wealthy overseas Chinese formed, for example, the Nanyang Chinese National Salvation Movement (Nanyang huaqiao jiuguo yundong) in 1937 to boycott Japanese goods and to raise funds for war resistance. They also proved to be avid consumers of National Product goods.

The advertisement campaign in the *New Union Times* illustrates Butterfly brand's reach into the Southeast Asian markets along patriotic Chinese diaspora networks and demonstrates Household Industries' global ambitions even while showcasing the company's (or its affiliate advertising company's) ability to localize campaigns to suit the immediate market. Although the two-month-long pitch was not a competition to choose which star should represent the Butterfly brand or nearly as glossy or high end in its production value as the Lux campaign, it was still a sustained campaign, featuring on a rotating basis four famous Chinese stars—Butterfly Wu, Xu Lai, Wang Renmei, and Li Lili. Wang Renmei, Xu Lai, and Li Lili were particularly well known to Singaporean Chinese audiences because of their earlier participation in the Bright Moon Song and Dance Troupe (Mingyue gewutuan). This troupe had traveled in the late 1920s to Southeast Asian cities, including Singapore, Bangkok, Malacca, Kuala Lumpur, and Jakarta in addition to the Chinese cities Beijing, Tianjin, and Manchuria. In 1931, with the advent of sound film, the Bright Moon Song and Dance Troupe was acquired by the Lianhua Film Company, which needed the skills of the troupe's singers for the new cinematic era, and the stars transitioned to film roles successfully (M. Zhang 1999, 146).

When Wang, Xu, and Li started to make movies in the 1930s, they capitalized on the wholesome image that they had cultivated during their time with the dance troupe. After starring in a host of successful films starting in 1932, Li Lili starred in *Queen of Sports* (*Tiyu huanghou*, 1934).[44] Directed by Sun Yu, *Queen of Sports* featured a female sports hero from the countryside who proved unspoiled by Shanghai capitalism. This role helped cement Li's reputation of wholesomeness, which converged with the NPM's pitch of nativist commodities as wholesome, pure alternatives to foreign commodities.[45] The other stars were also at the height of their careers during Household Industries' Singapore campaign. Wang Renmei's most notable film was *Song of the Fisherman* (*Yu guang qu*, 1934), directed by Cai Chusheng (1906–1968).[46] Xu Lai, who had helped Chen Diexian launch his Hangzhou hotel Dielai in 1927, was similarly an undeniable force in the industry in the early 1930s.

Household Industries' decision to rely on local affiliates to appropriate global marketing and advertising strategies and to muscle the Butterfly brand into the Singapore market via networks of diasporic patriotism was a smart one. As noted, the form of diasporic patriotism that facilitated the success of the company's nativist pitch cannot be seen as identical to domestic Chinese nationalism but needs to be understood in relation to the experience of the overseas Chinese in a multiethnic, multiracial colonial port city, where Chinese patriotism assumed a different connotation than patriotism within China. The localized campaign allowed the company to pitch its nativist products in a way that addressed the specific connotation of patriotism among the overseas

Chinese in Singapore. Such an approach ran parallel to Unilever's own global marketing approach in China (and elsewhere), which adapted a flexible template of employing movie stars to local audiences' tastes by using Chinese stars. Thus, with the ads in 1934, Singaporean-based marketers of Butterfly products were among many globally oriented actors who knew to tap into the transnational fan culture for Chinese film stars to generate brand attachment and to dominate the Singapore market. In this way, Butterfly brand—a National Products brand—went global.

CONCLUSION: THE GENUINE ARTICLE

Chen's marketing skills, so evidently on display in this chapter, demonstrate a considerable degree of savvy entrepreneurialism. From a less generous or more cynical perspective, they could evoke a more negative portrait of him as a showman with the ability to bluff and be cunning. In the entirely different context of nineteenth-century America, for example, these traits were often associated with robber barons, snake-oil salesmen, and other high-profile grifters. Perhaps the greatest showman of them all was circus entrepreneur P. T. Barnum, who brilliantly managed spectacle, was able to brand his endeavors and himself, and, indeed, as one scholar has put it, to engage consistently in "artful deception" in a new age of mass culture (Cook 2001).[47] Although Chen may not have been engaged in promotional schemes as slippery as some of Barnum's well-known hoaxes or scandalous curiosities, a quick comparison is worthwhile to highlight how Chen's tactics did indeed involve the willingness to engage in "artful deceptions" in order to pursue profit.

At the heart of Chen's "artful deceptions" was the mutually constitutive branding of person and object, which proved crucial in terms of its ability to engender a sense of authenticity for both the man and the objects he wanted to promote. To be sure, it was quite common for Chinese manufacturers to use the founder's biography to help market a good or product.[48] However, the Butterfly brand, if not entirely unique, is an exceptionally rich example. Having grasped the process of commodification through his serial novel writing, Chen applied similar strategies to his pharmaceutical commodities and hoped to do with his brand cosmetics what he had done so well as a writer. Working with his in-house marketing unit at Household Industries, Chen deployed his literary brand and reputation as a man of genuine sentiment to enhance the company's commercial and industrial endeavors. To authenticate the company's mass-produced cosmetics, Chen and this marketing unit played off of his studio names and his reputation as a romance novelist who trafficked generously in the stereotypical literary tropes of butterflies and mandarin ducks. His literary persona as a man of true sentiment helped him to forge consumer desire and brand loyalty for his Butterfly products as well as to stake a claim that his products were genuine and noble, as were his intentions to pursue profit.

The close relationship between trademark and the man as well as the substantial profits generated from such a relationship meant that Household Industries went to great lengths to claim legal and cultural ownership over this mark. To stake as exclusive a claim over the Butterfly name as possible, the company employed multiple strategies in the court of public opinion as well as in the legal courts. It pursued copycats, promoted trademark-infringement regulation, and disseminated industrial know-how on how to fight counterfeits. The company not only navigated the emerging global regime of trademark infringement but also acted as a promoter of nascent institutions for protecting intellectual property in China domestically. In an era when the state was rather anemic in its approach to this issue, Household Industries aggressively deployed legal means, marketplace tactics, and bully-pulpit power in the press.

Yet even as the company fought ferociously for exclusive ownership over the Butterfly name and for regulating trademark infringement more generally, it did not hesitate to "copy" marketing techniques from others when doing so suited its interests. The advertising campaign in the Singapore daily *New Union Times* demonstrates how Household Industries worked with a Singapore-based affiliate to pursue global aspirations by channeling fan loyalty to the Butterfly brand among overseas Chinese communities. In peddling the Butterfly brand, the affiliate—the Overseas Prosperity Company—adapted a model from an earlier Unilever campaign for Lux soap that appeared in Chinese dailies and proved willing to liberally borrow global strategies of marketing to forge the consumer attachment that marketers of mass-produced commodities so coveted. As in the making of the Household Industries trademark, where Chen's self-presentation as a genuine man of feeling in his novel writing lent the Butterfly brand a certain form of authenticity, this overseas ad campaign featuring some of China's most popular movie stars served to generate an illusion of genuineness to elicit brand loyalty among diaspora communities. It facilitated the relationship between the consuming subject—the modern consumer—and the consumed object—the commodity—that was predicated on a *sense* of genuine attachment, even if that attachment was in the end a simulacrum mediated through mass media and technologies of mass reproduction, a constant deferral of the authentic. The Butterfly brand had to establish itself as the genuine article precisely because it was one of many cosmetics brands worldwide. As a copycat campaign that was a layer removed from any purported original, the Household Industries campaign evoked the aura of authenticity of screen stars featured in the Unilever pitch to lure audiences, including ethnic Chinese consumers *outside* of China, through the elusive promise of achieving true Chineseness through the purchase of its National Products.

Although Chen and Barnum were separated by time and space, commonalities can thus be drawn between them. Each found success in periods marked by emerging mass culture and new levels of publicity and commerce. Both nineteenth-century America and early twentieth-century China witnessed the emergence of new techniques in printing and media, which were then used by cultural entrepreneurs to publish and publicize more inexpensively and to reach an audience wider than ever before. Both Chen and Barnum were savvy entrepreneurs and innovative adapters and became masters of marketing. Or, put less generously, both were tricksters and hustlers. They self-consciously managed their persona and brand to turn impressive profit. They dabbled in a range of careers, occupations, and fields in periods when new opportunities were emerging. Finally, each proved able to turn what might be considered deceitful behavior into a virtuous or respected trait. Barnum turned his reputation as a showman and profiteering into political fame and philanthropy during his lifetime. Chen portrayed his acts of copying foreign marketing techniques and manufacturing technology as patriotic and thus virtuous endeavors of emulation.

CHAPTER SIX

Compiling the Industrial Modern,
1930–1941

The preface to the domestic technologies collectanea *A Collection of Common Knowledge for the Household* (*Jiating changshi huibian*; hereafter, *A Collection of Common Knowledge*) lists its principles of compilation, one of which is given in the following excerpt:

> One can use boric acid (*pengsuan*) to gargle. But if you were to commit a simple mistake in miswriting a single character, you might write sulfuric acid (*liusuan*) or sodium nitrate (*xiaosuan*), which can lead to burning one's tongue and lips and even death. You can see how dangerous it is. Once there was a funny contributor who mixed a satirical piece in with the other articles that he contributed. In the piece, he wrote, "In order to stop a severe stomach ache, use *yushi* 礜石." In fact, *yushi* is [similar] to the word for arsenic (*pishi* 砒石), which certainly treats human life as a joke! The character 礜 (*yu*) furthermore is similar to the character 礬 (*fan*). Among our [country's] old ways, *fanshi* 礬石 [alunite] was used to cure stomach aches. [People would] grind *fanshi* and take it with water to treat gas pain. But if I wrote the character *yu* 礜 by mistake and the proofreader were to miss this, it would be disastrous. Thus, we must prohibit the pirating (*fanyin*) of this book in order to avoid misleading people. If you want a reprint, you can always order [it] by mail from me. (Chen Diexian 1935–1941, 1:2)

Chen Diexian was the compiler of this series and in this principle warned against the dangers of false, misprinted words, subquality medicine, faulty chemical knowledge, as well as the pirating of texts. All such dangers had the potential to result in the loss of human life. His point here was not to discredit industrial science and modern medicine. In fact, throughout his career, Chen was invested, both literally and figuratively, in promoting industrial modernity, its attendant objects, and related knowledge regimes. Yet in this text he acknowledged, if not actively generated, unease about new forms of knowledge and materials, as if to legitimate the publication of his text. One slip of the brush can transform the compound *fanshi* to *yushi* and thereby turn a beneficial medicine into an agent of death. Or, as Chen put it, "the difference of a single word can reverse benefit to harm" (Chen Diexian 1935–1941, 1:2). The difference between life and death, therefore, not only was dependent on the appropriate use of chemistry or the right application of biomedicine but also turned on authoritative, reliable editing and compilation of scientific and medicinal knowledge, something that readers could trust Chen to provide.

This passage is representative of textual strategies that Chen employed in three series on household science, medicine, and industrial technology during the 1930s. All three served to legitimate certain industrial goods and helped to assuage anxiety about inauthentic knowledge and false things. *A Collection of Common Knowledge* was published for both the general reader and industrialists. Its series of booklets on domestic matters was published under Chen's pen name "Tianxuwosheng" from 1935 to 1941 and was actually an eight-volume compilation of the "Common Knowledge for the Household" column in *Shenbao's* literary supplement *Free Talk*, discussed in chapter 3.[1] *Mr. Mei's New Compilation of Tested Prescriptions* (*Meishi yanfang xinbian*), published by the in-house press at Household Industries in 1934, with a second edition in 1937, was a second serial publication. Also published under the pen name "Tianxuwosheng," this seven-volume reprint was based on a publication from 1878 by Mei Qizhao, governor of Zhejiang at the time, which was itself a recompilation of a collection titled *A New Compilation of Tested Prescriptions* (*Yanfang xinbian*) from 1846.[2] Chen's third serial of the 1930s was *Collectanea on How to Acquire Wealth in Industry* (*Shiye zhi fu congshu*, 1933).[3] Targeting industrialists and manufacturers, *Wealth in*

Industry was a multivolume compilation of the Ministry of Agriculture and Commerce's earlier journal, *Industry in Laymen's Terms* (*Shiye qianshuo*1915–1925) and was printed by Xinhua Press in Shanghai.

Overlapping with a key motivation behind Chen's earlier how-to columns and common-knowledge bulletins, these three series were similarly meant to help promote his industrial products and confer legitimacy to himself, though in these later collectanea he did so as an established patriotic industrialist. Yet they did more than that. The 1930s—more so than the 1910s, when he first started publishing *xiao gongyi* writings—were an era when words, texts, and things were mass-produced, often copied, and counterfeited and pirated to what was increasingly seen to be an alarming degree. In this context, concerns about what constituted a real, authentic product rather than a fake or counterfeit emerged. What rendered a product authentically and fully "native" was another persistent worry, even with the drafting and dissemination of the National Products Standards in 1928, which sought to define what constituted a true "native" good (Gerth 2004, 192–200). Thus, if concern about industrialization and what constituted a truly native product had existed in the 1910s when Chen first started publishing how-to columns, ambivalence about inauthentic knowledge and pirated things in China had deepened considerably by the 1930s. In this era of heightened anxiety, these serial publications emphasized the relationship between sincere and trustworthy editing, the production of authoritative scientific and technical knowledge, and virtuous and genuine production of mass commodities and industrial goods.

These publications were also for sale. Accordingly, Chen had to secure the trust of his readers and convince them that his texts guaranteed the necessary knowledge for them to navigate an anxiety-ridden age of industrial materialism. Steven Shapin (1994) writes about the social life of the brotherhood of gentlemanly science associated with the Royal Society in seventeenth-century Britain. He identifies how these gentlemen's reputation for purported disinterestedness and apparent lack of commercial motive made them appear to be credible seekers of truth and was at the core of their ability to foster the mutual trust in each other needed to verify and guarantee their scientific claims. However, these claims of trustworthiness predicated upon the gentlemen's "freedom" from commercial concerns and ability to function freely in a moral economy served, in fact, to mask very concrete material interests. In the very different context of early-twentieth-century China, Chen was similarly seeking to guarantee the trustworthiness of his claims about science and industry, but his economic motive was central insofar as his knowledge was explicitly meant to facilitate commercial and industrial ends. Yet he, too, predicated the credibility of his knowledge production on the masking of some of the overt commercial goals of his publications and on the evocation of the moral authority of specific lettered strategies. What also needs to be noted is that whereas Shapin's gentlemen worked within a face-to-face setting, Chen's claims to credibility had to be established through the mediation of mass media. He thus depended on an array of textual strategies and methods of compilation to guarantee that the information on industrial arts and modern science he was selling was trustworthy, authentic, and nativist.

Thus, Chen's ability to compile and edit such information would serve as the ultimate guarantor. The personal care he took in vetting and editing such information was crucial. He married long-standing textual strategies of compiling and recompiling information and knowledge with a new emphasis on hands-on empirical verification (*shiyan*) and the goals of industrial and commercial pursuits. By claiming moral authority through textual competence, Chen legitimated the incorporation of modern science, industrially manufactured goods, and practices of production into daily life. He forwarded a discourse of effective copying and innovative adaptation of foreign technological knowledge as the basis of national production. He also promoted certain forms of commerce as patriotic, technology and industry as honorable, and native production and products as virtuous—attributes he wanted to associate with his own line of Butterfly products. Taken together, these three publications can be seen as a coherent textual gathering of the principles of vernacular industrialism that he had refined over the years and yet gained newfound urgency in the 1930s.

THE PROMISE AND PERIL OF INDUSTRIAL MODERNITY IN THE 1930s

By the third decade of the twentieth century, the need to identify authentic goods emerged in a context marked by unease. China's light industry had become relatively robust and competitive, and urban centers were marked by a far more sophisticated commercial culture than had existed at the turn of the century. Industrial products affected the lives of ordinary Chinese in very prosaic yet fundamental ways. It was precisely this newfound and widespread materiality that was generating anxiety, however. The flood of modern commodities and the specter of faulty industrial goods started to loom large. A shadow economy arose consisting of broadly circulated untrustworthy commodities, substandard medicinal items, and pirated and foreign goods. With the distinction between brands of mass-produced products indiscernible beyond their trademark, a market of copies and fakes emerged. Both domestic brands and international products were being widely copied. There was some acceptance of a "two-tier" economy whereby cheap imitations targeting the less-affluent market (which made up most of China's market) were tolerated even by some Western companies, in part because they felt that the shoddy, cheap imitation products could not be confused with their own brands (Dikötter 2007, 44–47). Yet the copy culture that had long thrived in China's commercial and cultural markets was perceived as increasingly problematic.[4] For international companies, concerns about Chinese pirating and copying quickly developed, and legal and even diplomatic entanglements arose over trademark-infringement and counterfeiting cases (e.g., Lean 2018). As we saw in chapter 5, domestic concern with copying was growing, and Chen's own company, Household Industries, sought to contain copycats. Finally, the unsettling integration of Chinese markets into the global capitalist market had also spurred the intensification of the highly politicized "buy and manufacture native" movement.

Along with this ambivalence about the profusion of mass-produced things, there was also a rise in skepticism toward modern science more generally. In the aftermath of World War I and with the start of yet another world war in Europe, intellectual ambivalence about Western science and technology in China deepened.[5] As science spread more widely, the general population found the newness and esoteric nature of such knowledge to be a source of unease. New domains and products of science and industry coexisted, often confusingly, with indigenous and historical technologies and knowledge regimes. Chinese medicine, local technologies, and other "folkloric knowledge" were being challenged by modern biomedicine and industry and yet continued to persist and thrive.[6] As in other countries where modern advertising resulted in the sudden rise and popularity of patent medicines, the sudden explosion of patent medicine in China's urban markets also engendered considerable apprehension about quackery and subpar quality.[7] The ability to distinguish between good and bad science and to identify false promises and misinformation became increasingly necessary.

To add to this picture, the 1930s saw a profusion of mechanically reproduced texts and print material, which also resulted in discomfort. The spread of new words and texts engendered the circulation of illicit texts and a growing concern about the spread of false information and untrustworthy knowledge. With the growing influence and adaptation of copyright and intellectual-property rights, the notion of owning ideas and words was gaining currency in the early twentieth century. So too was the related idea that the author (rather than the owner of the physical means of production or the actual printing blocks, usually booksellers' guilds) directly owned his or her creative work. This meant that copying texts without attributing one's source, once a relatively common practice in China, was becoming increasingly problematic.[8] Pirated texts became a social and cultural concern as brand-name authors, such as Chen's fellow butterfly-fiction writer Zhang Henshui (1895–1967) and others, were being copied left and right.[9]

In response to the general overabundance of words, including false and pirated ones, large-scale print projects were undertaken to give coherence to new terms, ideas, and language. Encyclopedia projects and the publication of *congshu*, collectanea or integrated series, were in vogue. The compilation of a Shanghai slang dictionary strove to make sense of Shanghai's confusing vernacular.[10] The Nationalist regime's public-library movement resulted in the Shanghai publication of the *Encyclopedia Minicollectanea (Baike xiao congshu)*. The publication of textbooks was also big business, as China's new public-education system saw that certain forms of knowledge were to be disseminated systematically via textbooks to form China's new citizenry (Culp 2007). Several such commercial print projects more specifically sought to render science accessible and legible to a far broader literate urban audience. Wang Yunwu, the editor of the Commercial Press in the 1930s, for example, actively commissioned leading intellectuals to compile and publish *congshu* associated with particular fields of knowledge, including the sciences (Culp 2019, 59).

In this context, it was as a successful entrepreneur *and* editor that Chen had a particularly good vantage point from which to detect and assuage social anxiety about false things and words in the worlds of both knowledge and commerce. In his capacity as a captain of industry, he had been witnessing his own brand-marked commodities stolen and counterfeited by smaller-scale merchants. As an editor and commercial writer, he was cognizant of widespread plagiarization of literary products and dissemination of false knowledge. To address anxiety about deceitful things and words as well as false ownership over both, Chen returned to his lettered roots and published serial collections. In an era when markets were perilous, when knowledge could be false and science questionable, Chen's series emphasized empirical and textual verification to offer a sense of security and strategy for survival.

A COLLECTION OF COMMON KNOWLEDGE: THE POLITICS OF VERIFICATION

Chen Diexian's faith in using editorial strategies to give order to industrial knowledge was unequivocally evident in his compilation *A Collection of Common Knowledge*. It compiled the submissions to his earlier *Shenbao* column with the same title, discussed in chapter 3. However, published a decade later, the compilation served more than its predecessor to assuage anxiety regarding inauthentic (industrially produced) things and words. To tease out the politics of this reprinting, we can focus our attention on its preface and changes in content. The publication was invested in promoting modern industrial goods and scientific know-how and yet exhibited a degree of apprehension about industrial modernity that was not as pronounced in the earlier column. To address the apprehension, the serial publication guaranteed the trustworthiness of its information by assuring readers that the material had been vetted and tested empirically in practice. Once armed with such texts, readers would, so the collectanea promised, be able to navigate a dubious world of misinformation, counterfeits, fakes, and copied commodities.

Who might have read such collectanea? Actual readership is difficult to determine. We know from Chen's prefatory comments that the target audience had followed his writings on technology and medicine in newspapers over the years and had written letters to the editor with personal observations and feedback (Chen Diexian 1935–1941, 1:1). Thus, some readers of the collectanea were the same as those of the earlier newspaper column. As for new readers, they were not that different, sharing a similar background. Internal textual evidence furthermore suggests that the readership was not a general one or petty urbanite in nature. Rather, it was likely a fairly tight-knit group of like-minded merchants, men of letters, consumers of technological knowledge, and new industrialists.

Chen stated in the preface the purpose behind publishing *A Collection of Common Knowledge*, noting that he selected and published "articles on household practice in order to contribute to society" (Chen Diexian 1935–1941, 1:1). This involved recataloging selections from the earlier column and adding new material. Additions included a bulletin on new recipes for cooking Chinese and Western foods and one on "indispensable industrial knowledge" (*gongye xuzhi*) that included various manufacturing methods that should be used in industry. Also new were a section on collected bits of beneficial wisdom, which posted scholarly research and included a Q&A forum, and, finally, a section called "Miscellaneous Jottings" on medical prescriptions. This section on medical prescriptions claimed to "post all kinds of cures and medicines that have been tested in practice and proven effective in the past half year, and that have been well-received by readers, including several rare cures" (I:1).

The eclecticism that characterized the earlier column continued to inform the compilation. There was, for example, an assortment of knowledge about how to cure and heal. The bewildering market of cures available in practice in China was reproduced in the text. Various cures for the affliction of *luoli*, a skin disease that can result in rotting sores and pustules all over the upper torso and neck, were offered (Chen Diexian 1935–1941, 2:74),[11] ranging from Chinese herbal medicine concoctions to local remedies, including a soup made up of cat meat and a paste that required small pellets of white mice feces and could be rubbed on the sores. Other entries were more informed by modern medicine and often included chemical information. The excerpt on using alunite powder to cure stomachaches, discussed at the start of this chapter, is one such entry. Entries on teeth and mouth care specified how to treat tooth rot with chemical products (see, e.g., 7:5 and 7:55).

Eclectic in its epistemological orientation, this collectanea nonetheless exhibited a degree of coherence not found in the earlier newspaper column. By compiling the scattered articles of the column published over a long period into a single series, Chen imposed a new order on the information. A collectanea, which collects knowledge and preserves it in a series format, is far more permanent than a newspaper column, which prioritizes the constant production of new knowledge to be consumed (and presumably jettisoned) on a daily or weekly basis. Also unlike the newspaper column, the series was published with a unifying preface. Editorial intervention was evident in the ordering of the content. Though a reader was not likely to read through the entire series or do so in one sitting, he or she would be able to reference the information at his or her convenience and be exposed to the logic of Chen's compilation through the table of contents and preface. Entries were collected and organized thematically into volumes, with the organizational logic laid out explicitly. For example, entries on the human body that had been scattered randomly over the run of the earlier newspaper column were physically collected together for the series and listed under one section in the table of contents. The entries were further subdivided according to particular parts of the body. Remedies for ailments related to the head were grouped together; those related to the throat constituted another subgroup. Chen moreover made clear that giving the information coherency was a primary motivation behind the compilation and warranted the reediting. He had received letters complaining about the difficulty of reading the original *Shenbao* column and encouraging him to reedit the information in a single series "in order to meet the needs of daily household use" (Chen Diexian 1935–1941, 1:1).

Thematically, certain foci are more manifest in the compilation than in the earlier column. Industrial knowledge and attendant goods in particular came to loom large. The original newspaper column had already identified *gongyi*, industrial arts, as a fundamental organizing category and included entries on the industrial uses of water and how to make one's own soap, artificial ivory tusks, toilet paper, different kinds of perfumed oils, and potassium nitrate. In the later compilation, the preface points out that one of the reasons for the reprinting was the need to verify the information specifically in the section on industrial arts. As the earlier *Shenbao* column did, the series treats *gongyi* as something close to "industrial folkloric craft" with its emphasis on methods of self-manufacturing industrial items. Chen's long-term commitment to spreading science and modern production know-how to his compatriots was still a sincere motivation. As noted, a new bulletin titled "Indispensable Industrial Knowledge" was added to the compilation, and the knowledge gained from such a section, it was implied, would enable the reader to discern false from true, good from bad, and copy from original—a crucial skill in this era of instability and overwhelming materialism. Finally, such knowledge would allow for the consumer to recognize even more the merits of Chen's brand. The publication appeared to promote goods that Household Industries sold as premade daily-use commodities notably by including information on how to manufacture them.

The prominence of industrial knowledge in the publication suggests that a large portion of the audience for the publication consisted of industrialists, perhaps even more so than the newspaper column. The collectanea had to pitch itself to a potential readership, be sold as a self-contained commodity, and could not assume the casual readers that a column in the *Shenbao* would have enjoyed. Thus, the compilation more explicitly positioned itself as relevant for fellow manufacturers, would-be industrialists, and consumers of technological information. The introductions to the segments on industrial arts (*gongyibu*) stated explicitly that industrialists constituted the intended audience, addressing this readership as "good friends in the world of industry, who help each other" (Chen Diexian 1935–41, 4:121). At another point, Chen urged China's industrial world not to spread itself too thin but to specialize in the production of one kind of product and excel in it: "A common problem with the industrial sector is that it wants quantity but it doesn't specialize. . . . If you make one thing and can sell it far and wide, then you can enjoy endless benefits. If you look at one thing and then try another, then it is 'in the morning it is three and in the evening it is four,' and I can predict you will not succeed" (4:121). Words of advice from his own years of experience were woven in to help attract the targeted audience.

Notably, Chen sought to mobilize his targeted readers to participate in vetting the knowledge he was compiling. He did so by promoting the notion of *shiyan* as a virtue that was fitting for this new industrial age. In modern Chinese, *shiyan* means scientific experimentation, but at the turn of the twentieth century the term had multiple connotations.

Early Republican editors such as Bao Tianxiao of the *Women's Eastern Times* drew from a global interest in promoting empiricism and lived experience as the basis of knowledge and thus published bulletins on *shiyantan*, or "accounts of experience," that described or discussed the scientific and practical dimensions of daily life (Judge 2015, 79–114). These editors were inspired by Japanese journals, which starting in the 1890s had featured sections on "accounts of experience," *jinkkendan* (Judge 2015, 90). At the same time, the use of the term *shiyan* along the lines of experimentation was also starting to appear. Writings by New Culture intellectuals who were advocates of promoting modern science increasingly used the term in this way. According to the *Comprehensive Chinese Word Dictionary* (*Hanyu dacidian*), the intellectuals Liang Qichao, Hu Shi, and Guo Moruo used the term to refer to the scientific process of forming a hypothesis and carrying out an activity to interrogate or examine that hypothesis. The entry for *shiyan* lists examples of this use in particular phrases, including "carrying out experiments" and "chemical experimentation" (Luo 1995, 3:1621). Lu Xun used the term to connote something based in reality or practice that disproves previous assumptions.[12]

In Chen's writings, the term *shiyan* assumed the slightly different if related meaning of something being verified against or confirmed by reality or practice. In addressing fellow industrialists, Chen expended energy in reviewing at great length in the preface the publication's compilation principles to demonstrate that the information was properly cataloged and, thus, that the publication overall was transparent and authoritative.[13] In these principles, he featured the notion of *shiyan* as a guarantor of the authenticity of the material presented in the collectanea. The knowledge in the serial, Chen specifically contended, had been vetted along the lines of whether it qualified as *shiyan* and, as such, was worthy of compilation. He singled out the *gongyi* section: "The part on the industrial arts (*gongyi*) in particular has undergone the test of application in reality (*shiyan*) by multiple readers, and each entry has been confirmed by reports of success and accomplishment" (Chen Diexian 1935–1941, 1:2). Here, the ideal of *shiyan* is a theory of testing or verifying general prescriptions, printed recipes, and universal principles against local practice and context-specific adaptation. Furthermore, Chen made a point of noting that in addition to his own personal verification, the content was scrutinized by a number of readers who had put such knowledge into practice, and the entries were then confirmed through their positive results and reports of satisfaction. Thus, his readers had the authority to engage in *shiyan*, vet the information through practice, and thereby help authenticate the collectanea's information.

The third principle of the preface provided a vivid if unconventional explication of the concept of *shiyan*. It used a cooking metaphor to validate skills associated with a social class different from that of Chen and his readers, including the ability to rely on one's senses to improvise and adapt:

> In these entries, the manufacturing procedures and the medicinal portions need to be adapted to circumstance. Thus, at different times, depending on the particular conditions, decide what is appropriate. . . . [S]uch an approach is similar to using a recipe in cooking. For example, if you have to fry or sauté fish and determine how much oil, salt, sauce and vinegar you need to use, there are not very precise portions [one can identify]. In fact, following a recipe mechanically does not live up to what even your kitchen maidservant does. As the heat of the stove always needs to be adjusted accordingly, one cannot be a stickler for rules. . . . In music, recording the score and identifying the beat in a scholarly manner is not enough to play music. You need to have technique in your fingers, and the beat needs to be alive and nimble. . . . It is not simply a matter of memorizing the score but depends on one's ability to feel the music.
> (Chen Diexian 1935–1941, 1:2)

In the face of an ongoing series of political and national failures, a discourse critical of effete, ineffectual, and even corrupt literati holding back China's progress had gained currency by the early twentieth century. One of the most trenchant elements of the critique was that classical literati culture had focused myopically on textual moral knowledge and in its reverence for the classics had passively received knowledge and had failed to look forward and engage in new, practical, and progressive knowledge. In this context, Chen's statement can be understood as a challenge to the conventional "scholarly manner" of elite readers and instead calling upon them to adopt appropriate strategies and skill sets for a new, industrial era, even if doing so meant drawing inspiration from an entirely different class of people. Specifically, he drew an analogy between how one should approach the collectanea's knowledge with the willingness to be flexible and the same skill used in cooking—a skill long associated with the lower classes, as the mention of the maidservant makes clear. The reference to the ability to *feel* music rather than merely execute it mechanically reiterated the idea that improvisation and adaptability in application were virtues relevant in the modern age and central to the practice of *shiyan*. His compilation was to be deployed in a daring, improvisational manner, its user flexibly adapting the information to new environments.

By making this point about the need to improvise, Chen Diexian portrayed himself as someone who genuinely knew what was involved in the production process. Written recipes in Chinese manufacturing history have long been an unimportant part of production processes and, at most, served as a trademark of sorts. Embodied knowledge passed down in kinship relations through apprenticeship in workshops was far more significant. In his examination of papermakers in Jiajiang, Sichuan, in the twentieth century, Jacob Eyferth (2009) points out that although recipes for pulp production and other techniques existed and that such knowledge tended to be the exclusive property of workshop owners who shared or concealed it at will, more often than not recipes were unnecessary for the actual production process. Knowledge on paper making was and continues to be shaped by the practice of manufacturing, which demands the ability to respond intuitively to variations and anomalies in production as well as constant experimentation and tinkering (Eyferth 2009, 47). Similarly, in the history of producing herbal medicines, recipes were often valuable objects, kept secrets passed down only through the family line. But there also existed knowledge that was not found in fixed recipes, passed through apprenticeship relations and the generations: experimenting with quantities, innovating herbal mixtures, and honing one's ability to "read" and respond accordingly to the particular situation, which in the case of medicine would be the subtle variation of each patient's condition. By urging readers to avoid being overly mechanical in their application of recipes, even while he provided recipes and manufacturing formulas in written form, Chen alluded to the reality in many production and manufacturing processes—namely, the limited applicability of the recipe and the need to rely also on embodied knowledge and improvise.

Yet even while Chen promoted his readers' hands-on experience and their ability to improvise and vet, the ultimate guarantor was still him, the editor of the compilation. Chen's expertise as an editor *and* as an industrialist was greater than that of his reader-practitioners. He was the one individual who could engage in *both* the sensorial practice of know-how and the hands-on vetting process of compiling and editing the reader's experiences into textual knowledge for all to access. Thus, even while Chen sought to show that he had the genuine and subtle appreciation for the art of manufacturing and the ability to verify knowledge through one's senses, he also established himself as *the* expert who could uniquely compile and collect the information for print. The passage on cooking and music served to appropriate everyday practices and their perceived virtues in production and manufacturing processes for urban readers, even while the compiler and his readers differentiated themselves through the tasteful editing and textual compilation of know-how. Furthermore, Chen's claim regarding authentic production processes and improvisational sensorial skill was ultimately ironic given the fact that many of the compiled entries were in fact translations of Western or Japanese articles on manufacturing. His relationship with manufacturing processes was thus mediated by a layer of textual intervention. For readers, Chen's editing added yet another layer.

For Chen and his readers, however, there was no contradiction or irony. Indeed, the preface seemed to suggest that the editorial compilation process was a means to vet and verify or, put differently, a textual mode of *shiyan*. In the second principle of compilation, Chen articulated the ideal of *shiyan* as practice or reality-based know-how rather than erudite book knowledge, but then he proceeded to point out the importance of the compilation process in identifying such knowledge and in rendering this publication unique in the print market. He wrote, "All entries in this edition are based in practice and proven to be efficacious (*shiyan youxiao*). . . . [T]hese [entries] were collected from earlier publications, and I, the editor, relied upon my knowledge to discriminate and select accordingly. I believe it is impossible to speak of similar books on the market in the same breath" (Chen Diexian 1935–1941, 1:1).

To guarantee his product, Chen detailed exactly what editorial practices were undertaken. In one principle, he noted, "Originally there were several articles, all including names of those who contributed the articles. . . . Those with mistakes have been corrected. . . . There were some cases where I discovered repetitions when I was proofreading. I also supplemented certain articles according to my own knowledge [of the topic]" (1:1). By keeping the names or pen names of the original authors or contributors of entries (providing them at the end of the entries), he underscored the collaborative effort of the compilation, credited individual contributors, yet ultimately upheld his own authority as the overall editor and compiler. This allowed him, on the one hand, to qualify possible mistakes by his contributors and, on the other hand, to boast of his meticulous review and proofreading of each entry in order to guarantee the trustworthiness of the information.

MR. MEI'S PRESCRIPTIONS: MAKING FAMILY SECRETS PUBLIC

Chen Diexian's collectanea *Mr. Mei's New Compilation of Tested Prescriptions* (hereafter *Mr. Mei's Prescriptions*), published first in 1934 and then again in a second edition in 1937, similarly functioned as a guide for readers to navigate forms of knowledge—in this case, medical knowledge.[14] Like *A Collection of Common Knowledge*, the series exhibited and capitalized upon the unease regarding the nature of commodified knowledge and the possibility of slick and false claims about medicine. To address this unease, the publication established its sincerity and trustworthiness by putting forward claims of transparency and by citing the authority of generationally transmitted and personally vetted knowledge.

The publication primarily collects and compiles medical and pharmaceutical information and is divided into sections on body parts: eyes, face, teeth, tongue, hair, ears, cheeks and mouth, throat and larynx, head, nose, and neck. Among the three compendia discussed in this chapter, the prefatory material in *Mr. Mei's Prescriptions* is less vernacular than that of the other two, evoking a more classical sensibility, which stemmed in part from the fact that the original text had been compiled in the nineteenth century as opposed to more recently (the 1910s in the case of the contents of *A Collection of Common Knowledge*). As mentioned earlier, this *congshu*—printed twice in the 1930s—was a recompilation of Zhejiang governor Mei Qizhao's republication in 1878 of an even earlier text, *Mr. Bao's New Compilation of Tested Prescriptions*. Published in 1846 by Hunanese official and medical knowledge compiler Bao Xiang'ao (born sometime between 1806 and 1816), *Mr. Bao's Prescriptions* was a commonly owned household reference book prolifically reprinted in more than a dozen different editions, including the one by Mei Qizhao in which Mei expanded, edited, and rearranged the material from head to foot.[15] Chen's reprinting was thus one of a long line of reprints.

As in *A Collection of Common Knowledge*, the prefatory material in Chen's reprint of *Mr. Mei's Prescriptions* sought to authenticate the content of the series by citing the editor's personal investment in the compilation. According to the preface, Chen had spent three months compiling the text, writing three thousand words as soon as he would wake up, from 6:00 to 9:00 a.m. each morning. Then, because of other obligations, he would not return to the task until the evening, at which point he would labor under the light of the lamps, with "my old eyesight, and a fog in front of my eyes" (Chen Diexian [1934] 1937, second page of preface).[16] After the text was printed the first time, in 1934, Chen discovered that there were still many mistakes, and so he decided to redo it. The careful recounting of the physical toil of editing the material, the complicated nature of the compilation process, the meticulous standards he held the text to, and his commitment to broadcasting the information widely was meant to confer authority and legitimacy to the publication and to promote the authority of his compilation work more generally.

Chen further made a personal investment in the publication when he directly linked some of the prescriptions collected in the series to his own family and provided eyewitness testimonial of the efficacy of the information. In explaining why he had bothered to reedit and publish Mr. Mei's compilation of *Mr. Bao's Prescriptions*, he wrote:

> My late father, who was talented at medicine, inherited the one copy [of *Mr. Bao's Prescriptions*] that our household had saved. [With it], he saved many people during the Taiping Rebellion era. When I was seven, my father passed away, and my later mother raised the four

of us. As a child, I saw my mother soak hibiscus flowers in thick brine every year. In the summer, if any child had a sore or boil, she would apply [the brine], and they would recover quickly. She would also [soak a] newborn rat in vegetable oil. If someone was injured by hot liquid or fire, this could immediately stop the pain. . . . Much of this I have tried myself . . . [and] all these [prescriptions] are collected and kept in a treasury. Thus, within our family, we regard this collection [of prescriptions] as a small pharmacy. . . . After reading [other] volumes on my bookshelf, I realize that all of them are based on *Mr. Mei's Tested Prescription.*
(Chen Diexian [1934] 1937, first page of preface)

In this passage, Chen proffered family transmission of recipes, personal eyewitness of the remedies' efficacy, and his own testing as proof of the publication's quality. He carefully described how he had personally inherited a copy from his late father, a gentleman doctor who had saved many people during the Taiping rebellion. In mentioning his father's noble medical endeavors in the past, he legitimated his own personal authority in passing down medical information. He went on to recite the various home remedies that his parents had once used and to list those that he had tried. Just as he had promoted the concept of *shiyan*, or practice, in the preface to *A Collection of Common Knowledge*, here his reference to witnessing his mother soak hibiscus flowers in brine to heal sores and then trying out such remedies turned on the assumption that personal application of recipes was crucial.

Even while Chen Diexian upheld family secrets and transmission through generations as a means to guarantee the trustworthiness of the knowledge, he also underscored that he was making those secrets transparent and public through the modern press for the sake of strengthening the nation. In the preface to the second edition, Chen wrote that whereas gentry doctors in the past had tended to pass their knowledge only to their sons and not even to their daughters, he decided to make the knowledge public and turn the volume into a household pharmaceutical treasury (*jiating yaoku*) for the public to consume (Chen Diexian [1934] 1937, second page of preface). He had taken this same rhetorical position many years earlier: announcing that he was publishing and thus making widely available family-based domestic knowledge. In "The

Warehouse" column entry on hair tonic from January 1915, quoted at length in chapter 2, for example, he stated that his intention in providing the recipe was to dispel any myths that there was a "secret technique" involved in making hair tonic (Chen Diexian 1915, vol. 1 [September], 5).

China had a long history of using clan rules, guilds, and secrecy to protect family manufacturing processes in the imperial period (Alford 1995, 16–17), and citing the status of clan and inherited knowledge to verify manufacturing, production, or medical know-how had long been practiced in Chinese literary history. By the late Ming, the gentleman-doctor would frequently publish his family secrets. With the boom in commercial publishing during the seventeenth century, books on medicine proved extremely popular and profitable (Furth 1999, 156–57). Case-history collections, popular vernacular works that brought together literati knowledge and folk knowledge from villages, manuscripts on medical knowledge, old pharmacy texts, printed household handbooks in easy-to-consult format, and sections on medicine in popular almanacs were consumed avidly. Successful local practitioners and literate physicians—many of whom came from hereditary lineages of family practitioners—would publish hitherto "secret" family traditions to bolster their prestige. Similar tropes persisted in nineteenth-century medical texts. In the nineteenth-century Hangzhou print market, Bao Xiang'ao's *A New Compilation of Tested Prescriptions* (*Yanfang xinbian*), the original text that was the basis of Mei Qizhao's reprint, which Chen was now reprinting once again, was a popular publication.[17] Bao authorized his compilation of "tested prescriptions," or *yanfang*, by arguing for the need to publicize effective healing techniques that had been passed down for generations. Such rhetorical posturing enabled a late-imperial learned gentleman who sought to publish medical knowledge and present himself as an amateur doctor to challenge the authority of professional physicians who worked for pay and were considered venal and greedy (Y. Wu 2010, 71–72).

Like his late-Ming and Qing predecessors, Chen could very well have been motivated by a desire to bolster his reputation and spread his sales with the promise of publicizing the "authentic" family knowledge that had resulted from relying on *A New Compilation of Tested Prescriptions*. Yet we should look seriously at how a strategy of invoking the authority of inherited family knowledge while at the same time boasting of a willingness to publicize this know-how gained new significance with the arrival of mechanized printing technology starting in the late nineteenth century. In the art world, for example, the 1870s were a time when artist sketchbooks, once serving as a trade secret for artists, became lithographically reproduced and sold openly, and this shift was indicative of a larger change in how the authority of a text or the fame of the artist was no longer premised on a regime of exclusivity and secrecy but came to turn on transparency and openness (Hay 1998). Similar trends took place in the world of literary production in the late nineteenth century, where a writer's claim to fame was longer dependent on the exclusive access to a novel's manuscript but instead was a "consequence of regular appeals to a wide audience" (Des Forges 2009, 41).

By the 1930s, Chen, a creature of the mass media, sought to employ the power of the modern press and commercial print market to democratize what had hitherto been more exclusively owned production knowledge. Yet at the same time he was also fully cognizant of the considerable growing ambivalence about the power of mass media and its ability to generate false and misleading knowledge. As a professional butterfly-fiction brand author, he knew that the mechanical reproduction of printed texts invited abuse and that literary products could easily be pirated in an era when copyright laws were nascent. In this context, Chen's self-portrayal of sincerity proved useful. In an age when the printed word could deceive in unprecedented ways, his assurance that the content of his *congshu* stemmed from trustworthy inherited family knowledge that he had personally invested in verifying and making transparent constituted a means to guarantee that his transmission of virtuous knowledge was *genuine.*

By extension, Chen's rhetorical claims in his preface gained meaning vis-à-vis social doubt about the commodification of knowledge. In an era of rampant capitalism, when anxiety about profit making as well as about false goods was widespread, a disavowal of the motivation of cold calculation was evident in the preface. To be sure, *Mr. Mei's Prescriptions*, a Household Industries publication, was a potential commodity that could generate profit. It moreover featured many remedies, medicines, and toiletries that Household Industries produced and sold, thereby serving to promote consumer desire for the company's products. And yet Chen nevertheless felt compelled to spend time emphasizing his sincere ethical motivation behind the publication of *Mr. Mei's Prescriptions* and de-emphasizing the cold motive of profit.

> These [prescriptions] are not advertisements.... [Rather], I am recording my sincerity here for you to know. Don't use the heart of a small person (*xiaoren*) to evaluate the stomach of a gentleman (*junzi*) (i.e., do not use your standards to judge me). When I first planned to print this, I donated my own 1,000 yuan and planned to print 2,000 copies. When I came to print it, they had me change [the page size], so we needed more paper, and as a result the price was higher.... If there is profit, we will print more and therefore can pass this knowledge on forever.... As for my wish, I hope that this kind of moral behavior can allow the sick and poor to benefit as well as help those who are jobless.
> (Chen Diexian [1934] 1937, second page of preface)

As if anticipating criticism, Chen warned readers not to use the heart of a "small person" but instead to judge what were on his part honorable, gentlemanly motivations. "Small person" was a direct allusion to Confucius's famous saying "The mind of the superior man is conversant with righteousness; the mind of the mean man is conversant with gain (*junzi yuyu yi, xiaoren yuyu li*)," which underscored Chen's claim that he was acting not out of the pursuit of profit but in a sincere and righteous fashion.[18] He then shifted to a more defensive posture, explaining that if profit happened to be made on the publication, it would be reinvested into the reprinting and hence enable the further dissemination of this important know-how. The passage set up the terms of this posture with its claim that "these [compiled prescriptions] are not advertisements" and noted, "I am recording my sincerity here for you." For Chen, engaging in the dissemination of medical knowledge for profit was hardly exclusive from ethical conduct of the highest order. In an era when texts and knowledge proliferated on the market, it was important for him to render the publication as close to a noncommodity as possible. By doing so, he could imply that the text's content was more authoritative than any of the commodified and, hence, somehow less trustworthy medical knowledge readily available for purchase at the time.

In an era when much knowledge was perceived as commodified, impersonal, and potentially deceitful, Chen's evocation of the authority of inherited family knowledge allowed him to assert the trustworthiness of his reprint and its content. The tension in the rhetorical gesture of sharing family knowledge—namely, the evocation of "family secrets" versus the claim of making such knowledge public—gained new significance in the modern period. With mechanized printing technologies and the rise of a mass media, publicizing knowledge was far easier and could have far more of an impact, but at the same time such tools to print such knowledge proved perilous with the threat of piracy and misinformation. Social anxiety regarding the power of media was intense, and the promise of "genuine" knowledge anchored in family-based know-how became all the more compelling. Thus, as was the case with *A Collection of Common Knowledge*, concern with falsity and the desire to authenticate the knowledge being presented profoundly informed Chen's agenda in *Mr. Mei's Prescriptions*.

WEALTH IN INDUSTRY: NATIVE PRODUCTION AND NATIONAL AUTHENTICITY

By the 1930s, Chen Diexian had firmly established himself as a leading industrialist and architect of the NPM.[19] In this capacity, he sought to mobilize widespread patriotic consumption and to promote domestic, autarkic production to counter fraudulent enemy commodities and imperialist merchants. Yet what exactly constituted a true "National Product" was an issue. The NPM had been struggling with determining product purity from the start as manufacturers expressed considerable concern about the fact that products were often hybrid—for example, fabric made of Japanese cloth but from Chinese cotton. By 1928, the movement formulated a set of standards to provide the foundation for defining what made a product Chinese and what exactly deserved a "National Product" label. Certificates issued by Minister of Industry and Commerce Kong Xiangxi would be based on these standards and serve to stamp the authenticity of a product. Four basic components involved in the manufacturing of a product were considered crucial in determining purity: capital, management, raw materials, and labor. Products were graded based on the degree to which these four components were authentically "Chinese" (Gerth 2004, 187–200).

Chen compiled *Wealth in Industry* in this context and published it in 1933. This publication consisted primarily of advice and tips for China's industrial development. It was divided into several parts, each section titled "How to Acquire Wealth in [X] Sector," whether the sector was agriculture, forestry, industry, commerce, mining, husbandry, fishing, or the silkworm production. Entries included "The Method to Improve the Picking and Manufacturing of Tea Leaves" in the agriculture section, "The Benefits of Individual Forest Management" in the forestry section, and "Merchants Should Not Pirate Shop Names" in the part on commerce. In the section on industry, there were several entries on how to manufacture toiletries, including "The Substantial Profit of Toothpowder and Cosmetics," "The Method for Manufacturing Rouge," and "Using Lye Water to Make Good Soap."

The preface of the publication explicitly linked virtuous commerce and industrial development to the betterment of society and strengthening the nation and stated outright that the information in the text was compiled for patriotic purposes. Chen noted that the compendium's agenda and, indeed, much of its content was from the Ministry of Agriculture and Commerce publications of 1915–1925. He then detailed how he had improved the original textbooks to generate the current publication:

> The original series was published in 118 volumes. . . . I compiled and categorized each volume. . . . We should treat this [republication] as public gospel. We need to let every family and household know of [the series] in order to promote interest [in industry]. If industrialists of all ranks know what [proper knowledge] to secure . . . people will have jobs, and we will progress [as a country]. Our masses will work hard and resist imports. Indeed, if we had had the support of the masses [on these counts by now], would we have been attacked by outside goods [as we have been] and be heading toward extinction each day?! . . . In the past two years, our economy has been spiraling down; the unemployment rate is affecting the entire

nation to a frightening degree. . . . [But] there are many roads to
prosperity. . . . It is up to those of us who have the will.
(Chen Diexian 1933b, 1–2)

The passage asserted the importance of compilation in making the
information "public gospel" for all industrialists. Compilation became the
means for Chen to verify the information and make that knowledge
accessible to Chinese manufacturers and industrialists. He then called
upon industrialists to use this information to provide the masses with
jobs, something much needed given China's worsening economic situation. To underscore the urgency of the matter, he used the metaphor of
war to describe economic competition and the threat of foreign commodities and thereby raised the specter of national and economic exter-
mination in the charged atmosphere of the NPM. Finally, Chen made evident the demand for such information and invoked the power of the
press: "Every time I receive a letter, I am treated as an old hand, but I can't
respond to everyone's requests individually, so I have urged the Xinhua
Press to reprint this book with a thousand copies for industrialists to
study" (Chen Diexian 1933b, 2).[20] Arguably, such authorial disingenuous-
ness was unremarkable in the era's literary culture; yet the declaration
still underscores how he sought to make the practices of modern editing
and printing crucial to the efforts to save the nation through industry.

Several of the entries explicitly mentioned the NPM. In the commerce section, "A Discussion on Whether to Display a 'National Products' [Mark] in Addition to the Trademark" pushed for using a National
Products mark in addition to trademarks (Chen Diexian 1933b, 1:32). In
"A Discussion on How the Promotion of National Products Must Start
from Improving Manpower," an entry in the industry section, Chen not
only sought to merge commercial and capitalist interests with a nationalist agenda of manufacturing native goods but also obliquely addressed
class tensions in China's industrialization, if only to elide them (3:46–54).
One of the more powerful political responses to the growing anxiety
about capitalism, industrialization, and imperialism in China in the
1920s was the mobilization of workers. Both the Chinese Communist
Party and the GMD actively engaged in labor mobilization against capitalists and imperialists (Tsin 1999). But by the 1930s, with the ascent of
the GMD Right and Chiang Kai-shek to the national stage, mass and

labor mobilization had dampened substantially. It thus may be no accident that in this brief entry no mention is made of the social costs of industrial modernity and the rise of social cleavages, political tensions, or the politicization of class warfare in China's cities. The issue of alienation between the human individual and his labor with the production of national commodities, a trenchant critique among the Chinese Left, was apparent only in the text's resounding silence on the matter. The entry in effect assumed the inevitable unity between labor and manpower, subsuming class tension into the agenda of nativist production. Given that *Wealth in Industry* was a publication for industrialists and capitalists, such an elision of class politics is not surprising.

Another fundamental impulse behind the compilation was the desire to present a narrative of social unity and national authenticity that notably did not hinge upon the use of indigenous Chinese production methods but could indeed rely upon the capacity to imitate cutting-edge technology from abroad. An understanding of production resting on emulation rather than on nativist invention can be found, for example, in "To Manufacture an Imitation (*Fangzao*) of the Small Foreign Knife," an entry in the section on industry (Chen Diexian 1933b, 1:7–8). The contributor of this particular entry was Zhang Yingxu, who noted that locally made knives were vulgar in their shape and had thus failed to attract buyers.[21] Consumers were flocking to Western-produced knives. To turn the flow of profit back to his fellow countrymen, Zhang promised to present a method "that does not require an engineer or the building of a factory." It was "effortless and simple to accomplish" and "in less than ten days" would result in "locally made, new-style 'small foreign knives' sold on the street" (1:8). That method entailed building on preexisting industry to turn it into something new. It was a method of adaptation and improvement (*gailiang*), and Zhang used a neighborhood in Beijing where knives and scissors shops were plentiful to make his point. He noted that existing blade stores could copy the Western-style blades, shops that made traditional handles could produce the handles for the new knife, copper artisans could make the copper nails and springs, and electroplating factories could assume the responsibility of electroplating the nickel. He urged patience and appealed to his readers' sense of nationalism: "This [method] will count on patriotic gentlemen. . . . For those who are manufacturing this kind of thing, you must not become discouraged halfway because there is no immediate profit. Those who buy, you cannot refuse its purchase simply because the price is a bit more expensive. You must be willing to improve industry along the way and have the will to promote national products" (Chen Diexian 1933b, 1:9). Patience, determination, and skillful copying were of the essence.

Some contributors were quite adamant about promoting masterful copying. In a discussion of the imitation of the Western ink pot and small knives, the contributor, who used the pen name "Shisuyongren" (literally "Vulgar and Mediocre Man"), exhorted against *slavish* copying of Western manufacturers. Rather, he promoted skilled copying that turned on the diligent research of craftsmanship (*gongyi*) in terms of grasping both the craft's knowledge *and* its tools. Chinese manufacturers needed to accomplish this, even if it meant studying the manufacturing of foreign objects. His entry included a written description of the technology behind producing knives and inkpots and a detailed diagram of the Western goods, which he expected readers to copy. Shisu Yongren stated that as a person who did not do any manufacturing, he could only contribute this small technique (*xiao jishu*), a contribution that was textual in nature, and he called upon big industrialists (*da gongyi zhizao jia*) to study the text carefully and act accordingly (Chen Diexian 1933b, 3:19–22). He wrote, "This is what Confucius had reasoned: 'If you want your industry (*gong*) to be excellent, you must first sharpen your tools (*Gong yu shan qi shi, bi xian li qi qi*).' . . . If we want to compete, we cannot simply copy Westerners; we also need to research [their methods] and have quality tools with which to manufacture" (3:22). The author exhorted Chinese manufacturers to emulate foreign technologies or objects, a pursuit he presented with little hesitation and found to be utterly unproblematic. What he considered problematic was the inability or failure to make industrial goods domestically. Masterful, well-researched, and thus well-executed replication of superior technologies, even if they were foreign, was the solution to China's halting industry.

Precedents for Chen's promotion of innovative nativist adaptation of foreign technologies can be found in China's modern history. In an article on the late-nineteenth-century Jiangnan Arsenal, Meng Yue notes the importance of the concept of adapting or duplicating—*fangzhi*—in the process of weapons production, which was focused on technological learning and training with the ultimate goal of cultivating technological creativity (1999, 20–23). To be sure, Meng's approach is revisionist, and as many earlier scholars writing on the arsenal have noted, there was considerable failure at the arsenals, with bombs notoriously failing to explode.[22] Yet Meng's contribution lies precisely in eschewing the issue of success versus failure in an assessment of the arsenal. In doing so, she is able to investigate what did occur, including the emergence of a discourse and practice of *fangzhi*. She shows that creativity in technological production at the arsenal was heavily dependent on duplication of Western knowledge and technology. The process of adaptation and duplication (*fangzhi*) was complex and included research, sample making (of parts of a weapon), and testing for efficacy. Such practices created the space for creativity, allowed for innovation, and resulted in products and models being remade, and the practice of *gaizao* or "remaking" was heralded as key to this progress.

Wealth in Industry demonstrates that half a century after the Jiangnan Arsenal, the notion of duplicating Western technological knowledge for creative and nationalistic industrial endeavors remained relevant, even urgent. China's copy culture in the Republican era was characterized by a great deal of imitation of Western products that served a large swath of the population that would never have been able to purchase expensive imports (Dikötter 2007, 38–42). In this context, copying (*fangzao*) was not always seen as problematic or immediately identified as a legal infringement. Moreover, duplication of foreign goods was central to the NPM. Thus, it is hardly surprising that in his technological treatises Chen, a leader of the NPM, not only had little problem with adept copying but also actively encouraged it. His endeavors as a pharmaceutical giant owed their success to a form of undeclared import substitution by his company—the substituting of "Western goods" (*yanghuo*) such as soap and toothpowder with native versions of those goods.

Just as Chen's industrial endeavors helped recategorize "Western goods" into quintessentially native products, his editorial activities in these domestic manuals and industrial treatises presented expert copying of foreign know-how as the foundation of authentic nativist production. Accordingly, *Wealth in Industry* exhibited a strong concern regarding false, nonnative industrial goods and promised that its compiled information would place readers in the position to draw sharp lines between virtuous native goods and politically fraught, dubious "enemy commodities" (*dihuo*). Yet even as this publication demarcated enemy goods from native products, it was a call to arms to industrialists to engage in a form of virtuous and skilled copying in order to strengthen national industry. A discourse of *fangzao*, copying, emerged that was indicative of this agenda of import substitution for the purposes of building national industry. The virtues of tinkering, adaptation, and improvement were at the heart of artful copying. Authentic production was thus defined as the manufacturing of native goods even if achieved through local imitation and skillful emulation of foreign manufacturing methods. Such an assumption conformed to the National Products Standards formally issued by the NPM in 1928, where the source of the technology behind the production of the product was never considered in the grading of the product's "Chinese-ness."

CONCLUSION: THE POLITICS OF COMPILATION

Using textual strategies of compilation to bring order to material and textual abundance was certainly not new to the twentieth century. In the seventeenth century, Chinese literate elites compiled lists and edited catalogs to make sense of overwhelming commercialism and materialism, restore the moral fabric of society, and reaffirm their literati identity vis-à-vis newly powerful merchants (e.g., Clunas 2004, 2007). The mere ability to acquire luxury objects did not define status. Rather, the ability to investigate things and, by extension, the natural world through textual knowledge was the key factor in establishing taste.[23] The practice of investigating things (*gewu zhizhi*) furthermore generated an abiding interest in managing everyday life through texts such as daily encyclopedias and in exploring the pharmaceutical world through comprehensive texts such as *The Compendium of Materia Medica* (*Bencao gangmu*) (as discussed in Elman 2005).

With the Self-Strengthening Movement of the latter half of the nineteenth century, the act of translation became conjoined with the act of compilation as intellectual labor necessary to generate new knowledge, and the compound *bianyi*, literally meaning "compilation and translation," gained currency. Compilation and translation were crucial in publishing the collectanea on modern science and technology as part of the

Foreign Affairs Movement, which sought to bring order to the profusion of new forms of knowledge (as well as of new and foreign things) (Elman 2005). In a period when China's central government was weakened considerably and no longer sponsoring statewide encyclopedic projects of compilation as it had in the eighteenth century,[24] new institutions such as translation bureaus and arsenals run by regional leaders took the lead in publishing collectanea and compendia on new knowledge. After the fall of the Qing, new commercial presses took over the task of knowledge compilation and translation. At the turn of the twentieth century, Shanghai's Commercial Press editors and writers employed the practice of *bianyi* to categorize all forms of knowledge, including modern science and industry. Commercial and cultural players such as Jiangnan philologists, dislocated reform-minded scholars, industrialists, entrepreneurs, and artisans, all fleeing the Taiping Uprising and migrating to Shanghai in search of new opportunities, sought "to preserve semiotic and textual diversity as much as [they] could in the face of universal modernity" and did so through the process of *bianyi*, "a specific cultural procedure of combining and restructuring words and texts" (Meng 2006, 33). They compiled Chinese dictionaries and encyclopedias and in doing so rendered new terms and new ideas translated from Japan and the West in a way that both resonated with and at times subverted or defied modern (Western) epistemological hegemony. Their acts rested on the belief in the power and politics of compilation—namely, that effective editing and compilation could legitimate, authenticate, and adapt new, indispensable knowledge for China's modernization.

Chen inherited this earlier generation's faith in the power of *bianyi* in legitimating and domesticating new knowledge. In the 1910s, Chen and other writers and editors had used the power of print to present industrial and scientific production knowledge as the legitimate basis for new forms of elite knowledge. After the start of the new Republic of China and as China's modern industry was just starting to develop, readers and editors at the time were driven by a considerable sense of optimism and enthusiasm in their production and consumption of "how-to" writings. Future industrialists ready to set off on bold, entrepreneurial initiatives consumed these pieces for tips. Self-fashioning urbanites appreciated these writings for their cosmopolitan flair. In contrast, the technological compendia and household manuals of the 1930s struck a more cautionary tone. These later publications continued to promote industrial and domestic science as the foundation for China's commercial and by extension political strength. However, they also exhibited a degree of apprehension about industrial science and slick words even while they promoted both manufactured goods and commodified knowledge. The use of this tension was clever. With newfound anxieties about deceptive words, false knowledge, and questionable commodities emerging in the 1930s, it became ever more pressing to address the authority and authenticity or genuineness of one's goods and words. By generating unease about industrial modernity and about (others') mechanically reproduced words, the collection publications rendered themselves indispensable with their assurances that they could serve as trustworthy textual guides by which to navigate industrial discontent. *A Collection of Common Knowledge* became a source of information and comfort with its promise to assuage anxiety through guarantees of transparency and the editorial feat of compilation, which was in turn based on readers' participation through *shiyan*, hands-on vetting. *Mr. Mei's Prescriptions* similarly attested to its own sincerity by assuring that the entries were qualitatively different from commercial advertisements but were genuine precisely because they had been vetted and passed down through the generations, claims that gained poignancy in an age of anxiety about insincere and false knowledge.

In *Wealth in Industry*, Chen grounded its authority and trustworthiness in its ability to define truly authentic nativist goods from counterfeit items, foreign goods, and hybrid commodities that were not "native" enough. By the 1930s, this distinction would turn on the domestic process of production and not on the provenance of the manufacturing knowledge or any nativist invention. Indeed, for vernacular industrialists such as Chen, skillful copying of foreign technologies was in fact crucial in the making of an authentically native good. *Wealth in Industry* was thus essentially a treatise on industrial innovation and adept copying, helping validate what Chen did in practice. It sought to define authentic or real production know-how not as the search for original or native technological knowledge per se but rather as hands-on and masterful ownership of knowledge, even if that knowledge originated from outside China. Industrial innovation and the artful copying and adaptation of technologies were hardly at odds with each other.

Instead, artful imitation of foreign technologies and ingenious use of indigenous knowledge applied to industrial innovation and strengthening the nation qualified as virtuous forms of nativist manufacturing. Finally, the endorsement of such tactics of adaptation of (foreign) technologies as the basis of innovation and national strength, which was so characteristic of Chen's publications, the National Products Movement, and Republican-era vernacular industrialism more generally, would survive beyond Chen's death. Indeed, some of these tactics appear to continue in the Mao era, when the revolutionary state endorsed autarkic and local industrial practices in revolutionary campaigns such as the Great Leap Forward (1958–1962) to devastating effect. In the contemporary moment as well, practices of "rogue manufacturing" that turn on strategic emulation and artful adaptation play a crucial role in helping fuel China's economic ascent in the global economy of our twenty-first-century moment.

Conclusion

[Tianxuwosheng] used his knowledge of chemistry and industry to establish new enterprises, and the gentle wind and dancing butterflies spread his praises. [He] wrote about his long journeys in Yunnan[,] . . . where he was inspired to travel and make his mark despite his advanced age.

[He] cultivated his moral character by composing literature. Even more impressive is that [his] heroic spirit was similar to that of [General] Yuanlong. [He] had no regrets in life beyond the fact that his country is not yet united.

Respectfully yours, Yan Duhe

—TIANXUWOSHENG JINIAN KAN

The butterflies of the Yangzi River danced and sank in the dream of Zhuangzi; the sound of the cuckoos in Sichuan was muffled on the day when pear blossoms fell.

Your unworthy nephew, Jiang Guangfu

—TIANXUWOSHENG JINIAN KAN

Chen Diexian passed away at the age of sixty-one on March 24, 1940. The epigraphs are elegiac couplets written to commemorate his life and collected in *A Memorial Volume for Tianxuwosheng* (*Tianxuwosheng jinian kan*, 1940).[1] The first one points to his chemical and industrial enterprises as well as his literary accomplishments. It also commemorates his lifelong patriotism. The second evokes his Zhuangziesque reputation and his namesake and brand, butterflies, in memorium. Longer eulogies in this publication elaborate on his accomplishments in the realms of literature and industry. One eulogist wrote:

He invented dental and facial cleansing powder to establish House-hold Industries and undermined the market for imported dental powder to restore the country's economic might. He went on to manufacture various kinds of cosmetics, wine, medicine, paper, soda water, juice, and the fire extinguisher and achieved great commercial success. . . . In literature, he could write prose, poems, *ci* poetry, verses, and novels. . . . His knowledge was incredibly broad, from astrology and geology to the three religions and nine schools of thought. He did not read English or formally study chemistry, but when he talked to you about chemistry, he was like a bottle of water spilling over, more knowledgeable than any chemist. . . . Whenever he was asked a question, he would share all he knew . . . it was truly touching that he inspired the younger generation the way that he did.
(*Tianxuwosheng jinian kan* 1940, 24–25)[2]

The passage praises Chen's broad and deep knowledge and underscores how as a generalist he appreciated all knowledge yet knew more than the professional and how he inspired the next generation by making this knowledge widely known. These memorials celebrate his life and paint a portrait of a remarkable man.

By all accounts, Chen remained active until his passing. He continued, for example, to publish on *xiao gongyi* throughout his later years. "An Exquisite Method for Manufacturing Table Salt" appeared as late as 1939 in a publication aptly titled *Xiao gongyi* (Chen Diexian 1939, 2). Echoing the principles that Chen had followed in his earlier *xiao gongyi* publications, this journal was explicit in its aim to disseminate scientific knowledge as "common knowledge" (*changshi*) that could be consumed by top university professors as well as ordinary readers, all of whom were encouraged to send letters to the editors and engage with the journal. Chen also remained at the helm of Household Industries until his death. The company faced some financial challenges during the early and mid-1930s but was able to revive its fortunes later in the decade. With the outbreak of the War of Resistance in 1937, Japan bombed Chen's factories in Shanghai, forcing him to relocate the company first to Hankou and then to Sichuan and Yunnan.[3] In 1938, at age sixty, Chen went back to Shanghai. The city was still under occupation by the Japanese during the war, but he decided nonetheless to return to be with his wife, who had fallen ill (*Tianxuwosheng jinian kan* 1940, 25–26). There, he was to die of an illness two years later, in 1940.

If the eulogies and couplets celebrate his life unequivocally, there is evidence of failure and disappointment between the lines. One eulogy titled "A Lament for Mr. Tianxuwosheng" recounts the destruction of his factories at the start of the war against Japan. It notes how until the Battle of Shanghai broke out, Chen devoted his final years to establishing the Butterfly Mosquito Coil Factory (Wudipai wenxiang chang) in Zhejiang, the Liyong Paper Mill (Liyong zaozhi chang) in Wuxi, and the Association for Machine-Made Domestic Goods Factories (Jizhi guohuo gongchang lianhehui) with fellow industrialists such as Xiang Songmao (1880–1932) (*Tianxuwosheng jinian kan* 1940, 4). His dental-powder factory in Shanghai was the first to be bombed, and the others faced devastation not much later. The eulogist grieves over the loss of those factories the most because they had long faced difficulty and had only just started to thrive. Such an account hints that even before the war not all was smooth in Chen's businesses. The eulogy then waxes sentimental in describing how Chen refused to give up even as he retreated inland. "[In] Hankou, . . . he relied on his rich experience and used the local natural resources to manufacture articles of everyday use. After Hankou fell into a state of emergency, . . . he arrived in Chongqing, where he strove to organize . . . local workers so that they would be self-reliant" (*Tianxuwosheng jinian kan* 1940, 25–26). Although this passage presents Chen's efforts as acts of patriotism in a period of war, one can imagine that Chen had little choice but to scramble, build new factories after his earlier ones had been destroyed in Shanghai, and exploit local labor. The chronology of his life featured at the start of the memorial publication and compiled by his children further hints at disappointment. The entry for the year 1939 notes how his eldest son rallied to raise funds and erect factories for the manufacture of paper when he heard the aged Chen mention regretfully that his painstaking efforts to manufacture paper never really met with success (*Tianxuwosheng jinian kan* 1940, 6). The final entry then describes how he had been a serious drinker all his life and that such drinking took a toll in his final years (7).

Household Industries survived the war and Chen's death in 1940. It relocated in Shanghai and regained a new lease on life after 1949. It renewed its attention to manufacturing Butterfly Toothpowder and Butterfly Cream, increasing production of the two commodities especially after 1951. Household Industries not only resurrected its manufacturing but also expanded sales into the northern and northeastern parts of China. Because of the invention and spread of toothpaste, however, overall sales of toothpowder remained lower than the highest amounts sold prior to 1949 (Shanghai shi tongjibu 1957, 136). And like other private companies, Household Industries did not survive past the 1950s. By 1956, it became a joint-state enterprise with the government and moved into the old factory of China Chemical Industries Co. At that point, it effectively ceased to exist as Household Industries (Chen Xiaocui, Fan, and Zhou 1982, 225–226).

As this focused inquiry into Chen Diexian and his company draws to a close, it is worthwhile to revisit the broader significance of Chen's efforts in vernacular industrialism. To be sure, the kind of vernacular industrialism Chen Diexian exemplified did not stop with Chen's death or the demise of Household Industries. Nor does it characterize all Republican-era industrial and scientific activity. In fact, the more familiar story has long been about formal forms of industry and science developed and pursued by a host of actors, from regional elites to the state and a growing corps of professional engineers, scientists, and other related experts. By 1927, with the rise of the Nationalist Party state, state investment in the building of industry became much more deliberate, and the People's Republic of China state only intensified top-down investment of industry building—especially heavy industry—under the first Five-Year Plan. By the 1950s, Chinese bodies were increasingly likely to be engaged in heavy and machine industry than in light industry and in mechanized manufacturing than hand and artisanal production. By that time as well, Chinese brains were regularly trained in the formal disciplines of chemistry, physics, and other fields of modern science.

It is thus precisely the purported unconventionality of Chen's practices that are worth our attention, especially because they force us to reexamine our current categories of analyses that render them not normative. The reality is that in the early twentieth century, Chen's practices were quite familiar and widespread. Obstacles to securing resources for manufacturing were considerable, and formal fields of knowledge such as chemistry and physics were not yet institutionalized. Individuals such as Chen engaged regularly in vernacular industrial practices often outside state-sanctioned or formal arenas. Some of these practices came to bear upon formal industry and science, though at times in unanticipated ways. Tinkering and commercialized knowledge work did not constitute somehow lesser, frivolous activities outside of formal industrial and scientific work but could indeed be compatible with productive industrial endeavors. With few resources coming from the government, vernacular industrialists such as Chen accessed and produced manufacturing know-how as "common knowledge," emulated both domestic and foreign technologies and recipes, and adapted them to local conditions by repurposing preexisting materia medica traditions. They mechanized by copying foreign machines and slowly gained a foothold in China's light-manufacturing sector (which, to be sure, had a lower technological entry barrier). If successful, these industrialists often scaled up. For Chen, this meant moving from experimenting with brine on the seashore to engaging in machine production of magnesium carbonate and finished products and ultimately emerging as a successful Chinese company able to compete in global pharmaceutical markets. Chen was hardly alone in mixing these vernacular practices with formal industrial work. Reverse-engineering foreign machinery to produce more suitable domestic mechanized looms was a regular practice on the floors of mechanized textile-manufacturing factories in Republican-era Shanghai (Yi forthcoming).

Yet even as some of Chen's knowledge work and tinkering did lead to the growth of formal industry, they also often assumed other social and cultural functions, whether shaping taste and demarcating social distinction or facilitating a nativist political message. The chemistry explored in the pages of *xiao gongyi* publications was not always exclusively geared toward conducting modern science or improving upon the next best manufacturing recipe. It was also being used for Daoist alchemical experimentation, which already had a long history in China. It was applied to inner-chamber experimentation, which helped define one's tasteful standing vis-à-vis the emergence of a market of mass-manufactured products. By showcasing the multifaceted nature of the tinkering and knowledge production pursued by

Chen and others like him, the concept of vernacular industrialism allows us to avoid any sort of teleological reading of these practices as merely "protoindustrial."

The notion of vernacular industry is useful in other ways, too. It allows us to expand the definition of the kinds of work that might be involved in industrial manufacturing. Chen's multifaceted endeavors provide a perfect opportunity to understand the *array* of labor involved in vernacular industrialism, whether material and mental, legal and commercial, or pharmacological and pharmaceutical. As a prolific chronicler, compiler, and editor of new knowledge and trends, Chen illustrates how knowledge work was central to the development of industry and commerce in China. The mechanical reproduction of words was crucial in the rendering of production knowledge—including brand formulas—as "common knowledge" for nonspecialists to access. In turn, this access to know-how provided many with a modest yet important entry point into light manufacturing in a resource-scarce and relatively inhospitable time for industry building. It would also allow local actors such as Chen to challenge emerging global regimes of ownership and industrial property by turning the practice of translating and adapting foreign technologies for local ends and nativist manufacturing into a virtue.

A related point is how vernacular industrialism encourages a broader view of industrial modernity insofar as it focuses not only on production but also on regimes of consumption and ownership. As a manufacturer of everyday commodities, such as toothpowder and cosmetics, Chen Diexian provides a particularly compelling case for exploring how new ways to make, consume, and possess things affected both formal industrial development and everyday society. Modern manufacturing generated a profusion of near-identical industrial goods that an ever-larger, more anonymous group of consumers could consume. At the same time and perhaps as a reaction, the rise of mechanized production generated the curious rise in the popularity of homemade, hand-based production of cosmetics and toiletries among elites eager to demarcate themselves from the mass consumer. Chen encouraged and capitalized on this DIY makers' impulse through his how-to columns. In terms of ownership, new-style industrialists both promoted and subverted emerging regimes of industrial propriety. Chen promoted legal institutionalization of the modern brand and trademark, which were central to the creation of brand loyalty for mass-produced daily-use items. At the same time, he deployed and praised practices of copying and virtuous imitation of foreign technologies for the sake of strengthening national manufacturing.

Finally, Chen Diexian's vernacular industrialism provides an interesting, early-twentieth-century Chinese case study through which we can appreciate the complex ways in which the rise of industry, the impact of global commerce, and the adaptation of modern science shaped modern China. As imperialist violence prompted China to integrate rapidly into an international capitalist economy and exposed it to new, scientific ways of understanding the natural world, Chen embraced translated technologies and pursued industrial endeavors with an open curiosity and a healthy dose of optimism, even if under the banner of patriotism. Yet ambivalence and growing cynicism about the promise of science and industrial progress emerged for Chen personally as well for China more broadly, especially after World War I. Chen, ever the marketer, was attentive to this evolving landscape, worked to manage the anxiety, and sought to profit from it. As a native industrialist, he founded his empire by drawing from foreign technologies and ways of building industry, yet he did so with an explicit anti-imperialist agenda that sought to present Chinese brands of toiletries as "authentic" in contrast to fraudulent enemy goods.

One might argue that aspects of Chen's vernacular industrialism such as its DIY ethos, hands-on tinkering, and strategic emulation can be found in multiple contexts. They can certainly be seen in most preindustrial artisanal contexts. They characterize amateur inventors seeking a breakthrough, technicians supplementing their laboratory equipment with everyday materials or combining different instruments, and DIY hobbyists crafting an anticonsumerist status in today's postindustrial world. The common characteristic is the rearranging of preexisting elements to form new assemblages—often with a new purpose and function. Creativity, virtuosity, and luck are often part of the formula. In times of shortage, such traits can help compensate for lack of resources. Such practices, moreover, have the potential to serve as a critique of capitalism. The production of new things out of recycled waste can function, for example, to disrupt capitalist chains of profit. Yet, despite the seeming ubiquity of these practices, examining the emergence of vernacular industrialism within the specific context of modern China is significant insofar as these practices have come to be strongly associated with specifically *Chinese* manufacturing in the modern and contemporary world.

To illuminate the modern association of these practices specifically with China, I end with some thoughts about the implications that vernacular industrialism might have for our understanding of China in the Maoist period (1949–1976) as well as in the current era. Although it might be tempting to regard Chen's efforts in the Republican era as merely symptomatic of a transitional phase, the ideological importance and material practices of vernacular industrialism did not wane over time. Take, for example, the Great Leap Forward campaign (1958–1962), a highly utopian, if ultimately destructive, experiment unleashed by Mao and radicalized further by zealous local cadres that sought to deepen the revolution and exponentially increase China's agricultural and industrial capacity. The campaign did so in radical fashion by attempting to mobilize rural populations to engage in large-scale infrastructural and industrial projects, such as irrigation and dam building. This industrial experimentation was meant to continue Mao's "permanent revolution," prevent China from sliding back into bureaucratic capitalist tendencies that were emerging under the First Five-year Plan of the 1950s, and propel China forward into communism. Waving the banner "Red and expert," Great Leap ideologues emphasized mass science and technologies as the means to enable China to leap frog ahead of the industrial world, especially in steel production. To make the industrial leap in steel production, local Communist Party authorities launched campaigns to mobilize ordinary Chinese to build their own furnaces and collect and smelt iron with the goal of overtaking Great Britain's steel production. The campaigns were hailed as exemplary examples of mass science and local, nativist efforts. In the end, these economic, industrial, and social efforts of the Great Leap were an unmitigated disaster. The backyard furnaces utterly failed in the production of high-quality steel. With the political pressure to demonstrate the revolutionary commitment to the Great Leap and avoid being labeled "rightists" or "defeatists," rural cadres throughout China overinflated the amounts of their grain production. This overinflation, in turn, resulted in a devastating famine that claimed the lives of an estimated twenty million people between 1959 and 1962. Meanwhile, little serious advancement was made in industrial production, and the population was left exhausted and disillusioned. Politically speaking, Mao Zedong was at least temporarily disempowered until he was able to regain political supremacy with the Cultural Revolution in 1966.

Although the industrial practices of the Great Leap are conventionally dismissed as ending in disaster, it is nonetheless worthwhile to take the ideological significances of these practices seriously and to consider them in conjunction with Republican-era vernacular industrialism. To be sure, there are considerable differences. The latter period's efforts were a state-sponsored socialist campaign focused on heavy industry rather than on light-industrial endeavors pursued by private merchants. The ideological orientation was also obviously radically divergent. In the socialist era, the pursuit of profit—central if at times obliquely veiled in Chen's efforts—had become deemed a core part of the hedonistic materialism of capitalism that was fundamentally under attack. A far more pronounced condemnation of much of Western science as "bourgeois" was also the case in the socialist period. Thus, at first sight, there seems little in common between the massive production of industrial steel propagated by the Chinese Communists and the playful experimentation with cuttlefish that Chen Diexian embraced.

Yet, despite differences, the Great Leap nonetheless endorsed many of the virtues that had gained relevance during the Republican era, including autarky, localism, adaptation, and persistent tinkering, even as they acquired new meaning. The relevance of local adaptation and autarky, for instance, can be found in "The Strength of the Masses Is Limitless" (1958), an account of steel production during the Great Leap in central Hunan Province:

> In Lunghui County, deputy secretary of the county party committee, Hsieh Kuo, set up experimental furnaces at Shihmen but failed to produce iron in 22 successive attempts. He persisted, studying and trying again and again, and finally he produced in all five local furnaces. . . . Leaders of co-ops, peasants, men and women of all ages, workers, government officials, and soldiers are all trying their skill with experimental furnaces. . . . When they first began to work

in iron and steel production, many people wanted to have "foreign" blast furnaces. They were not interested in these small native furnaces[;] . . . that line of thinking would result in producing less, slower , more expensively, and not so well, and it would not lead to production on a mass basis.

(Yin [1958] 2013, 416–417)

The backyard furnace campaigns celebrated self-reliance and persistent tinkering and experimentation as virtues. In an era of Cold War geopolitics, these promises of autarkic industrialism as well as the emblematic narrative of continued experimentation eventually leading to hard-fought success proved extremely powerful in helping generate a movement as radical as the Great Leap. Revolutionary industrial work was branded as nativist in orientation, while tinkering with backyard furnaces by the masses outside of the confines of elite or professional forums was hailed as part of the mass line.[4]

Arguably even more illuminating is a comparison between Chen's vernacular industrialism and the industrial practices that have helped fuel China's recent ascent as an economic global powerhouse and are often associated with the notion of *shanzhai*. The term *shanzhai* is often translated as "knockoff" or even "local imitation," but it originally was a literary term that referred romantically to the mountain strongholds in which rogue heroes pursued extralegal justice beyond the reach of authorities. The term and its romantic evocation of bandits have been used effectively to describe the manufacturing culture of underground factories located in manufacturing hubs such as Shenzhen that deliver rogue imitations of brand products. These products are not passed off as ripoffs or fakes but rather as lower-priced versions of famous brands with more or alternative features.[5] As China has emerged as a global economic force—both the world's factory and a vast marketplace—at the turn of the twenty-first century, its increasingly market-oriented economy has unleashed tremendous energy and entrepreneurial production of such copies. Smaller Chinese manufacturers experiment with and adapt more expensive brands in order to add features to the emulated brand item without having to abide by costly regulations or pay value-added taxes (Gerth 2010, 154). Cell phones, MP3 players, and computers are quintessential *shanzhai* objects, but so are food, fashion accessories, aircraft parts, cars, and even amusement parks (Lin 2011, 3). The *shanzhai* culture emerging in Shenzhen's electronic markets furthermore moves beyond the purely industrial into the realm of aesthetics, with new forms of artwork and creativity in the area, including the large-scale production of "ready-made," hand-painted copies of masters' paintings, which turn on bespoke copying (Wong 2014).

China's large-scale counterfeiting and rogue manufacturing practices have predictably generated international headlines portraying China as a quintessential copier in the contemporary world. Despite the occurrence of counterfeiting worldwide, China has become identified as *the* place unable to innovate and add productively and originally to the global economy, dwarfing all other places in the Western imagination as the most egregious offender in the production of fakes.[6] Some scholars, although more measured, premise their analysis of China's counterfeiting on the assumption that such copying practices constitute illicit and problematic behavior that needs to be contained. The political scientist Andrew Mertha (2005), for example, has shown how exogenous foreign pressure on China to police counterfeiting is less important and less effective than efforts by local bureaucracies, which are crucial in ensuring (or not ensuring) the enforcement of intellectual-property rights on the ground. Although he acknowledges that historical reasons for the counterfeiting exist, including the fact that as a "late-developing" country China has wanted to increase the diffusion of technologies to catch up, his ultimate point of departure remains that enforcement of anticounterfeiting efforts is desirable.[7] The historian Karl Gerth (2010) has also pointed to the massive counterfeiting that characterizes China in the first decades of the twenty-first century, and he notes that with weak protections and massive manufacturing capacity the country has been so rife with copies that it has emerged as a global superpower in the production and consumption of fakes (with the complicity of foreign consumers). He notes, too, that even if the national government (often in the face of international pressure) attempts to enforce intellectual-property rights, localities are often driven by the prospect of high profits in fakes to avoid such enforcement (138). Ultimately, Gerth rings a cautionary note and suggests that the counterfeit culture has generated a situation in which Chinese consumers live in a world of uncertainty (133).

To be sure, some of the fake manufacturing has created scares, notably in the arenas of medicine and food products, recently including baby formula (Gerth 2010, 144–148). However, one might note, as Frank Dikötter (2007) does for an earlier period, that as sophisticated markets for fakes emerge, an equally sophisticated army of savvy consumers who handily navigate these markets emerges as well. As factory workers have started to achieve new levels of consuming power, they have generated an insatiable appetite for the very *shanzhai* goods that many of them are producing, with many consumers preferring them over the more expensive international brand names (Lin 2011, 18–20). Moreover, an entire infrastructure supports the counterfeit market, is quite systematized and global, and spans cities such as Shenzhen, Shanghai, Taipei, and New York, even while it is deeply embedded in local networks and shopping cultures (Lin 2011, 35–56). Consumers browsing from Canal Street in New York to Petaling Street in Kuala Lampur navigate marketplaces of fakes. They know what malls, markets, alleys, and department stores carry counterfeit goods and where to buy higher-quality fakes or lesser-quality items. In a trip to a massive Shanghai mall dedicated solely to selling "copy" eyeglass frames in 2005, I saw stalls upon stalls of glass frames that were divided into the categories "first-tier fake," "second-tier fake," and "third-tier fake." These distinctions were evident in price and quality as well as in the frames' ability to capture the "look" of a "genuine" Prada or Gucci brand of eyewear. As Dikötter notes for the early twentieth century, the lower-priced fakes allow those who would never buy the brand-name item because they can't afford it to "aspire" to and even to help advertise the "real" brand to a much larger potential consuming audience.

From the perspective of production as well, an alternative discourse around *shanzhai* has emerged, both domestically and internationally, that casts *shanzhai* in an increasingly positive and even rosy light. Some of the coverage risks being overly celebratory and may help forward, if unwittingly, both the agenda of the Chinese state and neoliberal interests, which are increasingly intertwined especially after China's entrance into the World Trade Organization in 2001.[8] Journalists, for example, have praised the manufacturing culture of *shanzhai* in Shenzhen by likening the city to Silicon Valley and celebrating the area as a tech "nirvana" (Whitwell 2014; Rivers 2018). *Shanzhai* practices are increasingly linked to celebratory accounts of new forms of makers' movements. In 2015, the Chinese government implemented a policy characterized by the slogan "mass makerspace—mass entrepreneurship—mass innovation."[9] As part of the government's push to build a new innovation economy in China, this policy promoted the buildup of incubator spaces and the cultivation of an entrepreneurial mindset among Chinese citizens and generated interest in *shanzhai* production as an example of such makers' communities. Neoliberal interests have attached themselves to such movements as well, with large global firms such as Intel providing direct support of makers' initiatives in southern China.[10] These developments and endorsements draw from a larger global discourse on makers' cultures that is often rendered as the romantic picture of garage inventors, fashionable incubators, and startup entrepreneurism that has emerged with the rise of the technology ecosystems of places such as Silicon Valley.

Scholars have similarly started to offer a positive view of *shanzhai*, even while aiming to approach it from a critical perspective. Adopting a science-and-technology studies perspective, some present *shanzhai* as design and manufacturing activities that combine a DIY ethos with practices of emulation and collaboration. They show how Shenzhen-based companies such as Beijing Genomics Institute (Huada jiyin), a DNA-sequencing research institute have drawn from the city's *shanzhai* ecology and free flow of resources to establish themselves as creative, hybrid corporations that are competitive globally (see, e.g., Stevens 2018). One scholar argues for the possibility that counterfeiting communities, especially *shanzhai* producers, can bring into view alternatives to global neoliberalism, something the postsocialist state seeking to shore up its legitimacy in ways that conform to contemporary intellectual-property-rights regimes has failed to do (F. Yang 2016, 23–25). Others note how communities of makers have taken advantage of free access to resources and knowledge to engage in experimental technological production and innovative design (see, e.g., Lindtner, Greenspan, and Li 2014). They point to how open-source hardware advocates who are part of such makers' movements claim to be creating "hackerspaces with Chinese characteristics" that root their innovation in reuse and resourcefulness. They see their endeavors as the "future of making" and as having the potential to unsettle global (i.e., Western) narratives on industrial production and technology innovation (Lindtner 2015, 856–858). Some scholars (see, e.g., Lindtner, Bardzell, and Bardzell 2016) even argue that the study of the making cultures of China (and Taiwan), including but not limited to the *shanzhai* practices, can be the basis of an "anticipatory design" approach, which seeks to speculate about the democratic potential of new technologies in generating social justice. Advocates of such an approach seem to want to recover aspects of what they identify as the utopian techno-solutionism embedded in *shanzhai* practices and related makers' movements as a way forward to more equitable and sustainable manufacturing and technology practices.

These recent science-and-technology and anthropological studies are helpful especially insofar as they inquire into how epistemology (how to know in this new world of technology) and ethics (how to act in this increasingly globalized market) are inextricably linked. They identify how local practices of innovation rest on copying, hacking, and defying normative practices of the formal intellectual-property rights regime. These practices then help articulate pathways by which makers with underwhelming or few resources or capital can nonetheless gain a foothold in the global economy and even destabilize established chains of capital. There has recently emerged, however, a concern for the need to remain vigilant about how overly positive endorsements of makers' cultures might serve to mask the Chinese state's agenda, the expansion of neoliberal ideals, and the perpetuation of exploitative practices. Some sound the alarm about how the Chinese government and multinational corporations are interested in co-opting these grassroots makers' movements. More rosy depictions might also overlook how social inequity along gender lines and rural–urban divisions in factory towns and more middle-class incubator hubs persist.[11] Some scholars who were initially optimistic regarding the potential of these new makers' communities now document exploitative labor practices along gender and racialized lines.[12]

It is worthwhile to place Chen Diexian's vernacular industrialism alongside this contemporary *shanzhai* manufacturing, precisely because the implications of this contemporary phenomenon continue to be assessed in both scholarly and journalistic circles and are at the center of increasingly fraught U.S.-China trade relations. Making a connection between the two does *not* mean drawing a straight or direct line of causality from Chen's early-twentieth-century vernacular industrialism to twenty-first-century *shanzhai*. Rather, a consideration of the two together can serve to remind contemporary observers that *shanzhai* practices of strategic emulation, hands-on tinkering, "open-source" know-how, assembling and incremental improvement to remake technology all have a far longer history in China and were thus not always tied to contemporary neoliberal interests and postsocialist ideals per se. Such a historical perspective might help temper some of the more extreme assessments of the significance of contemporary *shanzhai*, whether they are sounding dire warnings that *shanzhai* is indicative of quintessential Chinese counterfeiting that precludes all innovation or are naively celebrating the emancipatory nature of China's new makers' movements.

Furthermore, when considering the two periods side by side, we can see how and why practices of DIY tinkering, copying, improving, and reassembling have come to be so closely associated with modern China and why they have come to be seen as "rogue" in global discourses, both in a derogatory and romanticized manner. Republican-era vernacular industrialism and contemporary *shanzhai* manufacturing overlap insofar as they emerged during moments of China's entry or reentry into global capitalism. Yet real differences between the two moments that bookend the long twentieth century exist and reflect some of the variant political implications behind not just the manufacturing cultures but also the divergent place of China vis-à-vis global capitalism *and* the differences between capitalism in the two eras. In the earlier moment, the nascent Republic of China was struggling with what were unremitting economic and political imperialist pressures while being ripped apart by internal warfare and political fragmentation. Despite this inhospitable context, vernacular industrialists such as Chen were able to adapt new forms of industrial manufacturing that emerged with global developments in chemistry and physics to generate a patriotic and anti-imperialist National Products Movement, in which "rogue" practices for the purposes of import substitution were deemed necessary. Republican-era vernacular industrialism broadcast a powerful anti-imperialist sentiment that aligned with a nativist movement during a period when China had a weak central state. At the same time, these acts of patriotism were not always purely patriotic and, as we have seen with Chen, could at the same time serve concrete marketing purposes, which could then become the basis of considerable power and wealth.

The contemporary moment offers us a different iteration of China and its relationship with global capitalism. Today's *shanzhai* and counterfeit manufacturing have emerged during a period when a strong postsocialist authoritarian state has been eager to reenter global capitalism and has adopted policies that have enabled China to do this extremely successfully. Practices of *shanzhai* copying and adapting electronic and digital technologies of the current postindustrial global economy have been part of this success, helping fuel China's ascent as an economic powerhouse. At times, the global reach of *shanzhai* production in terms of the markets it penetrates allows it to defy or subvert the postsocialist state's central goal of aligning China's national economy with global neoliberal institutions. At other times, the state is co-opting *shanzhai* for its own agenda. Regardless, the success of such forms of "Chinese" production has generated anxiety among global competitors, an anxiety that in the current moment is resulting in increased tension between China and the United States. However, the very fact that these practices are both historically and currently unsettling can be productively generative. Chen's vernacular industrialism in the early twentieth century and today's *shanzhai* force us to rethink conventional narratives and normative ways of understanding ownership, innovation, and what constitutes industrial work and industrial development. And in doing so, they allow us to maintain an ever-critical perspective on our ways of knowing the world, both past and present.

Glossary

baihua 白話
baihua bao 白話報
baihuawen 白話文
Baike xiao congshu 百科小叢書
Ban Zhao 班昭
bao ren zhong 報人鐘
Bao Tianxiao 包天笑
Bao Xiang'ao 鮑相璈
Baomushe 飽目社
Bencao gangmu 本草綱目
bianji 編輯
bianyi 編譯
bo 博
bolan 博覽
bowu 博物
bowuguan 博物館
bowuyuan 博物園
boxue 博學
Bu Zixia 卜子夏
Cai Chusheng 蔡楚生
Cai Yuanpei 蔡元培
caiyong 採用

camian yafen 擦面牙粉

Cansang 蠶桑

Cao Xueqin 曹雪芹

chan 產

changshi 常識

Chaoran 超然

Chen Cidie 陳次蝶

Chen Diexian 陳碟仙

Chen Dingshan 陳定山

Chen Fuyuan 陳福元

Chen Qu 陳蘧

Chen Shousong 陳壽嵩

Chen Xiaocui 陳小翠

Chen Xu 陳栩

Chen Yanyan 陳燕燕

Chen Yingning 陳櫻寧

chi 尺

chibi 赤鼻

chidu 尺牘

chuanshen 傳神

congshu 叢書

cui 萃

Cuili gongsi 萃利公司

da gongyi zhizao jia 大工藝製造家

da jiating 大家庭

Dafeng bohe gongsi 大豐薄荷公司

Daguanbao 大觀報

Dai 戴

Dasheng diyi shachang 大生第一紗廠

Daxue 大學

De Xiansheng 德先生

di 敵

Dianshizhai huabao 點石齋畫報

Dianyin huabao 電音畫報

Die 蝶

Dielai 蝶來

Dieshuang 蝶霜

dihuo 敵貨

Ding Chuwo 丁初我

Dingshang 頂上

dingxiangyou 丁香油

Dongfang zazhi 東方雜誌

Du Jiutian 杜就田

Du Xunhe 杜荀鶴

duiyi 對譯

Ershi shijie zhuzuolin she 二十世界著作林社

faming 發明

fan 礬

Fang Yexian 方液仙

fangsuan 肪酸

fangzao 仿造

fangzhi 仿製

fanshi 礬石

fanyin 翻印

fei 肥

feizao 肥皂

Fu'ermosi zhentan'an quanji 福爾摩斯偵探案全集

Funü shibao 婦女時報

Funü zazhi 婦女雜誌

gailiang 改良

gailiang yinzi qi 改良引字器

gaizao 改造

gewu 格物

gewu zhizhi 格物致知

gong 工

gong yu shan qi shi, bi xian li qi qi 工欲善其事，必先利其器

Gongshang xuebao 工商學報

gongye 工業

gongye shiyansuo 工業實驗所

gongye xuzhi 工業須知

gongyi 工藝

gongyibu 工藝部

gongyi huaxue 工藝化學

gongyiju 工藝局

guan 官

Guangfu hui 光復會

Guanyin fen 觀音粉

guifang 閨房

guige 閨閣

guixiu 閨秀

guixiu zuojia 閨秀作家

guiyou 閨友

guo 國

Guo Moruo 郭沫若

guohuo 國貨

guohuo zhi yinzhe 國貨之隱者

guwan 古玩

Haishiling 海士苓

hao 號

He Gongdan 何公旦

Hebei sheng gongye shiyansuo 河北省工業試驗所

"Hei die" "黑蝶"

Hengchanghou 恆昌厚

hong 紅

Hongloumeng 紅樓夢

Hu 胡

hu 蝴

huchi shengpin 護齒聖品

Hu Die 胡蝶

Hu Guangsu 胡光驌

Hu Xianglin 胡翔林

hua 華

Hua Chishi 華痴石

Hua-Ying yaofang 華英藥房

Huada jiyin 华大基因

Hua'nan 華南

Hua'nan huaxue gongyeshe 華南化學工業社

Huang Chanhua 黃懺華

Huang Gongdu 黃公度

huaqiao 華僑

Huaqiu 花球

Huaxue gongyi 化學工藝

huaxuejia 化學家

huayan 化驗

huayan shi 化驗師

hudie 蝴蝶

hui 會

Huiquan qishui chang 惠泉汽水廠

huishe 會社

jia 家

Jia Baoyu　賈寶玉

Jiandao　箭刀

"Jiang jin jiu"　"將近酒"

jiao　角

jiashu　家書

jiating　家庭

"Jiating changshi"　"家庭常識"

Jiating changshi huibian　家庭常識彙編

Jiating gongyeshe gufen lianhe gongsi　家庭工業社股份聯合公司

"Jiating xinshi"　"家庭新識"

jiating yaoku　家庭藥庫

Jiating zhihe chang　家庭製盒廠

jiazheng　家政

jin　斤

Jin Ping Mei cihua　金瓶梅辭話

Jingangshi　金剛石

Jingshi youmin xiyisuo　京師遊民習藝所

Jinhua　進化

jinkkendan　實驗談

jiu wenren　舊文人

Jizhi guohuo gongchang lianhehui　機製國貨工廠聯合會

juhua guo　菊花鍋

junzi　君子

junzi yuyu yi, xiaoren yuyu li　君子喻於義，小人喻於利

Kefa da yaofang　科發大藥房

kexue　科學

kexue xiao changshi　科學小常識

Kexue yiqi guan　科學儀器館

Kexue zazhi　科學雜誌

Kong Xiangxi　孔祥熙

Kongque huagongshe　孔雀化工社

ku　庫

Kuang Yu　匡予

kulu　苦滷

Lai　來

lan　覽

Leizhuuan　淚珠緣

li　利

li　理

Li Bai　李白

Li Chuangjue　李長覺

Li Hongjun　淡紅君

Li Lili　黎莉莉

liang　兩

Liang Qichao　梁啟超

Liang Saizhen　梁賽珍

Libailiu　禮拜六

Lihua youxian gongsi　利華有限公司

Lin Daiyu　林黛玉

Lin Lübin　林履彬

Lin Qi　林啟

Lin Shu　林紓

Lishi　力士

Liu Bannong　劉半農

Liu E　劉鶚

liushui zuoye　流水作業

liusuan　硫酸

lixue　理學

Liyong zaozhi chang　利用造紙廠

Lu Shi'e　陸士鄂

Lu Xun　魯迅

luoli　瘰癧

lü　綠

lü　氯

Lü Bicheng　呂碧城

lühuana　綠化鈉

lühuana　氯化鈉

Mei Qizhao　梅啓照

Meida huaxue gongyeshe　美大化學工業社

meigui lu　玫瑰露

Meili shuang　媚梨霜

Meishi yanfang xinbian　梅氏验方新编

meishu　美術

Meixing gongsi　美星公司

minsheng　民生

Mingyue gewutuan　明月歌舞团

nangeng nüzhi　男耕女織

Nanyang　南洋

Nanyang huaqiao jiuguo yundong　南洋華僑救國運動

Nanyang zhuzao chang　南洋燭皂廠

nei 內

nianpu 年譜

Nü'er shuang 女兒霜

Nü'er you 女兒油

nüshi 女士

Nüzi huaxue jiaokeshu 女子化學教科書

Nüzi shijie 女子世界

Nüzi wuli jiaokeshu 女子物理教科書

Ōkohira (or Ōkobira) 大河平鶴山

pai 牌

palmyŏng 發明

Pang Yuanji 龐元濟

pengsuan 硼酸

penwuqi 噴霧器

Pianzhi Sheng 駢枝生

pishi 砒石

qi 气

Qiantang 錢塘

qiao 巧

Qiaoxing gongsi 僑興公司

qing 清

qing 氫

qing meitan yang 輕鎂炭養

qing meitan yang 氫鎂炭氧

qinghao 青蒿

Qinghefang 清河坊

qinglin 青燐

qingshu 情書

qiren 奇人

"Qiwu lun" "齊物論"

qiyuan 漆園

qiyuan li 漆園吏

qiyuan xuxu 漆園栩栩

Quchenshi da yaofang 屈臣氏大藥房

qulishelin 屈里設林

Riguang 日光

Ruan Lingyu 阮玲玉

ruyi 儒醫

Sai Sei Do 濟生堂

Sai Xiansheng 賽先生

Sanhuapai xuehuagao　三花牌雪花膏

Sanjia qu　三家曲

Sanxing　三星

shang　商

Shanghai huaxue gongyi zhuanmen xuexiao　上海化學工藝專門學校

shangpin　上品

shanzhai　山寨

she　社

shen　神

Shen Jiuchen　沈九成

Shenbao　申報

Shengli gailiang zaozhi chang　省立改良造紙廠

shenhua　神話

shidaifu　士大夫

shijian　石鹼

shishang　士商

Shisuyongren　世俗庸人

shiyan　試驗

shiyan　實驗

shiyan fa　試驗法

shiyan ji　試驗計

shiyan youxiao　實驗有效

shiyantan　實驗談

shiye　實業

Shiye qianshuo　實業勸說

Shiye zazhi　實業雜誌

Shiye zhi fu congshu　實業之福叢書

Shiyebu yuekan　實業部月刊

shiyejia　實業家

Shizipai　獅子牌

shou　手

shou gongyi　手工藝

shu er buzuo　述而不作

Shuanglun　雙輪

Shuangmeimo　雙美嚜

shuilong　水龍

Shunchang jizhi shifen chang　順昌機製石粉廠

shurupin　輸入品

Siku quanshu　四庫全書

Siming shixue hui　四明實學會

Sin kok min jit po　新國民日報

Song chuang zaji　松窗雜記

Song-Hu shangbu weisheng ju　淞滬商部衛生局

songxiang　松香

sui xi wenyan wu yi baihua　雖係文言無異白話

Sun Yu　孫瑜

Taichang　太常

Taichangxiandie　太常仙蝶

tanci　彈詞

Tiangong kaiwu　天工開物

Tianxuwosheng　天虛我生

ting　庭

Tiyu huanghou　体育皇后

Tuhua xinbao　圖畫新報

wai　外

Wang Dungen　王鈍根

Wang Mengzou　汪孟邹

Wang Renmei　王人美

Wang Taijun　汪泰鈞

Wang Yunwu　王雲五

wanju　玩具

weisheng　衛生

wen　文

wenshi ziliao　文史資料

wenyuan　文苑

wu　物

wu　無

Wu (in dialect)　胡

wu (in dialect)　蝴

Wu Juemi　吳覺迷

Wu Yin　吳隱

Wu Yizhu　吳彝珠

Wuchang heji gongsi　武昌和濟公司

Wudipai　無敵牌

Wudipai bohe chang　無敵牌薄荷廠

Wudipai jingji bi　無敵牌經濟筆

Wudipai pingmian jiaoyinji　無敵牌平面膠印機

Wudipai wenxiang chang　無敵牌蚊香廠

Wudipai yafen　無敵牌牙粉

Wuhu kexue tushushe　蕪湖科學圖書社

wuli 物理

Wuzhou da yaofang 五洲大藥房

xi 惜

"Xi hua" "惜花"

Xi Meng 希孟

Xiang Songmao 項松茂

xiangpi che 象皮車

Xiangmao 祥茂

xiangshui chui 香水吹

xiangzao 香皂

xiansheng 先生

Xianshi huazhuangpin chang 先施化妝品廠

xiao 小

xiao gongyi 小工藝

xiao jiating 小家庭

xiao jishu 小技術

Xiaocui 小翠

Xiaodie 小蝶

xiaohao pin 消耗品

xiaoren 小人

xiaosuan 硝酸

Xiashilian 夏士蓮

Xie Zhuchen 謝鑄陳

Xihong 惜紅

Xihongsheng 惜紅生

Xiling 西泠

Xiling sanjia 西泠三家

Xin guomin ribao 新國民日報

Xin Nüxing 新女性

xing 行

Xinhua bohe chang gufen youxian gongsi 新華薄荷廠股份有限公司

xinxue 新學

xishou fa 吸收法

xiucai 秀才

xiuxian 休閒

Xu Gongming 徐公明

Xu Lai 徐來

Xu Qinfang 徐琴芳

Xu Shou 徐壽

Xu Zhuodai 徐卓呆

xue 學

Xueludun yaohang 薛魯敦药行

Xuesheng xinza 學生新雜

xuewen 學文

xueyi 學藝

xuxu 栩栩

Xuyuan 栩園

yaji 雅集

yang 養

yang 氧

Yang Xinghua 楊醒華

yanghong 洋紅

yanghuo 洋貨

yangjingbang 洋涇浜

yaoku 藥庫

yao shuilong 藥水龍

ye 業

Ye Mingdong 葉明東

yeji 野雞

yi 藝

Yifeng 益豐

yingchou wen 應酬文

yingliang 英兩

yishu 藝術

yixue 藝學

yiyi 意譯

Yonghe shiye gongsi 永和實業公司

You Huaigao 尤懷高

Youmin xiyi yuekan 遊民習藝月刊

you quwei 有趣味

youxi 遊戲

Youxi zazhi 遊戲雜誌

yu 礜

Yu guang qu 漁光曲

Yu Ziyi 俞子夷

yuan 元

Yuan Meiyun 袁美雲

Yuan Shikai 袁世凱

yuanyang hudie pai xiaoshuo 鴛鴦蝴蝶派小說

yushi 礜石

zaodou　澡豆

Zeng Guofan　曾國藩

Zeng Wenzheng　曾文正

Zeng Zhaolun　曾昭伦

Zhang Henshui　張恨水

Zhang Jian　張謇

Zhang Yingxu　張瑛緒

Zhang Yi'ou　張軼歐

Zhang Zhimin　張之銘

Zhao Lian　昭槤

Zhao Yan　趙顏

Zhen Zhen　真真

Zhendan jiqi tie gongchang　震旦機器鐵工廠

Zheng Mantuo　鄭曼陀

zhenqing　真情

Zhentan shijie　偵探世界

Zhentan yuekan　偵探月刊

zhi　知

zhiguai　志怪

zhishi　知事

zhishi fenzi　知識份子

zhizao　製造

zhizuo　製作

zhong　中

Zhong-Xi shuyuan　中西書院

Zhong-Xi yixueyuan　中西醫學院

Zhong Xianchang　鐘顯圏

Zhongguo diyi zhimei chang　中國第一製鎂廠

Zhongguo feizao gufen youxian gongsi　中國肥皂股份有限公司

Zhongguo huaxue gongyeshe　中國化學工業社

Zhongguo suan chang gufen youxian gongsi　中國酸廠股份有限公司

Zhongguo xiongdi gongyeshe　中國兄弟工業社

Zhongyang weisheng shiyansuo　中央衛生實驗所

Zhou Shoujuan　周瘦鵑

Zhu Shouju　朱瘦菊

Zhu Shu　朱恕

Zhuang Yumei　庄禹梅

"Zhuang Zhou meng die"　"莊周夢蝶"

zhuangyuan　狀元

Zhuangzi　莊子

zhulan 珠蘭

zhuzhici 竹枝詞

zi 字

Zimei hua 姊妹花

ziran kexue 自然科學

Ziye 子夜

Ziyoutan 自由談

Notes

INTRODUCTION

1. Examples of other individuals who were classically trained but who engaged in industry or commerce include so-called literati industrialists, such as Zhang Jian (1853–1929), a *zhuangyuan* (someone who earned the top position in the Qing imperial examinations) who founded the Nantong Dasheng Textile Industry (Köll 2003), established China's first museum in 1905, and became the minister of industry and commerce by 1913. Figures such as Xu Shou (1818–1884) were self-taught Jiangnan technological masters who were well versed in the classics and populated Self-Strengthening Movement arsenals, which I discuss later (Reardon-Anderson 1991, 17–28; Meng 1999, esp. 26–27). Another late-Qing transitional figure is the author, editor, and entrepreneur Liu E (1857–1909), who, after giving up a civil-service career, authored the immensely popular novel *The Travels of Laocan* (*Laocan youji*, 1907) and engaged in an array of entrepreneurial efforts, including working on salt production in Liaodong, the running-water supply in Beijing, and real estate in Shanghai (Kwong 2001, 360–365). A later example closer in age to Chen Diexian is Xu Zhuodai (1880–1958/1961?), a famous satirist who was also known as the "king" of soy sauce (Rea 2015, 18–19).

2. For such a characterization, James Reardon-Anderson notes that "the bookishness [of the late imperial period], the preoccupation with philosophical and literary subjects, denigration of manual and technical skills, and undue respect for established authority often left the classically trained scholar unfit for the laboratory, field, or workbench" (1991, 6).

3. For a description of a particularly virulent struggle and attack against a classically trained yet commercially oriented "man of letters" by New Culture intellectuals, see Hill 2013, 192–230. For a discussion of New Culture criticisms of literary products by old-style literati, including frivolous romance novels and journals such as *Women's Eastern Times* (*Fünu shibao*), see Judge 2015, 46–48.

4. For studies that demonstrate the importance of classically trained scholars in the burgeoning print markets of early-twentieth-century Shanghai, see, for example, Reed 2004, Culp 2016, Hill 2013, and Judge 2015.

5. For "medicine men," see Cochran 2006 and Scheid 2007. For a new breed of professional editors, see Reed 2004 and Culp 2016. For maverick entrepreneurs, see Hill 2013 on Lin Shu, the translator and promoter of "commodified classicism"; Fong 2015 on Lü Bicheng, a woman of letters, Buddhist, and businesswoman; Rea 2015b, 18–19, on the writer and soy sauce manufacturer Xu Zhuodai. For inventors and typewriter enthusiasts, see Mullaney 2017. For a list of early industrialists, including Chen Diexian, who were "far-sighted people, [and who] began to advocate the establishment of home industries for China," see the memoirs of the Hong Kong industrialist H. C. Ting (Ting 1974, 17). Finally, for more on "cultural entrepreneurs," or men and women who were turning to a range of commercial pursuits during this period, see Rea 2015b.

6. Jung Lee discusses Korean self-made inventors, such as Sŏ Kwang-uk, who received a patent for his wind-powered water pump; Yi Sŏngwon, a shoemaker by trade who invented a kind of glue; and the so-called Oriental Edison, Son Ch'angsik (2013, 788–791). Thomas Smith (1988) discusses earlier Tokogawa-era technologists in Japan, such as Ōkura Nagatsune, obscure men who never held office, had some acquaintance with the classics, but were concerned primarily with material problems and improving protoindustrial technologies.

7. In addition to sources that provide insight into Chen's material manufacturing work, I have selected writings by Chen (whether fictional, poetic, or how-to) based on whether they touched upon chemistry, manufacturing, technology, or commerce and profit.

8. For example, see Chen Dingshan [1955] 1967, 182.

9. Consider, for example, how writings on *xiao gongyi* in women's journals have either been completely overlooked by literary scholars who have focused on these journals' poetry or essays instead or treated too narrowly by historians who have referred to them as advice for housewives to engage in efficient domestic labor (e.g., Orliski 2003).

10. For a more detailed discussion of the significance of this culture of amusement, see chapters 1 and 2. For other studies that discuss the culture of play in urban

China from the 1890s to the 1910s, see C. Yeh 2006 and Rea 2015a, 40–77. For Chen's investment in this culture of play, or *youxi*, consider how one of the journals he published in Shanghai in 1913–1915 was titled the *Pastime* (*Youxi zazhi*; it was originally titled *Ziyou zazhi*, or *Liberty Magazine*, and then renamed *Youxi zazhi* after the first two issues were published). For more on the journal and Chen's involvement in it, see H. Lee 2007a.

11. Formal laboratories did not really emerge until the 1930s or even later in China. Reardon-Anderson notes that the Chinese were not able to set up their own substantial laboratories and academic programs until serious state resources were available during the Nanjing decade (1991, 175–207, 230–286). Guo Baozhang (1995) points out that Zeng Zhaolun, who was trained in America and was appointed the head of the chemical department at Beida, had to purchase the equipment to start a lab when he returned to China in 1931 and found that there was not one fully equipped lab in Chinese universities.

12. For more on the rise of professional fields and the increasing control of the state that led to the formalization of knowledge production in early-twentieth-century China, see, for example, Culp, U, and Yeh 2016.

13. The foundational study of "everyday technology" is David Arnold's book *Everyday Technology: Machines and the Making of India's Modernity* (2013). For a similar study in the Chinese context, see Dikötter 2007. Also see Mukharji 2016 for a study that examines how Ayurvedic physicians in colonial India appropriated small-scale techno-objects to legitimate their practice and to allow them to present a new way of understanding the body that braided the preexisting Ayurvedic tradition with Western science and biomedicine.

14. These approaches, for example, might preclude such questions as how handwork is involved in mechanized production or how the "hand" and the "machine" as categories might have been mutually constituted in industrial settings. They thereby forego the opportunity to interrogate how we define our conceptualization of the machine and hand. For an excellent exploration that raises these sorts of questions by examining the handwork in the manufacturing of textile machinery in early-twentieth-century Shanghai, see Yi forthcoming.

15. Meng Yue provides a similar characterization of the approach taken by Reardon-Anderson (1991) and by other scholars such as Du Shiran and his colleagues (1991), Albert Feuerwerker (1958), and Ting-yi Guo and Kwang-Ching Liu (1978). She notes that this kind of scholarship has tended to identify the "origins" of the Jiangnan arsenals with the Foreign Affairs Movement and to characterize these arsenals as derivative of Western industry (1999, 14–16, 24). For an account that describes modern science and medicine in China as being transmitted primarily from America, see Buck 1980.

16. Chinese journals and collectanea featuring translated knowledge associated with industrial development included the *Chinese Scientific Magazine* or *Chinese Scientific and Industrial Magazine* (*Gezhi huibian*, 1876–1892), edited by John Fryer and Xu Shou. For a full list, see Elman 2005, app. 8.

17. To be sure, there was some state sponsorship of industry during this period, and recent scholarship has been shedding light on some of these state efforts (e.g., Joyman Lee 2013).

18. For examples of a history-of-ideas approach to the study of modern science in China, see Kwok 1971 and Pusey 1983.

19. For more on the Science Society of China, see Buck 1980 and Reardon-Anderson 1991, 93–101.

20. For scholarship on modern geology, see G. Shen 2014; for forensics, Asen 2016; and for traditional Chinese medicine, Lei 2014.

21. Not all May Fourth thinkers embraced "Mr. Science," and among some there was considerable doubt about science and industrialization. This is evident in the debate over science and the philosophy of life in 1923 and in the reception of Rabindranath Tagore, whose speech on the problems of Western materialism and the strengths of Eastern spiritualism during a visit to China in 1924 was attractive to some intellectuals precisely because it tapped into their own post–World War I skepticism about capitalist production and the ties between industrialization and imperialism.

22. In a study of the commodity of tobacco in China, Carol Benedict (2011) similarly shows how small-scale, artisanal workshops in hand-rolling copycat cigarettes emerged to compete with the machine-manufactured cigarettes made by big transnational companies such as British American Tobacco in China. For Benedict, the introduction of modern industry in China was not merely a matter of replacing "traditional" forms of industrialization or mixing "traditional" institutions with "modern" ones but actually served to bring forth and encourage alternative forms of workshop-based and artisanal industry.

23. The literature on comparative industrialization and world history is vast. For the narrative that China was a late developer and lags behind the West, see the fundamental premise of the work by Joel Mokyr, who has written about the West's exceptionalism as recently as 2016 (e.g., Mokyr 2016). For a critique of this comparative approach behind studies seeking the origins of capitalism and science, see Rieppel, Lean, and Deringer 2018.

24. See, for example, the pioneering work by Pamela Smith (2004), which argues for the centrality of artisanal and bodily ways of knowing in the making of modern science.

25. For a more detailed discussion of "knowledge work" in these terms, see Rieppel, Lean, and Deringer 2018, esp. 13–19.

26. While Bernard Lightman (2007) uses the term *popularization*, I am somewhat reluctant to adopt it here. *Popularization* and the related term *dissemination* tend to imply straightforward transmission of information and fail to capture the complex process of knowledge production that occurs as knowledge circulates and travels. In contrast, this book sheds light on how knowledge was repurposed to address the concerns and interests of new readerships and assume multiple functions beyond mere transmission.

27. Joan Judge argues that "readers of high literary attainment" found the linguistic register of this new-style classical Chinese in women's magazines in the 1910s to be more accessible than the new national vernacular promoted by May Fourth intellectuals (2015, 47).

28. In the preface to a compilation of his business correspondence, *Model Correspondence on Industry and Commerce* (*Gongshangye chidu ou'cun*, 1928), a publication with which he sought to transmit his own experience in industry to readers, Chen (using the pseudonym "Tianxuwosheng") explicitly addressed his use of classical Chinese and noted that writing in the classical language (or his hybrid version) was no different than writing in the national vernacular (*baihua*). See the preface in Chen Diexian 1928.

29. In her discussion of how Republican-era women's journals were committed to "vernacularizing knowledge," Judge mentions publications by Chen, including the women's journal discussed in chapter 2 and the daily feature on household knowledge in *Shenbao* discussed in chapter 3, as being committed to "everyday knowledge" and "popular scientific knowledge" (2015, 42). Judge also sees these efforts made toward vernacularizing knowledge as distinct from the agendas of late-Qing reformism and May Fourth iconoclasm, especially in regard to their interest in the quotidian and the unabashed embrace of the commercial, even as they showed a commitment to reform (2015, 42).

30. Domestic appropriation of foreign goods was certainly not unprecedented (Benedict 2011), and exotica shaped everyday life as far back as the Tang dynasty, if not earlier (Schafer 1985). However, there have been particular historical moments of heightened anxiety about imported goods. Eighteenth-century recipes, for example, functioned to give order to new forms of material items that were circulating into the Qing Empire (Bian 2017). Though there had been a long history of foreign goods and exotica entering China, the mid–nineteenth century was a moment when industrially produced modern imports came to be associated with economic imperialism and China's declining geopolitical power, thereby generating intense distress. By the late nineteenth and early twentieth centuries, this intensification of foreign goods, especially those that were mass-produced, helped engender the National Products Movement (Gerth 2004; Dikötter 2007, 25).

31. The attempt to endow the market and commercial items with authenticity was symptomatic of global capitalism and hardly unique to China. Turn-of-the-twentieth-century England, for example, witnessed the rise of the "commodified authentic," both a commercial and literary trend that targeted a new middle class (Outka 2009). In a new, anxiety-ridden age of commerce, this class craved "tradition" that was ostensibly free of commercial taint even as members of the same class accessed that tradition through consumption. English marketers of lifestyle products from soap to home goods capitalized on this desire and presented their commodities as authentic, for example, in their ability to appeal to a pure nostalgic rural English past. In addition to Chen, other Chinese entrepreneurs were similarly appreciative of the power of consuming traditions. Lin Shu's cultural products constituted a form of "commodified classicism" that helped facilitate the ability of an emerging class of petty urbanites to negotiate new forms of knowledge through translation and to navigate the vicissitudes of modernity more generally (Hill 2013).

32. For another account that describes the need for Chinese businessmen in the early-twentieth-century medical market to engage in strategic political alliances and exploit political opportunities to guarantee favorable conditions for their entrepreneurial pursuits, see Cochran 2006, esp. 89–105 and 136–148.

33. See, for example, Hansen 2000 and Zhen Zhang 2005, which identify Shanghai cinema as a modern vernacular that provides the opportunity for participants to negotiate the meanings and experiences of their community and time by adapting global models to local conditions and for local purposes.

34. The recent global turn, for example, emphasizes instead exchange and fluidity among geographical regions and resists identifying discrete and fixed geographical origins for the "cosmopolitan" and "vernacular." Yet, notably, earlier formulations of vernacular carefully avoid any fixed notion of the "cosmopolitan." For example, Sheldon Pollack (2000) argues that the term *cosmopolitan* originated from the context of the Roman Imperium, where there was a distinct cosmos–polis binary, whereas in the Sanskrit universe, the subject of his analysis, there was no empire and thus no single polity against which vernaculars were defined. The vernacular, located at the regional, middle level, instead drew strategically on commonly circulating tropes that had emerged as cosmopolitan.

35. See, the *Oxford Dictionaries* definition of *tinker* at https://en.oxforddictionaries.com/definition/tinker.

36. For a cultural history of the representations of tinkers in Irish literature, see Burke 2009. For an anthropological account of travelers in Ireland in the twentieth century who lived off of tinkering and tin smithing and were targeted as the dregs of society by the settled Irish population, see Gmelch and Langan 1975.

My thanks to Mia Carter, University of Texas, Austin, for bringing this point to my attention and suggesting relevant literature.

37. See also Mokyr 2002 and 2009 and Jacob 2014.

38. George Basalla (1967) offers a view of evolutionary—rather than revolutionary—change in technology, though he still privileges the Industrial Revolution as the marker of true innovation. This privileging is implicit in his characterization of Chinese "stagnation" after the innovations of printing, gunpowder, and the compass (Basalla 1988, 169–176), an argument that belies a real lack of knowledge of innovation in craft and artifacts in Chinese material and technological culture.

39. Kenneth Pomeranz discusses how "divergence" between the most advanced countries in Europe and the most advanced regions in China in terms of economic development and technological innovation up until the eighteenth century was not as great as some comparative studies have suggested. If eighteenth-century Asia did not produce "macroinventions"—radical new ideas that by themselves suddenly altered production possibilities—Europe, argues Pomeranz, produced only a few between 1500 and 1750. Smaller technical improvements of various sorts continued to be made in different geographic and technological areas, with circulation of knowledge about dyes, for example, moving from European to Chinese innovators and back (2000, 47).

40. For a discussion of the multiple postcolonial and global responses to the Basalla evolutionary and diffusionist model, see Anderson 2018, 73. Warwick Anderson notes how, though George Basalla's essay "The Spread of Western Science" (1967) had become a convenient foil for the postcolonial turn in the history of science in the 1980s, it was nonetheless an example of "the good 'bad essay'" that proved extremely generative and forced the field to move in new directions regarding globalization and the travel of science.

41. This new discourse is considerably different from global discourses of intellectual property that have long seen China as being particularly guilty of acts such as copying, counterfeiting, and tinkering in back alleys to produce shoddy, knock-off products (on this change, see Lean 2018).

42. For the book that was published in conjunction with the opening exhibit at the explOratorium in 2014, see Wilkinson and Petrich 2013.

43. Creative coding and programming communities started emerging in the 1990s; they rely on "open sourcing," or collaborative sharing of coding information, facilitated by the rise of the internet, rather than on propriety software. This approach has now been identified as key in generating innovation in such communities.

44. Madeleine Dong argues for a notion of recycling that I find to be related to the concept of tinkering I use here to describe both Chen's textual and material work: "Recycling was not simply bringing back the old. Instead, it involved applying

labor to fragments of the past to rekindle and create new values to them" (2003, 206).

45. See Armitage and Guldi 2014 for *The History Manifesto*, a call for "big" history. For a powerful rebuttal, see "Exchange: On *The History Manifesto*" in the *American Historical Review* (Cohen and Mandler 2015).

46. For a sense of Needham's agenda, see Needham 1969, esp. 14–54, or review the multivolume work he directed, *Science and Civilisation in China* (Needham et al. 1954–2005). In this magisterial series, Needham was central in building the history of Chinese science and in generating an abundant interest in fields of knowledge and practice in imperial China that appear to correspond with modern definitions of science and technology.

47. For example, critics have rightly noted (e.g., Bray 1997; Hart 1999) how in his attempt to "recover" science in China Needham failed to historicize universalist claims of modern science or to recognize how the civilizational model within which he worked served only to perpetuate the idea that East Asian science is necessarily an "alternative" model and overlooked the transnational circulations informing the history of science in both China and the West.

48. The postcolonial turn in the 1980s and 1990s was fundamental in situating the study of science outside of civilizational and nation-state frames by examining the transmission of knowledge within the transnational networks of empire. The turn to global history has added to postcolonial scholarship by shedding light on the highly messy and convoluted pathways beyond the metropole–periphery binary through which ideas, things, and practices have traveled, often in multidirectional ways.

49. For example, see Raj 2007 on South Asian translators and go-betweens; Fan 2004 and Mueggler 2011 on Chinese and Naxi guides to British botanists; and Tilley 2011 on native informers to colonial anthropologists and scientists in early-twentieth-century Africa. Also see Schaffer et al. 2009.

50. On hydraulic metaphors in the globalization approach, see Anderson 2011. For the importance of recognizing friction and unevenness in the global turn in the history of science, see Fan 2012. For the value and dangers of focusing on travel and circulation in the global study of science, see Rieppel, Lean, and Deringer 2018, esp. 21–23.

1. UTILITY OF THE USELESS

1. For more on this culture of play, see the discussion in the text as well as Yeh 2006, esp. chap. 3, and Rea 2015a, 40–77.

2. Biographical information on Chen Diexian comes from Chen Dingshan [1955] 1967; Chen Xiaocui, Fan, and Zhou 1982; and Hanan 2000. Also, see Chen's

nianpu, or chronological record, in *Tianxuwosheng jinian kan* 1940, 1–7. Another source is *The Collected Works of Xuyuan* (*Xuyuan conggao*) (Chen Diexian n.d.), which his company Household Industries published, with an author's preface written in 1924 and a postface in 1927. Patrick Hanan characterizes the *jiwai shumu*, the bibliography of Chen's works in this publication, as an official biography (2000, 262 n. 2). The collection includes autobiographical poems by Chen, such as "My Life" ("Wo sheng pian").

3. Such a division of labor was typical of nineteenth-century grand families. During a period when success in the examination system was extremely difficult (and placement in office was hardly guaranteed even if one did succeed in the exam system), many families sought to ensure their survival by diversifying their interests. Male members would engage in a range of activities—scholarly, commercial, medical, and even military—while women turned to poetry, embroidery, and calligraphy and served as patrons to other female writers, often passing off profit-oriented pursuits as genteel scholarly enjoyment (Mann 2007).

4. "Xiaodie," the first pen name of Chen's eldest son, means "Little Butterfly," and "Cidie," his second son's name, means "Second Butterfly." Both sons' names were puns on the name "Diexian," which means "Butterfly Immortal." The significance of the term *butterfly* in Chen's names is discussed further in the text.

5. For more on the late-imperial category "gentry doctor" and specifically on gentry doctors in Hangzhou, see Y. Wu 2010.

6. For information on Chen becoming a *xiucai* candidate, see *Tianxuwosheng jinian kan* 1940, 3.

7. See Reed 2004, esp. chaps. 4–5.

8. A "courtesy name" is a name given to one in adulthood. For a list of some of Chen's courtesy names and sobriquets, see Gu Ying 2009, 2, and the biographical entry for Chen Diexian in "Zhejiang jinxiandai renwu lu" 1992, 230. Also see the entry for Tianxuwosheng in Chi 1998, 93.

9. Chen's sobriquet "Taichangxiandie" comes from the term *taichang xiandie*, which was first used during the Jiajing reign (r. 1521–1567) in the Qing and referred to butterflies living in the Taichang temple. During the Qing, the term accrued new meanings. For example, it came to refer to a spiritual being who could be seen only by worthy and noble individuals and became a symbol of luck for Qing examination takers (Zhu Jiaying 2015, 130, 132). My thanks to Gaoziyan Cui for help in doing the research on the courtesy names and other pen names discussed in the text.

10. The name "Xuyuan" was likely a combination of the terms *qiyuan* and *xuxu*. The term *xuxu* appears in the famous passage by Zhuangzi where he writes about dreaming to be a butterfly and not knowing whether he is a man dreaming to be a butterfly or a butterfly dreaming to be a man. See "The Adjustment of

Controversies" ("Qiwu lun") chapter of *Zhuangzi*, a foundational text of Daoism, for the sentence "Formerly, I, Zhuang Zhou, dreamed that I was a butterfly, a butterfly flying about, feeling that it was enjoying itself" (this translation is by James Legge and can be found at https://ctext.org/zhuangzi/adjustment-of-controversies). Notably, because Zhuangzi served as a *qiyuan li*, an official in charge of a place named Qiyuan, who refused to serve King Wei of Chu, the phrase *qiyuan* was also historically associated with recluses, a reputation that Chen was actively seeking to cultivate in the twentieth century. Authors and poets throughout the imperial period play with combinations of *qiyuan* and *xuxu* to evoke the "dreamscape" quality described in the passage from Zhuangzi. In the Northern Song, Huang Gongdu (1109–1156) wrote a poem that used the phrase *qiyuan xuxu* as a metaphor for dreamscape. The same phrase appeared in the poem "Black Butterflies" ("Hei die") by Zhao Lian (1776–1830), and in chapter 78 of *The Dream of the Red Chamber* (*Hongloumeng*), an eighteenth-century novel with which Chen was intimately familiar, the term *xuxu* is used to evoke a dreamscape.

11. "Xihong" was the name of the studio where Chen lived as a young man in Hangzhou. The two characters in the name, when placed together as the compound *xihong*, can be translated as "cherishing [the fading] rouge." This has a long literary history, conveying the sense of reminiscing about the past or the transient nature of youth and beauty. It can be found, for example, in the Tang dynasty poem "Cherishing Flowers" ("Xi hua"), which is located in volume 642 of *The Complete Tang Poems* (*Quan Tangshi*), a massive compilation of Tang poems commissioned in 1705 by the Kangxi emperor (r. 1661–1722) during the Qing dynasty.

12. The expression *chaoran* appears in *Commentary to the* Book of Changes *by Zixia* (*Zixia yizhuan*), supposedly written by one of Confucius's students, Bu Zixia (507 BCE–?). It also appears in the Daoist classic *Laozi*. In entry 26 of *Laozi*, a passage about a wise prince who maintains his throne by staying aloof, *chaoran* is used in the line "Although he [the prince] may have brilliant prospects to look at, he quietly remains [in his proper place], indifferent to them" (the English translation is by James Legge at https://ctext.org/dictionary.pl?if=en&id=11617). The term generally means being "above worldly considerations" and "holding oneself aloof from the world" and appears in all kinds of writings throughout the later dynasties.

13. I am using the Sinologist Patrick Hanan's eloquent rendering of the name "Tianxuwosheng" in English as "Heaven Bore Me in Vain" (1999, 1–2).

14. The poem from which the line is taken is emblematic of the ideal of romantic eccentricity as it calls for drinking one's life away cup after cup.

15. For more on the Bureau of Industry and the first issue of the *Zhili Industrial Gazetteer* (*Zhili gongyi zhi chubian*), see Zhou 1907. Many of the bureau's activities

were modeled on those carried out under the government-built bureaus and arsenals erected during the Self-Strengthening Movement. See Joyman Lee 2013 for
more on state-sponsored industrial efforts in late-Qing Tianjin and North China.

16. For more on this policy and the office of the industrial intendant, see Brennert
and Hagelsrom 1911, 420–421.

17. See, for example, Reardon-Anderson 1991, 17–25.

18. The inclination to treat elite studies of *bowu* as "protoscience" may stem in part
from what happened in Victorian England when professional science emerged
out of amateur activities. For example, Bernard Lightman (2007) argues that the
popularization of ideas of science, such as Darwin's theories, by male and female
journalists and writers was crucial in leading to the development of science as a
professional field in the latter half of the nineteenth-century, even if some of
these writings functioned to subvert the agenda of elite scientists and
naturalists.

19. Elegant gatherings were certainly not limited to Hangzhou and included ones
focused on an array of cultural activities. Late-imperial painting societies, for
example, held gatherings to encourage hands-on engagement with paintings
among intimate friends (Vinograd 1991, 184). Elegant poetry gatherings were
nostalgia-laden affairs throughout the early Republic that celebrated classical
poetry as part of a culture that was fast disappearing with the fall of the empire
and classical culture (Shengqing Wu 2008).

20. See Hill 2013, 53–57, for more on these Hangzhou reform circles.

21. See, for example, *Hangzhou baihuabao* [Hangzhou vernacular daily], January 16,
1907, 2.

22. See, for example, *Hangzhou baihuabao*, February 23, 1908, 6.

23. For a copy of the ad, see *Hangzhou baihuabao*, March 9, 1908, 1.

24. Another source notes that the Japanese consul's name was 大河平鶴山 (Chen
Xiaocui, Fan, and Zhou 1982, 212). The family name might be read as "Ōkohira"
or "Ōkobira," and the given name is most likely a literary sobriquet. Thanks to
David Lurie and Kim Brandt for help on trying to determine the proper reading
of this name. Unfortunately, I have not been able to locate any specific biographical information on this individual. For more on Japanese consuls in China
and more generally on early-twentieth-century Sino-Japanese contact, see
Brooks 2000, 16–28.

25. In a teasing and fun way, Chen Dingshan describes the Japanese man as "short
and hairy." In contrast, he describes his father in more sophisticated and refined
terms: "He had a long body and wore gold rimmed near-sighted spectacles. His
gown had long sleeves, and he often liked to add a vest. In his hands, he carried
a fan with a gold-colored peony. I often secretly wished that when I got big I
would be like my father in how he carried himself" (Chen Dingshan [1955] 1967,

181). These descriptive details were hardly accidental. The sartorial cues helped establish Chen Diexian as a lettered gentleman who could leisurely acquire new knowledge by inviting this Japanese man to tutor him in chemistry.

26. Hanan translates "Cuili" as "Gather Profit" (1999, 3).

27. See *Hangzhou baihuabao*, January 16, 1907, 2.

28. For more on reading rooms, especially at the Shanghai Polytechnic Institute, see Biggerstaff 1956 and Wright 1996.

29. Before the emergence of these scientific-appliance shops, consumers of scientific appliances and apparatuses had to turn to the pages of science journals to consume appliances figuratively or literally (through mail-order ads). These journals included the *Chinese Scientific and Industrial Magazine* (*Gezhi huibian*, 1876–1892), a publication of the China Polytechnic Institute that was edited by John Fryer and Xu Shou at the Jiangnan Arsenal during the Self-Strengthening Movement.

30. For more on Wang Mengzou and his enterprise, see M. Sun 2019, 26.

31. For more on the Ningbo connection and Zhong, see Zhuang 1963.

32. See Yu Ziyi 1981, 10–11, on the revolutionary history of the China Educational Supply Association and the Japanese imports.

33. For more on Zhang Zhiming and his involvement with the institution, see Zhang Zhiming 1947.

34. I discuss the role of emulation, or *fangzhi*, in innovation and the development of Chinese industry in later chapters. For more on repairing, reverse-engineering, and supplying replacement parts as the basis of industrial innovation in modern China, see chapter 4 and Yi forthcoming.

35. For more on this network and laboring in secrecy, see Yu Ziyi 1981, 10–11.

36. See *Xihu bolanhui rikan* [West Lake Expo daily] (Hangzhou), June 11, 1929, commercial page 2.

37. See, for example, Chen Diexian 1915, vol. 2 (February), 4. This was an entry in a how-to column discussed in chapter 2.

38. *Grand View* enjoyed a moderate circulation but was quickly shut down due to its critical view of the Boxer Uprising of 1900 (Haiyan Lee 2001, 320 n. 14).

39. For one of Chen's *tanci*, see *Peach Blossom Dream Rhyme Ballad*, published in 1900 and written when he was at the young age of fourteen (Hanan 2000, 264). For bamboo-branch poetry, see *Bamboo-Branch Poetry from the Gongchen Bridge* (*Gongchen qiao zhuzhici*) (Chen Diexian 1900), discussed in more detail later in this chapter.

40. Under his pen name "Chen Xu," Chen compiled and edited a nine-volume compilation of writing from the journal *Writing Forest* titled *The Writing Forest* (*Zhuzuolin*). For mention of foreign contributors to the journal, see Chen Xiaocui, Fan, and Zhou 1982, 211.

41. The *New Illustrated Pictorial* (*Tuhua xinbao*) is another example of a new-style illustrated journal that helped foster Chinese appreciation of science, technology, machines, and electricity in the 1880s.

42. The Gongchen Bridge is a famous stone bridge in Hangzhou that was built in 1631 during the Ming dynasty and refurbished in the late Qing in 1885, when Chen was a young boy.

43. By the end of the Qing, most bicycles used kerosene lamps as headlights. In the Republican era, a piece of red reflective stone was required at the back of a bicycle in several cities. Here aqua and crimson most likely refer to these two kinds of light, respectively.

44. Pianzhi Sheng, a Hangzhou literati and contemporary of Chen Diexian, wrote the poem "A Rubber-Wheeled Carriage [*Xiangpiche*] with Two Bridles," which he included in his poetry collection *The Songs of Gongchen Bridge* (*Gongchen qiao tage*) (for which Chen Diexian wrote a postscript). Both Chen's and Pianzhi's poems point to the presence of this kind of carriage around the Gongchen Bridge. For Pianzhi's poem, see Sun Zhonghuan 2009, 635. For more on the carriage, see He 2011, 42. My thanks to Yingtian He for pointing out this poem by Pianzhi Sheng and for the research on the carriage.

45. In the poem, the bell, *bao ren zhong*, refers specifically to the Bermuda carriage bell, which is operated by foot as a warning to pedestrians or oncoming vehicles.

46. Considerable work has been done on the rise of female workers in China and beyond. In the China field, most scholars have focused on factory girls in Shanghai. See, for example, Honig 1986.

47. My thanks to Weijing Lu for alerting me to this particular allusion.

48. As Craig Clunas (1997) argues, the aesthetic of *chuanshen* functioned to demarcate elites' class identity starting in the late Ming. Elites claimed that the aesthetic of *chuanshen* was better able to capture the individual's "real" spirit than more vulgar and commercial aesthetics that focused on figural or narrational representations.

49. I am using Patrick Hanan's felicitous translation for this book's title. The literal translation is closer to *The Bedevilment of Money*, but Hanan prefers *The Money Demon* (2000, 261).

50. Chen no doubt embellished details regarding the nature of relationships and personal encounters for dramatic effect and to conform to generic requirements.

51. For the English, I rely on Patrick Hanan's excellent translation (Chen 1999). For the original, see Chen Diexian 1981.

52. For more on the decline of China's grand families in the late nineteenth century, see Mann 2007. In this way, *The Money Demon* very much echoes the eighteenth-century novel *The Dream of the Red Chamber*, which is similarly about a grand family in decline and its inability to cope financially. In Chen's

nianpu, or chronological record, his son states that the technique Chen used in writing his novels was patterned after *The Dream* (*Tianxuwosheng jinian kan* 1940, 2). Even though *The Money Demon* is modeled after *The Dream* in certain respects, there are notable differences, including that in the classic novel Jia Baoyu never pursues profit because that task is handed off to others in the family. For Jia Baoyu, the main "tension" is not between profit and romantic escapism, but rather between official career and escapism. See the discussion in the text for more about how and why *The Money Demon* fashioned itself directly after *The Dream*.

PART II: MANUFACTURING KNOWLEDGE, 1914–1927

1. The late-imperial era had already seen the rise of individual fame and "brand-name" authors. The literary fame of late-Ming literatus Chen Jiru (1558–1639), for example, was similar to modern forms of celebrity (Greenbaum 2007). However, turn-of-the-twentieth-century China witnessed the rise of new forms of fame on a scale that was qualitatively different from earlier forms. The mass media played a crucial role in mediating fame and reputation in both the literary world and the commercial world.
2. A vast amount of work has been done on the role of compilation in late-imperial print culture and book history. For a pioneering study, see Elman 1984.
3. See, for example, Meng 2006, 31–64, on the labor of *bianyi* in the Republican era and M. Sun 2019, 96–133, on the significance of writing *and* editing (*bianxie*) for writers as prominent as Lu Xun (1881–1936).

2. ONE PART COW FAT, TWO PARTS SODA: RECIPES FOR THE INNER CHAMBERS, 1914–1915

1. I have not been able to identify who Mme. Xi Meng might be, and as I suggest in the text, she might even have been an imaginary reader.
2. The recipe does not provide a gloss for this ingredient. My translation of the Chinese is: "Refined plant oil; i.e., the self-manufactured oil from the previous issue's 'Method for Manufacturing Raw Materials.'"
3. Translation: "Finely powdered crimson pigment; needs to be self-manufactured."
4. Translation: "Rice Starch; i.e., the self-manufactured ground powder from this issue's 'Method for Manufacturing Raw Materials.'"
5. Xiaoqian Ji to Eugenia Lean, email, March 22, 2018.
6. Columns that introduced how-to tips on "practical affairs" (*shiye*), hygiene, or science (*ziran kexue*) for women could also be found in earlier women's magazines,

including the late-Qing radical journal with the same title as Chen's journal, *Women's World*.

7. For publication information and background on the *Ladies' Journal*, see Chiang 2006.

8. For these articles, see Ling 1915, Hui 1915, and Shen Ruiqing 1915, respectively.

9. The literature on recipes is vast. For a useful review of recipe studies in the European and especially early-modern context, see Leong 2013, 83–84. Also see Totelin 2009.

10. Perry Link to Eugenia Lean, verbal communication, March 27, 2006, Princeton University, Princeton, NJ.

11. Elaine Leong (2013) has shown how home-based, hand-written recipes of early-modern England were collectively authored manuscripts that treated know-how as unstable and thus invited commentary and testing by homemakers through generations. They were compiled by families and generated a small network in which people could recognize each other's handwriting and input. In terms of how Chen's pieces were consumed, it is entirely possible that these printed columns of recipes were ripped out of journals, circulated among more intimate networks, and accrued handwritten commentary, thus assuming qualities found in manuscript cultures.

12. For a rich study of the early Chinese periodical press via the women's journal *Women's Eastern Times*, see Judge 2015. Joan Judge notes that the generic richness, heterogeneity, and, indeed, unruliness of such journals—"from topical essays to readers' columns, from ancient-style poetry to translated fiction, from how-to articles to accounts of experience—[provided] a multiregistered response to the early Republic" (5). She notes that such journals were not feminist per se but better understood as "gendered journal[s] in which masculine norms determined the contours that women authors accepted, negotiated, occasionally defied and often modified. [They were] also a venue where new gendered practices—most notably the circulation of the words, images, and bodies of respectable women in public—were encouraged, decried, and refined" (4).

13. It is important to appreciate the extent of the mixed-gender nature of these journals lest we overlook the importance of the "woman's voice" as a powerful tool from which the modern subjectivities of both men and women were expressed. If an initial generation asserted that women's magazines were edited primarily by and for men, feminist scholarship has more recently offered a welcome corrective by engaging in a more careful examination of not only editors of these journals but also the magazines' contributors. See, for example, Chiang 2006 for a discussion of the gendered nature of the editorial staff of the *Ladies' Journal*.

14. For an example of such a characterization of these journals as solely targeting bourgeois housewives, see Orliski 2003.

15. This practice of men using women's pen names is not entirely surprising if one considers the long tradition of literati men assuming a woman's voice to express alternate views. Disaffected literati of the late Ming and early Qing saw the woman's voice as more genuine for expressing inner emotions, such as frustration, pathos, and anger, and hence more effective in articulating criticism of the failure of ideological orthodoxy. They would often ventriloquize the female persona of the suffering concubine or adopt a woman's voice in writing to articulate criticism of the failure of orthodoxy (Widmer 1992).

16. Chou Hsu-Chi, for example, suggests that the *Ladies' Journal* articles were translations from Western (English and American) journals or were cut from encyclopedias (2005, 126).

17. "Xi Meng" was used as a transliteration of the name of a female English poet who was introduced in the first issue of *Women's World* along with other foreign poets. See mention of her in *Nüzi shijie* [Women's world] 1, no. 1 (1914), table of contents. As an editor of the journal, Chen no doubt knew of this transliteration.

18. The *Manual of Therapeutics and Pharmacy* (Hunter 1915) was compiled by adding Indian and Chinese medicines to a translation of the fourteenth edition of Peter Squire's *Companion to the Latest Edition of the* British Pharmacopœia. The preface to this edition notes explicitly that the *British Pharmacopeia* (General Medical Council 1898)—which listed materials in Latin—was chosen for the translation of the manual because drugs in treaty ports were obtained mostly from England, and the preparations were based on British formulas (Hunter 1915, v). My thanks to Hu Yize for pointing me to both the *British Pharmacopoeia* and Hunter's *Manual of Therapeutics* and to the fact that they use the same Latin terms that appear in Chen's recipe.

19. These entries in "The Warehouse" on manufacturing cosmetics for women did not overlap with the journal's "Household" ("Jiating") section. The "Household" section drew more from home economics (*jiazheng*), a new field of knowledge emerging in the early twentieth century and modeled after Western fields of home economics and institutionalized in China in missionary schools and journals as a field explicitly meant for female household managers (Schneider 2011). The industrial arts pieces traced their genealogies back to the late-nineteenth-century arsenal texts on industrial production involving chemistry.

20. The second definition for *gongyi* offered in the Chinese dictionary *Comprehensive Chinese Word Dictionary* (*Hanyu dacidian* [Luo 1995]) coincides with this usage: "Taking original ingredients and half-finished products, add the methods of inputting labor to turn it into a product, and technology, etc."

21. For more on new-style pharmacies in China, see Cochran 2006, 16–17. Sherman Cochran contrasts traditional medicine stores or "old shoppes" to "new patent

medicine shops" or Western-style drugstores, which he describes in more detail in the later chapters of his book.

22. In Chinese history, not all spaces in the domestic arena were femininized. The literatus's studio, for example, was a distinctly male space within the household compound. But the inner chambers, or *guifang*, constituted a decidedly female part of the home.

23. This interest in playthings can be extended back to late-imperial China practices such as studying antiques, or *guwan* (literally "playing with antiques"), as a means to know the object.

24. For an article similar to the one on hair tonic, see Ling 1915. It has an entry on toothpowder that notes, "Recent word on the street has it that toothpowder being sold contains a small amount of sand, as well as the powder of the eggs of the sea mantis. . . . This easily causes harm" (17). It thus urges the readers to test the quality of store-bought toothpowder, warning that if the quality is poor, it could grind away one's enamel.

25. The stand-alone Public Health Bureau (Song-Hu shangbu weishengju) was established in Shanghai in 1925–1926. Nothing formal existed prior to that. For more on the institutional history of this Shanghai bureau, see Revells forthcoming, esp. chap. 5.

26. Unfortunately, not much is known about women's real consumption habits during this time and whether such exhortations would indeed coincide with or help encourage real consumer practice.

27. In a final paragraph describing exactly how to make "caustc [*sic*] soda," other English terms are introduced, including "Distilled Water," "Silver Nitrate," and the misspelled "Iron Sulppate" (Kuang 1915, vol. 3 [March], 4).

28. In his examination of instructional passages in Daoist publications on alchemy in early-twentieth-century Shanghai, Xun Liu argues that the mass-mediated transmission and communication through publications and letters meant that gender barriers between male teachers and female practitioners were broken down, making technical knowledge on alchemy more accessible to female followers and generating a sense of fellowship among male and female practitioners (2009, 255–264).

29. Chang Che-chia shows that from 1929 to 1931 a medical column in the *Ladies' Journal* received letters from readers not only in Shanghai, Guangzhou, and the Jiangnan area but also in Japan and Chongqing (2004, 153). This wide reach suggests the possibility that even in the 1910s the geographic distribution of the journal was not necessarily confined to the Shanghai area.

30. Some scholars note how readership and authorship changed from section to section within a single issue of the periodical. The *Ladies' Journal's* section on

writings by women, or the "literary garden" (*wenyuan*) section, featured the genteel female author, *guixiu zuojia*, as both its writer and its ideal consumer (Hu 2008, esp. 351–52), whereas other sections did not necessarily target the genteel woman specifically. Patrick Hanan (1999) makes a similar argument regarding *Women's World*.

31. The term *xueyi* combines *xue* from *xuewen*, "knowledge" or "learning," and *yi* from *yishu*, "skills." It might also be glossed as "science and arts" or "science and skill." The *Comprehensive Chinese Word Dictionary* (*Hanyu dacidian* [Luo 1995]) entry for *xueyi* gives a quote by Lu Xun, who used the term to refer to knowledge and skills that might be exhibited at a world expo—namely, those associated with the industrial arts.

32. In modern botany, *zhulan* is *Chloranthus spicatus*, or makino, a tree with fragrant, yellow, beadlike seeds.

33. That is, glycerin.

34. The strategic inclusion of English and chemical compounds in a sea of Chinese text served to inscribe in the words and compounds themselves a magical efficacy so that even if the reader did not understand the terms, the terms nonetheless had a degree of power, just as magical Daoist amulets might have in a very different context.

35. Hazeline Snow was one of the most popular vanishing face creams marketed in China's treaty ports at the time. It is notable that this article claims to divulge the recipe for manufacturing Hazeline Snow in 1915 with no apparent concern for intellectual-property rights. By the 1910s, Burroughs Wellcome & Co., the British manufacturer of Hazeline Snow, was already cracking down on counterfeit products and counterfeit use of its trademark in global markets (Lean 2018).

36. Glycerin is a neutral, colorless, thick liquid that freezes to a gummy paste and has a high boiling point. It can be dissolved in water or alcohol, but not in oils. Because many things will dissolve in glycerin more easily than they do in water or alcohol, it functions well as a solvent. Soap fats already contain glycerin, and it is when the fats and lye interact in the formation of soap that glycerin is the "by-product." The warning about handling glycerin was given probably because glycerin could be used to make nitroglycerin. But this warning was unnecessary because glycerin is not an explosive substance by itself and has to be turned into nitroglycerin before it can explode.

37. As the classical Confucian text *The Great Learning* (*Daxue*) explained, it is by grasping the nature of things that individuals can complete their knowledge and by extension that an imperial state can achieve its harmony. *Daxue* was one of the four canonical Confucian classics institutionalized in the Song dynasty as part of the civil-service-examination curriculum. Originally part of the *Book of*

the Rites, Daxue was authored by Confucius (551–479 BCE) in the sixth century BCE. For a history of the concept of *gewu zhizhi*, see Elman 2005.

38. The language in the journal articles included terms such as *shurupin* (import), *yanghuo* (Western goods), *shangpin* (top-grade goods), and *xiaohao pin* (consumable items). See, for example, Hui 1915, Ling 1915, and Shen Ruiqing 1915.

39. This correlation between personal hygiene and the nation's health was hardly unique to China and, indeed, was a global phenomenon. For related and comparative cases, see Hau 2003 on early-twentieth-century Germany and Stewart 2000 on nineteenth-century America.

40. For work on late-imperial medical and cosmetic recipes, see Ying Zhang 2017.

41. Tooth brushing, however, was not universal in the modern period. According to Frank Dikötter, *Beiping jiaowai zhi xiangcun jiating* (Families in the villages of Beijing's suburbs) noted in 1929 that not even one in three adults had a toothbrush; *Dingxian shehui gaikuang diaocha* (Investigation into the social conditions of Ding County) reported in 1933 that the habit of cleaning one's mouth was all but absent in Ding County, Hebei (2007, 210 n. 155).

42. See the entry "Soap, Household, and Laundry" in Williams 1933, 193–194. Although bar soap was classified as a foreign commodity, it spread fast and wide beyond the Jiangnan area starting in the late nineteenth century. As early as 1909, scented soaps as well as rouge, eau de cologne, toothpowder, and so on were widely available in Chengdu, Sichuan (Dikötter 2007, 57).

43. Since the Jin dynasty (265–420 CE), *zaodou*, a pig's ground pancreas mixed with beans and flavor, had been used as a detergent. There were also long-standing practices of using organic material such as oily pods from trees that were roasted, pulped, and molded into coarse balls of soap to wash clothes. Tea beans, burned soda, and potash were similarly used to create suds. Soda and potash had long been used in daily life in other forms of production practices as well, including paper making (Eyferth 2009, 24).

44. Thanks to I-Hsien Wu for directing me to these and the later references to rouge in *The Dream* (I-Hsien Wu to Eugenia Lean, email, March 20, 2015).

45. The title *Tiangong kaiwu* has conventionally been translated as *Exploitation of the Works of Nature*. More recently, scholars have noted that the use of "nature" in this translation is anachronistic. An alternative English title for the seventeenth-century text that avoids the anachronism is *The Works of Heaven and the Inception of Things*, recently used in an authoritative study of this work (Schäfer 2011). This chapter later gives a translation of the passage on the manufacturing of safflower cakes, often for rouge production, in *Tiangong kaiwu*'s chapter on dyes. For a recent Chinese edition of *Tiangong kaiwu*, see Song [1587–1661] 1976, and for a translation into modern Chinese, see Pan Jixing 1993.

46. My thanks to Xiaoqian Ji for pointing out that knowledge of the making of cosmetics can be found in an assortment of medical books and technological manuals of the late-imperial period (Xiaoqian Ji to Eugenia Lean, email, March 22, 2018).

47. In fact, for nonelite consumers, soap and cosmetics were easily available for purchase from street peddlers (see, e.g., Dikötter 2007, 51–52).

48. The ads for these three pharmacies can be found in *Funü zazhi* [Ladies' journal] 1 (1) (1915). In the Sai Sei Do ad, the inclusion of medical tools and medical containers suggests that the consumers targeted included not only household consumers but also pharmacists, other merchants, and small industrialists producing medicine, and the Sai Sei Do pharmacy was similar to the scientific-appliance shops discussed in chapter 1.

49. For more on the development of modern chemistry education, see Reardon-Anderson 1991, esp. chap. 5. For more on curriculum change (including the introduction of chemistry) in new-style high schools and middle schools, see Culp 2007, 29.

50. The fact that the term *flask* was transliterated speaks to the newness of this object for the Chinese and that a term had not yet been fixed for it in Chinese.

51. A Chinese tael is the equivalent of fifty grams. An "English tael," or *yingliang*, was the equivalent of one ounce, a unit of weight imported from England.

52. Domestic glass factories were just starting to open up around this time. The Kung Yih Glass Factory was founded in Shanghai in 1912 and focused on manufacturing bottles and glassware (*Handbook of Chinese Manufacturers* 1949, 173). It was not until the late 1930s that domestic factories manufactured a full array of chemical apparatuses and lab tools.

53. For the full list of equipment sold at the Chinese Educational Supply Association, see "Shanghai Kexue yiqiguan zizhipin mulu" 1917, 41–56. By the late 1920s (if not earlier), one could also purchase scientific apparatuses at companies such as the Commercial Press. An exhibit pamphlet from the late 1920s, *Descriptions of the Commercial Press Exhibit* (n.d.), noted that the Commercial Press not only sold its own publications but also imported books, stationary, and scientific appliances. The equipment included the barometer, the moving-coil galvanometer, the Wimhurst self-exciting influence machine, the oil vacuum pump, and the Chinese typewriter.

54. My thanks to Peter Hamilton for alerting me to H. C. Ting and his memoirs' mention of Chen Diexian (Ting 1974).

55. The company was also successful in manufacturing food-flavoring powder, including the Boddhisattva Powder (Guanyin fen), and Jiandao Soap. Later on, Fang came to be known as the king of National Products because of his anti-Japanese activism in the NPM. It was this same activism and his unwillingness

to work in collaboration with the pro-Japanese Wang Jingwei government that finally led to his assassination by secret agents in 1940. For an account of his involvement in the NPM, see Gerth 2004, 180–181.

56. For more on Wu Yizhu, see X. Liu 2009, esp. 56–58.

57. *Qinghao* is the herbal plant *Aritemisia apiacea*, widely found in Korea, Japan, and China.

58. For this translation, see Sung 1966, 77.

59. According to "Table of Chinese Weights" in the *Chinese Maritime Customs Foreign Trade Report* from 1915, a *liang* is a tael; sixteen *liang* are equivalent to one *jin* (catty); and 1,000 *liang* would be around 62.5 *jin* (*Zhonghua minguo haiguan huayang maoyi zongce* [1915] 1982, n.p.). With 100 *jin* (catties) the equivalent of 133.33 pounds, 62.5 *jin* would be around 83.33 pounds. Several weight systems were used in Shanghai in 1915. But because high-quality caustic soda (sodium hydroxide) would have been imported and sold in a pharmaceutical store, it is reasonable to use the customs report weight system to do the conversion.

60. The Capital Vagrant Workhouse's journal, *Vagrant Workhouse Monthly* (*Youmin xiyi yuekan*), is located in file J181-18-21936, Beijing Municipal Archives. The 1927 issue includes an advertisement for the workhouse in the front matter, which notes this information about the training provided in the workhouse's chemical workshops. Janet Chen was kind enough to share this material with me, and I follow her translations for the workhouse name and journal (Janet Chen to Eugenia Lean, email, May 13, 2009). The production of soap still required some equipment and training, so the Capital Vagrant Workhouse tended to be among the better-funded and functioning workhouses. When it ran out of money, it would revert to making matchboxes and straw sandals.

61. If we were to compare *Women's World* (*Nüzi shijie*) of 1915 with the late-Qing publication of the same title, the contrast could not be more marked. Founded by Ding Chuwo, the late-Qing journal was highly political and explicitly revolutionary in nature, exhorting women to leave the inner chambers. For more information on this early *Nüzi shijie*, see the entry by Xu Yuzhen in Ding 1982–1987, 1:461–73, and see the Chinese Women's Magazines in the Late Qing and Early Republican Period Database at https://kjc-sv034.kjc.uni-heidelberg.de/frauen zeitschriften/.

62. Haiyan Lee (2007a) has characterized *Pastime* as a literary "dime store" offering variegated parcels of entertainment and information that readers could consume individually in their homes—new spaces of commodified pleasure—even while they communed in their shared interest in such leisurely consumption. This characterization could easily be applied to *Women's World* and Chen's newspaper column "Common Knowledge for the Household," discussed in chapter 3.

63. Spectacular depictions of technology started to appear in late-nineteenth-century newspapers such as the *Dianshizhai Pictorial* (*Dianshizhai huabao*, 1884–1898), which featured depictions of wondrous science and technology, including the hot-air balloon and fire extinguishers quelling blazing fires. Weihong Bao describes how this newspaper featured pictorials of modern technologies, such as the fire engine and high-pressure water hoses alongside crowds and publics watching the spectacle of fire (2016, 81, 332).

64. For a characterization of the New Culture intellectuals' push for family reform as a primarily male agenda, see Glosser 2003, 49.

3. AN ENTERPRISE OF COMMON KNOWLEDGE: FIRE EXTINGUISHERS, 1916–1935

1. *Hot pot* is *juhua guo* in Chinese, which can be literally translated as "chrysanthemum hot pot." It uses wine as the fuel, and the foodstuff inside is arranged like a chrysanthemum—hence its name.

2. For mention of Chen's successful manufacturing of the fire extinguisher, see Chen Dingshan [1955] 1967, 192. For his pursuit of a patent, see a series of orders by Kong Xiangxi, the minister of the GMD Ministry of Industry and Commerce, on the patent request, including the decree (number 208) on September 11, 1928, *Gongshang gongbao* [Bulletin of industry and commerce] 1, no. 5 (1928): 29–30; the decree (number 275) on September 23, 1928, *Gongshang gongbao* 1, no. 6 (1928): 26–27; and the decree (number 370) on September 23, 1928, *Gongshang gongbao* 1, no. 7 (1928): 29–30.

3. Chen Dingshan, Chen Diexian's son, was born in 1897, so the incident he describes here would have occurred around 1905.

4. The seventeenth-century Dutch, including a highly innovative and technologically savvy fire chief of Amsterdam, Jan van der Heyden, were highly invested in developing such technologies, as were state authorities located in Peter the Great's eighteenth-century capital, St. Petersburg. For the Dutch, see Kuretsky 2012; for the Russian example, see Frierson 2012.

5. For more on Shanghai Polytechnic and on the journal, see Wright 1996 and Elman 2005, 308–319.

6. "Shiyong shuilong shuo" 1876 and "Miehuoqi shuoluo" 1877, respectively. For the image in the latter article, see page 5 of the issue.

7. For the ad, see *Gezhi huibian* [Chinese scientific and industrial magazine] 1 (4) (1876): 12.

8. The visual also appears on the final page of the article "Miehuoqi shuoluo" (1877).

9. For information on the Aurora Company, see *Handbook of Chinese Manufacturers* 1949, 247, 254. After the Kanto earthquake in Japan in 1923 engendered a huge urban conflagration, the need for fire extinguishers likely became all the more pressing throughout Asia.

10. The *Shenbao*—where the supplement was printed—was one of Shanghai's most important daily papers. By the early 1920s, its audience had grown beyond its earlier late-Qing clientele, which had generally been restricted to literati-officials, merchants, and industrialists—expanding beyond a local, regional scope to encompass a national audience, moving into the rural arena, and targeting women. For a discussion of Republican rural elites having access to modern newspapers such as the *Shenbao*, see Harrison 2005, 105. On women readers, see Mittler 2004, 245–311. According to the Shanghai city yearbook for 1935, the circulation for the *Shenbao* in 1934 was 150,000, with 40 percent distributed in Shanghai and 60 percent outside the city. These figures do not accurately reflect the actual number of readers, though, which was much greater because it was common practice for the newspaper to be posted on public reading boards for people to read communally.

11. The "spray bottle" consisted of two tubes, a horizontal glass tube, and the vertical taper tube. When one blew through the horizontal tube, the air flowed faster at the top of the vertical tube and thus had a lower pressure than the bottom part of the vertical tube. (The faster a fluid moves, the less pressure it exerts.) As a result, the water could be "sucked in" due to the difference in air pressure.

12. The name of the entry's contributor was often included in parentheses at the end of the entry. Here we see a contribution by someone named Yang Xinghua. When Chen contributed entries, he did so under his pen name "Tianxuwosheng," as he did in the sprayer entry.

13. See, for example, articles in the *Ladies' Journal* related to the *jiating*, whose topics ranged from household-management issues to marriage and family reform. The urgency associated with the reform of the *jiating* by the late 1910s may have stemmed directly from actual experiences that reformist intellectuals and writers had as they witnessed the decline of the grand family (*da jiating*). Individual brothers and their nuclear family units, once assembled together in a grand family invested in reproducing itself through the civil-service exam, were now forced to take on new professions and improvise in a period when family strategies (such as how to provide education for children) were still in flux. Many assumed writing for the reformist press as a means to support their smaller families. As a result, the reform of the modern home was of concern for many who came of age at the turn of the century, and it dominated discussions about social reform and rebuilding the Chinese nation (Chou 2005, 136–37).

14. Another example is "Wei jiuhuo yaoshui ji meihuo ji" [The matter of foam extinguishers and sand extinguishers], in Chen Diexian 1928, vol. *guihai*:36–38.

15. Ellen Widmer (1989) writes about a collection of model letters known as *Modern Letters* (*Chidu xinyu*) that was shared in the epistolary world of seventeenth-century Chinese women.

16. For more on the term *chidu*, see Richter 2013, 35–36. For more on the genre in the late-imperial and Republican periods, see Cai forthcoming.

17. *Model Correspondence* was featured in an advertisement in Chen's publication *Jilianhui kan* [Machinery Association journal] 97 (1934): 9. All four volumes of *Model Correspondence* were being sold at one yuan for each volume. The ad also included other titles by Chen, including *The Peppermint Industry* (Chen Diexian 1933a), discussed in chapter 4, whose individual volumes sold at five jiao a piece.

18. For more on the Shanghai School's goals, curricula, and student requirements, see the advertisement for the school on the inner cover of *Huaxue gongyi* [Chemical industry journal] 1 (2) (October 1922).

19. The *Scientific American* article referenced does not seem to be in the journal, at least not in the years 1922 or 1923, around the time that "Common Knowledge Chemists Should Possess" (Yu Ziming 1923) was published. Thus, the article might have been from a different source or was written by the author rather than translated, even though *Scientific American* was referenced.

20. By the 1930s, Chinese copies infringing upon the Xiangmao brand name were targeted by the British Foreign Office for counterfeiting. In 1922, however, the publication of the formula for Xiangmao soap production was apparently unproblematic.

21. See *Huaxue gongyi* 1 (1) (May 1922): 49–52. For other examples, see entries in some of the journal articles discussed in chapter 2, such as Shen 1915, which freely shared the recipe for manufacturing Hazeline Snow, a vanishing cream by Burroughs Wellcome & Co.

22. Standardization of scientific terminology started in China in 1915 under the auspices of the Joint Terminology Committee, which was part of the Jiangsu Provincial Education Association, a nonstate association based in Shanghai, run by a loose network of regional elites committed to institutionalizing medicine and science in China, and lasting until 1927. The Terminology Committee did not begin with chemistry in 1915, but rather with unifying the terminology of anatomical knowledge. For more on this standardization, see Luesink 2015.

23. For the term *lühuana* 氯化鈉, see the dictionary *Cihai* (literally, "The Sea of Words") (1936 ed.).

24. According to modern-day notation, the equal sign (=) in the reaction should be an arrow sign (→) instead. Also, some of the chemical reactions are unbalanced.

The second reaction, $4MgSO_4 + 4Na_2CO_3 + XH_2O = (3MgCO_3 + Mg [OH]_2 + XH_2O) + CO_2 + 2Na_2SO_4$, is not balanced correctly as written. The balanced reaction is $3MgSO_4 + 3Na_2CO_3 + 2H_2O \rightarrow 2MgCO_3 + Mg[OH]_2 + 1\ H_2O + 1CO_2 + 3Na_2SO_4$. The third reaction, $4MgCl_2 + 4Na_2CO_3 + XH_2O = [3MgCO_3 + Mg(OH)_2 + XH_2O] + CO_2 + 8NaCl$, is also not balanced and should be $3MgCl_2 + 3Na_2CO_3 + 2H_2O \rightarrow 2MgCO_3 + Mg(OH)_2 + 1H_2O + 1CO_2 + 6NaCl$. When balanced, the reactions are chemically sound. I thank Joseph Ulichny, an associate professor in the Department of Chemistry at Columbia University, for his help with assessing these reactions.

25. For more on the rise of formal chemical and other scientific labs in China in the 1930s, see Wright 2000, and on forensic laboratories see Asen 2016. For more on makeshift darkrooms, see the discussion of photography advocate and pioneer Du Jiutian in Y. Gu 2013, 129.

26. For more on the neologism *changshi*, see L. Liu 1995, app. B, 285.

27. Chen's daughter noted retrospectively how his articles and advertisements in "Common Knowledge" functioned to promote the NPM and helped generate business for Household Industries (Chen Xiaocui, Fan, and Zhou 1982, 219).

28. Between World War I and World War II, nation-states were ramping up air defense systems and preparing local citizen populations with the resources to defend themselves from bombing. Such a climate would have been amenable to the promotion of Butterfly Fire Extinguishers in the 1930s.

4. CHINESE CUTTLEFISH AND GLOBAL CIRCUITS: THE ASSOCIATION OF HOUSEHOLD INDUSTRIES

1. For another publication of the son's retrospective, see Chen Dingshan 1964. For another version of the cuttlefish account, see the *nianpu*, chronology, for Chen Diexian in *Tianxuwosheng jinian kan* 1940, 3. For other retrospective accounts on Chen using cuttlefish bones, see Zheng 1992 and Gu Yi 2009. For a contemporaneous account, see Zhang Yimin 1936. Chen Xiaocui, Fan Yanqiao, and Zhou Shoujuan discuss the urgency of Chen needing to find a cheaper source for raw materials than purchasing them at Western pharmacies (1982, 218).

2. The name "Jiating gongyeshe" was officially translated as the "Association for Domestic Industry" in its day. In *China Industrial Handbooks Kiangsu* (1933), the company was listed under this name. This name was also used regularly in the annual "Shanghai guohuo chang shangming lu" ("Shanghai manufacturers directory") that was included in the cosmetic section of the annual publication *Survey of China's National Products* (*Zhongguo guohuo diaocha ce* 1934–1947). See, for example, the listing of the company and the ad in the 1947 publication of the directory (file Y9-1-95-59, Shanghai Municipal Archives, 30, 36). The English

name renders the term *jiating* as "domestic." This is a good choice insofar as the company's products were "domestic" in two senses—first, as items for the home and, second, as NPM products. However, *jiating* in Chinese does not really convey "domestic" in the sense of "national" or "native" but is far closer in meaning to "home," "household," and "family." For this reason, this study uses the name "Association for Household Industries" or the abbreviated version "Household Industries." It is a more felicitous translation and captures the dual meaning of "home" and "native," if metaphorically. Others have translated the name as "Family Industries Ltd." (e.g., H. Lee 2001, n. 11) and "Household Enterprises" (e.g., Gerth 2004, 11).

3. On the uses of cuttlefish bones in Chinese medicine, see, for example, "Frequently Used Chinese Medicine" n.d.

4. *Mr. Mei's New Compilation of Tested Prescriptions*, a commonly owned household reference book that was originally published in 1846 by Bao Xiang'ao, a Hunanese official and medical-knowledge compiler, is an example of the kind of texts that Chen was exposed to when he was young. See "Preface to the Second Edition of *Mr. Mei's New Compilation of Tested Prescriptions*" in Chen Diexian [1934] 1937, Chen's recompilation of *Mr. Mei's New Compilation of Tested Prescriptions*, where he notes how this text was circulated among Hangzhou's gentry families, including his own.

5. Chen Dingshan, too, notes that his father's plan to use cuttlefish to produce calcium carbonate ran afoul when he realized that the amount of calcium carbonate in cuttlefish bones was not enough to warrant the efforts of extraction ([1955] 1967, 183).

6. For a full business history of Unilever, see Wilson 1954. For a general history of Unilever's overseas history, see Fieldhouse 1978.

7. According to his daughter, Chen did not originally start out with toothpowder. He first experimented with producing frostbite ointment, which, like toothpowder, was characterized by light initial investment and relatively simple techniques of production (Chen Xiaocui, Fan, and Zhou 1982, 217–18). Upon realizing that frostbite ointment was seasonally specific and not likely to turn as much of a profit as toothpowder, a commodity used daily year-round, Chen switched to toothpowder. Manufacturing toothpowder involved the simple mixing of materials such as magnesium carbonate, talcum powder, peppermint, and vanilla essence and so was easy to manufacture within a small-scale setting.

8. For more information on this company, see *China Industrial Handbooks* 1933, 498.

9. See Shanghai shi tongjibu 1957, 134, a handwritten report titled "The Historical Materials of the Association for Household Industries," by the Shanghai Bureau of Statistics (located in file B31-2-271, Shanghai Municipal Archives).

10. The start-up funds were initially 10,000 yuan. In February 1919, Household Industries' capital increased to 20,000 yuan and by 1920 totaled 100,000 yuan. See Shanghai shi tongjibu 1957, 134.

11. Household Industries was to move several times over the course of its existence, both within Shanghai and into the hinterland during war. In 1933, it was located on National Products Street in Shanghai (*Zhongguo guohuo diaocha ce* 1934, 235, file Y9-1-92-307, Shanghai Municipal Archives). For more information on this company in general, see *China Industrial Handbooks* 1933, 508; "Jiating Gongye-she" 1935, 115; *Zhongguo guohuo gongchang shilüe* 1935, 23–24, 117–118, 127–128; Zhang Yimin 1936.

12. Scholars of Chinese business history have long noted that the dominant form of business enterprise in modern China was the family firm (often led by a strong patriarch). For a recent study of a larger-scale family enterprise, see Cochran and Hsieh 2013.

13. For a comprehensive sense of small-scale enterprises in Zhejiang Province, see *China Industrial Handbook Kiangsu* 1933. For a discussion of small-scale tobacco and cigarette factories, see Benedict 2011.

14. This was hardly unique to Household Industries. Vertical integration through lineage trusts characterized, for example, the salt industry in Zigong, Sichuan (Zelin 2005).

15. See *Huaxue gongyi* [Chemical industry journal] 1 (2) (October 1922): 41.

16. For examples of Butterfly brand advertising in Southeast Asian newspapers, see the ad for Butterfly Cream in *Zonghui xinbao* [Union times] (Singapore), February 15, 1932, sec. 2, p. 1. See also a full advertising campaign for Butterfly Tooth-powder that ran in the *Union Times* in March and April 1934 and featured movie star endorsements—for example, one printed on April 2, 1934, sec. 2, p. 4, and another on April 6, 1934, sec. 1, p. 4.

17. For a table of the company's annual growth in terms of the overall monetary value of its production and its surplus gains from 1918–1956, see the handwritten report "The Historical Materials of the Association for Household Industries" compiled by the Shanghai Bureau of Statistics (Shanghai shi tongjibu 1957, 137). It also features tables that list the annual value of production per commodity, including hair oil, scented powder, blush, toothpaste, and so on (138–140).

18. For Household Industries' standing as a National Products company, see *Zhongguo guohuo diaocha ce* 1934, 235, file Y9-1-95-59, Shanghai Municipal Archives. For its lead position in manufacturing toothpaste, toothpowder, and so on, see *Zhongguo guohuo diaocha ce* 1934, 237–40. By 1931, there were a total of fifty cosmetic manufacturers in China (*China Industrial Handbooks* 1933, 499–501, 509–511). China Chemical Industries Co. was the most successful, especially its Three Star brand products, and drew most of its customers from Sichuan and

the Yangzi delta. Other notable companies were the Yung Woo Industrial Company (Yonghe shiye gongsi), Sincere Perfumery Factory (Xianshi huazhuangpin chang), Mei Sing Company (Meixing gongsi), Hua'nan Chemical Industry Company, China Brothers Company (Zhongguo xiongdi gongyeshe), and Peacock Chemical Industry Company (Kongque huagongshe).

19. For a detailed account of the company's situation leading up to World War II, during the war, and up to 1956, see Shanghai shi tongjibu 1957, 135–136.

20. See ordinance number 1834, *Jiangsu sheng gongbao* [Jiangsu Province bulletin] 2180 (January 1919): 9–10.

21. For the magnesium carbonate announcement, see *Anhui gongbao* [Anhui bulletin] 557 (December 1919): 5–6, and for the Meili face cream, see order number 479, *Jiangsu sheng gongbao* 3200 (November 1922): 3–4.

22. In-house machinery production was not that unusual. Chinese factories often preferred to purchase cheaper, imitation machinery made domestically even if it was inferior to imports (Dikötter 2007, 119). Much of this domestic imitation of imported machinery was accomplished through repair work, and the industrial foreman and their apprentices running the factory floors were often the ones who would then open native machine manufacturers and new machine shops (Reed 2004, 138–141).

23. As noted, the Republican state prior to the GMD had already started this policy of tax exemption for mechanized manufacturing, and Household Industries was a beneficiary as early as 1919. In claiming that it was only after the GMD came to power in 1927 that the government promoted mechanized production in Chinese industry through tax exemption to factories that produced industrial goods with machines, Chen Dingshan's chronology was off by quite a few years ([1955] 1967, 187).

24. For more on the revolutionary roots of "self-reliant science" in the Yan'an period, see Schmalzer 2015, 6. Sigrid Schmalzer also discusses how Maoist science in the Great Leap period emphasized self-reliance, nativism, and mass-labor mobilization and makes the case that the virtue of self-reliance persisted into the post-Mao and post–Cold War era (8–16). Chinese scientists who started to engage more actively in international scientific exchange in the post-Mao era emphasized Chinese uniqueness in science from which other (third-world) countries could learn.

25. For more on the "living rooms as factories" movement and related campaigns, see Hsiung 1996, 47–63.

26. For these prices, see the section "Items for the Household and for Industry" in China Educational Supply Association 1928, 55–58.

27. For more on the standardization efforts, see Gerth 2004, 192–200.

28. See the report "Columbia University Job 2019-018 Dental Powder Analysis," April 6, 2019, prepared by Ted Reuss and reviewed by Edgar Leone of Excel Laboratory Services. The Butterfly Toothpowder container was purchased from the auction house Old Goods Bazaar (Jiuhuo shangcheng) online at http://7788.com on January 21, 2019 (http://7788.com/pr/detail_5622_61218716.html).

29. See Bian 2017, especially 313–316, for exotica entering the Chinese materia medica corpus in the Qing. To be sure, the Chinese appetite for exotica reaches much farther back than the Qing dynasty. See Schafer 1985.

30. Such collaborative translation work was standard practice in the early-modern world as well (Harun Küçük to Eugenia Lean, personal communication, May 8, 2015). Translators often know enough of both the source language and the target language and so move from a lower-vernacular rendition to a classical version. These acts of translation thus create original work in the process. It is often labor for money but not at the expense of innovation and has implications for our understanding of intellectual labor.

31. Chen had worked for Lin in Lin's many for-profit cultural endeavors, serving as a "faculty" member for a write-in correspondence course in classical literature (Hill 2013, 176–79).

32. For the details on Chen's translation work, see Chen Xiaocui, Zhou, and Fan 1982, 213–214.

33. Such an approach evoked long-standing forms of literati work. Large compendium projects, such as the Hanlin Academy's compilation *The Emperor's Four Treasuries* (*Siku quanshu*) in the Qing, were large-scale collaborative efforts, with scores of scribes doing the compilation work and the main editors or compilers getting involved only at the level of polishing, editing, and writing a preface.

34. Chen Diexian's translation bureau was also a commercial endeavor. The manuscript fee he could secure was average if not on the high side, and he would split the fee with his team (Chen Xiaocui, Zhou, and Fan 1982, 213–214).

35. This publication was part of the Ministry of Agriculture and Commerce's push to develop light manufacturing in China. This push also included the establishment of the Bureau of Industrial Research in Beijing in 1915, which was dedicated to the analysis of native products, including cosmetics and dyes, and played a crucial role in promoting and building native industry.

36. For related ways of thinking about translation as a complex site of negotiating different epistemological traditions, see the foundational study *Translingual Practice* by Lydia Liu (1995) and *Hygienic Modernity* by Ruth Rogaski (2004), which draws on translingual practice to think about the translation of technologies and hygienic science in early-twentieth-century Tianjin.

37. For a discussion of Zhang Gao (1149—1227) as an example of a *ruyi* who embodied this trait, see Hinrichs 2013, esp. 66.

38. Chen's daughter and the other two compilers recount how in addition to Chen's ability to compose prescriptions, he also compiled books of prescriptions—both Chinese and Western—along with divination texts and food-recipe books, all related genres (Chen Xiaocui, Fan, and Zhou 1982, 210).

39. For more on W. G. Sewell, see Bickers and Seton 1996.

40. See the entries for the Dah Fong Peppermint Factory and the New China Peppermint Co., Ltd., in *Handbook of Chinese Manufacturers* 1949, 228 and 231.

41. *Pharmaceutical Record and Weekly Market Review* (New York) 6, no. 11 (June 1, 1886): 164.

42. For more on the appeal of detective fiction, see Kinkley 2000, 180–194.

43. According to Chen Dingshan, the Household Industries trademark image was registered with the Ministry of Agriculture and Industry in 1917 and remained unchanged for thirty-six years ([1955] 1967, 185).

44. The Korean term for "invention" was *palmyŏng*, a neologism from Japan, and the Chinese term, *faming*, was the same compound and also a neologism from Japan.

45. For more information on Hudnot, see Jones 2010, 29, and "Richard Hudnot" n.d.

46. The English brand name was "Butterfly Cream," shown on the packaging of the product in figure 4.3. A better translation of "Dieshuang" might be the more literal "Butterfly Frost Vanishing Cream," which captures the multiple meanings of the brand name in Chinese, with the cold cream being both *cold*, like frost, and *white*, like a woman's ideal skin. The literariness of the name speaks again to Chen's ability to turn his literary skills into a business resource.

47. For the pricing information, see Chen Xiaocui, Fan, and Zhou 1982, 223. Also see Zuo 2016, 169, which notes that Three Flowers sold for one yuan, whereas Chen's version sold initially at seven jiao and then at five jiao, half the price.

48. The alcohol content of the witch hazel and the carbon dioxide bubbles produced by carbonates in the cream were liable to evaporate, resulting in a loss of volume ("Hazeline Snow" n.d.). This problem may be what the complaint referred to.

49. Stearic acid is a saturated fatty acid and a waxy solid, and its chemical formula is $C_{17}H_{35}CO_2H$.

50. The sodium bicarbonate, an alkali, would release carbon dioxide during the manufacture to produce a cream with a foamy, snowy consistency. Fifty percent of the cream was hazeline, or witch hazel extract, which had purported medicinal attributes ("Hazeline Snow" n.d.). Hence, the name "Hazeline Snow."

51. See "Hazeline Snow" n.d. For more on the copying of Hazeline Snow and BW&C's attempt to police trademark infringement and to identify counterfeit versions worldwide, particularly in China, see Lean 2018.

52. In the decades following the U.S. Civil War, the rise of a drug industry characterized by modern laboratories and clinical science led to the emergence of
chemical patents as a legitimate means to stake claim over the manufacturing
processes of certain products. Prior to the Civil War, American physicians and
pharmacists saw medical patenting and the use of trademarks by drug manufacturers as unethical forms of monopoly. It was not really until the first decade
of the twentieth century that patent law came to be understood through a framework of intellectual-property rights that rested on the assumption of being able
to identify a "true and first" inventor (Gabriel 2014, 121–22). Similarly, in late-
nineteenth-century England, patent law was seen more along the lines of serving to grant the patent holder short-term rights to *monopoly* rather than property ownership (Arapostathis and Gooday 2013, xii).

53. Earlier accounts of how to manufacture Hazeline Snow did not seem to invite
similar scrutiny. The *Chemist and Druggist* issue for December 4, 1897, included
on page 884 a brief description of how to improve Hazeline Snow, and there
seemed to be no indication that the sharing of this information might constitute a legal or ethical violation.

54. For more on the role of alleged Chinese copycats in the making of a modern
industrial-property regime that sought to legalize exclusive corporate ownership
of brands in international trademark-infringement disputes, see Lean 2018.

55. The offset printing press features the printing technique of "offsetting" or transferring the inked image from a plate to a piece of rubber and then to the printing surface. Some offset presses combine this technique with the lithographic
process, which is based on the repulsion of oil and water. In this case, a flat pla-
nographic image carrier (where the image to be printed is located) draws ink
from ink rollers, and the nonprinting area attracts a water-based film, which
ensures that the nonprinting area remains ink free.

56. As Karl Gerth notes, nationalizing Chinese consumer culture was not always
easy (2004, 31–32).

57. See *Weisheng gongbao* [Hygiene bulletin] (Nanjing) 1 (4) (1929): 24.

58. See *Hebei shiye gongbao* [Hebei industry bulletin] 22 (1933): 21–23.

59. See *Gongshang gongbao* [Bulletin of industry and commerce] 1 (1930): 10.

60. The agendas of the two main biographical accounts of Chen's life (Dingshan
[1955] 1967; Chen Xiaocui, Fan, and Zhou 1982) were shaped by different politics, even if they converged in promoting entrepreneurism. The *wenshi ziliao*
(cultural and historical materials) account, an important site of ideological production, was published in 1982, a period of consolidation under the new Deng
regime. The state sought to promote entrepreneurism as part of "socialism with
Chinese characteristics," and regional editors, provincial compilers, and individual testimony givers negotiated state interests to articulate their respective

agendas—for example, accounts of migrant entrepreneurs to Manchuria (Fromm 2019, 45–95). The Dengist interest in promoting entrepreneurism was likely a factor behind Chen's daughter's decision to have her father's account memorialized. Public memory of industrial and commercial innovation in the 1930s would have a powerful resonance for the early 1980s. Chen's son's account was published in 1955 in Taiwan (and reprinted several times in the 1960s), where a commitment to turning Taiwan into a manufacturing center in East Asia similarly made Chen's biography compelling.

61. Kapil Raj has looked at local knowledge production in spaces where direct colonial encounters and "contact zones" existed, writing that "localities constantly reinvent themselves through grounding objects, skills, ideas and practices that circulate both within narrow regional or transcontinental—and indeed global—spaces" (2007, 21; also see Schaffer et al. 2009).

5. WHAT'S IN A NAME? FROM STUDIO APPELLATION TO COMMERCIAL TRADEMARK

1. If the Qing code did not provide much in the way of commercial law, the late-imperial state nonetheless often upheld the custom of protecting name brands, working with guilds and local authorities. Such practices allowed for considerable amount of leeway and flexibility on the part of the magistrates to manage and mediate business and commercial conflicts and relationships. See Qiu 2009, 78–81, for a discussion of commercial regulation of marks in the Suzhou and Songjiang cloth markets that had emerged out of customary practice.

2. In 1898, the British and French were the first to conclude an agreement for the mutual protection of their trademarks in China (Heuser 1975, 190). By 1902, the Mackay Treaty officially afforded protection to British trademarks (Zuo 2003). In 1903, U.S. and Japanese trademarks were granted legal protection.

3. In the United States, protection against the use of false geographical indications was long part of common law, but it was only with the Trademark Act of 1905 that it became part of federal statutory law. And with the Trademark Act of 1946 (the Lanham Act), certification marks were defined and protected.

4. Some scholars have characterized Western intervention in compiling China's modern Trademark Law in 1923 as exceptional and yet another example of the extent of Western imperialism in China (e.g., Zuo 2003, 51–56).

5. This image is from Shanghai jizhi guohuo gongchang lianhehui 1947, 44. It can be found also in a Household Industries ad that appeared in 1947 in the cosmetics section of the annual *Survey of China's National Products* (*Zhongguo guohuo diaocha ce* 1947, 36) and see the image in Wang Taijun 1924, inserted sleeve.

6. See "Jiating gongyeshe" 1935, 114. As a sport that was accessible primarily to China's privileged, cosmopolitan sectors of society, tennis more generally connoted a leisurely and luxurious lifestyle.

7. The Shanghaiese pronunciation of 蝴, the first character in the compound *hudie*, "butterfly," is *wu* in a third tone and is a homophone to the first character, *wu* 無 in Mandarin, in *wudi*, "peerless." The second character of *hudie*, 蝶, is pronounced in Shanghaiese as *di* in a fifth tone, which is a light, short tone. It is a homophone to the Mandarin pronunciation of 敵, *di*, though in Mandarin it is a third tone.

8. This trademark can be found in Shanghai jizhi guohuo gongchang lianhehui 1947, 44. The butterfly in this trademark differed slightly from the one featured in the colored logo for Butterfly Toothpowder.

9. For Zheng's style, see Laing 2004, 116–137, and for mention of Zheng painting for Chen Diexian, see Laing 2004, 126. Chen's son Dingshan knew Zheng well and could well have served as an intermediary between the artist and Household Industries. For more on that relationship, see Chen Dingshan 1964, 20–22, 117–119.

10. One alleged copycat was the Wuchang Heji Company, discussed in detail later in this chapter.

11. In the Ming–Qing commercial culture, trademarks for more high-end merchandise were characterized by texts rather than by images in part because of the lettered consumers' literary taste (J. Wu and Lien 2013, 256–258). This legacy of "literary," text-heavy trademarks persisted until the 1920s, especially for stores and products catering to more high-end consumers, who continued to take pride in their learnedness in an age of increased vernacularism (J. Wu and Lien 2013, 262–264). Chen's Butterfly mark, although not as text heavy as some other ads, nonetheless clearly played with words and puns and catered to a similar audience that appreciated China's classical literary culture.

12. This is the official registered trademark for the Butterfly brand, included in the publication titled *Dongya zhi bu shangbiao huikan* (Collection of Asian trademarks) in the early 1930s (Shiyebu shangbiaoju 1934, 30). Published by the Trademark Bureau of the Ministry of Industry and Commerce, the collection featured Chinese and Japanese marks registered in China. For more on this publication, see Zuo 1999, 28–30.

13. For more on the rise of commercial classicism in the early twentieth century, see Hill 2013.

14. The original Butterfly Toothpowder container was purchased on January 21, 2019, at the website for the auction house Old Goods Bazaar (Jiuhuo shangcheng) (http://7788.com/, item entry at http://7788.com/pr/detail_5622_61218716.html).

15. At the auction house where I found this object, there are at least seven other versions of this container available for purchase, all in varying conditions, some

quite poor. See, for example, the item at http://7788.com/pr/detail_auction_950 _16733166.html. Other containers were used for Butterfly Toothpowder, including the one featured as the item at http://7788.com/pr/detail_825_36822302.html. This one is a tin rather than a paper container. It features the English brand name "Butterfly" and a somewhat racially ambiguous face and torso of a modern woman, which suggests that the tin might have been used to attract foreign consumers.

16. Starting in the mid–nineteenth century, the Chinese state erected and sponsored institutions and bureaucratic offices such as the Jiangnan Arsenal to deal specifically with the industrial and commercial sectors. By the 1920s, attempts to justify and empower such offices and bureaus were ongoing, and the Jiangsu Industrial Bureau was one such bureau at the provincial level.

17. *Hu* is also a homophone in Shanghaiese to the first character in 無敵, Chen's brand. Thus, "Hu Die," the star's name, and "Wudi," part of Chen's brand name, although overlapping as homophones in Shanghaiese with the compound *hudie*, "butterfly," were entirely different characters in writing and did not overlap in Mandarin.

18. For more on the importance of appearing "real" and "genuine" in an era of mass-produced starlets in Shanghai's thriving film industry by the 1930s, see M. Chang 1999.

19. The Xiling Bridge, located in Hangzhou's famous West Lake, was infused with cultural authenticity by 1929. It was associated with the Xiling Seal Society, which in the first decade of the twentieth century became a renowned society for seal carving and appreciation that was suffused with nostalgic resonance for regional elites in Hangzhou. This very cultural authenticity became a marketable commodity, and the name "Xiling Seal Society" itself was a brand name (Lawrence 2014). Wu Yin (1867–1922), the founder of the Shanghai Xiling Seal Society, who migrated to Shanghai after the fall of the empire, as did Chen, presented himself similarly as a scholar and hermit recluse who rose above the vulgarities of commerce and politics to brand the society (Lawrence 2014, 93–96).

20. For an ad of the opening ceremony for the Butterfly Lodge, see *Shenbao*, April 4, 1934, 2, and April 5, 1934, 10. It featured an image of the butterfly. Photos of the opening ceremony featuring the stars appeared in urban journals and film magazines. See, for example, the first page of issue 10 of the *Illustrated Journal of Film* (*Dianyin huabao*) in 1934.

21. For the legal decision, see "Shiyebu suyuan juedingshu" 1933.

22. For more on this case against Hua'nan Chemical Company, see "Xingzheng susong caipan" 1936 and *Sifa gongbao* [Judicial bulletin] 119 (1936): 1–3. There were other cases. For a trademark dispute with the Huang'an Company that also took place in 1933, see *Shiye gongbao* [Ministry of Industry bulletin] 111–112 (1933): 10.

23. In 1927, Chen founded the Machine-Manufactured National Products Factory Association (Jizhi guohuo gongchang lianhehui) with fellow NPM merchants

such as Xiang Songmao and Shen Jiuchen (*Tianxuwosheng jinian kan* 1940, 4). The association produced the *Machinery Association Journal* (*Jilianhui kan*).

24. In a study of *Shenbao*, Barbara Mittler (2004) argues that in the earlier years foreign-style advertisements were often translated into Chinese style by using the language and visual conventions of traditional Chinese shop signs. By the 1930s, newspaper advertising had become big business, and the amount of space dedicated to newer-style advertisements that featured visual imagery grew substantially. Patent medicines and tobacco firms were among the most aggressive in introducing these pictorial ads.

25. In *Shenbao* advertisements, the shift toward targeting female readers intensified in the early 1910s (Mittler 2004, 264).

26. For this ad featuring Mae West, see, for example, *Cosmopolitan* 96, no. 5 (May 1934): 109.

27. In 1910, U.K. imports of "household and fancy soap" to China totaled 8,913 tons (Fieldhouse 1978, 341). By 1912, imports of English soap to China totaled more than 10,000 tons. Thus, one of Lever's most important proposals was to build joint works in China (Wilson 1954, 140–141), and so it founded the China Soap Company in Hong Kong in 1911 and opened a branch in Shanghai in 1923. In 1925, Lever launched its Sunlight (Riguang) brand in Shanghai, producing 4.2 tons of it in the first year of operation. In the 1930s, after Lever had merged with the Dutch company Margarine Unie to become Unilever, the company replaced Sunlight with the new brand Lux (Lishi), which succeeded in penetrating the urban Chinese market even more successfully than Sunlight.

28. These ad agencies included the China Commercial Advertising Agency Co. run by Charles William Millington. Another famous American advertiser in Shanghai was Carl Crow.

29. When Lever Brothers merged with the Netherlands-based company Margarine Union and developed into the diversified Anglo-Dutch giant Unilever, Lintas grew substantially to become an independent agency and began pursuing advertising accounts on its own. Lintas would often work with local Chinese artists to generate ads that appealed to local tastes. For this history, see "Lintas: Worldwide" n.d.

30. This use of film stars extended to Unilever's ad campaigns not just in China but also in Latin America (Jones 2010, 125–134).

31. For more on courtesans and late-Qing literati in Shanghai, see Hershatter 1997 and C. Yeh 2006. By the republican period, literati culture was on the decline, and both the image and the person of the courtesan—the product and symbol of that culture—increasingly invoked a sense of decadence. For more on how the Chinese movie star and Shanghai's movie culture were closely linked to the global cinematic culture, see Z. Zhang 2005.

32. Whereas a great deal has been written about the process by which stars have been commodified, what we see here is the converse—namely, how the process of adoring a human being (the movie star) was deployed to cultivate sentiment for an object. In other words, rather than the person becoming commodified in the process of commodity fetishism, the thing became anthropomorphized as the object of subjective attachment.

33. In China, this method of guaranteeing authenticity, the autograph, was very new. In the imperial past, the chop or seal had long authenticated social and political power. The singular hand of the emperor behind the imperial chop transmitted and authenticated imperial power, reproducing itself thousands of time in imperial China's bureaucratic culture, giving authority to the paperwork that constituted imperial communication. The literati, with their status verified by their success on the civil-service examination and thus having been figuratively "touched" or anointed by the emperor, also had the prestige and status to add authenticity and testimony to, for example, a painting by applying their personal chop. The modern use of signatures and autographs marked a shift away from the imperial economy of power upon which literati status rested to a new consumer society where mass production reigned.

34. The use of the headshot and signature emerged from the global regime of Hollywood and sought to give fans a sense of intimacy. The rather mediocre calligraphy of these signatures could very well have revealed that these women were not particularly well educated or classically trained. This did not necessarily count against them. Indeed, the lure of the movie star lay in the somewhat paradoxical combination of her being at once unattainable in her star status and at the same time seemingly accessible, ordinary, and "own-able" by all fans as a mass commodity (M. Chang 1999).

35. For more on Household Industries' use of a franchise system to manage its provincial branches, see Huameicunren 1922, 42.

36. For mention of this company, see any of the *New Union Times* ads in the 1934 campaign, discussed later in this chapter. For example, see *Zonghui xinbao* [New union times] (Singapore), March 21, 1934, sec. 4, 2; March 24, 1934, sec. 2, 4; and April 2, 1934, sec. 4, 2.

37. The title of this newspaper was changed back to *Union Times* (*Zonghui bao*) in 1939, and its final edition was published in 1946 (Kenley 2014, 587 n. 11).

38. See, for example, *Zonghui xinbao*, March 24, 1934, sec. 2, 4, and April 7, 1934, sec. 1, 5.

39. See, for example, *Zonghui xinbao*, March 28, 1934, sec. 1, 4, and April 3, 1934, sec. 1, 2.

40. For more on "Straits Chinese" and the multiethnic port of Singapore, see Chua 2012.

41. See, for example, Cochran 2006, which focuses on Chinese medicine men in particular.

42. For example, Sherman Cochran's (2006) work conceptualizes Chinese middlemen such as Chen as engaged in transplanting foreign models to Southeast Asian soil, if not to Chinese soil.

43. To be sure, in his discussion of Aw Boon-haw, an overseas Chinese entrepreneur who manufactured Tiger Balm, Cochran is careful to show how Aw was particularly adept at marketing his goods as "transcultural" to address the nature of his consuming constituency—using strategies such as recruiting artists who were transnational and transcultural (e.g., Guan Huinong based in Hong Kong), employing the Chinese and vernacular local language for his marketing, and allowing multicultural consumers to attach local meaning to the product (2006, chap. 5).

44. Li Lili starred in *Loving Blood of the Volcano* in 1932, directed by Sun Yu. This film was probably very popular in Singapore and Southeast Asia. It is set in the South Seas and features Li dancing, which played to her strengths. Sun Yu went on to direct Li in *Queen of Sports* in 1934 and *Big Road* in 1935, another film written specifically for Li, both of them blockbusters.

45. By 1935, Li Lili, perhaps more than any other movie star, embodied a healthy beauty that was becoming the ideal beauty promoted in magazines and consumer culture and that was clearly in line with the New Life Movement's emphasis on athletic culture. She secured this reputation after appearing in the film *Queen of Sports* in 1934, and Paul Pickowicz describes her allure in that film as stemming from the director's portrayal of her natural, robust sexuality: "His heroine is wholesome, but she is also frisky, and radiates a natural spontaneous sexuality" (1991, 51).

46. For a biography of Wang Renmei, see Meyer 2013.

47. For a study of Barnum's hoaxes and nineteenth-century Americans' fascination with fraud and deception, see Cook 2001. For a study of one of Barnum's most famous hoaxes, the exhibition of Joice Heth (the supposedly 161-year-old "nursing mammy" of George Washington), and its relationship with race, see Reiss 2010.

48. Karl Gerth, for example, discusses how biographical references were used regularly in the packaging of National Products, citing Wu Yunchu (1891–1953), whose person and biography converged with the product on the labels of his flavor enhancing powder made of monosodium glutamate, MSG (2004, 352–354).

6. COMPILING THE INDUSTRIAL MODERN, 1930–1941

1. Each volume was published and distributed abroad and domestically, totaling more than ten thousand copies (Chen Dingshan [1955] 1967, 182). Keep in mind that these publications were probably shared and collectively read in households, so actual readership was even larger.

2. For the reprint history, see the first page of "Preface to the Second Edition of *Mr. Mei's New Compilation of Tested Prescriptions*" in Chen Diexian [1934] 1937. Mei Qizhao, who received the status of a *jinshi* degree holder in 1852, served as the provincial governor of Zhejiang from 1877 to 1879. For biographical information on Mei, see Qian 1980, 2:1718–1720, and Zhu and Xie 1980, 3:2809.

3. Probably a few thousand copies of *Wealth in Industry* were sold. We know that one thousand more copies were printed after the first printing. See Chen Diexian 1933b, 1.

4. A vibrant copy culture and late-imperial practices of emulating foreign imports conditioned the Republican-era practices of copying for purposes of strengthening China's manufacturing sector and substituting foreign goods with local imitations (see Dikötter 2007, 30–48).

5. An example of this intellectual ambivalence can be found in the famous debates on science and metaphysics in 1924, arguably a turning point among intellectuals with the articulation of a critique of the universality of modern science.

6. See, for example, Lei 2014, which discusses how Chinese healing practices were reorganized into the unified field of Chinese traditional medicine in juxtaposition to modern biomedicine.

7. For more on the rise of the popularity of patent medicines in the consumer culture of early-twentieth-century China, see Lean 1995.

8. For a discussion of the uneven adaptation of copyright in early-twentieth-century China, see M. Sun 2019, 134–169. Myra Sun notes how the emerging notion of author-centered ownership did not completely displace the practice of defining ownership according to who owned the print blocks, which remained quite persistent.

9. See Des Forges 2009, 46, 48–49, on the pirating of fiction written by well-known brand-name authors such as Zhang Henshui, Zhu Shouju (1892–1966), and Zhou Shoujuan (1895–1968). Zhou Shoujuan was a close friend of Chen Diexian; he penned a eulogy for Chen when Chen passed in 1940 (*Tianxuwosheng jinian kan* 1940, 24–25) and worked with Chen's daughter on a retrospective account, which was published in 1982 (Chen Xiaocui, Fan, and Zhou 1982). Chen would surely have known of Zhou's fiction being pirated.

10. My thanks to Christopher Rea (personal communication, March 21, 2009) for pointing out this dictionary to me.

11. According to *Chinese Historical Illness Terminology*, volume 1 of Zhang Zhibin and Paul Unschuld's *Dictionary of the* Ben Cao Gang Mu, the English translation of *louli* is "scrofula pervasion illness" (2015, 329). It is a pathological condition in which swellings the size of plums appear on the neck or in the armpits and, if they open, can fester and take a long time to heal.

12. It is important to note, too, that the related term and homophone *shiyan* 試驗 also appeared in texts during that time and was closer in meaning to "testing" or "examining."

13. In Chinese literary history, the preface to *A Collection of Common Knowledge* (Chen Diexian 1935–1941) is similar to what Gérard Genette (1997) has described as a "paratext." For Genette, paratexts, or elements in a published work that accompany the main body of the text, including prefatory material, provide a space or zone where editors or authors can assume a strong authorial voice with the intent to intervene in and shape the reading process. Chen Diexian treated his prefaces in these collectanea much like the paratexts that Genette describes. However, although much of his preface to *A Collection of Common Knowledge* conforms to Genette's definition, certain aspects of it seem unique to the Chinese literary tradition, including the use of principles of compilation to authenticate a publication's content. Another characteristic of the Chinese preface that might be more specific to the Chinese tradition is its inclusion of material not only by the author or editor but also by the author's or editor's friends or network of famous associates to authenticate a text.

14. In "Preface to the Second Edition of *Mr. Mei's New Compilation of Tested Prescriptions*," Chen noted that with the reprint he had printed a total of three thousand copies of this book, in addition to the one thousand copies printed by the Sanyou Corporation, for an estimated four thousand copies circulating in the market in the mid-1930s (Chen Diexian [1934] 1937, first page of preface).

15. For a discussion of *Mr. Bao's Prescriptions*, see Y. Wu 2010, 71–72.

16. Such a portrayal conformed to the new social image of the professional writer that Chen sought to project, which coincided with the fictional trope that Alexander Des Forges has described as arising initially in fiction in 1909 (2009, 49): namely, the productive figure of the professional writer in Shanghai's urbanscape, often depicted as hunched over his writing desk, hard at work. As Des Forges notes, this image was in response to the anxiety surrounding the rise in the number of professional (for-pay) writers.

17. The first edition of Bao Xiang'ao's *Yanfang xinbian* was published in 1846; it was expanded and edited by Mei Qizhao in 1878. For a modern critical edition, see Bao Xiang'ao [1846] 1990.

18. For Confucius's saying, see the Liren section of *The Analects*. The translation used here is by James Legge (https://ctext.org/analects/li-ren, line 16).

19. In this capacity, Chen, for example, published the *Journal of the Shanghai Machine-Based National Products Association* (*Shanghai jizhi guohuo lianhehui huikan*) starting in 1930.

20. In the preface to the *Wealth in Industry*, Chen mentioned that because of popular demand, yet another one thousand copies of the book were to be printed

(Chen Diexian 1933b, 1). We can assume that the actual number of readers was most likely greater than the number of copies published because texts were shared and knowledge in the texts was transmitted verbally and practically. That said, editors regularly claimed that their publication was so popular that a large number of readers had demanded its reprinting.

21. For *Wealth in Industry*, Chen collected entries from a range of contributors, serving primarily as an editor rather than as author or compiler of each and every entry.

22. See also Elman 2005, 355–395, for a reassessment of earlier narratives of "failure" and an argument that although the Jiangnan Arsenal was considered rather innovative in its day, it was the Sino-Japanese War in 1894–1895 that "refracted" the stories of the arsenal in particular and of the Self-Strengthening Movement in general into narratives of failure.

23. Craig Clunas has nicely linked this encyclopedic and classificatory interest in collecting information on the pharmacopoeia of the Ming to the popularity of the medicine cabinet and its multiple drawers, which physically separated elements of the world of pharmacology into sections (2007, 112–113).

24. Eighteenth-century state projects included the Qing state's Four Treasuries (Siku quanshu) project. For more on the state sponsorship of such projects and their social impact in Jiangnan, see Elman 1984.

CONCLUSION

1. For more obituaries and published eulogies, see, for example, Zhou Shoujuan 1940 and Wang Cangping 1940. "Yuanlong" is the stylistic name of Chen Deng (170–208 CE) of the Three Kingdoms period (220–280 CE). He was bestowed the title "General Fubo" for contributing to the capture of warlord Lü Bu. His contemporaries praised him for his heroic spirit and unparalleled civil and military skills.

2. This excerpt comes from Zhou Shoujuan's eulogy "Mourning the Death of Tianxuwosheng, Mr. Chen Diexian" ("Daonian Tianxuwosheng Chen Xuyuan," 1940).

3. For details on the problems the company faced during the 1930s, see Chen Xiaocui, Fan and Zhou 1982, 224–225, and Shanghai shi tongjibu 1957, 135. For mention of the Japanese bombing of Chen's factories, see Zheng 1992, 11. Zheng Yimei notes, perhaps somewhat apocryphally, that Japan deliberately bombed Chen's factories because his toothpowder had overpowered the Japanese Lion brand on the market. For details on the relocation of Household Industries and how branches of the company fared during the war, see Shanghai shi tongjibu 1957, 135–136, and Chen Dingshan [1955] 1967, 194–202.

4. These attributes were identified as characterizing activities not just specific to the Great Leap. A recent investigation into People's Republic of China medical aid missions to rural Algeria in the 1960s and 1970s, for example, shows how the Chinese doctors' practices of improvisation, adaptation, and reliance upon local resources—methods that emerged in the face of scarcity and lack of resources— came to be touted as key characteristics of "Chinese socialist medicine" worthy of being exported abroad (Zou 2019). See also work on amateur radio technologists and their tinkering in the Maoist era (Y. Yang forthcoming).

5. For a study of Shenzhen as a conducive site for *shanzhai* production because barriers to technological production are relatively low there and technologies, knowledge, and materials flow relatively freely, see Stevens 2018, 90–95.

6. Yang Fan refers to the "endless news outbursts about Chinese counterfeits" as part of a rise of a new global discourse on "faked in China," which is bound to fears of China's ascent as a global powerhouse (2016, 2, 17–18).

7. For Mertha's discussion of the historical context leading up to counterfeiting in China today, see Mertha 2005, 25.

8. For more on how neoliberalism has helped shore up the Chinese state's legitimacy, especially after China's entry into the World Trade Organization, see Yang 2016, esp. 20–25.

9. For more on mass making in China and the government's involvement, see Lindtner, Bardzell, and Bardzell 2016, 1395–1396, and Stevens 2018, 92–93.

10. On the Chinese government's investment in China's making culture and Intel's investment of millions of U.S. dollars in South China to sponsor China's "mass makerspace" initiative, see Lindtner, Bardzell, and Bardzell 2016, 1396.

11. For an account that *is* sensitive to how gender and access to mobility might limit or enable a "maker," see Wong 2014, 125–132, which focuses on a Dafen painter making to order copies of iconic paintings or images for far-flung customers around the world.

12. For more on exploitative practices and inequalities along gendered and racialized lines in makers' cultures in Shenzhen, see Lindtner forthcoming, especially chapters 3 and 5. In the introduction to this forthcoming book, Silvia Lindtner thoughtfully acknowledges how she had initially been swept up in the techno-optimism surrounding these makers' communities and their practices. Over time, however, she grew increasingly ambivalent about their liberatory potential and now powerfully documents the new forms of exploitation these communities generate, even as they serve as an alternative to individualist notions of authorship, ownership, and empowerment that underpin Western tech movements. My thanks to Silvia Lindtner for sharing her manuscript with me.

References

ARCHIVES

Hangzhou Library, Ancient Books Collection, Hangzhou
Shanghai Municipal Archives
Wellcome Institute Archives, London

PUBLISHED AND OTHER CITED SOURCES

Alford, William P. 1995. *To Steal a Book Is an Elegant Offense: Intellectual Property Law in Chinese Civilization*. Stanford, CA: Stanford University Press.

Anderson, Warwick. 2011. "'Looking for Newton? From Hydraulic Societies to the Hydraulics of Globalization." In *Force, Movement, Intensity: The Newtonian Imagination and the Humanities and Social Sciences*, ed. Ghassan Hage and Emma Kowal, 128–135. Melbourne: Melbourne University Press.

——. 2018. "Remembering the Spread of Western Science." *Historical Records of Australian Science* 29:73–81. http://www.publish.csiro.au/hr/HR17027.

Anhui gongbao 安徽公報 [Anhui bulletin]. 1919.

Arapostathis, Stathis, and Graeme Gooday. 2013. *Patently Contestable: Electrical Technologies and Inventor Identities on Trial in Britain*. Cambridge, MA: Harvard University Press.

Armitage, David, and Jo Guldi. 2014. *The History Manifesto*. https://www.cambridge.org/core/services/aop-file-manager/file/57594fd0fab864a459dc7785.

Arnold, David. 2013. *Everyday Technology: Machines and the Making of India's Modernity*. Chicago: University of Chicago Press.

Asen, Daniel. 2016. *Death in Beijing: Murder and Forensic Science in Republican China*. Cambridge: Cambridge University Press.

Bankoff, Greg, Uwe Lübken, and Jordan Sand. 2012. Introduction to *Flammable Cities: Urban Conflagration and the Making of the Modern World*, ed. Greg Bankoff, Uwe Lübken, and Jordan Sand, 3–20. Madison: University of Wisconsin Press.

Bao, Weihong. 2005. "A Panoramic Worldview: Probing the Visuality of *Dianshizhai huabao*." *Journal of Modern Chinese Literature* 32 (March): 405–459.

——. 2016. *Fiery Cinema: The Emergence of an Affective Medium in China, 1915–1945*. Minneapolis: University of Minnesota Press.

Bao Xiang'ao 鲍相璈. [1846] 1990. *Yanfang xinbian* 驗方新編 [A new compilation of tested prescriptions]. Beijing: Renming weisheng chubanshe.

Basalla, George. 1967. "The Spread of Western Science." *Science* 156:611–622.

——. 1988. *The Evolution of Technology*. Cambridge: Cambridge University Press.

Benedict, Carol. 2011. *Golden-Silk Smoke: A History of Tobacco in China, 1550–2010*. Berkeley: University of California Press.

Bi Yuan 毕苑. 2010. *Jianzao changshi: Jiaokeshu yu jindai Zhongguo wenhua zhuanxing* 建造常识：教科书与近代中国文化转型 [Making common sense: Textbooks and the transformation of Chinese culture]. Fuzhou: Fujian kiaoyu chubanshe.

Bian, He. 2017. "An Ever-Expanding Pharmacy: Zhao Xuemin and the Conditions for New Knowledge in Eighteenth-Century China." *Harvard Journal of Asiatic Studies* 77 (2): 287–319.

Bickers, Robert, and Rosemary Seton, eds. 1996. *Missionary Encounters: Sources and Issues*. Richmond, U.K.: Curzon Press.

Biggerstaff, Knight. 1956. "Shanghai Polytechnic Institution and Reading Room: An Attempt to Introduce Western Science and Technology to the Chinese." *Pacific Historical Review* 25 (2) (May): 127–149.

Bray, Francesca. 1997. *Technology and Gender: Fabrics of Power in Late Imperial China*. Berkeley: University of California Press.

Brennert, H. S., and V. V. Hagelsrom. 1911. *Present Day Political Organization of China*. New York: Paragon Press.

Brooks, Barbara. 2000. *Japan's Imperial Diplomacy: Consuls, Treaty Ports, and War in China, 1895–1938*. Honolulu: Hawai'i University Press.

Buck, Peter. 1980. *American Science and Modern China, 1876–1936*. Cambridge: Cambridge University Press.

Burke, Mary. 2009. *"Tinkers": Synge and the Cultural History of the Irish Traveller*. Oxford: Oxford University Press.

Cai, Danni. Forthcoming. "Letter-Writing Manuals in Late Imperial and Republican China." PhD diss., McGill University.

Cao Xueqin. 1977. *The Story of the Stone*. Trans. David Hawkes. New York: Penguin Books.

Cassel, Par. 2011. *Grounds of Judgment: Extraterritoriality and Imperial Power in Nineteenth-Century China and Japan*. Oxford: Oxford University Press.

Chang Che-chia 張哲嘉. 2004. "*Funü zazhi* zhong de 'yishi weisheng guwen'" "婦女雜誌" 中的<醫事衛生顧問> ["Advice on Medicine and Hygiene" column in the *Ladies' Journal*]. *Jindai Zhongguo funü shi yanjiu* 近代中國婦女史研究 12 (December): 145–168.

Chang, Michael G. 1999. "The Good, the Bad, and the Beautiful: Movie Actresses and Public Discourse in Shanghai, 1920s–1930s." In *Cinema and Urban Culture in Shanghai, 1922–1943*, ed. Yinjing Zhang, 128–159. Stanford, CA: Stanford University Press.

Chemist and Druggist (London). 1897.

Chen Diexian 陳蝶仙 (pseud. Chen Xu 陳栩). 1900. *Gongchen qiao zhuzhici* 拱宸橋竹枝詞 [Bamboo-branch poetry from the Gongchen bridge]. 2 vols. Hangzhou: Daguanbao guan.

—— (pseud. Tianxuwosheng 天虛我生), contrib. 1915. "Huazhuangpin zhizao ku" 化妝品製造庫 [The warehouse for cosmetic production] (column). Ed. Chen Diexian. *Nüzi shijie* 女子世界 1–5 (January–May).

—— (pseud. Tianxuwosheng 天虛我生), comp. and ed. 1928. *Gongshangye chidu ou'cun* 工商業尺牘偶存 [Model correspondence on industry and commerce]. Shanghai: Jiating gongyeshe.

—— (pseud. Tianxuwosheng 天虛我生), trans. 1933a. *Bohe gongye* 薄荷工業 [Peppermint industry]. Shanghai: Jiating gongyeshe.

—— (pseud. Tianxuwosheng 天虛我生), ed. 1933b. *Shiye zhi fu congshu* 實業致富叢書 [Collectanea on how to acquire wealth in industry]. 5 vols. Shanghai: Xinhua Press.

—— (pseud. Tianxuwosheng 天虛我生). 1934. "Shangbiao fa you buchong zhi biyao" 商標法有補充之必要 [The need to supplement trademark law]. *Jilianhui kan* 機聯會刊 97:2–5.

—— (pseud. Tianxuwosheng 天虛我生), ed. 1935–1941. *Jiating changshi huibian* 家庭常識彙編 [A collection of common knowledge for the household]. 8 vols. Shanghai: Jiating gongyeshe.

—— (pseud. Tianxuwosheng 天虛我生), ed. [1934] 1937. *Meishi yanfang xinbian* 梅氏驗方新編 [Mr. Mei's new compilation of tested prescriptions]. Shanghai: Jiating gongyeshe.

—— (pseud. Tianxuwosheng 天虛我生). 1939. "Jingzhi shiyan fa" 精製實驗法 [An exquisite method for manufacturing table salt]. *Xiao gongyi* 小工藝 1 (7) (March): 2.

—— (pseud. Tianxuwosheng 天虛我生). 1981. *Huangjin sui* 黃金祟 [The money demon]. Taipei: Guangwen shuju.

——. 1999. *The Money Demon: An Autobiographical Romance.* Trans. Patrick Hanan. Honolulu: University of Hawai'i Press.

—— (pseud. Tianxuwosheng 天虛我生). n.d. *Xuyuan conggao* 栩園叢稿 [The collected works of Xuyuan]. Comp. Zhisheng Zhou. Shanghai: Jiating gongyeshe.

Chen Dingshan 陳定山. 1964. *Chun Shen jiuwen* 春申舊聞 [Old stories of early Shanghai]. Taipei: Chenguang yuekanshe.

——. [1955] 1967. "Wode fuqin Tianxuwosheng—Guohuo zhi yinzhe" 我的父親天虛我生 — 國貨之隱者 [My father, Tianxuwosheng—recluse of the National Products Movement]. In *Chun Shen jiuwen* 春申舊聞 [Old stories of early Shanghai], 180–204. Taipei: Shijie wenwu.

Chen Duxiu. 1919. "Ben zhi zui'an zhi dabianshu" 本誌罪案之答辯書 [This magazine's reply to charges against it]. *Xin Qingnian* 新青年 6 (1) (January 15): 10–11.

Chen, Janet. 2012. *Guilty of Indigence: The Urban Poor in China, 1900–1953.* Princeton, NJ: Princeton University Press.

Chen Pingyuan 陈平原. 2010. *Zhongguo xiaoshuo xushi moshi de zhuanbian* 中国小说叙事模式的转变 [The transformation of narrative modes in Chinese fiction]. Beijing: Peking University Press.

Chen Xiaocui, Fan Yanqiao, and Zhou Shoujuan 陈小翠, 范烟桥, 周瘦鹃. 1982. "Tianxuwosheng yu Wudipai yafen" 天虛我生与无敌牌牙粉 [Tianxuwosheng and Butterfly Toothpowder]. In *Wenshi ziliao jingxuan* 文史资料精选 [Selection of cultural and historical materials], vol. 80, ed. Zhongguo renmin zhengzhi xieshang huiyi quanguo weiyuanhui wenshi ziliao yanjiu weiyuanhui 中国人民政治协商会议全国委员会文史资料研究委员会, 209–226. Beijing: Zhongguo wenshi chubanshe.

Chi Xiuyun 池秀云. 1998. *Lidai mingren shiming biehao cidian* 历代名人室名别号辞典 [The dictionary of pen-names of historical personages]. Taiyuan: Shaanxi guji chubanshe.

Chiang, Yung-chen. 2006. "Womanhood, Motherhood, and Biology: The Early Phases of the *Ladies' Journal*, 1915–25." *Gender & History* 18 (3) (November): 519–545.

China Educational Supply Association, ed. 1928. *Catalogue of Education Supplies.* Shanghai: China Educational Supply Association Press.

China Industrial Handbooks Kiangsu. 1933. Shanghai: Bureau of Foreign Trade, Ministry of Industry.

China Press (Shanghai). 1933.

Chou Hsu-Chi 周敘琪. 2005. "Yuedu yu shenghuo: Yun Daiying de jiating shenghuo yu 'Funü zazhi' zhi guanxi" 閱讀與生活: 惲代英的家庭生活與《婦女雜誌》之關係 [Reading and lifestyle: Yun Daiying's family life and its relationship with the *Ladies' Journal*]. *Si yu yan: renwen yu shehui kexue zazhi* 思與言：人文與社會科學雜誌 43 (3) (September): 107–190.

Chow, Kai-wing. 2004. *Publishing, Culture, and Power in Early Modern China Publishing.* Stanford, CA: Stanford University Press.

Chua, Ai Lin. 2012. "Nation, Race, and Language: Discussing Transnational Identities in Colonial Singapore, Circa 1930." *Modern Asian Studies* 46 (2) (March): 283–302.

Claypool, Lisa. 2005. "Zhang Jian and China's First Museum." *Journal of Asian Studies* 64 (3): 567–604.

Clunas, Craig. 1997. *Pictures and Visuality in Early Modern China.* Princeton, NJ: Princeton University Press, 1997.

——. 2004. *Superfluous Things: Material Culture and Social Status in Early Modern China.* Honolulu: University of Hawai'i Press.

——. 2007. *Empire of Great Brightness: Visual and Material Cultures of Ming China, 1368–1644.* Honolulu: University of Hawai'i Press.

Cochran, Sherman. 2006. *Chinese Medicine Men: Consumer Cultures in China and Southeast Asia.* Cambridge, MA: Harvard University Press.

Cochran, Sherman, and Andrew Hsieh. 2013. *The Lius of Shanghai.* Cambridge, MA: Harvard University Press.

Cohen, Deborah, and Peter Mandler. 2015. "Exchange: On *The History Manifesto*." American Historical Review 120 (2): 530–542.

Cook, James. 2001. *The Arts of Deception: Playing with Fraud in the Age of Barnum.* Cambridge, MA: Harvard University Press.

Cosmopolitan. 1934.

Culp, Robert. 2007. *Articulating Citizenship: Civic Education and Student Politics in Southeastern China, 1912–1940.* Cambridge, MA: Harvard University Asia Center.

——. 2016. "Mass Production of Knowledge and the Industrialization of Mental Labor: The Rise of the Petty Intellectual." In *Knowledge Acts in Modern China: Ideas, Institutions, and Identities,* ed. Robert Culp, Eddie U, and Wen-hsin Yeh, 207–241. Berkeley: Institute of East Asian Studies, University of California Press.

——. 2019. *The Power of Print in Modern China: Intellectuals and Industrial Publishing from the End of Empire to Maoist State Socialism.* New York: Columbia University Press.

Culp, Robert, Eddie U, and Wen-hsin Yeh, eds. 2016. *Knowledge Acts in Modern China: Ideas, Institutions, and Identities.* Berkeley: Institute of East Asian Studies, University of California Press.

Dagongbao 大公報 [L'Impartial] (Tianjin). 1932.

Darmon, Reed. 2004. *Made in China.* San Francisco: Chronicle Books.

Des Forges, Alexander. 2009. "Professional Anxiety, Brand Names, and Wild Chickens: From 1909." In *Rethinking Chinese Popular Culture,* ed. Carlos Rojas and Eileen Chow, 40–53. New York: Routledge.

Descriptions of the Commercial Press Exhibit. n.d. Shanghai: Commercial Press.

Dianyin huabao 電音畫報 [Illustrated journal of film]. 1934.

Dikötter, Frank. 2007. *Exotic Commodities: Modern Objects and Everyday Life in China.* New York: Columbia University Press.

Ding Shouhe 丁守和, ed. 1982–1987. *Xinhai geming shiqi qikan jieshao* 辛亥革命时期期刊介绍 [Introduction to periodicals of the 1911 revolutionary period]. 5 vols. Beijing: Renmin chubanshe.

Dong, Madeleine. 2003. *Republican Beiping: The City and Its History.* Berkeley: University of California Press.

Du Shiran 杜石然, Lin Qingyuan 林庆元, Guo Jinbin 郭金彬. 1991. *Yangwu yundong yu Zhongguo jindai keji* 洋务运动与中国近代科技 [The Foreign Affairs Movement and China's modern science and technology]. Shenyang: Liaoning jiaoyu chubanshe.

Edgerton, David. 2007. *The Shock of the Old: Technology and Global History Since 1900.* Oxford: Oxford University Press.

Elman, Benjamin. 1984. *From Philosophy to Philology: Intellectual and Social Aspects of Change in Late Imperial China.* Cambridge, MA: Harvard University Asia Center.

——. 2005. *On Their Own Terms: Science in China, 1550–1900.* Cambridge, MA: Harvard University Press.

Eyferth, Jacob. 2009. *Eating Rice from Bamboo Roots: The Social History of a Community of Handicraft Papermakers in Rural Sichuan, 1920s–2000.* Cambridge, MA: Harvard University Asia Center.

Fa Chang 法常. 1922. "Quan guoren sheli huaxue yanjiusuo" 勸國人設立化學研究所 [Urging my countrymen to establish a chemical research institute]. *Huaxue gongyi* 化學工藝 1 (5) (May): 5–11.

Fan, Fa-ti. 2004. *British Naturalists in Qing China: Science, Empire, and Cultural Encounter.* Cambridge, MA: Harvard University Press.

——. 2012. "The Global Turn in the History of Science." *East Asian Science, Technology, and Society Journal* 6:249–258.

Fang Chaoheng 方朝珩. 1922. "Xiangmaopai feizao tian shiliao zhi diaocha" 祥茂牌肥皂填實料之調查 [Investigation of Xiangmao soap's ingredients]. *Huaxue gongyi* 化學工藝 1 (2) (October): 44–46.

Fernsebner, Susan. 2003. "A People's Plaything: Toys, Childhood, and Chinese Identity, 1909–1933." *Postcolonial Studies* 6 (3) (November): 269–293.

Feuerwerker, Albert. 1958. *China's Early Industrialization: Sheng Hsuan-huai (1844–1916) and Mandarin Enterprise.* Cambridge, MA: Harvard University Press.

Fieldhouse, D. K. 1978. *Unilever Overseas: The Anatomy of a Multinational 1895–1965.* Stanford, CA: Hoover Institution Press.

Fong, Grace. 2015. "Between the Literatus and the New Woman: Lü Bicheng as Cultural Entrepreneur." In *The Business of Culture: Cultural Entrepreneurs in China and Southeast Asia, 1900–65*, ed. Christopher Rea and Nicolai Volland, 35–61. Vancouver: University of British Columbia Press.

"Frequently Used Chinese Medicine: Cuttlebone." n.d. The Medical Needle (Yibian). http://yibian.hopto.org/yao/?yno=499.

Frierson, Cathy A. 2012. "Imperial Russia's Urban Fire Regimes, 1700–1905." In *Flammable Cities: Urban Conflagration and the Making of the Modern World*, ed. Greg Bankoff, Uwe Lübken, and Jordan Sand, 102–124. Madison: University of Wisconsin Press.

Fromm, Martin. 2019. *Borderland Memories: Searching for Historical Identity in Post-Mao China*. Cambridge: Cambridge University Press.

Funü zazhi 婦女雜誌 [Ladies' journal] (Shanghai). 1915.

Furth, Charlotte. 1999. *A Flourishing Yin: Gender in China's Medical History, 960–1665*. Berkeley: University of California Press.

Gabriel, Joseph M. 2014. *Medical Monopoly: Intellectual Property Rights and the Origins of the Modern Pharmaceutical Industry*. Chicago: University of Chicago Press.

General Medical Council, United Kingdom. 1898. *British Pharmacopoeia*. London: Spottiswoode.

Genette, Gérard. 1997. *Paratext: Thresholds of Interpretation*. Cambridge: Cambridge University Press.

Gernet, Jacques. 1962. *Daily Life in China on the Eve of the Mongol Invasion, 1250–1276*. Stanford, CA: Stanford University Press.

Gerth, Karl. 2004. *China Made: Consumer Culture and the Creation of the Nation*. Cambridge, MA: Harvard University Asia Center.

——. 2010. *As China Goes, so Goes the World: How Chinese Consumers Are Transforming Everything*. New York: Hill and Wang.

Gezhi huibian 格致彙編 [Chinese scientific and industrial magazine] (Shanghai). 1876–1877.

Glosser, Susan. 2003. *Chinese Visions of Family and State, 1915–1953*. Berkeley: University of California Press.

Gmelch, Sharon, and Pat Langan. 1975. *Tinkers and Travellers*. Dublin: O'Brien Press.

Gongshang gongbao 工商公報 [Bulletin of industry and commerce] (Nanjing). 1930.

Gordin, Michael. 2015. *Scientific Babel: How Science Was Done Before and After Global English*. Chicago: University of Chicago Press.

Greenbaum, Jamie. 2007. *Chen Jiru (1558–1639)*. Leiden: Brill Academic.

Gu, Yi. 2013. "What's in a Name? Photography and the Reinvention of Visual Truth in China." *Art Bulletin* 95 (1) (March): 120–138.

Gu Ying 顧穎, ed. 2009. "Xunzhao Chen Diexian" 尋找陳蝶仙 [Finding Chen Diexian]. Xinhuanet, December 19. http://big5.xinhuanet.com/gate/big5/www.zj.xinhuanet .com/website/2009-12/19/content_18467086.htm.

Gunning, Thomas. 1995. "Tracing the Individual Body AKA Photography, Detectives, Early Cinema, and the Body of Modernity." In *Cinema and the Invention of Modern Life*, ed. Vanessa R. Schwartz and Leo Charney, 15–45. Berkeley: University of California Press.

Guo Baozhang 郭保章. 1995. *Zhongguo xiandai huaxue shilue* 中国现代化学史略 [The history of modern chemistry in China]. Nanning: Guangxi jiaoyu chubanshe.

Guo Shangbao 郭上寶. 1922. "Zhong-Ying yaofang suo shou zhi dongqingyou. Shi tianra pin, liushi renzao pin?" 中英藥方所售之冬青油.是天然品, 柳是人造品? [Is the wintergreen oil by the China-British Pharmacy a natural product or a man-made product?]. *Huaxue gongyi* 化學工藝 1 (2) (October): 46–47.

Guo, Ting-yi, and Kwang-Ching Liu. 1978. "Self-Strengthening: The Pursuit of Western Technology." In *The Cambridge History of China*, vol. 10: *Late Ch'ing, 1800–1911, Part 1*, ed. John K. Fairbank, 491–542. Cambridge: Cambridge University Press.

Hanan, Patrick. 1999. Introduction to Chen Diexian, *The Money Demon: An Autobiographical Romance*, ed. and trans. Patrick Hanan, 1–11. Honolulu: University of Hawai'i Press.

——. 2000. "An Autobiographical Romance of Chen Diexian." *Lingnan Journal of Chinese Studies* 2:261–282.

Handbook of Chinese Manufacturers. 1949. Shanghai: Foreign Trade Association of China.

Hangzhou baihuabao 杭州白畫報 [Hangzhou vernacular daily]. 1907–1909.

Hansen, Miriam. 2000. "Fallen Women, Rising Stars, New Horizons: Shanghai Silent Film as Vernacular Modernism." *Film Quarterly* 54 (1): 10–22.

Harrison, Henrietta. 2005. *The Man Awakened from Dreams: One Man's Life in a North China Village 1857–1942*. Stanford, CA: Stanford University Press.

Hart, Roger. 1999. "Beyond Science and Civilization: A Post-Needham Critique." *East Asian Science, Technology, and Medicine* 16:88–114.

Hau, Michael. 2003. *A Cult of Health and Beauty in Germany: A Social History, 1890–1930*. Chicago: University of Chicago Press.

Hay, Jonathan. 1998. "Painters and Publishing in Late Nineteenth Century Shanghai." In *Art at the Close of China's Empire*, ed. Chou Ju-hsi, 173–175. Phoebus Occasional Papers in Art History. Tempe: Arizona State University Press.

"Hazeline Snow." n.d. Cosmetics and Skin. http://www.cosmeticsandskin.com/aba /hazeline-snow.php.

"Hazeline Snow, a Toilet Cream." 1907. *National Druggist* 37 (8) (August): 272.

"Hazeline Snow a Trade-Mark, and Name Not Public Property." 1907. *National Druggist* 37 (12) (December): 411.

He Wangfang 何王芳. 2011. *Minguo Hangzhou shehui shenghuo* 民國杭州社會生活 [Republican-era Hangzhou's social lifestyle]. Hangzhou: Hangzhou chubanshe.

Hebei shiye gongbao 河北實業公報 [Hebei industry bulletin] (Baoding). 1933.

Hershatter, Gail. 1997. *Dangerous Pleasures: Prostitution and Modernity in Twentieth-Century Shanghai.* Berkeley: University of California Press.

Heuser, Robert. 1975. "The Chinese Trademark Law of 1904: A Preliminary Study in Extraterritoriality, Competition, and Late Ch'ing Law Reform." *Oriens Extremus* 22 (2) (December): 183–210.

Hill, Michael Gibbs. 2013. *Lin Shu, Inc.: Translation and the Making of Modern Chinese Culture.* Oxford: Oxford University Press.

Hinrichs, T. J. (Ai Tijie 艾缇捷). 2013. "Yi ru yi yi de Zhang Gao" 亦儒亦医的张杲 [The *ru*-ness and *yi*-ness of Zhang Gao]. *Zhongguo shehui lishi pinglun* 中国社会历史评论 4:65–76.

Honig, Emily. 1986. *Sisters and Strangers: Women in the Shanghai Cotton Mills, 1919–1949.* Stanford, CA: Stanford University Press.

Hsiung, Ping-Chun. 1996. *Living Rooms as Factories: Class, Gender, and the Satellite Factory System in Taiwan.* Philadelphia: Temple University Press.

Hu, Siao-Chen. 2008. "Construction of Gender and Genre in the 1910s New Media: Evidence from the *Ladies' Journal.*" In *Different Worlds of Discourse: Transformations of Gender and Genre in Late Qing and Early Republican China*, ed. Nanxiu Qian, Grace S. Fong, and Richard J. Smith, 349–382. Leiden: Brill Academic.

"Hu shang Chen Diexian jihua gailiang zao zhi yuanliao" 滬商陳蝶仙計劃改良造紙原料 [Shanghai merchant Chen Diexian improves the raw materials for manufacturing paper]. 1936. *Shiyebu yuekan* 實業部月刊 1 (3): 107.

Huameicunren 畫楳村人. 1922. "Jiating gongyeshe gaizhuang" 家庭工業社概況 [A survey of the Association for Household Industries]. *Huaxue gongyi* 化学工藝 1 (2) (October): 41–44.

Huaxue gongyi 化學工藝 [Chemical industry journal] (Shanghai). 1922–1923.

Hui Xia 蕙霞. 1915. "Yanzhi zhizao fa" 臙脂製造法 [Method for making rouge]. *Funü zazhi* 婦女雜誌 1 (3) (March): 15–16.

Hung, Eva. 1998. "Sherlock Holmes in Early Twentieth Century China (1896–1916): Fiction as Educational Tool." In *Translators' Strategies and Creativity*, ed. Anne Beylard-Ozeroff, Jana Kralova, and Barbara Moser-Mercer, 71–79. Amsterdam: John Benjamins Press.

Hunter, S. A. 洪士提反, ed. 1915. *Wanguo yaofang* 萬國藥房 [A manual of therapeutics and pharmacy in the Chinese language]. Shanghai: Meihua shuguan.

Huntington, Rania. 2003. "The Weird in the Newspaper." In *Writing and Materiality in China: Essays in Honor of Patrick Hanan*, ed. Judith T. Zeitlin and Lydia H. Liu, 341–396. Cambridge, MA: Harvard University Asia Center.

Jacob, Margaret C. 2014. *The First Knowledge Economy: Human Capital and the European Economy, 1750–1850*. Cambridge: Cambridge University Press.

Jacob, Margaret C., and Larry Stewart. 2004. *Practical Matter: Newton's Science in the Service of Industry and Empire*. Cambridge, MA: Harvard University Press.

Jiangsu sheng gongbao 江蘇省公報 [Jiangsu Province bulletin] (Nanjing). 1919–1922.

"Jiating gongyeshe" 家庭工業社 [The Association for Household Industries]. 1935. *Gongshang shiliao* 公商史料 1 (December): 113–118.

"Jiating gongyeshe biaoyan miehuoji" 家庭工業社表演滅火機 [The Association for Household Industries demonstrates the fire extinguisher]. 1935. *Xianxun zhoukan* 縣訓周刊 5:46.

"Jiating gongyeshe qianhui? Zhi yingye" 家庭工業社阡回?址營業 [Has the Association for Household Industries moved back? The business address]. 1942. *Xinan shiye tongxun* 西南實業通訊 5 (1): 70.

Jilianhui kan 機聯會刊 [Machinery Association journal] (Shanghai). 1934.

Jones, Geoffry. 2010. *Beauty Imagined: A History of the Global Beauty Industry*. Oxford: Oxford University Press.

Judge, Joan. 2015. *Republican Lens: Gender, Visuality, and Experience in the Early Chinese Periodical Press*. Berkeley: University of California Press.

Kenley, David. 2014. "Advertising Community: *Union Times* and Singapore's Vernacular Public Sphere, 1906–1939." *Journal of World History* 25 (4) (December): 583–609.

Kinkley, Jeffrey. 2000. *Chinese Justice, the Fiction: Law and Literature in Modern China*. Stanford, CA: Stanford University Press.

Köll, Elisabeth. 2003. *From Cotton Mill to Business Empire: The Emergence of Regional Enterprises in Modern China*. Cambridge, MA: Harvard University Asia Center.

Kuang Yu, contrib. 1915. "Huazhuangpin zhizao ku" [The warehouse for cosmetic production], ed. Chen Diexian. *Nüzi shijie* 女子世界 3–4 (March–April).

Kuretsky, Susan Donahue. 2012. "Jan van der Heyden and the Origins of Modern Firefighting: Art and Technology in Seventeenth-Century Amsterdam." In *Flammable Cities: Urban Conflagration and the Making of the Modern World*, ed. Greg Bankoff, Uwe Lübken, and Jordan Sand, 23–43. Madison: University of Wisconsin Press.

Kwok, D. W. Y. 1971. *Scientism in Chinese Thought, 1900–1950*. New York: Biblo and Tannen.

Kwong, Luke S. K. 2001. "Self and Society in Modern China: Liu E (1857–1909) and *Laocan Youji.*" *T'oung Pao* 87:360–392.

Laing, Ellen Johnston. 2004. *Selling Happiness: Calendar Posters and Visual Culture in Early-Twentieth-Century Shanghai*. Honolulu: University of Hawai'i Press.

Lawrence, Elizabeth. 2014. "The Chinese Seal in the Making, 1904–1937." PhD diss., Columbia University.

Lean, Eugenia. 1995. "The Modern Elixir: Medicine as a Consumer Item in the Early Twentieth-Century Press." *UCLA Historical Journal* 15:65–92.

——. 2018. "The Making of a Chinese Copycat: Trademarks and Recipes in Early Twentieth-Century Global Science and Capitalism." *Osiris* 33 (1): 271–293.

Lee, Haiyan. 2001. "All the Feelings That Are Fit to Print: The Community of Sentiment and the Literary Public Sphere in China, 1900–1918." *Modern China* 27 (3) (July): 291–327.

——. 2007a. "'A Dime Store of Words': *Liberty* Magazine and the Cultural Logic of the Popular Press." *Twentieth-Century China* 33 (1) (November): 53–79.

——. 2007b. *Revolution of the Heart: A Genealogy of Love in China, 1900–1950.* Stanford, CA: Stanford University Press.

Lee, Joyman. 2013. "Where Imperialism Could Not Reach: Chinese Industrial Policy and Japan, 1900–1940." PhD diss., Yale University.

Lee, Jung. 2013. "Invention Without Science: 'Korean Edisons' and the Changing Understanding of Technology in Colonial Korea." *Technology and Culture* 54 (4) (October): 782–814.

Lee, Seung-Joon. 2011. *Gourmets in the Land of Famine: The Culture and Politics of Rice in Modern China.* Stanford, CA: Stanford University Press.

Lei, Sean Hsiang-lin. 2014. *Neither Donkey nor Horse: Medicine in the Struggle Over China's Modernity.* Chicago: University of Chicago Press.

Leong, Elaine. 2013. "Collecting Knowledge for the Family: Recipes, Gender, and Practical Knowledge in the Early Modern English Household." *Centaurus* 55 (2): 81–103.

Lightman, Bernard. 2007. *Victorian Popularizers of Science: Designing Nature for New Audiences.* Chicago: University of Chicago Press.

Lin, Jessica Yi-Chieh. 2011. *Fake Stuff: China and the Rise of Counterfeit Goods.* New York: Routledge Taylor and Francis Group.

Lindtner, Silvia. 2015. "Hacking with Chinese Characteristics: The Promises of the Maker Movement Against China's Manufacturing Culture." *Science, Technology, and Human Values* 40 (5): 854–879.

——. Forthcoming. *Prototype Nation: China, the Maker Movement, and the Promise of Entrepreneurial Living.* Princeton, NJ: Princeton University Press.

Lindtner, Silvia, Shaowen Bardzell, and Jeffrey Bardzell. 2016. "Reconstituting the Utopian Vision of Making: HCI After Technosolutionism." Unpublished manuscript. https://static1.squarespace.com/static/52842f7de4b0b6141ccb7766/t/57 36afobd51cd47f818fa04a/1463201551143/p1390-lindtner.pdf.

Lindtner, Silvia, Anna Greenspan, and David Li. 2014. "Shanzhai: China's Collaborative Electronics-Design Ecosystem." *Atlantic*, May 18. https://www.the atlantic.com/technology/archive/2014/05/chinas-mass-production-system/37 0898/.

Ling Ruizhu 淩蕊珠. 1915. "Huazhuangpin zhizaofa lüeshuo" 化妝品製造法略說 [A brief explanation of the methods to make cosmetics]. *Funü zazhi* 婦女雜誌 1 (1) (January): 15–18.

Link, Perry. 1981. *Mandarin Ducks and Butterflies: Popular Fiction in Early Twentieth-Century Chinese Cities.* Berkeley: University of California Press.

"Lintas: Worldwide." n.d. Company-Histories.com. http://www.company-histories .com/Lintas-Worldwide-Company-History.html.

Liu, Lydia. 1995. *Translingual Practice.* Stanford, CA: Stanford University Press.

Liu, Xun. 2009. *Daoist Modern: Innovation, Lay Practice, and the Community of Inner Alchemy in Republican Shanghai.* Cambridge, MA: Harvard University Asian Center.

Lü Heng 慮恆. 1922. "Yong huazhuangpin ying ju zhi changshi" 用化妝品應具之常識 [Common knowledge one needs to use cosmetics]. *Huaxue gongyi* 化學工藝 1 (2) (October): 18–20.

Luesink, David. 2015. "State Power, Governmentality, and the (Mis)Remembrance of Chinese Medicine." In *Historical Epistemology and the Making of Chinese Medicine*, ed. Howard Chiang, 160–188. Manchester: Manchester University Press.

Luo Zhufeng 罗竹风. 1995. *Hanyu dacidian* 漢語大辭典 [Comprehensive Chinese word dictionary]. Shanghai: Hanyu dacidian.

Mann, Susan. 2007. *Talented Women of the Zhang Family.* Berkeley: University of California Press.

McKeown, Adam. 2001. *Chinese Migrant Networks and Cultural Change: Peru, Chicago, and Hawai'i 1900–1936.* Chicago: University of Chicago Press.

Meng, Yue. 1994. "A Playful Discourse, Its Site, and Its Subject: 'Free Chat' on the *Shen Daily*, 1911–1918." Master's thesis, University of California at Los Angeles.

——. 1999. "Hybrid Science Versus Modernity: The Practice of the Jiangnan Arsenal, 1864–1897." *East Asian Science, Technology, and Medicine* 16:13–52.

——. 2006. *Shanghai and the Edges of Empires.* Minneapolis: University of Minnesota Press.

Mertha, Andrew. 2005. *The Politics of Piracy: Intellectual Property in Contemporary China.* Ithaca, NY: Cornell University Press.

Meyer, Richard. 2013. *Wang Renmei: The Wildcat of Shanghai.* Hong Kong: Hong Kong University Press.

"Miehuoqi shuoluo" [An account of the fire extinguisher]. 1877. *Gezhi huibian* 格致彙編 1 (11): 1–11.

Mittler, Barbara. 2004. *A Newspaper for China? Power, Identity, and Change in Shanghai's News Media, 1872–1912.* Cambridge, MA: Harvard University Asia Center.

Mokyr, Joel. 1990. *The Lever of Riches: Technological Creativity and Economic Progress.* Oxford: Oxford University Press.

——. 2002. *The Gifts of Athena: The Historical Origins of the Knowledge Economy.* Princeton, NJ: Princeton University Press.

——. 2009. *The Enlightened Economy: An Economic History of Britain, 1700–1850.* New Haven, CT: Yale University Press.

——. 2016. *A Culture of Growth: The Origins of the Modern Economy.* Princeton, NJ: Princeton University Press.

Mueggler, Erik. 2011. *The Paper Road: Archive and Experience in the Botanical Exploration of West China and Tibet.* Berkeley: University of California Press.

Mukharji, Projit. 2016. *Doctoring Tradition: Ayurveda, Small Technologies, and Braided Science.* Chicago: University of Chicago Press.

Mullaney, Thomas. 2017. *The Chinese Typewriter: A History.* Cambridge, MA: MIT Press.

Muscolino, Micah. 2009. *Fishing Wars and Environmental Change in Late Imperial and Modern China.* Cambridge, MA: Harvard University Asia Center.

National Druggist (St. Louis, MO). 1907.

Needham, Joseph. 1969. *The Grand Titration: Science and Society in East and West.* London: Allen and Unwin.

Needham, Joseph, et al., eds. 1954–2016. *Science and Civilisation in China.* 7 vols. as of 2016. Cambridge: Cambridge University Press.

Nivard, Jacqueline. 1984. "Women and the Women's Press: The Case of the *Ladies' Journal* (*Funü zazhi*) 1915–1931." *Republican China* 10 (1b) (November): 37–55.

Nüzi shijie 女子世界 [Women's world] (Shanghai). 1914–1915.

Orliski, Constance. 2003. "The Bourgeois Housewife as Laborer in Late Qing and Early Republican Shanghai." *Nan Nü* 5 (1): 43–68.

Outka, Elizabeth. 2009. *Consuming Traditions: Modernity, Modernism, and the Commodified Authentic.* Oxford: Oxford University Press.

Pan Jianguo 潘建国. 2003. "*Gongshangye chidu ou'cun* suo zai yuanyang hudie pai xiaoshuojia shiliao jikao" 《工商业尺读偶存》所在鸳鸯蝴蝶派小说家史料辑考 [A study of *Model Correspondence on Industry and Commerce* as historical material for authors of butterfly and mandarin duck fiction]. *Ming-Qing xiaoshuo yanjiu* 明清小說研究 3 (69): 233–246.

Pan Jixing 潘吉星. 1993. *Tiangong kaiwu yizhu* 天工開物译注 [An annotated translation of the *Tiangong kaiwu* into modern Chinese]. Shanghai: Guji chubanshe.

Pharmaceutical Record and Weekly Market Review (New York). 1886.

Pickowicz, Paul. 1991. "The Theme of Spiritual Pollution in Chinese Films of the 1930s." *Modern China* 17 (1) (January): 38–75.

Pinkstone, John. 2000. *Ways of Knowing: A New History of Science, Technology, and Medicine.* Chicago: University of Chicago Press.

Pollack, Sheldon. 2000. "Cosmopolitan and Vernacular in History." *Public Culture* 12 (3) (September): 591–625.

Pomeranz, Kenneth. 2000. *The Great Divergence: China, Europe, and the Making of the Modern World Economy*. Princeton, NJ: Princeton University Press.

Pusey, James Reeve. 1983. *China and Charles Darwin*. Cambridge, MA: Harvard University Press.

Qian Shifu 錢實甫, ed. 1980. *Qingdai zhiguan nianbiao* 清代職官年表 [The chronology of Qing-era officialdom]. 4 vols. Beijing: Zhonghua shuju.

Qiu Pengsheng 邱澎生. 2009. "Faxue zhuanjia, Suzhou shangren tuanti yu Qingdai Zhongguo de 'xiguanfa' wenti" 法学专家，苏州商人团体与清代中国的 "习惯法"问题 [Legal professions, Suzhou merchant associations, and the "customary law" issue in Qing China]. *Peking University Law Review* 10 (1): 68–88.

Quanguo shougongyi pin zhanlanhui bianjizu 全國手工藝品展覽會編輯組 [Editorial Group of the National Exhibit of Handicraft Goods], eds. 1937. *Quanguo shougongyi pin zhanlanhui gailan* 全國手工藝品展覽會概覽 [Overview of the national exhibit of handicraft goods]. Nanjing: Quanguo shougongyi pin zhanlanhui.

Raj, Kapil. 2007. *Relocating Modern Science: Circulation and the Construction of Knowledge in South Asia and Europe, 1650–1900*. Houndmills, U.K.: Palgrave Macmillan.

Rea, Christopher. 2015a. *The Age of Irreverence: A New History of Laughter in China*. Berkeley: University of California Press.

——. 2015b. "Enter the Cultural Entrepreneur." In *The Business of Culture: Cultural Entrepreneurs in China and Southeast Asia, 1900–65*, ed. Christopher Rea and Nicolai Volland, 9–32. Vancouver: University of British Columbia Press.

Rea, Christopher, and Nicolai Volland, eds. 2015. *The Business of Culture: Cultural Entrepreneurs in China and Southeast Asia, 1900–65*. Vancouver: University of British Columbia Press.

Reardon-Anderson, James. 1991. *The Study of Change: Chemistry in China, 1840–1949*. Cambridge: Cambridge University Press.

Reed, Christopher. 2004. *Gutenberg in Shanghai: Chinese Print Capitalism, 1876–1937*. Honolulu: University of Hawai'i Press.

Reiss, Benjamin. 2010. *The Showman and the Slave: Race, Death, and Memory in Barnum's America*. Cambridge, MA: Harvard University Press.

Revells, Tristan. Forthcoming. "From Bad Booze to Biofuel: Alcohol, Global Standards, and China's First Alternative Energy Industry (1890–1946)." PhD diss., Columbia University.

Rhoads, Edward J. M. 2012. "Cycles of Cathay: A History of the Bicycle in China." *Transfers* 2 (2) (June): 95–120.

"Richard Hudnot." n.d. Cosmetics and Skin. http://www.cosmeticsandskin.com/companies/richard-hudnut.php.

Richter, Antje. 2013. *Letters and Epistolary Culture in Early Medieval China*. Seattle: University of Washington Press.

Rieppel, Lukas, Eugenia Lean, and William Deringer. 2018. Introduction to "The Entangled Histories of Science and Capitalism," ed. Lukas Rieppel, William Deringer, and Eugenia Lean. Special issue of *Osiris* 33 (1): 1–24.

Rivers, Matt. 2018. "Inside China's Silicon Valley: From Copycats to Innovation." CNN, November 22. https://www.cnn.com/2018/11/22/tech/china-tech-inno vation-shenzhen/index.html.

Rogaski, Ruth. 2004. *Hygienic Modernity: Meanings of Health and Disease in Treaty-Port China*. Berkeley: University of California Press.

Ross, Kerry. 2015. *Photography for Everyone: The Cultural Lives of Cameras and Consumers in Early Twentieth-Century Japan*. Stanford, CA: Stanford University Press.

Rowe, William. 1992. *Hankow: Commerce and Society in a Chinese City, 1796–1889*. Stanford, CA: Stanford University Press.

Schäfer, Dagmar. 2011. *The Crafting of the 10,000 Things: Knowledge and Technology in Seventeenth-Century China*. Chicago: University of Chicago Press.

Schafer, Edward. 1985. *The Golden Peaches of Samarkand*. Berkeley: University of California Press.

Schaffer, Simon, Lissa Roberts, Kapil Raj, and James Delbourgo, eds. 2009. *The Brokered World: Go-Betweens and Global Intelligence 1770–1820*. Sagamore Beach, MA: Watson.

Scheid, Volker. 2007. *Currents of Tradition in Chinese Medicine, 1626–2006*. Seattle: Eastland Press.

Schmalzer, Sigrid. 2015. "Self-Reliant Science: The Impact of the Cold War on Science in Socialist China." In *Science and Technology in the Cold War*, ed. Naomi Oreskes and John Krige, 1–35. Cambridge, MA: MIT Press Scholarship. https://mitpress.universitypressscholarship.com/view/10.7551/mitpress/97802620279 53.001.0001/upso-9780262027953-chapter-3.

Schneider, Helen. 2011. *Keeping the Nation's House: Domestic Management and the Making of Modern China*. Vancouver: University of British Columbia Press.

Sewell, W. G. 1972. "A Chemist in China." *Chemistry in Britain* 8 (12) (December): 529–533.

Shang, Wei. 2006. "The Making of the Everyday World: *Jin Ping Mei Cihua* and Encyclopedias for Daily Use." In *Dynastic Crisis and Cultural Innovation: From the Late Ming to the Late Qing and Beyond*, ed. David Wang and Wei Shang, 63–92. Cambridge, MA: Harvard University Asia Center.

Shanghai jizhi guohuo gongchang lianhehui 上海機制國貨工廠聯合會 [Shanghai Association for Machine-Made Domestic Goods Factories], ed. 1947. "Jiating gongyeshe gufen youxian gongsi" 家庭工業社股份有限公司 [Association for Household Industries Joint Stock Limited Co.]. In *Zhongguo guohuo gongchang quanmao chubian* 中國國貨工廠全貌初編 [The complete overview of China's national goods factories, volume 1], 40–45. Shanghai: Shanghai Association for Machine-Made Domestic Goods Factories.

"Shanghai Kexue yiqiguan zizhipin mulu" 上海科學儀器館自製品目錄 [The inventory of self-manufactured goods at the China Educational Supply Association Ltd]. 1917. *Jiangsu sheng gongbao* 江蘇省公報 1153:9.

Shanghai shi tongjibu 上海市統計部 [Shanghai Bureau of Statistics]. 1957. "Gongsi heying Jiating gongyeshe lishi ziliao" 公司合營家庭工業社歷史資料 [The historical materials of the Association for Household Industries]. Unpublished manuscript, file B31-2-271, Shanghai Archives.

Shao, Qin. 2003. *Culturing Modernity: The Nantong Model, 1890–1930.* Stanford, CA: Stanford University Press.

Shapin, Steven. 1994. *A Social History of Truth: Civility and Science in Seventeenth-Century England.* Chicago: University of Chicago Press.

Shen, Grace. 2014. *Unearthing the Nation: Modern Geology and Nationalism in Republican China, 1911–1949.* Chicago: University of Chicago Press.

Shen Ruiqing 沈瑞清. 1915. "Huazhuangpin zhizao fa" 化妝品製造法 [Method for manufacturing cosmetics]. *Funü zazhi* 婦女雜誌 1 (5) (May): 18–25.

Shenbao 申報 [Shun-Pao]. 1916–1934.

Shi Naiwen 史乃文. 1934. "Shangbiao buyun jieyue, Hu Die tichu shangsu you shibai" 商標不允解約, 胡蝶提出上訴又失敗 [Trademark, not allowed to end the contract, Hu Die fails again in her appeal]. *Diansheng* 電聲 3 (15): 238.

Shiye gongbao 實業公報 [Ministry of Industry bulletin] (Nanjing). 1933.

Shiye qianshuo 實業淺說 [Industry in layman's terms] (Beijing). 1915–1925.

Shiyebu shangbiaoju 實業部商標局 [Trademark Bureau of the Ministry of Industry], ed. 1934. *Dongya zhi bu shangbiao huikan* 東亞之部商標匯刊 [Collection of Asian trademarks]. Shanghai: Zhonghua shuju.

"Shiyebu suyuan juedingshu, suzi di liu wu hao" 實業部訴願決定書，訴字第六五號 [Ministry of Industry's appeal decision, Decision Number 65]. 1933. *Shiye gongbao* 實業公報 150:1–7.

Shiyebu yuekan 實業部月刊 [Monthly bulletin of the Ministry of Industry] (Nanjing). 1936–1937.

"Shiyong shuilong shuo" [An explanation of how to use the fire extinguisher]. 1876. *Gezhi huibian* 格致彙編 (Shanghai) 1 (2) (1876): 7–8.

Sifa gongbao 司法公報 [Judicial bulletin] (Nanjing). 1936.

"Sinian yilai wei huo yiwen; Hu Die wei shangbiao choujin xing song" 四年以來未獲一文；胡蝶為商標酬金興訟 [For the past four years, no compensation; Hu Die files suit for trademark remuneration]. 1936. *Diansheng* 電聲 5 (33): 824.

Smith, Pamela. 2004. *The Body of the Artisan: Art and Experience in the Scientific Revolution.* Chicago: University of Chicago Press.

Smith, Thomas. 1988. *Native Sources of Japanese Industrialization, 1750–1920*. Berkeley: University of California Press.

Song Yingxin 宋應星. [1587–1661] 1976. *Tiangong kaiwu* 天工開物 [The works of heaven and the inception of things]. Guangzhou: Guangdong renmin.

Stevens, Hallam. 2018. "Starting Up Biology in China: Performances of Life at BGI." *Osiris* 33 (1): 85–106.

Stewart, Mary Lynn. 2000. *For Health and Beauty: Physical Culture for Frenchwomen, 1880s–1930s*. Baltimore: Johns Hopkins University Press.

Sun, Myra. 2019. "Fictions of Authorship: Literary Modernity and the Cultural Politics of the Author in Late Qing and Republican China." PhD diss., Columbia University.

Sun Zhonghuan 孫忠焕, ed. 2009. *Hangzhou yunhe wenxian jicheng* 杭州运河文献集成 [Collected documents of Hangzhou's canal]. Hangzhou: Hangzhou chubanshe.

Sung, Ying-hsing. 1966. *Chinese Technology in the Seventeenth Century: T'ien-Kung K'ai-Wu*. Trans. E. tu Zen Sun and Shiou-chuan Sun. University Park: Pennsylvania State University.

Swislocki, Mark. 2008. *Culinary Nostalgia: Regional Food Culture and the Urban Experience in Shanghai*. Stanford, CA: Stanford University Press.

Tianxuwosheng jinian kan 天虛我生紀念刊 [A memorial volume for Tianxuwosheng]. 1940. Shanghai: Zixiu zhoukan yinshe.

Tilley, Helen. 2011. *Africa as a Living Laboratory: Empire, Development, and the Problem of Scientific Knowledge, 1870–1950*. Chicago: University of Chicago Press.

Ting, H. C. 1974. *Truth and Facts: Recollections of a Hong Kong Industrialist*. Hong Kong: New Island Printing.

Totelin, L. M. V. 2009. *Hippocratic Recipes: Oral and Written Transmission of Pharmacological Knowledge in Fifth- and Fourth-Century Greece*. Leiden: Brill Academic.

Tsai, Hui-yi Caroline. 2014. "Displaying 'Everyday Modernity'—and What Is Beyond? Haircut Hygiene in the 1925 Taipei Police Exhibition." Paper presented at the conference "Beyond Modernity: Understanding Change in China," Columbia University, New York, September 19–20.

Tsin, Michael. 1999. *Nation, Governance, and Modernity in China: Canton, 1900–1927*. Stanford, CA: Stanford University Press.

Vinograd, Richard. 1991. "Private Art and Public Knowledge in Later Chinese Painting." In *Images of Memory: On Remembering and Representation*, ed. Susanne Küchlerand Walter Melion, 176–202. Washington, DC: Smithsonian Institution Press.

Wan Qingli 万青力. 2001. "Meishujia, qiyejia Chen Xiaodie: Minguo shiqi Shanghai huatan yanjiu zhi yi" 美术家，企业家陈小蝶-民国时期上海花坛研究之一 [Artist,

industrialist Chen Xiaodie: Research on the Republican-era Shanghai art scene].
In *Haipai huihua yanjiu wenji* 海派绘画研究文集 [Collected works on the research
of the Shanghai painting school], 9–29. Shanghai: Shuhua chubanshe, 2001.

Wang Cangping 王滄萍. 1940. "Ku Tianxuwosheng xiansheng" 哭天虛我生先生
[Mourning Mr. Tianxuwosheng]. In *Tianxuwosheng jinian kan* 天虛我生紀念刊
[A memorial volume for Tianxuwosheng], 25. Shanghai: Zixiu zhoukan yinshe.

Wang, Di. 2003. "The Rhythm of the City: Everyday Chengdu in Nineteenth-Century
Bamboo-Branch Poetry." *Late Imperial China* 24 (1) (June): 33–78.

Wang, Hui. 2006. "Discursive Community and the Genealogy of Scientific Categories." In *Everyday Modernity in China*, ed. Madeleine Dong and Joshua Goldstein,
80–117. Seattle: University of Washington Press.

Wang Taijun 汪泰鈞. 1924. "Shangbiao wenti" 商標問題 [The question of trademarks].
Gongshang xuebao 工商學報 2:16–18.

Weisheng gongbao 衛生公報 [Hygiene bulletin] (Nanjing). 1929.

Whitwell, Tom. 2014. "Inside Shenzhen: China's Silicon Valley." *Guardian*, June 13.
https://www.theguardian.com/cities/2014/jun/13/inside-shenzen-china-silicon
-valley-tech-nirvana-pearl-river.

Widmer, Ellen. 1989. "The Epistolary World of Female Talent in Seventeenth-Century
China." *Late Imperial China* 10 (2) (December): 1–43.

——. 1992. "Xiaoqing's Literary Legacy and the Place of the Woman Writer in Late
Imperial China." *Late Imperial China* 13 (1) (June): 111–155.

Wilkinson, Karen, and Mike Petrich. 2013. *The Art of Tinkering*. San Francisco: Wel-
don Owen.

Williams, C. A. S. 1933. *Manual of Chinese Products*. Peiping: Kwang Yuen Press.

Wilson, Charles. 1954. *The History of Unilever: A Study in Economic Growth and
Social Change*. London: Cassell.

Wong, Winnie. 2014. *Van Gogh on Demand: China and the Readymade*. Chicago:
University of Chicago Press.

Wright, David. 1996. "John Fryer and the Shanghai Polytechnic: Making Space for
Science in Nineteenth-Century China." *British Journal for the History of Science*
29 (1): 1–16.

——. 2000. *Translating Science: The Transmission of Western Chemistry Into Late
Imperial China, 1840–1900*. Leiden: Brill Academic.

Wu Chengluo 吳承洛. 1924. "Cong Shanghai huaxue gongyi zhanlanhui guancha
Zhongguo huaxue gongye zhi xianzhuang" 從上海化學工藝展覽會觀察中國化學工
業之現狀 [Viewing the situation of China's chemical industry from the perspective of the Shanghai chemical industry's expo]. *Zhonghua huaxue gongyehui
huizhi* 中華化學工業會誌 2 (1): 7–59.

Wu, Jen-shu, and Ling-ling Lien. 2013. "From Viewing to Reading: The Evolution of
Visual Advertising in Late Imperial China." In *Visualizing China, 1845–1965:*

Moving and Still Images in Historical Narratives, ed. Christian Henriot and Wenhsin Yeh, 231–266. Leiden: Brill Academic.

Wu, Shellen. 2015. *Empires of Coal: Fueling China's Entry Into the Modern World Order, 1860–1920*. Stanford, CA: Stanford University Press.

Wu, Shengqing. 2008. "Contested *Fengya*: Classical-Style Poetry Clubs in Early Republican China." In *Literary Societies of Republican China*, ed. Kirk Denton and Michel Hockx, 15–46. New York: Lexington Books.

Wu, Yi-li. 2010. *Reproducing Women: Medicine, Metaphor, and Childbirth in Late Imperial China*. Berkeley: University of California Press.

"Wudibi" 無敵筆 [The Butterfly Pen]. 1935. *Shiye zazhi* 實業雜誌 207:20.

Wythoff, Grant. 2016. Introduction to Hugo Gernsback, *The Perversity of Things: Hugo Gernsback on Media, Tinkering, and Scientifiction*, ed. Grant Wythoff, 1–49. Minneapolis: University of Minnesota Press.

Xiao gongyi 小工藝 [Light industry] (Shanghai). 1939.

Xihu bolanhui rikan 西湖博覽會日刊 [West Lake Expo daily] (Hangzhou). 1929.

"Xingzheng susong caipan" 行政訴訟裁判 [The judgment of the Ministry of Judicial Administration]. 1936. *Sifa gongbao* 司法公報 119:51–53.

Xu Shoudie 許瘦蝶. 1948. "Ji Chen Diexian" 記陳蝶仙 [A note on Chen Diexian]. *Yong'an yuekan* 永安月刊 104:43–44.

Xu, Xiaoqun. 2000. *Chinese Professionals and the Republican State: The Rise of Professional Associations in Shanghai, 1912–1937*. Cambridge: Cambridge University Press.

Yang, Fan. 2016. *Faked in China: Nation Branding, Counterfeit Culture, and Globalization*. Bloomington: Indiana University Press.

Yang, Timothy. 2013. "Market, Medicine, and Empire: Hoshi Pharmaceuticals in the Interwar Years." PhD diss., Columbia University.

Yang, Yingchuan. Forthcoming. "Revolution on Air: Radio Technology, Socialist Culture, and China's Global Engagement." PhD diss., Columbia University.

Yao Jiayu. 姚家玉. 1934. "Hu Die shangbiao'an bai su; tichu fei yue zhi dongji yu neimu" 胡蝶商標案敗訴, 提出廢約之動機與內幕 [Hu Die's defeat in the trademark lawsuit; the motivation and inside scoop behind the contract's annullment]. *Diansheng* 電聲 3 (2): 25.

Ye Mingdong. 葉明東. 1923. "Jiating gongyeshe zong guancha" 家庭工業社總觀察 [A complete survey of Household Industries]. *Jingji huibao* 經濟匯報 2 (2): 43–48.

Yeh, Catherine. 2006. *Shanghai Love: Courtesans, Intellectuals, and Entertainment Culture, 1850–1910*. Seattle: University of Washington Press.

Yeh, Wen-hsin. 2007. *Shanghai Splendor: A Cultural History, 1843–1949*. Berkeley: University of California Press.

Yi, Yuan. Forthcoming. "Malfunctioning Machinery: The Global Making of Chinese Cotton Mills." PhD diss., Columbia University.

Yin Zeming. [1958] 2013. "The Strength of the Masses is Limitless." In *The Search for Modern China: A Documentary Collection*, ed. Janet Chen, Pei-kai Cheng, and Michael Lestz, with Jonathan Spence, 415–418. New York: Norton.

Youmin xiyi yuekan 游民習藝月刊 [Vagrant work training monthly] (Beijing). 1927.

Yu Ziming. 俞自明. 1923. "Huaxuejia yingyou zhi changshi" 化學家應有之常識 [Common knowledge chemists should possess]. *Huaxue gongyi* 化學工藝 1 (3) (May): 57–59.

Yu Ziyi 俞子夷. 1990. "Cai Yuanpei xiansheng he caochuang shi de Guangfu hui" 蔡元培先生和草创时的光复会 [Mr. Cai Yuanpei and the founding of the Guangfu Association]. In *Wenshi ziliao jingxuan* 文史资料精选 [Selection of cultural and historical materials],vol. 2, ed.Wenshi ziliao xuanji bianjibu 文史资料选集编辑部, 323–336. Beijing: Zhongguo wenshi chubanshe.

Zelin, Madeleine. 2005. *The Merchants of Zigong: Industrial Enterprise in Early Modern China*. New York: Columbia University Press.

Zhang Yimin 章亦敏. 1936. "Jiating gongyeshe zhi gaikuang" 家庭工業社之概況 [The general situation of the Association for Household Industries]. *Zhejiang shangwu* 浙江商務 1 (4): 55–58.

Zhang, Ying. 2017. "Household Healing: Rituals, Recipes, and Morals in Late Imperial China." PhD diss., Johns Hopkins University.

Zhang Yi'ou, ed. 張軼歐, ed. 1921. "Shanghai jiatingshe Wudipai camian yanfen jiamao yinggai gai gan weibian" 上海家庭社無敵牌擦面牙粉假冒影戯改[sic]干未便 [Shanghai Household Industries Peerless brand face and toothpowder trademark cannot be copied]. *Jiangsu shiye yuekan* 江蘇實業月刊 29 (August): 44–45.

Zhang, Zhen. 2005. *An Amorous History of the Silver Screen: Shanghai Cinema 1896–1937*. Chicago: University of Chicago Press.

Zhang Zhibin, and Paul Unschuld, eds. 2015. *Dictionary of the* Ben Cao Gang Mu. Vol. 1: *Chinese Historical Illness Terminology*. Berkeley: University of California Press.

Zhang Zhiming 張之銘. 1947. "Chuangli kexu yiqiguan zhi jingguo" 創立科學儀器館之經過 [The process of creating the Scientific Appliance Shop]. *Yiwen* 儀文 1:23–24.

"Zhe sheng gailiang zhiliao" 浙省改良紙料 [Zhejiang Province's reformed paper]. 1937. *Guoji maoyi qingbao* 國際貿易情報 28 (2): 48.

"Zhejiang jinxiandai renwu lu" 浙江近现代人物录 [A record of modern personages of Zhejiang province]. 1992. In *Zhejiang wenshi ziliao xuanji* 浙江文史资料选辑 [Selection of Zhejiang cultural and historical materials], vol. 48, ed. Zhejiang sheng zhengxie wenshi ziliao weiyuanhui 浙江省政协文史资料委员会, 230. Hangzhou:Zhejiang renmin chubanshe.

Zheng Yimei 鄭逸梅. 1992. *Yiyuan suowen* 艺苑琐闻 [Scraps from the art garden]. Chengdu: Sichuan renmin chubanshe.

Zhong Xiangping 仲向平. 2013. *Hangzhou yunhe lishi jianzhu* 杭州运河历史建筑 [Historical buildings of the Hangzhou canal]. Hangzhou: Hangzhou chubanshe.

Zhongguo guohuo diaocha ce 中國國貨調查冊 [Survey of China's National Products]. 1934–1947. Shanghai: Shanghai guohuo jieshao hui baoguan.

Zhongguo guohuo gongchang shilüe 中國國貨工廠史略 [A historical sketch of China's National Product factories]. 1935. Shanghai: Guohuo shiye chubanshe.

Zhonghua minguo haiguan huayang maoyi zongce 中華民國海關華洋貿易總冊 [*Chinese maritime customs foreign trade report*]. [1915] 1982. Taipei: Guoshiguan.

Zhou Er'run 周爾潤, ed. 1907. *Zhili gongyi zhi chubian* 直隸工藝志初編 [Zhili industrial gazetteer, first edition]. China: Zhili gongyi zongju.

Zhou Shoujuan 周瘦鵑. 1940. "Daonian Tianxuwosheng Chen Xuyuan" 悼念天虛我生陳栩園先生 [Mourning Tianxuwosheng Chen Xuyuan]. In *Tianxuwosheng jinian kan* 天虛我生紀念刊 [A memorial volume for Tianxuwosheng], 24–25. Shanghai: Zixiu zhoukan yinshe

Zhu Baojiong 朱保烱, and Xie Peilin 謝沛霖, eds. 1980. *Ming Qing jinshi timing beilu suoyin* 明清進士題名碑錄索引 [The roster of successful *jinshi* degree holders in the Ming–Qing period]. 2 vols. Shanghai: Shanghai guji chubanshe.

Zhu Jiaying 朱家英. 2015. "Qingdai wenren yu Taichangxiandie gushi de yanbian" 清代文人与太常仙蝶故事的演变 [Qing literati and the evolution of the story of Taichangxiandie]. *Zhongguo dianji yu wenhua* 中国典籍与文化 1 (2): 129–133.

Zhuang Yumei 庄禹梅. 1963. "Guanyu Ningbo lü Hu tongxianghui" 关于宁波旅沪同乡会 [About Ningbo's native-place association in Shanghai]. In *Wenshi ziliao jingxuan* 文史资料精选 [Selection of cultural and historical materials], vol. 34, ed. Zhongguo renmin zhengzhi xieshang huiyi quanguo weiyuanhui wenshi ziliao yanjiu weiyuanhui 中国人民政治协商会议全国委员会文史资料研究委员会, 262–263. Beijing: Wenshi ziliao chubanshe.

Zonghui xinbao 總匯新報 [New union times] (Singapore). 1934.

Zou, Dongxin. 2019. "Socialist Medicine and Maoist Humanitarianism: Chinese Medical Missions to Algeria, 1963–1984." PhD diss., Columbia University.

Zuo Xuchu 左旭初. 1999. *Lao shangbiao* 老商标 [Old trademarks]. Shanghai: Shanghai huabao chubanshe.

——. 2003. *Zhongguo jindai shangbiao jianshi* 中国近代商标简史 [The brief history of modern trademarks in China]. Shanghai: Xuelin chubanshe.

——. 2016. *Minguo huazhuangpin baozhuang: Yishu sheji yanjiu* 民国化妆品包装：艺术设计研究 [Republican-era cosmetics packaging: Artistic design studies]. Shanghai: Lixing kuaiji chubanshe.

Index

Anglo-Chinese Dispensary (Hua-Ying yaofang; Shanghai), 53, 78, 84, 86
Anhui Industrial Journal, 184
arsenals, 12–13, 50, 156, 182, 271, 305n1, 320n19; emulation in, 268–69. *See also* Jiangnan Arsenal
Association for Household Industries Co., Ltd. *See* Household Industries
Association for Machine-Made Domestic Goods Factories (Jizhi guohuo gongchang lianhehui), 277
audience: for advertising, 232–33, 243; for *Collection of Common Knowledge*, 250–51, 253; for "Common Knowledge," 133–36, 152; for film stars, 228–29; for films, 237–38; for *Free Talk*, 132; for mass media, 57, 81, 262; for *Model Correspondence*, 144–45; for new knowledge, 102–14, 118, 309n26; for professional journals, 145–46; for recipes, 101, 102–14, 106; for science texts, 249–50; sharing of publications by, 81, 341n1, 344n20; for *Shenbao*, 327n12; for *Wealth in Industry*, 267; women as, 91, 92; for women's magazines, 102–14, 321nn29–30
Aurora Company (Zhendan jiqi tie gongchang), 125
authenticity: and advertising, 62, 158, 230–31, 233, 249, 263, 272; anxiety about, 247–50, 264, 272, 281; of Butterfly brand, 62, 241, 243, 247, 253; of Chen's persona, 204–5, 242–43; and Chen's textual strategies, 245, 247, 250; and *Collection of Common Knowledge*, 250, 253; and commodification of knowledge, 262–64, 310n31; and compilation, 245–47, 271; and

editorial work, 245–47, 250, 257–58, 266, 271; and emulation, 247, 272–73; and experimentation, 254, 272; and film, 230–31; and Hangzhou, 221, 338n19; and import substitution, 269–70; and mass production, 230–31, 241–42, 246; of medical knowledge, 258–64; of native vs. foreign products, 155–59, 246, 264–70; of new knowledge, 245–47; and seals vs. signatures, 340n33; of sentiment, 67, 204–5
authorship: brand-name, 64, 69, 73–74, 249, 318n1a, 342n9; female, 82, 92, 321n30; and ownership, 342n8; of professional writers, 72–73, 75, 181, 343n16
Aw Boon-haw, 238, 341n43

Bamboo-Branch Poetry from the Gongchen Bridge (*Gongchen qiao zhuzhici*; Chen Diexian), 58–64
Ban Zhao, 115
Bao, Weihong, 57, 326n63
Bao Tianxiao, 73, 74, 82, 254
Bao Xiang'ao, 259, 261, 330n4
Barnum, P. T., 241, 243
Basalla, George, 311n38, 311n40
Beijing Genomics Institute (Huada jiyin), 287
Benedict, Carol, 214, 308n22
bianji. *See* editorial work
bianyi (compilation and translation), 74, 83, 196, 270–71, 280
"Bicycle, The" ("Jiaotache"; Chen Diexian), 58, 317n43
Big Road (film), 341n44
bodily practices, 9, 10, 19, 34, 94, 130
bowu. *See* broad learning; natural studies

Boxer Uprising (1900), 206, 316n38
boxue. See broad learning
branding, 16–26, 204–43; and advertising, 226–27; and authenticity, 241, 243, 247, 253, 262; of authors, 64, 69, 73–74, 249, 318n1a, 342n9; and butterfly fiction, 23–24, 74, 159; and Chen Diexian, 16–17, 22–26, 62, 70, 73–74, 91, 159, 220; and common knowledge, 149, 205, 280; and consumer loyalty, 205, 233, 281; and copying, 195–96, 248–49, 250; in cosmetic industry, 241–42; of fiction, 205, 241–42, 249; and language, 21–22, 334n46; legal protection for, 24, 25, 30, 149, 196, 205–6, 280–81, 328n20, 336n1; and nativism, 23–24, 158, 166, 202; and *shanzhai* culture, 284–90, 286; and traditional culture, 70, 221, 338n19. *See also* trademarks
"Brief Explanation on Methods for Making Cosmetics" (*Ladies' Journal* article), 92–93, 94
"Bright Moon Mirror Photography" ("Mingyuejing zhaoxiang"; Chen Diexian), 61–64
Bright Moon Song and Dance Troupe (Mingyue gewutuan), 240
"Bring on the Wine" (Li Bai), 42
Britain, 21, 319n11, 320n18; amateur scientists in, 246–47, 315n18; commodified authentic in, 310n31; and Great Leap Forward, 282; and intellectual property rights, 206, 214, 328n20, 335n52, 336n2
British American Tobacco, 15, 151, 156, 214, 308n22
British Foreign Office, 206, 328n20
British Pharmacopoeia, 84, 320n18

broad learning (*boxue, bowu*), 43–47, 69, 96, 133–34, 138, 150, 315n18
"Bulletin on the Trademark Question" (Chen Diexian), 224–25
Bureau of Industrial Research, 156, 333n35
Burroughs Wellcome & Co. (BW&C), 193, 194, 195–96, 214, 322n35
Butterfly (Wudipai) brand: advertising of, 32, 159, 225–26, 228, 234–41, 331n16; authenticity of, 62, 241, 243, 247, 253; and butterfly fiction, 23–24, 74, 159; and Chen Diexian, 41, 43, 275; cosmopolitanism of, 208–9; and language, 208, 337n7, 338n17; and literati culture, 210–11, 213; logo of, 190–91, 208, 209; protection of, 214–25, 334n43; in Southeast Asia, 331n16; tax exemptions for, 172–73; trademark of, 190–91, 204, 205–20, 337n12; and Zhuangzi, 42–43, 68
Butterfly Cream, 192, 193, 225–26, 278, 334n46
butterfly fiction (Mandarin duck and butterfly fiction; *yuanyang hudie pai xiaoshuo*), 22, 82, 205, 262; and branding, 23–24, 74, 159; sentiment in, 64–65
Butterfly fire extinguisher (Wudipai yao shuilong), 16, 121, 122, 125, 153, 329n28
Butterfly Flat Offset Printing Press, 197
Butterfly Lodge (Dielai), 221, 240
Butterfly Mosquito Coil Factory (Wudipai wenxiang chang), 277
Butterfly Pen, 201
Butterfly Peppermint Factory (Wudipai bohe chang), 170

Butterfly Toothpowder, 2, 120–21, 168–81, 278; and cuttlefish bones, 40, 161–62, 164, 165, 176, 178, 180, 330n5; packaging of, 207–8, 212–13; trademark of, 190–91, 212

Butterfly Wu (Hu Die), 205, 220–25, 228, 230, 231, 240

Bu Zixia, 314n12

Cai Chusheng, 240

Cai Yuanpei, 47, 52–53

calcium carbonate, 7, 162–64, 177, 181, 182, 187, 330n5

Cansang Academy, 46, 47

Cao Xueqin, 63, 98–99

capitalism: anxiety about, 158, 262, 308n21; and authenticity, 262, 310n31; and Chen Diexian, 17–18, 25, 280, 281; vs. DIY culture, 281; and elites, 3, 67, 118; global, 17, 26, 31–33, 80, 96–97, 205–6, 248, 280, 281, 287–88, 290, 310n31; and Great Leap Forward, 283; and home manufacturing, 80, 88–89; and industry, 6, 280; and intellectual property rights, 31, 205–6, 248; and national strength, 96–97; and native products, 176, 248, 266; print, 71–76; and *shanzhai* culture, 287, 288, 290; and tinkering, 29–30; vs. vernacular industrialism, 17–18, 280

Capital Vagrant Workhouse (Jingshi youmin xiyisuo), 113, 325n60

Central Hygiene Experimentation Insititute (Zhongyang weisheng shiyan suo), 200

chemical industry, 12, 145–50, 151

Chemical Industry Journal (*Huaxue gongyi*), 145–50

"Chemist in China, A" (Sewell), 102, 185

chemistry, 11–12; amateur, 9, 16, 107; and broad learning, 44, 45; and Chen Diexian, 1, 2, 5, 7–9, 16, 21, 23, 24, 26, 37, 47–48, 119, 164, 181, 275, 276; in Chen's publications, 131, 134, 143, 145, 251; and crime novels, 189; and Daoism, 108; education in, 102, 106–7; and elites, 16, 50; experiments with, 2, 8, 9, 20, 37, 50, 118, 177, 189; in home manufacturing, 82, 84, 85, 87, 92, 93–94, 97, 101, 103, 108–9, 114, 116; and intellectual property rights, 8, 335n52; and manufacturing, 7–9; of poisons, 52; publications on, 184, 185–86; and revolutionaries, 52–54; sources of ingredients for, 7, 15, 20, 26, 40, 52–54, 77–78, 177; terms in, 78, 84, 94, 187, 320n18, 322n34; and vernacular industrialism, 164, 279, 289; in women's magazines, 82, 85, 92, 93–94. *See also* cosmetics

Chen, Janet, 113

Chen Cidie (son), 38

Chen Deng (Yuanlong), 275, 344n1

Chen Diexian, 1–11, 18–32; darker side of, 25, 179–80, 181; early life of, 37–41; eulogies for, 275–77; knowledge work of, 18–22; marketing skills of, 6, 23–24, 25, 26, 241–43; names of, 41–43, 70, 165, 204–5, 313nn4–10, 314nn11–12; as "native products recluse" (*guohuo zhi yinzhe*), 164; persona of, 24–25, 37–38, 40, 42–43, 163–64, 173–74, 204, 205, 220, 225, 242, 243; physical description of, 315n25; plays by, 74, 75; sources on, 1, 5, 20, 164–65, 175, 202; as

colonialism: and film, 25, 237; Japanese, 130; in Korea, 5, 189–90; and modernity, 26; and nativism, 176, 203, 336n61; and science, 9–10, 28, 33, 311n40, 312n48; in Singapore, 237, 240. *See also* imperialism

Commercial Press (Shangwu yinshuguan), 72, 79, 249–50, 271, 324n53

commercialization: and authenticity, 310n31; of cities, 46, 100, 248; and elites, 2, 4–5, 21, 39, 43, 46, 66, 67, 69–70; of entertainment, 22–23, 39; and home manufacturing, 80, 100–101; and vernacular industrialism, 34, 281

commodification: of film stars, 230, 340n32; of knowledge, 80, 91, 258, 262–64, 272, 310n31; of literature, 56, 71, 137, 241

commodified authentic, the, 310n31

commodified classicism, 143–44, 182, 306n5, 310n31

common knowledge (*changshi*), 120–54; and branding, 149, 205, 280; in Chen's publications, 2, 8, 126–38, 142, 144, 185, 203, 276; and fire extinguisher, 121–22; vs. intellectual property rights, 30, 121, 149; and manufacturing, 2, 145, 149; in mass media, 23, 82; vs. professional expertise, 21, 133–36, 138, 145–50, 152–53; and translation, 187, 203; and vernacular industrialism, 279

"Common Knowledge Chemists Should Possess" (Yu Ziming), 146

"Common Knowledge for the Household" ("Common Knowledge"; "Jiating changshi"; *Shenbao* column; Chen Diexian), 75, 121, 126–38, 246, 325n62; audience for, 133–36, 152;

compilation of, 131, 245, 250–53; and *Model Correspondence*, 143, 144, 145; and NPM, 329n27; and oral transmission, 129; vs. specialization, 21, 133–34, 138, 149–50; topics in, 128–31, 136–38

Companion to the Latest Edition of the British Pharmacopoeia (Squire), 320n18

Compendium of Materia Medica (Bencao gangmu), 185, 270

compilation, 244–74; and adaptation, 31, 72, 74, 85, 185; and authenticity, 245–47, 271; by Chen, 20, 75, 122, 244–47; politics of, 270–73; in Qing period, 333n33; of recipes, 81, 83, 85, 334n38; and *shiyan*, 257–58; and technology, 157, 271–72; and translation (*bianyi*), 74, 83, 196, 270–71, 280. See also *Collection of Common Knowledge for the Household*; *Wealth in Industry*

Compilation of Laws (Falü huibian), 75

Comprehensive Chinese Word Dictionary (Hanyu dacidian), 254

Conan Doyle, Arthur, 188

Confucianism, 14, 67; vs. Daoism, 41, 43; and elite, 3, 4, 322n37; and women, 95, 96, 114, 132

Confucius, 268

connoisseurship: of Chen, 16, 40, 47; and commercialization, 46, 72; in "Common Knowledge," 131–32, 134; and technology, 3, 4–5, 6, 30, 44, 69, 96, 113, 114, 117

consumers, 3, 18, 133, 155–56, 280; and gender, 21, 321n26; and knowledge, 21–22; loyalty of, 205, 225–27, 233, 242, 243, 281; and *shanzhai* culture, 285–86 copying. *See* emulation

corporations: foreign, 15, 31, 166; international, 15, 248–49, 287; joint limited, 158, 184; joint-state, 156, 278; new, 13, 48–55. *See also particular organizations*

correlative cosmology, 133

correspondence schools, 75–76

cosmetic industry, 166–67, 188, 331n18; branding in, 241–42; Household Industries in, 191–96; local raw materials for, 176, 177, 180

cosmetics: advertising of, 159, 225–27, 229; Butterfly-brand, 24, 32, 159, 225–27, 239, 241–43; Chen on, 20, 21, 265; counterfeits of, 214; domestic production of, 107, 108–9, 113–14, 145–46, 198, 324n47; home manufacturing of, 77–80, 92–95, 97–100, 116–17, 145, 280; homemade vs. store-bought, 89–90, 101; moral ambivalence of, 95–96; recipes for, 77–119; reverse-engineering of, 15, 193–95; rouge, 108–11. *See also* hair products; "Warehouse for Cosmetic Production"

counterfeiting: anxiety about, 23, 155–57, 158, 159, 248–49, 258; and British Foreign Office, 206, 328n20; of Butterfly trademark, 214–20; Chinese, 311n41, 335n54, 345n6; and *Collection of Common Knowledge*, 250; vs. emulation, 184; and Household Industries, 158, 159, 248; of knowledge, 245–47; legal cases on, 221–25; and legal ownership, 158, 242; and medical knowledge, 258, 264; and *shanzhai* culture, 284–90; of trademarks, 205, 206, 265, 322n35.

See also intellectual property rights

courtesans, 56, 58, 63, 67, 68, 228, 339n31

courtesy letters (*yingchou wen*), 75

Crow, Carl, 339n28

Culp, Robert, 72

Cultural Revolution (1966–1976), 283

cuttlefish bones, 2, 15, 40, 176, 178, 180, 186, 283; calcium carbonate in, 7, 162–64, 187, 330n5; story of, 161–65

Dah Fong Peppermint Factory (Dafeng bohe gongsi), 187

Dai Jitao, 158

Daoism, 314n12; and alchemy, 107, 108, 279, 321n28; and Chen's persona, 41–43, 164–65

Darwin, Charles, 315n18

Dasheng textile mills, 12, 15, 156

Daughter Cold Cream (Nü'er shuang), 191

depression, global economic, 158–59

Des Forges, Alexander, 72, 343n16

Diamond (Jingangshi) brand, 167, 208

Dianshizhai Pictorial (Dianshizhai huabao), 56–57, 326n63

Dietrichs, Eugene, 188

Diexian (Butterfly Immortal; Chen Diexian), 41, 43

Dikötter, Frank, 169, 286, 323n41

Ding Bing, 60

Ding Chuwo, 325n61

DIY (do-it-yourself) culture, 28–29, 89, 202, 280, 281, 287, 289

Dong, Madeleine, 311n44

Dream of the Red Chamber (Honglou-meng; Cao Xueqin), 63, 67–68, 314n10, 317n52; on homemade cosmetics, 98–100

Du Jiutian, 107–8
Du Xunhe, 61
Du Yaquan, 107–8

Eastern Miscellany (*Dongfang zazhi*; journal), 108
Economy Report (*Jingji huibao*), 173
Edison, Thomas, 1, 4
editorial work (*bianji*), 20, 72, 74, 181, 280; and authenticity, 245–47, 250, 257–58, 266, 271; of Chen, 5, 6, 75, 122, 167, 259; and Chen's family, 168
education: in chemistry, 102, 106–7; foreign, 136; and industrialization, 44, 113, 145; in missionary schools, 102, 150; for women, 92, 102. *See also* textbooks
elegant gatherings (*yaji*), 37, 40, 44–47, 55–56, 69, 70, 315n19; and Gather Benefit Company, 47, 49
elite, educated: amateur ideal of, 30, 46; and capitalism, 3, 67, 118; and *chuanshen*, 62, 317n48; and civil-service exams, 39, 66, 117, 327n13, 340n33; and commercialization, 3–5, 21, 39, 43, 46, 66, 67, 69–70; and common knowledge, 132, 144, 152; and Confucianism, 3, 4, 322n37; cosmopolitan, 117, 119, 271; and culture of play, 38, 63, 69, 116–18, 132; experimentation by, 16, 31, 115, 255–57; female, 4, 7, 77, 82, 85, 92, 114, 115–19, 306n5, 320n15, 322n30; as gentry merchants (*shishang*), 39; in Hangzhou, 43–47, 49–51; and home manufacturing, 80, 100, 185–86, 280; and industry, 2, 21, 44, 66, 305n1; literati culture of, 204, 210–11, 213, 225, 255–57, 305n2; as literati physicians (*ruyi*),

185, 261; and mass media, 39–40, 118; and movie stars, 228; networks of, 40, 45–46, 145; and new knowledge, 49–50, 69–70; and professional writers, 72–73, 75, 181, 343n16; and professionalization of knowledge, 150–51; and profits, 40, 66–70, 118, 313n3; reformist, 3, 12, 22–23, 119, 306n3; and science, 16, 50, 151, 249, 328n22; and seals vs. signatures, 340n33; and sensorial knowledge, 255–57; textual strategies of, 270–71; urban, 4–5, 7, 16, 31, 39, 66–67, 80, 92, 108, 132, 228–29, 249, 257, 271; and Western learning, 46–47, 69
Emperor's Four Treasuries (*Siku quanshu*), 333n33
emulation (*fangzhi, fangzao*): in arsenals, 268–69; and authenticity, 247, 272–73; and branding, 195–96, 248–49, 250; and Chen, 16, 17, 20, 144, 165, 243, 267–70, 281; vs. counterfeiting, 184; and *Dream of the Red Chamber*, 67; and fire extinguisher, 122, 126; of foreign products, 24, 31–32, 111, 187, 189, 196, 267–70, 273, 279, 342n4; and innovation, 32, 189–96, 316n34; of marketing techniques, 242, 243; and native products, 267–70, 272–73, 279; and *shanzhai* culture, 284, 287, 289; of texts, 20, 72, 74, 85; and tinkering, 27, 31, 187; vs. trademark law, 2, 281
Encyclopedia Minicollectanea (*Baike xiao congshu*), 249
encyclopedias, 99, 100, 129, 249–50, 270, 271
English language, 90, 103, 187, 208, 235, 237, 322n34

film stars: in advertising, 205, 220–24, 227–37, 240, 241, 243, 339n30; audience for, 228–29; commodification of, 230, 340n32; signatures of, 340n34

fire extinguishers, foam (*yao shuilong*), 120–54, 327n9; advertising for, 124, 153–54; Butterfly-brand, 16, 121, 122, 125, 153, 329n28; Chen on, 126–27, 139–40, 142; in Chen's eulogies, 276; Chen's tinkering with, 16, 20, 26, 30, 48–49, 122–26; as common knowledge, 127; foreign, 123, 124, 125; patent for, 121, 122, 125; in pictorials, 326n63

firefighting, 123–24, 126–27, 326n4

Foreign Affairs Movement, 271, 307n15

Four Brights Practical Studies Association (Siming shixue hui), 51

Four Treasuries (*Siku quanshu*), 344n24

France, 123, 197, 336n2

Free Talk (*Ziyoutan*; *Shenbao* literary supplement), 73, 75, 82, 120, 127, 131–32, 245. *See also* "Common Knowledge for the Household"

French language, 133, 183, 195

Fryer, John, 124, 182, 308n16, 316n29

Gather Benefit Company (Cuili gongsi; scientific-appliance shop), 6, 47–51, 69; and revolutionaries, 54–55

gender, 46, 60, 66, 91, 221, 321n28; of consumers, 21, 321n26; and magazine production, 81–83, 319nn12–13; and skill (*qiao*), 114–15. *See also* women

Genette, Gérard, 343n13

German language, 187

Gernsback, Hugo, 29–30, 31

Gerth, Karl, 285, 341n48

glassware industry, 103, 169, 191–93, 324n52. *See also* scientific equipment

gongyi. *See* industrial arts

"Gongyi Cotton Mill" ("Gongyi shachang"; Chen Diexian), 59–60, 62

"good wives and wise mothers," 102

government, Nationalist: and adaptation of foreign products, 17, 196, 198–99, 202; and Household Industries, 174, 175, 199–200; and intellectual property rights, 206, 214, 215–16, 221, 242; local offices of, 215–17; and modern laboratories, 151; and overseas Chinese, 238; and public libraries, 249; regulation by, 200–201, 202; support of industry by, 12, 156, 167, 184, 278, 279, 308n17, 315n15, 338n16; tax exemptions from, 172–73, 332n23. *See also* Guomindang; Ministry of Agriculture and Commerce

Grand View (*Daguanbao*; newspaper), 55, 73, 316n38

Grand View Publishing House (Daguanbao guan), 46, 50, 55–56, 68

Great Five Continents Drugstore (Wuzhou da yaofang), 101, 147, 177

Great Leap Forward (1958–1962), 175, 273, 282–84, 332n24

Great Learning (*Daxue*), 322n37

Guan Huinong, 341n43

Guomindang (Nationalist Party; GMD), 158, 236, 266–67

Guo Moruo, 254

hair products, 146, 261; homemade vs. store-bought, 88–90; recipes for, 77–79, 83–84, 88, 91, 103, 105, 187, 188

Household Industries (*continued*)
205–20; vernacular industrialism of,
15, 16, 17; and World War II, 170, 171,
276–77. *See also* Butterfly (Wudipai)
brand
Hsieh Kuo, 283–84
Hua Chishi, 55
Hua'nan Chemical Industry Company
(hua'nan huxue gongyeshe), 221–25,
338n22
Huang Chanhua, 108
Huang Gongdu, 314n10
Hudnot, Richard, 191
Hu Guangsu, 136
Hui Springs Soda Water Factory, 198
Hui Xia, 108
Hu Shi, 22, 254
Hu Xianglin, 172
hygiene, 92, 98, 127, 200; in advertising,
229, 236; in "Common Knowledge,"
130, 131, 133; and national strength,
96–97, 323n39

Illustrated Newspaper of Fiction
(*Xiaoshuo huabao*), 73
Imperial Maritime Customs, 206
Imperial Patent Office (Japan), 5, 189
imperialism, 2, 11; and Chen, 15, 281;
and extraterritoriality, 48; and
industrialization, 14, 19, 158, 166,
308n21; Japanese, 4, 96, 166, 168;
and national strength, 96–97; vs.
nativism, 26, 167, 177, 202, 266,
309n30; and trademarks, 205–6,
336n4; and vernacular industrialism, 17, 289
imports, foreign: advertising of, 225,
236; anxiety about, 96, 157, 309n30;
boycotts of, 239; emulation of, 24,
31–32, 111, 187, 189, 196, 267–70, 273,

279, 342n4; exotic, 181, 309n30,
333n29; and intellectual property
rights, 158, 206, 214, 248–49,
328n20, 335n52, 336n2; Japanese, 52,
167, 168, 177, 191, 225, 239, 324n55; of
lab equipment, 103–4; recipes for,
191, 193–96; in Southeast Asia, 235;
tax exemptions for, 172, 180. *See also*
native (*guohuo*) vs. foreign (*yanghuo*) products
import substitution, 269–70, 289,
342n4
improvement (*gailiang*, *gaizao*): and
Chen, 17, 154, 165, 267–70; and
import substitution, 270; vs.
innovation, 28, 32, 34, 189–96,
201–3; as knowledge work, 20; and
nativist industry, 197–201; and
shanzhai culture, 289; and tinkering, 26, 29–30; and translation,
184–85
India, 98
industrial arts (*gongyi*), 6–7, 113, 118,
119, 128, 254, 268, 320n20; publications on, 92, 144, 184, 252–53
industrialists, new (*shiyejia*), 132, 150,
203, 216, 271; and Chen's persona,
204; and Chen's publications, 114,
118, 122, 134, 138, 140–41, 144, 251,
265, 267; literati, 2, 44, 305n1
industrialization: alternative forms of,
11–18; anxiety about, 158; vs.
backyard furnaces, 283–84; and
Chen's tinkering, 123; in China vs.
Europe, 311n39; and coal, 19; and
entrepreneurs, 4–5, 12, 38–39, 44;
formal vs. vernacular, 10–11, 13,
14–15, 17, 151, 278–79; historiography of, 12–13, 32–34; nativist, 31, 137,
149, 167, 176, 197–201; and new

media, 61; state-sponsored, 12, 44, 156, 167, 184, 278, 279, 308n17, 315n15, 338n16

Industrial Revolution, 19, 27, 311n38

industrial testing bureaus (*gongye shiyan suo*), 200

industry, light (*xiao gongyi*): Chen's publications on, 26, 131, 135, 136–37, 138–39, 144, 154, 158, 159, 276, 280; development of, 155, 167, 247–48; and Great Leap Forward, 283; knowledge work in, 20, 76; and national power, 137–38; publications on, 26, 30, 158, 184, 198–99, 201, 246, 276, 279; in Qing period, 40, 44; in Republican period, 166–67, 333n35; and vernacular industrialism, 6–8, 151, 279–80. *See also* chemical industry; cosmetic industry; glassware industry; pharmaceutical industry; textile industry

Industry and Commerce Report, 201

Industry in Laymen's Terms (*Shiye qianshuo*), 184, 198–99, 246

Industry Journal (*Shiye zazhi*), 201

Intel, 287, 345n10

intellectual property rights: anxiety about, 249; and Chen Diexian, 149–50, 280–81; vs. common knowledge, 30, 121, 149; and DIY culture, 28; and fire extinguishers, 121, 122, 125; global regimes of, 7–8, 158, 196, 205, 224, 280, 311n41; in Japan, 5, 189; laws on, 2, 158, 195–96, 205, 206, 215–16, 218, 219, 224–25, 280–81, 336n2; vs. open sourcing, 28, 287, 289, 311n43; and patents, 5, 121, 122, 125, 147, 189–90, 195–96, 201, 335n52; and printing technology, 262, 342n8; and *shanzhai*

culture, 285, 287, 288; and the state, 205, 242; and tinkering, 26–32, 30, 201. *See also* trademarks

International Mixed Court (Shanghai), 48

internet, 28, 311n43

invention (*faming*; innovation), 334n44; vs. adaptation, 8, 43, 76, 189–96, 201–3; and Chen, 2, 5, 201–3; vs. emulation, 32, 189–96, 316n34; and experimentation, 189–96, 201–3; vs. improvement, 28, 32, 34, 189–96, 201–3; in Korea, 5, 189–90, 191, 306n6; of technology, 27–28, 190; and tinkering, 27, 201–3

investigation of things (*gewu zhizhi*), 96, 270

Japan: and Butterfly Toothpowder, 207–8; Chinese conflicts with, 12, 47–48, 167, 324n55, 344n22; companies from, 101, 166–67, 324n48, 344n3; "good wives and wise mothers" from, 102; and Household Industries, 31, 276–77; imperialism of, 4, 96, 130, 166, 168; imports from, 52, 167, 168, 177, 191, 225, 239, 324n55; and intellectual property rights, 5, 189, 336n2; inventors in, 306n6; Kanto earthquake in, 327n9; new knowledge from, 47–48, 55, 271; publications from, 48, 53, 185–86, 187, 254

Japanese language: neologisms from, 151, 210, 334n44; translations to and from, 55, 74, 83, 102, 108, 137, 185–86, 187, 203, 257

Jiang Guangfu, 275

Jiangnan Arsenal, 53, 182, 268–69, 307n15, 316n29, 338n16, 344n22

Jiangnan region, 43, 45, 55, 56; cosmo-
politanism of, 208–9; culture of play
in, 38, 63, 69, 116
Jiangsu Industrial Bureau, 215, 216,
338n16
Jiangsu Industrial Monthly (*Jiangsu
shiye yuekan*), 215
Jiating gongyeshe gufen lianhe gongsi.
See Household Industries
Journal de Phamacie d'Anvers, 195–96
journalism, 55–56, 150. *See also*
newspapers
Journal of Industry and Commerce
(*Gongshang xuebao*), 211–12
*Journal of the Shanghai Machine-Based
National Products Association*
(*Shanghai jizhi guohuo lianhehui
huikan*), 343n19
journals: how-to columns in, 3, 6, 16,
24, 54, 246, 271, 280; on industry,
145–50, 184, 188, 195–96, 201,
211–12, 224–25, 276, 308n16, 328n17,
339n23, 343n19; Japanese, 254;
literary, 76, 82, 316n40; new, 14, 79,
317n41; pictorial, 56–57, 317n41,
326n63; popular, 107, 132, 188;
professional, 145–50, 153; scientific,
13, 107, 124, 125, 126, 146, 187–88,
316n29, 328n19; and Self-
Strengthening Movement, 316n29;
state-sponsored, 184. See also *Free
Talk*; *Pastime*; women's magazines
Judge, Joan, 309n27, 309n29, 319n12
Judge Bao, 188

Kanto earthquake (Japan; 1923), 327n9
knowledge: alternative forms of, 11, 13;
anxiety about, 250, 264, 272;
authenticity of, 43, 245–47, 258–64,
310n31; colonial vs. local, 9, 203,

336n61; commodification of, 80, 91,
258, 262–64, 272, 310n31; and
consumers, 21–22; economy of, 27;
embodied, 9, 10, 19; expert, 21,
133–36, 138, 145–50, 152–53;
folkloric vs. modern, 248–49, 261;
global, 34, 164, 187–88, 196; in home
manufacturing, 80, 81, 94, 97, 101;
medical, 127, 150, 152, 258–64; in
Ming encyclopedias, 100; and
national strength, 96–97, 137, 153;
and nativism, 24, 151, 265; ownership of, 146–47; production of, 72,
156; professionalization of, 150–54;
279; secret, 137, 258–64; sensorial,
87–88, 94, 255–57; and *shanzhai*
culture, 288; sharing of, 28, 29,
125–26, 137, 180, 260–61; textual vs.
tacit transmission of, 98–99;
traditional female, 92; translation
of, 181–89; transmission of, 28,
258–64, 309n26, 312n48; vernacularization of, 82, 309n29
knowledge, new: audience for, 102–14,
118; authenticity of, 245–47; and
branding, 18–26, 70; compilation of,
74, 270–73; and culture of play, 118;
and elite, 43–47, 49–50, 69–70; and
emulation, 272–73; and Gather
Benefit Company, 49–50; from
Japan, 55; and marvelous (*zhiguai*)
tales, 56; and *Model Correspondence*, 144–45; and national
strength, 96–97; networks of, 47–55;
and new companies, 48–55; and
printing, 72, 76; purchase of, 90–91;
and revolution, 51–52; and texts,
55–64; and vernacular industrialism, 279–80; and women, 85, 92, 93,
116, 118

knowledge work, 18–26, 34; and language, 22, 26; and material work, 3, 20, 26; new forms of, 71–76; in Shanghai, 71–76; translations as, 182–83

Koelkel & Schroeder Ltd. (Kefa da yaofang; Shanghai), 53, 78

KOFA Dispensary (Shanghai), 53, 78, 84, 86

Kong Xiangxi, 201, 264, 326n2

Korea, 5, 189–90, 191, 306n6

Korean language, 334n44

Kuang Yu, 91

labor, 265, 277; mobilization of, 266–67, 332n24; of women, 59–60, 169, 175

laboratories, 307n11; equipment for, 103–5; home, 108, 151; modern, 151, 174, 335n52. *See also* scientific equipment

Ladies' Journal (*Funü zazhi*), 79, 80, 82, 91–97, 320n16, 327n13; audience for, 113, 115, 116, 321nn29–30; recipes in, 92–95, 108, 110–11, 193, 196

languages, foreign: and Chen, 183, 203; in recipes, 90, 103, 187, 194, 322n34; in romanized alphabet, 94; in women's magazines, 78, 83–84, 94. *See also* Chinese language; English language; French language; Japanese language; translation

Lanham Act (U.S.; Trademark Act of 1946), 336n3

Laozi, 314n12

Latin language, 78, 84, 94, 187, 320n18

Lee, Haiyan, 65, 325n62

Lee, Jung, 189, 191, 306n6

Legalism, 41

Lessons for Women (*Nü jie*; Ban Zhao), 115

Lever Brothers (Lihua youxian gongsi), 166, 228, 339n27, 339n29

Liang Qichao, 254

Liang Saizhen, 231

Lianhua Film Company, 240

Li Bai, 42

Li Chuangjue, 183

Lightman, Bernard, 309n26, 315n18

Li Hongjun, 135–36

Li Lili, 228, 231, 232, 233, 236, 240, 341nn44–45

L'Impartial (*Dagongbao*; newspaper), 228, 233

Lindtner, Silvia, 345n12

Ling Ruizhu, 92–93, 94

Link, Perry, 81

Lin Lübin, 201

Lin Qi, 46

Lin Shu, 47, 182, 183, 306n5, 310n31

Lintas (Lever International Advertising Services), 228, 339n29

Lion (Shizi) brand, 163, 167, 208, 344n3

literature, 1–2, 5, 6, 8, 18–19, 38; "court case" (*gong'an xiaoshuo*), 188; high vs. low-brow, 22; new genres of, 57, 72; and new media, 71–76; and print technology, 23, 262. *See also* authorship; butterfly fiction; fiction; poetry; *particular titles*

lithography, 50, 56, 57, 231, 233, 262, 335n55

Liu Bannong, 188

Liu E, 305n1

Liyong Paper Mill (Liyong zaozhi chang), 277

Loving Blood of the Volcano (film), 341n44

Lü Bicheng, 306n5

Lumière, Louis, 60–61, 62

Lu Shi'e, 72–73

Lux (Lishi) Soap, 339n27; advertising campaign for, 227–34, 235, 239, 242

Lu Xun, 318n3a, 322n31

new knowledge, 56–57, 71–76; new technologies for, 21–22, 26, 50, 56, 57, 123, 197, 231, 233, 262, 264, 335n55; and panoramic perception, 57; and trademark enforcement, 215–20, 224; and vernacular industrialism, 25–26. *See also* journals; newspapers

medicine: and amateurism, 138; and authenticity, 258–64; Ayurvedic, 307n13; Chinese socialist, 345n4; as common knowledge, 127, 152; family knowledge about, 258–64; literati physicians (*ruyi*) in, 185, 261; patent, 225, 249, 339n24; and politics, 310n32; professionalization of, 150; traditional, 20, 38, 97, 185, 251, 256, 342n6; traditional vs. modern, 133, 248–49; and treaty ports, 320n18. See also *Mr. Mei's New Compilation of Tested Prescriptions*; pharmaceutical industry

Meida Chemical Industry (Meida huaxue gongyeshe), 216

Mei Qizhao, 245, 259, 342n2, 343n17

Memorial Volume for Tianxuwosheng (*Tianxuwosheng jinian kan*), 275–77

Meng Yue, 131–32, 268–69, 307n15

Mertha, Andrew, 285

"Method for Making Rouge" (*Ladies' Journal* article), 93–94, 108

"Method for Manufacturing Cosmetics" (Shen Ruiqing), 103

"Method for Producing Cosmetics" (Shen Ruiqing; *Ladies' Journal* article), 94–95, 193

"Method for the Refined Production of Cosmetic Soap" (Kuang Yu), 111–12

Midnight (*Ziye*; Mao Dun), 158

Millington, Charles William, 339n28

Ministry of Agriculture and Commerce, 156, 172, 184, 198–99, 215–16, 265, 333n35

Ministry of Industry (GMD), 199–200, 201, 221

missionaries, Western, 11, 12, 102, 150, 182

model correspondence (*chidu*), 16, 20, 138–45, 153

Model Correspondence on Industry and Commerce (*Gongshangye chidu ou'cun*; Chen Diexian), 121, 138–45, 153, 309n28, 328n17; commodified classicism of, 143–44, 310n31; and professionalization, 152; and trademark enforcement, 217–20

Modern Letters (*Chidu xinyu*), 328n14

modernity: advertising of, 235; anxiety about, 247–50, 272; and Chen Diexian, 5, 37, 156–57, 250, 267; colonial, 26; and compilation, 271; cosmopolitan, 208–9; and films, 25–26; of household, 132; of Household Industries, 174; industrial, 3, 5, 9, 10, 25, 114, 156–57, 244–74, 280; and May Fourth movement, 14; of Shanghai, 25, 37; and translation, 310n31; vernacular, 18, 25–26; and women, 114, 115

Moism, 41

Mokyr, Joel, 27

Money Demon, The (*Huangjin sui*; Chen Diexian), 64–69, 73, 205

Monthly Bulletin of the Ministry of Industry (*Shiyebu yuekan*), 199

"Mountain Tree, The" (*Zhuangzi*), 37, 41–42

Mr. Bao's New Compilation of Tested Prescriptions (Bao Xiang'ao), 259

natural studies (*bowu*), 45, 96, 133

Needham, Joseph, 32, 312nn46–47

neo-Confucianism (*lixue*), 95, 114

neoliberalism, 287, 288, 289, 290, 345n8

New China Peppermint Co., Ltd. (Xinhua bohe chang gufen youxian gongsi), 187

New Compilation of Tested Prescriptions (*Yanfang xinbian*; Bao Xiang'ao), 245, 261

New Culture Movement, 70, 74, 141, 151, 153, 254; and elite, 3, 119, 306n3; and language, 22; and May Fourth Movement, 14; and women, 115, 132

New Hunan Newspaper (*Xiangzhong xinbao*), 73

New Illustrated Pictorial (*Tuhua xinbao*), 317n41

"New Knowledge for the Household" (*Shenbao* column), 120–21, 127

New Life Movement, 341n45

New People's Daily (*Sin kok min jit po*; *Xin guomin ribao*), 236

New Pharmaceutical Manual, The (Dietrichs), 188

New Policies (late Qing), 44, 113

New Shanghai (*Xin Shanghai*; Lu Shi'e), 72–73

newspapers: advertising in, 225–41, 339n24; and Chen Diexian, 39, 40, 55, 71, 73, 316n38; columns in, 21, 30, 73, 77–80, 120–21, 127; language of, 22, 46; serialized fiction in, 72, 73; in Southeast Asia, 235–36; and trademark enforcement, 217–20. *See also* "Common Knowledge for the Household"; *Shenbao*; "Warehouse for Cosmetic Production"

New Student Journal (*Xuesheng xinza*), 79

New Union Times (*Zonghui xinbao*), 235–36, 237, 239, 242

New Woman (Xin nüxing), 115

New Youth (*Xin qingnian*; journal), 14

Ningbo, 7, 11, 25, 68, 161–62, 169, 178

Ningbo Native-Place Association (Ningbo tongxianghui), 51

Ningbo Vernacular Daily (*Ningbo baihua ribao*), 46–47

occupations, new, 146, 150, 203

Odes of Three Rarities (*Sanjia qu*), 55–56

Ōkura Nagatsune, 306n6

open sourcing, 28, 287, 289, 311n43

overseas Chinese (*huaqiao*): advertising to, 235–41, 242, 243; and GMD, 238; and Household Industries, 17, 159; nationalism of, 239, 240–41; in Southeast Asia, 238–39

Overseas Prosperity Company (Qiaoxing gongsi), 235, 242

Pang Yuanji, 60

paper manufacturing, 12, 198, 199–200, 256

paratexts, 343n13

Pastime (*Youxi zazhi*; journal), 73–74, 75, 116, 307n10, 325n62

patent medicines, 225, 249, 339n24

Peking Union Medical College, 102

People's Republic of China (PRC): Deng era in, 335n60; First Five-Year Plan of, 278, 282; Great Leap Forward in, 175, 273, 282–84, 332n24; industrialization in, 175–76, 278; Maoist period (1949–1976) in, 282–84; *shanzhai* culture in, 273, 284–90; *wenshi ziliao* accounts from, 164, 168, 179, 335n60 peppermint, 186–87, 198

Peppermint Industry, The (Bohe gongye), 137, 163, 165, 186–87, 328n17

pharmaceutical industry, 3, 241; and Household Industries, 172, 279; and intellectual-property law, 195–96, 214, 335n52; Japanese in China, 166–67; journals for, 149, 188; and *Model Correspondence*, 142–43

Pharmaceutical Record and Weekly Market Review, 188

pharmacies, 78, 128, 130; advertising for, 100–101, 324n48; Japanese, 101, 324n48; Western, 86, 87, 101, 177

pharmacology, traditional, 31, 344n23; and Chen, 131, 162, 181, 184–85, 279

photocopy machine, 123, 197

photography, 48, 61–64, 133, 136, 151, 229; and authenticity, 230–31; and chemistry, 107–8; and portraiture, 61–62

physicians, literati (*ruyi*), 185, 261

physics, 7, 93, 114, 177; in "Common Knowledge," 131, 134–35; and home manufacturing, 87–88, 101; in *Model Correspondence*, 142, 143, 145; and vernacular industrialism, 279, 289

Pianzhi Sheng, 317n44

Pickowicz, Paul, 341n45

Pine Window Jottings (Song chuang zaji; Du Xunhe), 61, 62

"Plan for a Fire Brigade's Use of the Fire Extinguisher" (Chen Diexian), 126–27

play (*youxi*), culture of, 7–9, 321n23; and Chen, 16, 63; and "Common Knowledge," 134, 137; and *Dream of the Red Chamber*, 67; and elite, 38, 63, 69, 116–18, 132; and

experimentation, 7, 9, 116; in Jiangnan region, 38, 63, 69, 116; and manufacturing, 23, 87, 116; and poetry, 63, 87; and science, 8, 23

Playful Magazine (Youxi Bao), 132

Plum in the Golden Vase (Jin Ping Mei cihua), 100

poetry: bamboo-branch, 15, 21, 40, 55–64, 69; and Chen, 3, 5, 6, 7, 37, 38, 58–64, 70, 74, 276; and culture of play, 63, 87; elegant gatherings for, 315n19; and new technology, 55–64; rhyme ballads (*tanci*), 56; on technology, 21, 40

poisons, 52, 54

Pollack, Sheldon, 310n34

Pomeranz, Kenneth, 311n39

portraiture (*shenhua*), 61–62

print culture, 3, 4, 26, 76, 81

printing: and Chen, 15, 149–50; and Household Industries, 170; lithographic, 50, 56, 57, 231, 233, 262, 335n55; market for, 12, 100, 145, 149–50, 153; and new knowledge, 71–76; new technologies for, 21, 23, 26, 50, 56, 57, 62, 81, 123, 197, 231, 233, 262, 264, 335n55, 342n8; offset, 26, 123, 197, 335n55. *See also* publishing, commercial

production, mass, 6, 18, 37, 118, 155–59; and advertising, 225, 242; and authenticity, 230–31, 241–42, 246; vs. backyard furnaces, 283–84; of culture, 72; and intellectual property rights, 205, 206, 248–49; of texts, 246, 249–50; and tinkering, 29–30

products: authentic vs. fake, 155–57, 158, 159, 281; daily-use, 155, 157, 199; enemy (*dihuo*), 18, 23, 24, 26, 155–56,

reformers, 309n29; elite, 3, 12, 22–23, 119, 306n3; and Gather Benefit Company, 49–50; on household, 132, 133, 327n13; on hygiene, 97; and profits, 69–70; and women, 60, 115. *See also* May Fourth Movement; New Culture Movement

Reforms of 1898, 51

Republican period (1911–1949), 71–243; chaos in, 4, 8, 156; industry in, 12, 166–67, 278, 333n35; intellectual property rights in, 204–43, 269; vs. Maoist period, 282–84; Nanjing decade in, 12, 307n11; science in, 13; vernacular industrialism of, 289; women in, 115–16, 118

Retrocession Association (Guangfu hui), 52

reverse engineering, 31, 130, 193–98, 203, 279; of cosmetics, 193–95; of machinery, 332n22

Revolution of 1911, 4, 54

revolutionaries, anti-Manchu, 46, 47, 51–55

Riba Manufacturing Soap Warehouse, 166

Rockefeller Foundation, 102

Royal Society (Britain), 246–47

Ruan Lingyu, 228, 231, 233

"Rubber-Wheeled Carriage" ("Xiang-piche"; Chen Diexian), 59

Sai Sei Do (Japanese pharmacy), 101, 324n48

salt merchants, 12, 178–80

Saturday (*Libailiu*; journal), 82

Schloten, H. (Xueludun yaohang), 142

science (*kexue*): and alchemy, 107; amateur, 6, 16, 80, 107, 281, 315n18; anxiety about, 248–49, 250, 272,

342n5; audience for, 249–50; and colonialism, 9–10, 28, 33, 311n40, 312n48; in "Common Knowledge," 130–31, 134; and detective fiction, 188–89; and elite, 16, 44, 50, 151, 249, 328n22; English popularizers of, 21; experimental, 1–2, 6; and Great Leap Forward, 283, 332n24; historiography of, 19, 28, 32–33, 311n40, 312n48; institutionalization of, 13–14, 102, 279; languages of, 84; Maoist, 332n24; and May Fourth Movement, 14, 23, 118–19, 308n21; and national strength, 130–31; professionalization of, 23, 102, 150–54, 279; vs. profits, 246–47; terminology for, 328n22; vernacular, 9, 278–79; Western vs. Chinese, 27, 32–33; in women's magazines, 82. *See also* chemistry; experimentation; physics

Science (*Kexue*; journal), 13

Science Society of China, 13

Scientific American (journal), 146, 328n19

scientific-appliance shops, 6, 39, 47, 69, 316n29, 324n48. *See also* China Educational Supply Association Ltd.

scientific equipment, 44, 281, 324n53; in "Common Knowledge," 128, 130; for home manufacturing, 90, 101, 103–6, 114; for photography, 108

seal script, 210–11

self-cultivation, 30, 44, 107, 108

Self-Strengthening Movement, 11–12, 24, 156, 316n29, 344n22; and elites, 43, 305n1; and government, 44, 315n15; and translations, 74, 182, 270; and women, 118 sentiment (*qing*), 40–41; in advertising, 225–27, 231, 233, 242, 340n32; and Butterfly brand, 220, 225, 226–27; and Chen's persona, 204–5, 242–43; and *Dream of the Red Chamber*, 67, 98; in fiction, 64–65, 68–71

Sewell, W. G., 102, 185, 186

Shanghai: Chen Diexian in, 20, 21, 39, 54, 73, 121, 277; commercialization of, 46, 100, 158; cosmopolitanism of, 208–9; entertainment in, 26, 72, 208–9, 228, 310n33; and Hangzhou, 54–55; Household Industries in, 171, 174, 278, 331n11; intellectual labor in, 12, 71–76, 271; modernity of, 25, 37; pharmacies in, 53, 78, 84, 85, 86; Self-Strengthening Movement in, 11; *shanzhai* culture in, 286. See also *Shenbao*

Shanghai Industrial Arts Expo (1924), 151

Shanghai Polytechnic, 124

Shanghai School of Chemical Industries, 145

shanzhai culture, 284–90

Shapin, Steven, 246–47

Shaw brothers, 236

Shenbao (*Shanghai News*): advertising in, 225, 226, 228, 230, 233, 339nn24–25; audience for, 327n12; industrial arts column in, 120–21; literary supplement of, 73, 75, 82, 120, 127, 131–32, 245; *Money Demon* in, 64–69, 73, 205; and vernacularization of knowledge, 309n29. *See also* "Common Knowledge for the Household"

Shen Jiuchen, 339n23

Shen Ruiqing, 94–95, 103

Shenzhen, 28, 284, 285, 286, 287, 345n5

Sherlock Holmes mysteries, 74, 188–89

Shisu Yongren, 268

shiyan. *See* experimentation

Singapore, 235–38, 240–41, 242

Sino-Japanese War (1895), 12, 47–48, 344n22

Smith, Thomas, 306n6

soap, 324n47, 328n20, 339n27; advertising of, 227–34, 235, 239, 242; foreign vs. traditional, 98, 323nn42–43; manufacturing of, 111–12, 146, 147, 166, 167, 177

social status, 16, 40, 44, 150, 266–67, 270; and home manufacturing, 77, 80, 89, 100, 185–86, 280; in Japan, 133; and *shiyan*, 255–56; and vernacular industrialism, 9, 279. *See also* elite, educated

soda bottle caps, 197–98

Sŏ Kwang-uk, 306n6

Son Ch'angsik, 306n6

Song of the Fisherman (*Yu guang qu*; film), 240

Songs of Gongchen Bridge (*Gongchen qiao tage*; Pianzhi Sheng), 317n44

Southeast Asia, 341n42; advertising in, 235–41; Butterfly brand in, 331n16; film in, 26, 236–37, 341n44; Household Industries in, 2, 17, 32, 158, 159, 167, 170

specialization, 127, 136; vs. "Common Knowledge," 21, 133–34, 138, 149–50

Squire, Peter, 320n18

steam engines, 124

"Strength of the Masses Is Limitless, The" (Yin Zeming), 283–84

Sun, Myra, 342n8

Sun Yu, 240, 341n44

Supreme Court Verdicts in Civil and Criminal Cases (*Daliyuan minxing-shi panjue li*), 75

Tagore, Rabindranath, 308n21

Taipei Police Exhibition (1925), 130

Taiping Uprising (1850–1864), 4, 46, 143, 259, 260, 271

Taiwan, 130, 176, 286, 288, 336n60

tax exemptions, 25, 172–73, 175, 180, 332n23

Teardrop Destiny (*Leizhuyuan*; serialized novel; Chen Diexian), 56, 67–68, 73

technology: in advertising, 229, 231, 233, 243; anxiety about, 21, 281; Chinese typewriter, 123, 324n53; and compilation, 157, 271–72; and connoisseurship, 3, 4–5, 6, 30, 44, 69, 96, 113, 114, 117; depictions of, 118, 125, 126, 326n63; digital, 290; emulation of, 24, 31–32, 111, 157, 267–70, 272–73; everyday, 9–10, 57; of firefighting, 123–24; foreign, 11–12, 24, 31–32, 40, 111, 164, 267–70, 311n39; industrial, 14–15, 18, 245; invention of, 27–28, 190; for media, 21–22, 56, 60; in *Model Correspondence*, 142–43; open-source, 28, 287, 289, 311n43; photocopying, 123, 197; and poetry, 21, 40, 55–64; for printing, 21, 23, 26, 50, 56, 57, 62, 81, 123, 197, 231, 233, 262, 264, 335n55, 342n8; and property rights, 31–32; steam, 124; tinkering with, 29–30, 37; traditional vs. modern, 248; transmission of, 9–10; and women, 116. *See also* fire extinguishers, foam; photography

technology transfer, 34, 203

Terminology Committee, Joint (Jiangsu Provincial Education Association), 328n22

textbooks, 22, 51; chemistry, 185–86; vs. *Model Correspondence*, 138, 144, 153; new, 131, 138, 144, 149, 153, 249; translated, 55, 102

textile industry, 167, 169, 170, 279

texts: authenticity of, 245–47, 249, 250, 257–58, 266, 271; emulation of, 20, 72, 74, 85; on experimentation, 247, 253–58, 260; and fire extinguisher, 121–22; foreign scientific, 83, 182–89; fungibility of, 72; and home manufacturing, 88, 98–99; on household management, 114–15; mass production of, 246, 249–50; mechanical reproduction of, 23, 26, 29–30, 37, 81, 249, 280; and new knowledge, 55–64; state-sponsored, 184; strategic use of, 21, 34, 76, 156, 245, 247, 250, 270–71; tinkering with, 29–30, 184; and trademarks, 210–13, 337n11. *See also* printing; publishing, commercial

Three Flowers Vanishing Cream (Sanhuapai xuehuagao), 191, 192

Three Western Rarities (Xiling sanjia), 55

Tiger Balm, 238, 341n43

Ting, H. C., 106, 108, 306n5

tinkering: by Chen, 26–32, 48–49, 123, 144, 154, 165, 186, 281; and crime novels, 189; and Great Leap Forward, 283–84; and Household Industries, 157; and import substitution, 270; and innovation, 201–3; and intellectual property rights, 26–32, 201; and Irish tinkers, 27, 310n36; with magnesium carbonate, 176–81; and nativist industry, 197–201; and recipes, 114, 256; and recycling, 311n44; by

Unilever, 159, 214, 235, 241, 243, 339nn27–30; and Lux Soap, 227–34, 242

United States, 136, 227; Chinese relations with, 288, 290; intellectual-property laws in, 195, 335n52, 336nn2–3

Vaseline, 88, 90

vernacular industrialism, 6–11, 279–82; vs. capitalism, 17–18, 280; and chemistry, 164, 279, 289; of Chen Diexian, 3, 6, 7–11, 15–22, 25–26, 34, 76, 126, 144, 154, 164, 176, 247, 273, 281; and commercialization, 34, 281; vs. formal industrialization, 10–15, 17, 151, 278–79; and light industry, 6–8, 151, 279–80; vs. mechanization, 172; and media, 25–26; and nativism, 166, 172, 202, 279, 280, 289; and *shanzhai* culture, 284–90; and tinkering, 27–32, 279, 281

vernacular modernism, 25–26

Versailles, Treaty of, 14

Wang Dungen, 73, 74, 75, 82

Wang Jingwei, 325n55

Wang Mengzou, 51

Wang Renmei, 228, 236, 240

Wang Taijun, 204, 211–12

Wang Yunwu, 249

"Warehouse for Cosmetic Production" ("Huazhuangpin zhizao ku"; *Women's World* column), 81, 85–94, 97, 180, 261; vs. *Chemical Industry Journal*, 148; and "Common Knowledge," 130, 132; and culture of play, 116, 118; hair tonic recipe in, 77–79, 187–88; illustration from, 105; and *Model Correspondence*, 145

Watson (soda water), 198

Watson's Pharmacy (Quchenshi da yaofang), 101

Wealth in Industry (*Collectanea on How to Acquire Wealth in Industry; Shiye zhi fu congshu*), 245–46, 265–70, 272; preface to, 343n20

West, Mae, 227

West China Union (Chengdu), 102

Western learning, 46–47, 69, 182

women: advertising for, 226–34, 339n25; and application of recipes, 106, 108; as audience, 91, 92; as authors, 82, 92, 321n30; and Confucianism, 95, 96, 114, 132; as consumers, 21, 321n26; culture of, 86–87; education for, 92, 102; elite, 4, 7, 77, 82, 85, 92, 114, 115–19, 306n5, 320n15, 322n30; experimentation by, 7, 116, 118, 279; as factory workers, 59–60; as film stars, 205, 220–24, 227–37, 240, 241, 243, 339n30, 340n34; and footbinding, 97, 115; genteel (*guixiu*), 77, 82, 85, 115–19, 322n30; home manufacturing by, 77–91, 175; inner chambers of, 85–87, 89, 92, 94, 97, 109, 115–19, 132, 321n22; liberation of, 132, 325n61; model letters for, 328n14; and New Culture Movement, 115, 132; and new knowledge, 85–91, 92, 93, 116, 118

Women's Eastern Times (*Funü shibao*), 82, 116, 254, 306n3, 319n12

women's magazines: audience for, 102–14, 115, 116, 321nn29–30; authorship of, 321n30; chemistry in, 21, 82, 85, 92, 93–94; foreign languages in, 78, 83–84, 94; gendered production of, 81–83, 319nn12–13; how-to columns in, 6,

Selected Titles
(Complete list at: http://weai.columbia.edu/publications/studies-weai/)

Fighting for Virtue: Justice and Politics in Thailand, by Duncan McCargo. Cornell University Press, 2020.

Beyond the Steppe Frontier: A History of the Sino-Russian Border, by Sören Urbansky. Princeton University Press, 2020.

Pirates and Publishers: A Social History of Copyright in Modern China, by Fei-Hsien Wang. Princeton University Press, 2019.

The Typographic Imagination: Reading and Writing in Japan's Age of Modern Print Media, by Nathan Shockey. Columbia University Press, 2019.

Down and Out in Saigon: Stories of the Poor in a Colonial City, by Haydon Cherry. Yale University Press, 2019.

Beauty in the Age of Empire: Japan, Egypt, and the Global History of Aesthetic Education, by Raja Adal. Columbia University Press, 2019.

Mass Vaccination: Citizens' Bodies and State Power in Modern China, by Mary Augusta Brazelton. Cornell University Press, 2019.

Residual Futures: The Urban Ecologies of Literary and Visual Media of 1960s and 1970s Japan, by Franz Prichard. Columbia University Press, 2019.

The Making of Japanese Settler Colonialism: Malthusianism and Trans-Pacific Migration, 1868–1961, by Sidney Xu Lu. Cambridge University Press, 2019.

The Power of Print in Modern China: Intellectuals and Industrial Publishing from the End of Empire to Maoist State Socialism, by Robert Culp. Columbia University Press, 2019.

Beyond the Asylum: Mental Illness in French Colonial Vietnam, by Claire E. Edington. Cornell University Press, 2019.

Borderland Memories: Searching for Historical Identity in Post-Mao China, by Martin Fromm. Cambridge University Press, 2019.

Sovereignty Experiments: Korean Migrants and the Building of Borders in Northeast Asia, 1860–1949, by Alyssa M. Park. Cornell University Press, 2019.

The Greater East Asia Co-prosperity Sphere: When Total Empire Met Total War, by Jeremy A. Yellen. Cornell University Press, 2019.

Thought Crime: Ideology and State Power in Interwar Japan, by Max Ward. Duke University Press, 2019.

Statebuilding by Imposition: Resistance and Control in Colonial Taiwan and the Philippines, by Reo Matsuzaki. Cornell University Press, 2019.

Nation-Empire: Ideology and Rural Youth Mobilization in Japan and Its Colonies, by Sayaka Chatani. Cornell University Press, 2019.

Fixing Landscape: A Techno-poetic History of China's Three Gorges, by Corey Byrnes. Columbia University Press, 2019.

The Invention of Madness: State, Society, and the Insane in Modern China, by Emily Baum. University of Chicago Press, 2018.

Japan's Imperial Underworlds: Intimate Encounters at the Borders of Empire, by David Ambaras. Cambridge University Press, 2018.

Heroes and Toilers: Work as Life in Postwar North Korea, 1953–1961, by Cheehyung Harrison Kim. Columbia University Press, 2018.

Electrified Voices: How the Telephone, Phonograph, and Radio Shaped Modern Japan, 1868–1945, by Kerim Yasar. Columbia University Press, 2018.

Making Two Vietnams: War and Youth Identities, 1965–1975, by Olga Dror. Cambridge University Press, 2018.

A Misunderstood Friendship: Mao Zedong, Kim Il-sung, and Sino–North Korean Relations, 1949–1976, by Zhihua Shen and Yafeng Xia. Columbia University Press, 2018.

Playing by the Informal Rules: Why the Chinese Regime Remains Stable Despite Rising Protests, by Yao Li. Cambridge University Press, 2018.

Raising China's Revolutionaries: Modernizing Childhood for Cosmopolitan Nationalists and Liberated Comrades, by Margaret Mih Tillman. Columbia University Press, 2018.

Buddhas and Ancestors: Religion and Wealth in Fourteenth-Century Korea, by Juhn Y. Ahn. University of Washington Press, 2018.

Idly Scribbling Rhymers: Poetry, Print, and Community in Nineteenth-Century Japan, by Robert Tuck. Columbia University Press, 2018.

China's War on Smuggling: Law, Economic Life, and the Making of the Modern State, 1842–1965, by Philip Thai. Columbia University Press, 2018.

Forging the Golden Urn: The Qing Empire and the Politics of Reincarnation in Tibet, by Max Oidtmann. Columbia University Press, 2018.

The Battle for Fortune: State-Led Development, Personhood, and Power Among Tibetans in China, by Charlene Makley. Cornell University Press, 2018.

Aesthetic Life: Beauty and Art in Modern Japan, by Miya Elise Mizuta Lippit. Harvard University Asia Center, 2018.

Where the Party Rules: The Rank and File of China's Communist State, by Daniel Koss. Cambridge University Press, 2018.

Resurrecting Nagasaki: Reconstruction and the Formation of Atomic Narratives, by Chad R. Diehl. Cornell University Press, 2018.

China's Philological Turn: Scholars, Textualism, and the Dao in the Eighteenth Century, by Ori Sela. Columbia University Press, 2018.

Making Time: Astronomical Time Measurement in Tokugawa Japan, by Yulia Frumer. University of Chicago Press, 2018.

Mobilizing Without the Masses: Control and Contention in China, by Diana Fu. Cambridge University Press, 2018.

Post-Fascist Japan: Political Culture in Kamakura After the Second World War, by Laura Hein. Bloomsbury, 2018.

China's Conservative Revolution: The Quest for a New Order, 1927–1949, by Brian Tsui. Cambridge University Press, 2018.

Promiscuous Media: Film and Visual Culture in Imperial Japan, 1926–1945, by Hikari Hori. Cornell University Press, 2018.

The End of Japanese Cinema: Industrial Genres, National Times, and Media Ecologies, by Alexander Zahlten. Duke University Press, 2017.

The Chinese Typewriter: A History, by Thomas S. Mullaney. MIT Press, 2017.

Forgotten Disease: Illnesses Transformed in Chinese Medicine, by Hilary A. Smith. Stanford University Press, 2017.

Borrowing Together: Microfinance and Cultivating Social Ties, by Becky Yang Hsu. Cambridge University Press, 2017.

Food of Sinful Demons: Meat, Vegetarianism, and the Limits of Buddhism in Tibet, by Geoffrey Barstow. Columbia University Press, 2017.

Youth for Nation: Culture and Protest in Cold War South Korea, by Charles R. Kim. University of Hawai'i Press, 2017.

Socialist Cosmopolitanism: The Chinese Literary Universe, 1945–1965, by Nicolai Volland. Columbia University Press, 2017.

The Social Life of Inkstones: Artisans and Scholars in Early Qing China, by Dorothy Ko. University of Washington Press, 2017.

Darwin, Dharma, and the Divine: Evolutionary Theory and Religion in Modern Japan, by G. Clinton Godart. University of Hawai'i Press, 2017.